"With the keen mind of a theologian and the warm heart of an evangelist, Robert Coleman displays how evangelism is the heartbeat of all theology. This work is biblical and practical—vintage Coleman!"

**Timothy K. Beougher**, Billy Graham Professor of Evangelism, Southern Baptist Theological Seminary

"I have waited over thirty-five years for this book! It was the life and teaching of Dr. Coleman that convinced me of the inseparable link between evangelism and theology, and this has resulted in several books that I have written. Now we have a comprehensive treatment from the master himself in the style of biblical and theological writing that is devotionally rich and practically helpful, which we have come to expect from Robert Coleman."

**Ajith Fernando**, national director, Youth for Christ, Sri Lanka

"Here is the theology of the Gospel in classic Wesleyan dress, vividly presented by one of its most honored veteran expositors. All who love the Lord will find this a heartwarming read."

**J. I. Packer**, Board of Governors Professor of Theology, Regent College

"This magnificent study by Robert Coleman will undoubtedly become a classic among theologies of evangelism. With great personal sensitivity and elegant simplicity, he places the question of 'Why evangelism?' into a biblical and theological context that is larger than many of us know. His study could very well ignite an evangelical fire within our hearts. This is a genuinely inspiring and instructive book not to miss—a must-read."

**John A. Woodbridge**, research professor of church history and Christian thought, Trinity Evangelical Divinity School

"What rich wisdom learned from a life lived in the Word and in the teaching and practice of evangelism! Coleman's love for both the Gospel and the Christ of the Gospel is contagious. Read and learn and worship."

**—Dennis F. Kinlaw**, president, Francis Asbury Society

"When Robert Coleman and I taught together at Trinity Evangelical Divinity School, students would often tell me that his classes changed their lives, and I think that will also happen with those who read this book. He brings all the great doctrines of the Bible to bear on the topic to which he has devoted his life: the wonderful Gospel of salvation through Christ alone. Though Coleman writes from a Wesleyan/Arminian perspective, at many points he graciously explains the Calvinistic Reformed view and shows when both sides can agree regarding evangelism. He also warns against many false gospels today that deviate from the truth of the Bible. This book will awaken readers' hearts to proclaim the Gospel, and no doubt to worship God."

**Wayne Grudem**, research professor of theology and biblical studies, Phoenix Seminary

## Books by Robert E. Coleman

*The Master Plan of Evangelism*

*The Master Plan of Discipleship*

*Established by the Word*

*Introducing the Prayer Cell*

*Life in the Living Word*

*The Spirit and the Word*

*Dry Bones Can Live Again*

*One Divine Moment*

*Written in Blood*

*Evangelism in Perspective*

*They Meet the Master*

*The Mind of the Master*

*Songs of Heaven*

*Growing in the Word*

*The New Covenant*

*Heartbeat of Evangelism*

*Evangelism on the Cutting Edge*

*The Spark That Ignites*

*Nothing to Do but to Save Souls*

*The Great Commission Lifestyle*

*Let the Fire Fall*

*Singing with the Angels*

*The Coming World Revival*

*The Heart of the Gospel*

# THE HEART
# OF THE
# GOSPEL

### THE THEOLOGY BEHIND
### THE MASTER PLAN *of* EVANGELISM

## ROBERT E. COLEMAN

**BakerBooks**
*a division of Baker Publishing Group*
Grand Rapids, Michigan

Published by Baker Books
a division of Baker Publishing Group
P.O. Box 6287, Grand Rapids, MI 49516-6287
www.bakerbooks.com

Printed in the United States of America

Library of Congress Cataloging-in-Publication Data
Coleman, Robert Emerson, 1928–
    The heart of the Gospel : the theology behind the master plan of evangelism / Robert E. Coleman.
        p.   cm.
    Includes bibliographical references (p.    ) and index.
    ISBN 978-0-8010-1370-6 (pbk.)
    1. Evangelistic work—Philosophy. 2. Theology, Doctrinal. I. Title.
BV3790.C569 2011
269'.2—dc22                                                                    2010041216

11   12   13   14   15   16   17          7   6   5   4   3   2   1

To my students who have prayed for me and have given
me the humbling honor of being their teacher

# Contents

# Introduction

## Theology and Evangelism

Theology is the study of God. No subject is more instructive and elevating in the whole realm of human thought. Little wonder that it is called "Queen of the sciences." Based on the revelation given to mankind finally and perfectly disclosed in Jesus Christ, it surpasses all other sciences in its quest to know ultimate reality.

The word *theology* comes from two Greek terms, *theos* (God) and *logos* (discourse), thus literally meaning "God speaking." This corresponds to the impulse within the nature of God to make himself and his purposes known. That inherent desire to communicate bespeaks his love, which gives rise to evangelism—bearing Good News. And what greater news can one hear than to learn of the love of God and his Redeemer Son, whom to know aright is eternal life.

In their origins, then, theology and evangelism belong together. When the two are separated in practice, as so often happens, both suffer loss—theology loses direction and evangelism loses content. To use the analogy of C. E. Autrey: "Theology is to evangelism what the skeleton is to the body. Remove the skeleton and the body becomes a helpless quivering mass of jelly-like substance."[1] Looking at it another way, J. I. Packer observes, when theology is separated from evangelism, "it grows abstract and speculative, wayward in method, theoretical in interest and irresponsible in stance."[2] Perhaps James Denny says it best: "If evangelists were our theologians or theologians our evangelists, we should be nearer the ideal, for evangelism is in the last resort the judge of theology."[3]

### Evangelical Theology

The Gospel defines what is popularly called evangelical theology. Its fundamentals, according to J. I. Packer, are "the supremacy of Holy Scripture,

9

the majesty of Jesus Christ, the lordship of the Holy Spirit, the necessity of conversion, the priority of evangelism, and the importance of fellowship."[4]

John Stott reduces Packer's six essentials to three (the last three he believes are but elaborations of the first three). Thus, using the three persons of the Holy Trinity as a rubric, evangelical priorities are summed up in "the revealing initiative of God the Father, the redeeming work of God the Son and the transforming ministry of God the Holy Spirit."[5]

Some scholars see in the larger revelation of God's Good News a central core of salvation truth particularly in the preaching of the apostles. Prominent in the viewpoint is C. H. Dodd. He makes a distinction between preaching, the Greek term *kerygma*, meaning public proclamation to the non-Christian world, and teaching, the Greek word *didaskein*, addressed to the church.[6] In this view, much in revelation would not be strictly evangelistic, the audience determining what was appropriate. Michael Green, on the other hand, sees a much wider variety of ways the Gospel was presented.[7]

However one wants to define the essential message, evangelical theology gets its name from the Gospel. As John Stott says, "Both our theology (evangelism) and our activity (evangelizing) derive their meaning and their importance from the good news (the evangel)."[8]

For a concise formulation of the Gospel, based on the total revelation of God, one needs to go back to the great affirmations of Christendom hammered out in the first centuries of the church, particularly the Apostles', the Nicene, the Chalcedonian, and the Athanasian Creeds. To these early ecumenical statements could be added the confessions of faith developed through the history of the church, like the Thirty-nine Articles, the Westminster Confession, the New Hampshire Baptist Confession, and the Articles of Religion of the Methodist Church. More recent ecumenical proclamations of general acceptance among evangelical theologians would be the Lausanne Covenant and the Amsterdam Declaration: A Charter for Evangelism in the Twenty-First Century. Suffice it to say that evangelical theology and orthodox Christianity are cut from the same cloth.

It is in this full sense of divine revelation that I approach a theology of evangelism. Some parts of doctrine may have more immediate relevance to personal salvation, but everything that God has said has some bearing on his purpose to make a people to display his glory. Cut through evangelical theology anywhere, I believe, and it will bleed the Gospel.

### Scope of Evangelism

Let me clarify, however, that to me making known the Good News means more than making converts. Certainly that is primary, but the objective of the Gospel in the context of the Great Commission is to make disciples, that is, learners committed to following Christ, teaching them in turn to do the same, that through the process of multiplication, someday the nations will hear the Gospel (Matt. 28:18–20).

It is the vision of reaching the world with God's saving revelation that drives evangelism and evangelical theology. The Commission comes from him who has all authority, and therefore with the assurance that, however long it takes, God will accomplish his purpose.

Every believer enters into this mission. Making disciples is not a special gift or calling; it is a lifestyle of obedience incumbent on the whole body of Christ, the church.

## No Lack of Resources

The basic text for the study of God, of course, is the Bible, our only inerrant source of truth. Interpretations of Scripture in commentaries and theological formulations will vary, so it is helpful to compare notes. We can learn much from each other, especially in working through differing points of view.

In my own study, I have perused the writings of the early Christian fathers, then followed developing thought through church history, giving particular attention to the great reformers, while not forgetting voices of renewal from the Moravians, Pietists, Puritans, and Wesleyans. Many scholars of more recent vintage have also been consulted in an effort to understand the theological underpinnings of the Gospel.[9]

Giving my research more practical input, countless sermons also have been reviewed from preachers with a passion for souls. I have often told my students, the best way to understand theology is to see how it preaches.

Across the years, too, a number of books described as theologies of evangelism have appeared,[10] one of the most recent being the work of Lewis A. Drummond.[11] While I am appreciative of these works, my own study takes a more comprehensive approach and gives greater attention to application.

## Pattern of the Study

The book unfolds with some variation around the classical outline of systematic theology, beginning with the character of God the Father, his revelation, creation, and the fall of mankind. Moving to God the Son, attention centers on the incarnation, the life and death of Christ, his resurrection, and ascension. Then with the Holy Spirit in prominence, the focus is on the grace of God, conversion, the new life, sanctification, and eternal security. The study concludes with the church, Christ's return, the providence of God, and the coming glory.

Each chapter begins with a biblical résumé of the doctrine. This leads to the theological rationale, which in some instances brings out conflicting evangelical interpretations. Where pertinent, distinctions are made between Reformed and Arminian positions, and on some doctrines, differences with Roman Catholic dogma. The next section treats popular misconceptions of the Gospel that adversely affect evangelism. Finally, each chapter ends with a practical application of the doctrine. These observations are not exhaustive, but they capsule important issues. All that goes before in the chapter gives the background for these conclusions. Obviously one cannot make applications until first the theological basis is understood.

Initially, the chapters were delivered as lectures to my students. In that setting, clarity, brevity, and simplicity were all-important, as well as the frequent use of illustrations. When the oral presentations were rewritten and revised for this book format, I tried to follow these guidelines even more closely.

Much cannot be covered in a work of this size, of course. However, something left out in one chapter may be treated in another. Theology rests on the total revelation of God, so it all tends to come together in the end.

## A Burning Heart

Though this book had its origin in the classroom, its purpose is not academic. The study of theology, rightly pursued, becomes a spiritual exercise that leads into the heart of God, out of which flows his Gospel to a lost world he ever seeks to save. To feel the passion of God speaking makes one burn with the desire to tell the Good News to others.

I recall the German pastor Pregizer of Haiterbach once seeking to arouse his lethargic congregation by suddenly shouting in a Maundy Thursday sermon: "Fire! Fire! Fire!"

"Where?" the startled congregation asked.

Whereupon the pastor exclaimed, "In disciples' hearts!"[12]

It is my hope that tracing in these pages the story of the Gospel through the sequence of theology will ignite an evangelical fire in disciples' hearts.

# 1

# The Character of God

Evangelism is all about God. He is the evangelist. Making known the Gospel of salvation unveils the character of him who sits on the throne, the Lord God Almighty, Sovereign of the universe, who displays his glory in the redemption of a people made in his image to praise him forever. Getting to know this God and glorifying him is the purpose of evangelism.

## The God We Know

Let us acknowledge at the onset that God is too great for our finite minds to fathom. That was made clear when Moses asked God his name. His reply: "I Am Who I Am," or it could be translated, "I Am What I Am" or "I Will Be What I Will Be" (Exod. 3:14). Clearly only God can define who he is.[1]

### The Holy Trinity

Though still beyond full comprehension, God reveals himself in Scripture as Father, Son, and Holy Spirit. The presence of these three divine personalities begins to emerge in the Old Testament. Genesis records God saying, "Let us make man in our image," indicating a plurality of persons involved in the creation decision (Gen. 1:26; cf. 3:22; 11:7; Isa. 6:8). Likewise, there are instances where the word *God* or *Lord* is used to distinguish from another person acting as God (Pss. 10:1; 45:6–7; Hosea 1:7). In Isaiah 48:16, when the Messiah can be seen in the word *me*, it appears that the whole Trinity is recognized: "And now the Lord GOD has sent me, and his Spirit."

The New Testament brings the concept to culmination. It comes through constantly in the words of Jesus. For example: "It is not I alone who judge, but I and the Father who sent me" (John 8:16); "I will ask the Father, and he will give you another Helper, to be with you forever" (John 14:16); "When the Helper comes, whom I will send to you from the Father, the Spirit of truth, who proceeds from the Father, he will bear witness about me" (John 15:26). Other instances when all three persons are mentioned together in the Gospel narratives are at the baptism of Jesus (Matt. 3:16–17) and in the baptismal formula given by Jesus when he sent out his disciples with the Great Commission (Matt. 28:19). Indications of the Trinity could be multiplied through the New Testament (e.g., 1 Cor. 12:4–6; 2 Cor. 13:14; Eph. 4:4–6; 1 Pet. 1:2).

Theologians through the ages have sought to formulate the idea of a triune God into various creeds.[2] The Article in the Church of England would be typical: "There is but one living and true God, everlasting, without body, parts, or passion; of infinite power, wisdom, and goodness; the Maker and Preserver of all things both visible and invisible. And in unity of this Godhead there be three Persons, of one substance, power, and eternity: the Father, the Son, and the Holy Spirit."[3]

### The Photograph of God

However helpful this and other historic creeds may be, they leave much to the imagination. I heard of a little girl who was drawing a picture at school. Asked by her teacher what she was drawing, the little girl said that she was drawing a picture of God. "But, you know, dear," replied the teacher, "nobody really knows what God looks like." Without a pause, the little girl answered, "Well, they will when I get through."[4]

You may smile at the little girl's presumption, but her desire to objectify God's identity seems quite natural. Do you not try to visualize God in a personal way? That was in the mind of the disciples when Jesus told them that he was going to prepare a real place for them in heaven. But "how can we know the way there?" asked Thomas. Jesus replied, "I am the way, and the truth, and the life. No one comes to the Father except through me" (John 14:6).

Still not satisfied, Philip said, "Lord, show us the Father, and it is enough for us" (v. 8). As if to say, this teaching about God is fine, but put it in concrete terms, so we can see him with our eyes. "Jesus said to him, 'Have I been with you so long, and you still do not know me, Philip? Whoever has seen me has seen the Father'" (v. 9; cf. 1 John 1:1).

This is why any understanding of the Trinity begins with Jesus. He is the photograph of God, "the exact imprint of his nature" (Heb. 1:3), "the image of the invisible God" (Col. 1:15). In him, through the Holy Spirit, the eternal "Word became flesh and dwelt among us, and we have seen his glory, glory as of the only Son from the Father, full of grace and truth" (John 1:14).

### Interpersonal Relationships

To be sure, Jesus is the one seen in human form, but God is also present in the Father and the Spirit. Each of the three persons in whom the one God exists has their being in relation to the other two. The Father reveals himself in the Son who glorifies the Father on earth by accomplishing the work given him to do (John 17:4). This reciprocal love is given expression in the person of the Holy Spirit who receives his being from the self-giving love of the Father and the Son (John 15:26). The three persons of the Trinity are thus "pure relationality; they are relations in which the one nature of God works in three distinct and non-interchangeable ways."[5]

Within his relational being, God has eternal fellowship. Different from human beings who are always dependent on their Creator and Lord for completeness, the Sovereign God enjoys perfect communion and fulfillment within himself. The Father, Son, and Spirit in love "so co-inhere within each other that if you know one person of God, you know all three persons and have found all that God is."[6]

### Undivided Unity

The interaction of the Father, Son, and Spirit in no way implies the existence of three gods. This was made clear when the commandments were given by God to Moses, and it was repeated by Jesus: "Hear, O Israel: The LORD our God, the LORD is one" (Deut. 6:4; Mark 12:29).

Obviously, too, God cannot be divided into parts. All his characteristics fuse into his whole being. One characteristic may be more prominent in a particular situation, but every other aspect of deity is also present in his fully integrated personality.

Sometimes theologians speak of this unity as "singularity," in the sense that there is only one God, and not many. That he is by nature distinctively holy, of course, precludes his being among many gods. Signifying his separateness, over and over, the Bible declares that there is no other deity (e.g., Neh. 9:6; Ps. 86:10; Isa. 44:6; Zech. 14:9; 1 Cor. 8:4; James 2:19). Clearly there is "one God and Father of all, who is over all and through all and in all" (Eph. 4:6).

The Bible, without attempting to explain the mystery, simply shows the "togetherness" of God in three persons, equal in glory, one in essence, yet each separate from the other in consciousness and vocation.

### The Inexplicable Reality

Admittedly, the Trinity is a reality beyond human comprehension, but regardless of our inability to grasp its full-orbed glory, it does afford a means by which the nature and work of God can be interpreted.

Attempts to explain the One Divine Three take many forms. To T. A. Kantonen, the Trinity yields a subject, a predicate, and an object. The subject of course is the Revealer, God the Father; the predicate or act is the Revelation, God revealing himself in Christ; and the object is the impartation of himself to people in their historic existence, through the revealedness of the Spirit.[7] In some Reformed theology, an eternal covenant of redemption is believed to have taken place within the persons of the Trinity. The Father elects a people of Christ, the Son is entrusted their salvation, and the Holy Spirit carries out the application of redemption. Looking at the Trinity with a missiological eye, Timothy C. Tennent conceptualizes the Father as the sender or source of the mission, the incarnate Son as the historical embodiment of mission in the world, and the Holy Spirit as the enabling power of God for the mission.[8]

Others see God in his universal relations as the Father, unveiling himself as the Son, and in operation as the Spirit. From a different perspective, God is beyond us as the Father, among us as the Son, and within us as the Spirit. To use the illustration of electricity, the Father can be likened to the dynamo, the Son to the wire, and the Spirit to the power.

The triangle is another paradigm, their being one triangle with three sides. Some have seen the sun as analogous to the Father, the light of the sun to the Son, and its warmth to the Holy Spirit. Still others may point to the oneness of water, yet it is found in three states: ice, liquid, and vapor.

All these efforts to explain the Trinity of God still cannot adequately describe the Godhead. The commendable efforts of theologians to reduce this infinite truth to a simple formula fall as far short of the goal as the human mind is finite. But the wonder of it causes a wise person to reverence even more the greatness of God.

The Gospel evolves within the context of this revelation. In fact the doctrine of the blessed Holy Trinity, when seen in the light of redemption, becomes the summation of the Christian faith.

### The Personhood of God

Seeing Jesus, and the mutual love within the persons of the Holy Trinity, makes real the personhood of God. No mystical abstraction, no mechanical force, no cold system of law, God is a person and personally involved with his creation. He is described as the "Father of the fatherless" (Ps. 68:5); the "good shepherd" (John 10:11, 14); a counselor who "will guide you into all truth" (John 16:13). Human beings can know and love a person.

Have you noticed that throughout the Scriptures practically everything that is attributed to a person is also ascribed to God—he sees, he speaks, he hears, he teaches, he leads, he sends, he reproves, he takes, he receives, he governs, he reigns, he hates, he loves? These are human feelings and actions involving knowledgeable decisions.

To think of God as a person is to recognize that he is rational and voluntary in what he does. To put it another way, he is self-conscious, intelligent, a free moral being. Though unspoiled like humans, he has a mind and will by which his actions are determined.

The personhood of God enables us to understand how there can be unity within the plurality of the Trinity. A person, as we know ourselves, has many thoughts and activities, though in a very restricted sense. But God, as the ultimate person, who has no limitations, can involve himself as he pleases anytime and anywhere without any loss of his self-identity.

He acts in consistency with his nature; the person is who does the acting. It is this personal quality of God that gives purpose to all that happens in the universe, including the unfolding drama of redemption.

## Divine Attributes

Qualities that define the character of God are often called "attributes." Grouped in various ways, they help one approach an understanding of the unsearchable dimensions of the Almighty.

A young chaplain at one of the Oxford University Colleges made a practice of asking new students about their religious convictions. He was not surprised when occasionally a freshman would say, somewhat awkwardly, that he did not believe in the God that the chaplain believed in. The chaplain would then reply, "How interesting! Would you mind telling me in which god you do not believe?" After the student would give his reason for rejecting God, the chaplain would then smile, and more often than not, comment that he and the student had a great deal in common, for he did not believe in that kind of God either.[9] I expect that many of us would agree with the chaplain on hearing some of the strange notions of God put forth by confused and misguided unbelievers.

Of course, God is so incomparably perfect in his essence, and we are so bound by the limitations of our flesh, that our efforts to describe him are pitifully incomplete. It may actually be easier to think of God in the way he is not limited as we are.[10] Recognizing the contrast may help us see God as well as ourselves more realistically.

### Incommunicable Attributes

These qualities relate to the absolute existence of God and are termed "incommunicable" because in any real sense they cannot be shared with us.

17

Unlike us, *God is not limited by creation*. He is uncreated, self-existent in himself but not solitary. "The God who made the world and everything in it, being Lord of heaven and earth, does not live in temples made by man, nor is he served by human hands, as though he needed anything, since he himself gives to all mankind life and breath and everything" (Acts 17:24–25). Not bound by a physical body, as we are, his existence is pure being, more real than the material world. He "is spirit, and those who worship him must worship in spirit and truth" (John 4:24).

Consider, too, that *God is not limited by space*. He is omnipresent and imminent. "Do I not fill heaven and earth? declares the LORD" (Jer. 23:24; cf. Ps. 139:7–12). "The heavens, even the highest heavens, cannot contain" our God (1 Kings 8:27 NIV; 2 Chron. 6:18 NIV). To use the expression of H. Orton Wiley, God exists in "immensity of infinitude."[11] Not that he is everything he made, as pantheists contend, but he is always present in every part of creation.

Moreover, *God is not limited by time*; he is eternal, "the Alpha and the Omega" (Rev. 1:8), "who was and is and is to come" (Rev. 4:8), "the LORD [who] will reign forever and ever" (Exod. 15:18; cf. Ps. 9:7). Standing above time, free from all temporal distinctions, in his being there is no succession, no beginning or ending, no past or future—all is present in him, an eternal now. Time itself is of his making; it has its origin and its continuation within his will. With us time is an urgent factor, of course, but never with God. He is from "everlasting to everlasting" (Ps. 90:2).

Even more, *God is not limited by change*. He is immutable, "the same yesterday and today and forever" (Heb. 13:8). In the midst of the world's vicissitudes and decay, he says, "I the LORD do not change" (Mal. 3:6). The earth "will perish" and the works of mankind "will all wear out like a garment," but God will "remain the same" (Heb. 1:11–12 NIV). With him there is no variation "like shifting shadows" (James 1:17 NIV).

How reassuring it is to know that God will always be what he is. Though he can change in his actions toward people and nations, depending on their changes of behavior, he will never change in his character. His purposes are steadfast, never failing.

Try to comprehend also that *God is not limited by ignorance*. He is omniscient, possessing perfect knowledge of all things. "Nothing in all creation is hidden from God's sight. Everything is uncovered and laid bare before the eyes of him to whom we must give account" (Heb. 4:13 NIV). "God is light; in him there is no darkness at all" (1 John 1:5 NIV). "I make known the end from the beginning," he says, "from ancient times, what is still to come" (Isa. 46:10 NIV).

Because he "is perfect in knowledge" (Job 37:16), "the only wise God" (Rom. 16:27), he always acts in the best way to accomplish his goals. Even when finite creatures reject his desires, he knows in advance those contrary choices and has planned accordingly.[12] "Oh, the depth of the riches of the wisdom and knowledge of God! How unsearchable his judgments, and his paths beyond tracing out" (Rom. 11:33 NIV).

As if this difference with us were not enough, *God is not limited by any weakness.* He is omnipotent, the Lord Almighty, who "does all that he pleases" (Ps. 115:3). The prophet expressed it well: "Ah, Sovereign LORD, you have made the heavens and the earth by your great power and outstretched arm. Nothing is too hard for you" (Jer. 32:17 NIV). "Do you not know? Have you not heard? . . . He sits enthroned above the circle of the earth, and its people are like grasshoppers. He stretches out the heavens like a canopy, and spreads them out like a tent to live in. He brings princes to naught and reduces the rulers of this world to nothing" (Isa. 40:21–23 NIV).

Because of his invincible power, it was only natural for Jesus to remind his disciples that "with God all things are possible" (Matt. 19:26; cf. Luke 1:37). No way can his sovereign power be curtailed by man, "for the Lord our God the Almighty reigns" (Rev. 19:6).

What a mighty God we have! A realization of his self-existent attributes should fill a creature with awe. But more wonderful is the perfection of his moral character.

### Communicable Moral Attributes

The moral qualities of God are shared with us. And when we compare ourselves with him, they help us realize how, limited as we are, we can by his enabling partake of his character. We know that *God cannot be unjust.* He "is righteous in all his ways" (Ps. 145:17); "righteousness and justice are the foundation of his throne" (Ps. 97:2); "his works are perfect, and all his ways are just. A faithful God who does no wrong" (Deut. 32:4 NIV).

The moral order of the universe rests on this rock, the foundation of God's law. Because his character cannot be compromised, evil invariably invokes divine wrath. Yet judgment always is in accordance with justice. As Abraham put it, "Will not the Judge of all the earth do right?" (Gen. 18:25 NIV). Whatever the situation, we can be confident that the answer is in the affirmative.

Wonderful, too, is knowing that *God cannot deceive or be unfaithful,* for he is true (John 16:13). "It is impossible for [him] to lie" (Heb. 6:18). Since his "word is truth" (John 17:17), we can trust implicitly what he says. Therefore, what he promised he will do. The steadfastness of God is a corollary to his truthfulness. "Does he speak and then not act? Does he promise and not fulfill?" (Num. 23:19 NIV). The answer cannot be doubted, for God "keeps faith forever" (Ps. 146:6).

More blessed still is the assurance that *God cannot be defiled or contaminated by sin.* He is holy (Ps. 71:22), meaning that he is utterly separate from anything profane. As the prophet said, his "eyes are too pure to look on evil," or even to "tolerate wrong" (Hab. 1:13 NIV). Preeminently holiness defines the nature of God.

Descriptive of this character, when the Lord is seen sitting on his throne, the seraphim in his presence call to one another, "Holy, holy, holy is the LORD of hosts; the whole earth is full of his glory" (Isa. 6:3). So awesome is the flaming brightness of the glory of God that the seraphim, expressing their worship and humility, cover their faces and feet with their wings. The threefold repetition of their adoration here and in Revelation 4:8 was the Hebrew's way of emphasizing what was said—like an exclamation point in English. Interestingly, no other divine attribute receives this same emphatic acclamation in Scripture.

Though God is set apart from all other beings, in his desire to display his glory to himself, he wants persons made in his image to be like him: "You shall be holy, for I am holy" (1 Pet. 1:16; cf. Lev. 11:44). This quality of life distinguishes God's people and makes them different from the world. "You shall be to me," he declares, "a kingdom of priests and a holy nation" (Exod. 19:6). As we shall discuss later when considering sanctification, the making of saints lies at the heart of biblical evangelism and discipleship.[13]

Flowing out of God's holiness is an attribute that further defines his nature and the heartbeat of the Gospel. Wonder of wonders, *God cannot be unloving.* He "is love" (1 John 4:16), a quality determined by God himself, the subject, not by the recipients of his love. What it means is manifested perfectly in the relationship of the Father and the Son within the Holy Trinity (John 15:9; 17:24, 26).

Wrapped up in this attitude are the goodness and mercy and grace of God. "For the LORD is good; his steadfast love endures forever, and his faithfulness to all generations" (Ps. 100:5). He is "merciful and gracious, slow to anger, and abounding in steadfast love and faithfulness" (Exod. 34:6).

His love initiates our salvation, "not that we have loved God but that he loved us" (1 John 4:10). Calvary is the supreme demonstration of what this means, a self-giving love that would not let us go even "while we were still sinners" (Rom. 5:8; cf. John 3:16).

Having given so freely of himself, it is not surprising that God wants us to love like Jesus. This quality of character becomes the evidence that we are his disciples (John 14:23). Not only that, but his love for us while we were outcasts should overflow to our enemies (Matt. 5:43–45). That such love is expected certainly underscores the possibilities of divine grace apart from which there would be no hope for us all.

We can learn from the old farmer who had the weather vane of his barn inscribed with the words, "God is love." Asked, "Does that mean that God's love turns about as the arrow turns in the wind?" the farmer responded, "Oh, no, it means that whichever way the wind blows, God is still love."

## Some Common Misconceptions

Inadequate views of God undermine evangelism at its source. If the Author of salvation is imperfect in his nature, then that which he does must be defective. Hence any confusion with respect to God's character obscures the glory of the Gospel and finally questions its whole validity.

### Confounding the Holy Trinity

In some ways, all heresy involves disbelief in the Holy Trinity. Challenges to this doctrine have confronted the church from the beginning, yet these attacks have served to make the early fathers think through this truth, of which the great creeds of Christendom bear eloquent testimony.[14] Opponents usually strike at either the purity of the Godhead or the eternity of the persons in the Trinity.

Those attempting to destroy the unity will contend that the one God manifested himself, not as the Trinity of persons, but in three successive modes or forms. Those attacking the eternity of the Trinity regard the Son and Spirit as created beings, rather than coexistent with God.

Suffice it to say, theologies that dilute the oneness of the Father, Son, and Holy Spirit, or detract from the eternity of any member of the Holy Trinity, will only confound the redemptive mission of God.

### Depersonalizing God

Exponents of deism regard God as a sort of spiritual force or body of law that governs the universe, but he has no personal involvement in what he has made. He is seen as a sort of distant landlord so transcendent to creation that personal communion with him is impossible.[15] Reason is thought to be sufficient to answer all the questions of man, including what can be known about God. Anything miraculous is ruled out.[16]

It can be seen readily that this opinion eliminates the experiential side of the Gospel and makes salvation little more than the Hindu idea of Nirvana—the self-losing personal identity in the eternal principle of the cosmos.

### Downplaying Divine Sovereignty

Unthinking persons, infatuated with an exaggerated sense of self-sufficiency, like to subdue, or at least minimize, the awesome reality of God's almighty authority and control in the universe. His absolute rule over all things seems too overpowering. The title sometimes ascribed to God as "the man upstairs," while not used by sophisticated people, nevertheless reflects the idea in this humanistic bent of mind.

It amounts to sinful creatures trying to project human limitations on God, as if unlimited deity could be confined within the restrictions of our finite experience. God is looked on as a softhearted grandfather who will never do anything to disrupt the pleasure of his children. The Lord of heaven and earth is thought to be dependent on people for his administration of creation and accountable to us for what he does.

Such thinking represents the assertion of human arrogance and pride and is nothing less than blasphemy. For either God is all-powerful, unlimited by and independent from all others, or else he is not God at all.

### Evolution within the Character of God

Akin to this perversion, God may be looked upon as a person still in the process of growth, along with mankind. As God matures, it is claimed, so also do human beings, a teaching popularized in Mormonism: "What man is, God once was; what God is, man may become." With this concept of eternal progression, man will eventually evolve into godhood.

While magnifying the potential of human development, this idea entirely ignores the unchanging character of God and, like so many other heresies, has the effect of making God in man's image.

### Tampering with God's Complete Perfection

Persons in this error ignore any divine attribute that would correct a mistaken preconceived position and stress only qualities of God that support their opinion. For example, universalists who believe no one is ultimately lost like to emphasize divine love to the exclusion of his justice. On the other hand, those who see clearly God's justice may overlook his loving-kindness.

Admittedly, it is hard to keep every diverse attribute in balance. And, I suspect, all of us need more understanding. Still, despite the difficulty, whenever one attribute of God is exaggerated out of context with the perfection of his whole being, either by ignorance or unbelief, to that degree the application of the conclusion will be in error. Thankfully, persons who have full confidence in the absolute integrity of God are much better able to grow in grace and knowledge.

## Summary Applications

Applications of God's character will be seen as the scope of redemption unfolds in subsequent chapters. But some things need to be clear at the onset.

### 1. Evangelism flows out from God.

As the revelation of his character, God is self-authenticating. He needs no proof. He is God. The reality of his overruling presence is never in question. Of course, arguments for his existence,[17] and the reasonableness of the Christian faith, are easily found and can be helpful in presenting the Gospel.[18]

However, the Good News of salvation does not analyze the inner being of the Trinity of God; it simply bears witness to his manifestations as the Father, Son, and Holy Spirit. As to the relationship between the three persons of the Godhead and their respective functions, the Gospel is content to leave a mystery a mystery.[19] The mystery, of course, lies in the manner of the *how* of the Trinity, not the *fact* of it. We do not have to commit our faith to what is not disclosed, as John Wesley observed: "Would it not be absurd in me to deny the fact, because I do not understand the manner, that is, to reject what God has revealed, because I do not comprehend what he has not revealed."[20]

Indeed, this is the only position that makes sense. We are not surprised, then, at the way the apostles proclaimed the Trinity in their experience of God without getting bogged down in futile controversy. For example, in the sermon at Pentecost, Peter declares the councils of the Father, the work of Christ, and the promise of the Holy Spirit—all as facts—without even trying to show how God could have spoken through David or how Christ could have worked miracles or how the Holy Spirit comes (Acts 2:15–39).

Similarly, we do not have to answer every curious question about God in order to proclaim his holy majesty. We are called only to bear witness to his revelation. The Gospel is a testimony, not a critique.

Failure to make clear at the beginning the reality of the sovereign Being of God shrouds the message with uncertainty. This is the fallacy of theological liberalism, and all other schemes of human deductions that begin with the premise "know thyself." Man, of course, must know himself, but unless we first see our Creator and Savior, we are in no position to correctly evaluate ourselves as creatures of God. To start with man and seek to work up to God is in effect to start with a problem and to end up in confusion. Thus it usually happens that when finite man evolves his own theology on the basis of his limited knowledge and experience, he ends up limiting God and deifying himself. This is idolatry, and it takes from the Gospel of salvation all its meaning and purpose.

Evangelical truth, on the other hand, always starts with God—as fully disclosed in Christ through the Holy Spirit—and then as we see him in our image, we know not only how far short we have fallen from God's glory, but also what God wants us to be.

*2. The Triune God is perfect and complete within himself.*

God requires nothing to supplement his being. He is his own cause. He is his own reason. He is his own wisdom. He is his own activity. He is maximally perfect, so there can be no possible way for God to improve himself.

This dispels any notion that God needs us to help him out, as if our fellowship would fill some vacuum in his nature. Within the Trinity, God already enjoys absolute communion, so he never gets lonely.

23

More absurd is the idea that he has to consult with us in the discharge of his will. He may reason with us, but that is entirely his prerogative. The prophet expressed it well: "Who has measured the Spirit of the LORD, or what man shows him his counsel? Whom did he consult, and who made him understand? Who taught him the path of justice, and taught him knowledge, and showed him the way of understanding? . . . All the nations are as nothing before him, they are accounted by him as less than nothing and emptiness" (Isa. 40:13–14, 17).

### 3. God can do anything he wants to do.

All the resources of the cosmos are at God's command. Nothing in heaven and earth is beyond the reach of God's mighty arm. What, then, shall we say to these things? The apostle Paul answered it right: "If God is for us, who can be against us?" (Rom. 8:31).

But let us not think that we can set God's agenda. His sovereignty cannot be tamed. Just with one wave of his hand, if he pleases, he can strike every creature to the dust. As he said to Moses, "I wound and I heal; and there is none that can deliver out of my hand" (Deut. 32:39). To persons in rebellion against God, this is a terrifying thought. That feeling is depicted by Jonathan Edwards when preaching on the text, "Their foot shall slide in due time" (Deut. 32:35 KJV):

> There is no fortress that is any defense from the power of God. Though hand join in hand, and vast multitudes of God's enemies contrive and associate themselves, they are broken in pieces. They are as great heaps of chaff before the whirlwind; or large quantities of dry stubble before devouring flames. We find it easy to tread on and crush a worm that we see crawling on the earth; so it is easy for us to cut or singe a slender thread that anything hangs by: thus easy it is for God, when he pleases, to cast his enemies down to hell. What are we, that we should think to stand before him, at whose rebuke the earth trembles, and before whom the rocks are thrown down?[21]

### 4. God never makes mistakes.

Though human beings are helpless before God's power, whatever he does issues from the perfection of his character. Because he knows all things, and can see everything in light of his ultimate purpose for creation, "his way is perfect" (Ps. 18:30).

God is no less loving even when he executes judgment on sinners, for he is also just and must respect the demands of his own law of righteousness. And because he is holy, he can never excuse sin; nor can he be unmindful of it, since he is omniscient. God cannot violate his own nature, just as every attribute of his person is in perfect harmony with all the others. Such knowledge is too wonderful for us, but it is utterly consistent with God. Indeed, apart from this impeccable excellence of his character, he would not be God.

What a beautiful confidence this brings to a trusting disciple! Whether God be at work on his judgment of nations or on his care of a little sparrow that falls to the earth, it is the same mighty Lord who acts. An appreciation of this fact gives significance to everything that happens, just as it should cause us to walk softly before our God.

### 5. Bowing before God is the first requirement for salvation.

If God is, then everything that exists or happens must acknowledge his lordship. "Whoever would draw near to God must believe that he exists and that he rewards those who seek him" (Heb. 11:6).

This elemental truth comes through so clearly in the plea of God to his wayward people when he says, "Turn to me and be saved, all the ends of the earth! For I am God, and there is no other. By myself I have sworn; from my mouth has gone out in righteousness a word that shall not return: 'To me every knee shall bow, every tongue shall swear allegiance'" (Isa. 45:22–23).

Recognizing God's rightful claim on our lives, thus, becomes our initial step toward redemption. To presume that we can get along without God is idolatry of self—the essence of sin. We may seek to escape this fact, but no one can ever get beyond God's reach; not even in dying, for death only opens the door to a final reckoning with truth.

At the funeral of Louis XIV, the priest looked down at the casket containing the body of the once-powerful monarch of France, with the luxurious robes of royalty concealing the cold form within. Then turning to the assembled nobility present, he began his oration, "My friends, only God is great!" Indeed, this truth should be obvious to all. But if it is not realized on this earth, we may be sure that it is proclaimed in heaven, and to him "every knee shall bow" (Rom. 14:11).

### 6. The quest for truth begins on our knees.

Reverence for the Creator and Lord of the universe puts his creatures in a position to learn from him. "The fear of the LORD is the beginning of wisdom" (Ps. 111:10; cf. Job 28:28). Until this humility of the student is reached, learning in any form has not found its purpose or direction.

Unfortunately, in wanting wisdom, we can amass a lot of facts yet never come "to arrive at a knowledge of the truth" (2 Tim. 3:7). Facts must be assembled and related to the higher intelligence of God if they are to have pertinent significance. True wisdom has its origin in us when we cease to live in our own authority.

This was made vivid to me while pursuing an interest in oil painting after graduation from college. One day the teacher, trying to help me see an object critically, picked up a skull lying on the shelf and, placing it on an old, open, dusty college textbook, told me to paint what I saw. As I sat there looking intently at that replica of someone's ended life, resting on that emblem of human learning, it helped put my education in perspective. This is the reason that painting, though no work of art, across the years has hung on the wall of my office between academic degrees.

Sometimes students notice the painting and ask its meaning. I tell them to read the first three chapters of Paul's first letter to the church at Corinth, and they will understand. In these chapters the apostle explains that to this world the Gospel of the cross seems foolish and that to find the wisdom from above one must first bow before the Lord. In its most basic sense, education should make this clear to us—that all truth ultimately centers on God and that he alone gives meaning to our existence.

*7. Knowing God is the only happiness that can satisfy the human soul.*
In his "presence there is fullness of joy" and at his right hand "pleasures forevermore" (Ps. 16:11; cf. 1 Pet.1:8).

To comprehend his character is to feel the magnificence of glory. This realization broke in upon the consciousness of Jonathan Edwards one day as he read in the Bible: "Now unto the King eternal, immortal, invisible, the only wise God, be honour and glory for ever and ever" (1 Tim. 1:17 KJV). He said:

> There came into my soul, and was as it were diffused throughout, a sense of the glory of the divine Being; a new sense, quite different from anything I ever experienced before. Never any words of Scripture seemed to me as these words did. I thought with myself, how excellent a being that was; and how happy I should be if I might enjoy that God, and be rapt up to him in heaven; and be as it were swallowed up in him forever![22]

Knowing this God and enjoying him forever is the reason we exist, and making him known the blessing of our mission in life.

*8. The personhood of God finally revealed in Jesus brings his glory into the realm of our experience.*
Although this truth may be abused by those who think of God as a person limited like themselves, thus degrading his character and restricting his power, nevertheless, it is essential to the Gospel. God is a person—not confined to any human limitation—but still a person of intelligence and will, a person infinitely sovereign, yet a person whom we can know and experience.

Here we have a medium of communication and communion. Our finite minds may try to envision the infinite dimensions of God's reign, yet our imaginations at last are exhausted. His ways are so much higher than our ways that they cannot be fathomed by human deduction. But all of us can have a knowledge and love of a person, and though we stand in awe before him, we know that he understands and he cares.

The story is told of a little boy standing on a riverbank, waving his hand and calling to an approaching riverboat, "Here I am! Here I am!"

People noticed the boy and told him to go on home, that no one on that steamer would pay any attention to him. But the little boy did not seem to hear and just kept waving his hand and calling, "Here I am!"

Then to the surprise of everyone but the boy, that river steamboat suddenly turned and made its way to the riverbank. The stairway of the boat was lowered, the ship's captain came ashore, walked over to the little boy, put his arm around him, and together they walked up the stairway onto the deck of the boat.

The whistle blew and slowly the steamboat pulled away. As it churned back into the river, the little boy called to the astonished people watching on the bank, "I knew all along that this boat would stop for me, for the captain of this boat is my daddy."

That is the way it is with our Father God. An overwhelming feeling comes into the heart of those who accept this truth, realizing that he who was before the worlds were made; he whose will is the source of all law; he who is the life of all that live—the Creator of all that exists, the King of the universe, the Lord God Almighty—is our Father. He knows. He feels. He delights to make himself known. He gives us his hand, and we see that it is not the hand of a philosophical doctrine but rather the hand of a real person, the hand of God who finally took on himself the form of our flesh and walked among us in the person of Jesus Christ, who bore our sins away on the cross and who continues to minister to us now in the person of the Holy Spirit.

Oh, this is the hand of the Gospel! When it grips the heart, evangelism comes alive.

# 2

# Revelation and the Bible

A dramatic moment in the coronation of Queen Elizabeth II came when the moderator of the General Assembly of the Church of Scotland presented her with the Holy Bible. Then the Archbishop of Canterbury said, "Our gracious Queen: to keep your majesty ever mindful of the Laws and the Gospel of God as the Rule for the whole of life and government of Christian Princes, we present you with this Book, the most valuable thing the world affords."

More appropriate words could not have been spoken. For the Bible is a divine revelation, apart from which mankind would be lost without hope in this world.

## God Has Spoken

### Human Limitations

Because of the finiteness of man, until the Father God speaks,[1] we have no way of knowing who he is or his Gospel of salvation. We may read out of the natural world some insights into things as they are[2] but remain bewildered in the realm of absolute and eternal truth.

It is well enough to see God's fingerprints in the created universe (Ps. 19:1–5)—the grandeur of the mountains and the majesty of the starry heavens bespeak his power and glory—but that does not disclose his character. We can deduce from the harshness of the storm and the fierceness of the tiger that life is hard and full of sorrows, but that recognition does not tell us how to be comforted. Yes, we can conclude from observations in nature that everything has an ending, and the grave seems certain, but our basic questions remain unanswered: Who am I? How did I get here? What is the reason for my toil? Where am I going? How can I be saved?

Finding no solace in nature, we may turn to the study of history for answers. Indeed, the behavior of men and nations through the ages, to a discerning student, can teach much about morality. For example, we can see in the rise and fall of civilizations that nations crumble outwardly when corrupted within. Common laws of decency and righteousness seem engraved in the structure of human government, and we always suffer when these laws are violated. Yet the observation of this fall, apart from an interpretative revelation of God, does not tell us the meaning of those events or that God is personally interested in the salvation of people. History shows the working out of providence but does not reveal its purpose.

Nor does the study of human nature answer our deepest questions. The conscience of man is an instrument of direction, not of revelation.[3] God enables our reason to perceive truth, but even this illumination is related to interpreting his Word. Persons, without supernatural help, simply have no means of discovering the redemptive plan of God. The mind can see evidence of God's influence over his creatures; it can show the reality of human longings and aspirations unfilled by science; it can point to the need for a fuller revelation of truth, even its credibility; but it can never produce an eternal Gospel. The consciousness of need exists, but there is no certain knowledge of how to meet the need. Man's basic questions can be answered only by divine revelation.

### God Knows Our Helplessness

We can be grateful that, through his grace, God the Father has made himself and his purposes known. He realizes our human predicament—knows it better than we do—and in his omniscient understanding, he has spoken to us.

A God of infinite love cannot ignore the plight of persons perishing for lack of saving truth, nor can he withhold the knowledge of what we were made to be, and by heeding his Word, can become. It is like him to want the best for his people. Because of the perfection of his being, he cannot do otherwise.

And since God is rational, he can reason with persons created in his image. Moreover, because he is true, everything he says can be trusted, for by his nature, he cannot deceive or lie.

So what we believe about the character of God finally determines how we regard his Word. To have faith in a mighty God makes it easy to believe the Bible.

### Personal Revelation

What makes his revelation believable is that God speaks to us in the way that we can best understand—he speaks personally. Not to discount that God has spoken within the framework of nature, history, and human consciousness—

but in a special way, he has spoken to persons as a person. Special revelation thus centers in personality—the person of God expressing himself through an intelligent word (the medium disclosing the purpose of the one speaking).

The word of God supremely expressed in himself, of course, comes through Christ—the second person of the Holy Trinity—the incarnate or living Word. Whenever God is fully disclosed, Christ is the person of the Godhead seen. In this sense, he is "the Word" (John 1:1)—the fullness of God expressed in all his attributes, including his love, which ultimately issues in the cross and the salvation of mankind. The only way, thus, that anyone can know God personally and redemptively is through his Son, Jesus Christ. He is the saving Word of God, who could say: "I am the way, and the truth, and the life. No one comes to the Father except through me" (John 14:6).

In a different way, the Word was spoken personally by specially anointed men. The validity of their proclaimed word comes from its inspiration by God, attested by his authority, and ordained for a purpose in redemption culminating in Jesus. Preserving accurately this oral word, however, required a permanent record of what was said. Without such a reliable memorandum, the message could be easily lost or misinterpreted with the passing of time.

To protect the transmission of this Word, it was at last written in the language of men through the inspiration of the Holy Spirit in the Bible. Thus God preserved his redemptive message from extinction as well as error by seeing that it was committed to writing. Through these recorded words, people now have access to a trustworthy declaration of the Gospel of grace.

The Bible becomes both the *record* of what God has done to redeem a people for his glory and the *means* by which this work is realized in human personality from one generation to another. While differing in form, the Bible is nevertheless part of God's special or supernatural revelation. The living Word, the spoken word, and the written word interact, which means that in truth what the Bible says is the Word of God.

## Inspiration of the Bible

### Attested by the Spirit

The words recorded in Scripture were inspired by God, meaning the language of the Bible was sovereignly communicated "in words not taught by human wisdom but taught by the Spirit" (1 Cor. 2:13; cf. Num. 24:2; 1 Sam. 10:6; 2 Sam. 23:2; 2 Chron. 15:1; Jer. 36:2; Matt. 22:43; Acts 1:16; 2 Tim. 3:16; Heb. 3:7; 10:15; 1 Pet. 1:11). To put it another way, the Holy Spirit so worked in the memory, perception, and imagination of choice servants that they were enabled to grasp and express divine truth.[4]

The exact way this was done remains a mystery, like any other miracle. However, the fusion of the divine and human in one personality of Jesus Christ—also a work of the Holy Spirit—reflects the same mysterious power of God. The doctrine of the inspiration of Scripture is a corollary of the incarnation of Christ.

The personalities of the prophets and apostles were not violated when receiving revelation. Their frailties of the flesh may have been supplemented in the transmission, but they were not mere mechanical scribes of an impersonal word.[5] The men who wrote the Bible remained themselves. In fact their own peculiar temperament and education was used by the Holy Spirit to great advantage in giving color and pungency to the message. That a number of people representing many different backgrounds were chosen to write the Bible is evidence that God intended his Word to be recorded from the standpoint of varied human circumstances.

Notwithstanding the limitations of the biblical authors, the Holy Spirit saw to it that the language used got the idea across. It had the approval of God. As originally written, then, the Holy Scripture was without any error of fact. Not that there are no differences of style or grammar, nor word for word exactness in quoted statements or direct discourse. It does not imply the inclusion of every detail or of identical details in parallel narratives. Inerrancy means simply that the statements of Holy Scripture are entirely trustworthy.

Inspiration, of course, refers to the original documents, not to translations or versions, which are subject to error. However, even in the transmission of these texts, the Spirit of God has preserved from corruption the essential revelation. Although there is no original autograph known today, still the best scientific research has concluded that our present text is substantially the same as the original.

### The Answer to Human Need

More to the point, the Bible speaks to our basic needs. It is "profitable for teaching, for reproof, for correction, and for training in righteousness, that the man of God may be competent, equipped for every good work" (2 Tim. 3:16–17). There is no part of the sacred writings that, if properly understood, would not have relevance to our lives.

Although all Scripture is authorized by God, the immediate application varies according to the need. For example, God has caused some words of the devil to be recorded so that we might recognize how Satan operates and resist his insidious ways. Similarly, there are some false teachings in the Bible, like the advice of the comforters of Job, which God himself contradicted. Whatever is said, however, is accurately reported for our good.

A continuity of purpose flows through it all, from beginning to end, since the author of the whole Scripture is the same Spirit of truth. The Old Testament is the prophecy of the New, while the New Testament is the fulfillment of the Old. Any part of the written Word of God points to the living Word, the fullness of all truth—Jesus Christ.

The record is now completed and sealed (Deut. 4:2; 12:32; Rev. 22:18–19). Nothing more needs to be said that is not already revealed in the Word. Moreover, anything not read therein or proved thereby is not required to be believed as an article of faith by any person.

### Canon of Scripture

The inspired writings have been collected to form the canon of the Bible. These are the divinely authenticated books collected to form a "rule of faith" for the church. It originated with the collected writings of the Old Testament and was completed with the New Testament.

Books were accepted into the canon by virtue of their own intrinsic nature and authority. It is important to realize that the Bible is not an authorized assortment of books, but rather a collection of authorized books. Inspired writings were verified on the basis of who the writer was, what he said, and how his message lined up with the witness of the Spirit in human experience. Each book thus determined to be canonical had to evidence some recognizable prophetic or apostolic credential, express an aspect of the redemptive revelation of God embodied in Christ, and correspond to the spiritual discernment given to true believers.

The church, after careful examination and comparison, bound the inspired books into the Bible. It was not the work of a single council, but the combined experience of the whole church extending over several hundred years, finally being fixed in the fourth century. Many writings were found unfit to be included in the canon because they could not meet the qualifications. This period of time for testing in no way implied a gradual recognition. No writing was included in the Bible that was not fully inspired by the Spirit in the first place. The way that God has providentially guarded authentic Scripture is but an expression of his power to make known the Gospel.

## Interpreting Scripture

### Getting It Right

The words of Scripture must be correctly interpreted, of course. So God gives illumination to understand his revelation. The Spirit who inspired the writings continues to "guide . . . into all the truth" (John 16:13; cf. Neh. 9:20; Isa. 30:21; Luke 12:12; John 16:14, 26; 1 Cor. 2:13; 1 John 2:27). He so quickens the spiritual and mental powers of man that we can comprehend sacred truth. As such, this is an expression of God's prevenient grace.

Illumination enables a person to properly interpret and apply God's revelation; otherwise we could not understand the Bible. The Gospel simply does not make sense to the world. "The natural person does not accept the things of the Spirit of God, for they are folly to him, and he is not able to understand them because they are spiritually discerned" (1 Cor. 2:14; cf. 2 Cor. 4:3–4). God does not give his holy truth to arrogant and blasphemous persons content to walk in darkness.

### Seeking the Truth

Persons receive illumination to the degree they seek truth. To begin, we must believe that God has spoken personally to us in his Word. Only through the exercise of faith can the historical events of revelation have redemption power. "By faith we understand" (Heb. 11:3; cf. 11:6; 2 Cor. 4:18; 1 John 5:9–11). We hear God's message when we are receptive to his voice.

Take Abraham as an example. When God spoke to him, he "obeyed" and notwithstanding the difficulties of leaving everything behind, he "went out" in faith (Rom. 4:20–21; Heb. 11:8–12). Following God's command, he came to understand the meaning of the promise to raise up in his seed a posterity to the ends of the earth (Gen. 12:1–4)—an interpretation impossible through natural deduction.

The response of people to the life and teachings of Jesus is the supreme demonstration of this truth. Men crucified Christ because they did not believe his words, since to them it was incredible that God could reveal himself in such a sacrificial way. The fact that Jesus did not come down from the cross was to them proof of their logic. Although God had spoken finally in the personality of his Son, the world could not understand it because the world did not believe it. Those who do believe will do what Christ says, and thus prove that "the teaching is from God" (John 7:17).

In faith, then, we ask the Author of Scripture to give illumination. Spiritual perception is a gift of God, and like any other gift, mediated through the Spirit of Christ (John 14:26; 15:26; 16:13–14; cf. Matt. 11:25; 16:17). Apart from it we are blind (Matt. 15:14; 23:16–17, 19, 26; John 9:31–41; Rev. 3:17). So we must pray for spiritual perception and expect the Spirit to open our eyes to truth (Pss. 18:28; 25:5; 119:18, 130; Eph. 1:18; 1 Pet. 2:9). Thankfully, God is pleased to answer the believer's cry for wisdom (Ps. 48:14; Eph. 1:17; Col. 1:9; James 1:5).

This requires seeking to know God's will with a pure heart. Selfish and preconceived opinions must be abandoned, which means that we are willing to be taught, open to any new truth that God may be pleased to teach. To have our mind already made up is to invite prejudice to enter into the interpretation.

### Rules to Follow

Finally, the Bible must be studied according to its own rule. God expects us to use our created ability to reason. "Rightly handling the word of truth" means work—hard work (2 Tim. 2:15; cf. Acts 17:11). God does not give scriptural discernment to make Bible study unnecessary, but to make it fruitful.

The most elemental criteria of exegesis is to learn what the passage actually says. A knowledge of the original language is helpful, but not necessary if proper attention is given to word study. Each word of the Bible is inspired and therefore important. Of course, one must respect the literary style of Scripture and the historical character of the account. Basic rules of grammar and discourse also should be considered. The question always asked is: what does the passage affirm? There is no use trying to discover what the Bible means until first we know what it says. As a general rule, the words of the Bible should be understood as bearing their basic and plain literal sense unless a good reason can be given for why it should be otherwise.

Compare what God says elsewhere in the Bible about the same truth, "comparing spiritual things with spiritual" (1 Cor. 2:13 KJV). Scripture interprets Scripture, since God's Word is a unity, and he does not contradict himself. There is no error on earth that may not find apparent support from some isolated text, but no error can stand the light of the whole Scripture.

Keep in view always the salvation objective of the passage under study, a purpose ultimately fulfilled in God's incarnate Son. The Bible cannot be interpreted correctly except through the eyes of Jesus Christ, who became the master key in unlocking all the treasures of wisdom.

Of course, to accomplish its mission, truth learned must be applied to life. It is in the practice of the Word that the Bible comes alive and shows its power.

Following diligently these rules of interpretation, the believer will always receive illumination. However, we are still finite and can never expect to know all the mind of God—his thoughts are higher than our thoughts, "as the heavens are higher than the earth" (Isa. 55:9). For this reason it can be expected that many things will remain a mystery, but problems that may appear can be attributed to our lack of information or spiritual discernment rather than to the Bible. And as we grow in the grace and knowledge of our Lord and Savior, we trust that many things will become more understandable.

John Wesley, reflecting on the brevity of life in the light of eternity, expressed a profound aspiration:

> I want to know one thing, the way to heaven—how to land safe on the happy shore. God himself has condescended to teach the way. He hath written it down in a book. O give me that Book! At any price give me the Book of God! I have it. Here is knowledge enough for me. Let me be *homo unius libri*. I sit down alone: only God is here. In his presence I open, I read the Book; for this end, to find the way to heaven. Does anything appear dark or intricate? I lift up my heart to the Father of lights. . . . Thou hast said, "If any be willing to do thy will, he shall know." I am willing to do, let me know, thy will. I then search after and consider parallel passages of Scripture. . . . I meditate thereon, with all the attention and earnestness of which my mind is capable. If any doubt remains,

I consult whose who are experienced in the things of God, and then the writings whereby, being dead, yet they speak. And what I thus learn, that I teach.[6]

## Contradictory Views

### Problems of Relativism

Liberal humanism denies Scripture any supernatural authority. The Bible is viewed as entirely a human achievement—a book inspired by man, not God. Persons who wrote the Scriptures are believed to have had only their own wisdom and discernment. Consequently the Bible is said to reflect all the human limitations of knowledge, judgment, and morality.[7]

As to the theme of Scripture, it is regarded as man's aspirations after God, not the quest of God seeking to redeem a fallen race. Proponents of this view usually honor the Bible as one of the great books of literature, perhaps even the greatest because it does disclose the highest insights of the good, true, and beautiful yet attained by mankind; but it is merely the result of superior thoughts than may be seen elsewhere in literature.

However, some liberals believe that, through rare insight of the biblical writer, the truth of God did come through in certain instances, as in the Ten Commandments or the teachings of Jesus. This insight into God's nature is usually associated with the ethic of love or high morality. But as to how much of the Bible has even this superior value, it is ultimately a matter of human deduction. Following this same reasoning, the books forming the canon of Scripture were not accepted by virtue of the mark of divine inspiration on them, but because of their human insights into ethical monotheism.

The basic assumption of liberalism is always that God acts only within the framework of natural law. God is not believed to intervene personally into human history to save people. Special revelation is denied, since this would be inconsistent with natural law. Miracles are out of the question. Inherent in their thinking is the philosophy of pantheism, deism, and evolution, which argues for a progression of the race.

Pressed to its conclusion, liberalism repudiates the message and the proclamation of the Gospel. God is seen more as a force of law in creation than as a personal being vitally interested in man. Yet in an extreme view of divine imminence, these theologians actually defeat their emphasis on the goodness of God. For if, as they contend, God truly loves mankind, would he not want his people to know the highest good, namely himself? Yet they have tied God to natural phenomenon to such an extent that he is denied his sovereign power to make himself known personally to men.

Theological relativism results. Absolute authority in matters of truth is denied. Man becomes his own judge as to what is right and what is wrong. As circumstances change, so will one's view of truth. There is no fixed standard.

Man is left to determine his own salvation the best way he can. The whole interpretation of redemptive history is made fallible and full of error.

Most damaging is the denial of the finality and saving efficacy of the incarnate Word of God. Although Christ is usually adored as the purest specimen of mankind, he is merely the climax of human achievement. Ultimately, liberalism sinks in unbelief before the miraculous attestations of God's perfect and final revelation in his Son. They respect his moral teaching but refuse to accept his divine authority. Consequently these theologians can offer no sure redemption beyond themselves. They have no Gospel because they have no divine savior.

### Problems of Subjectivism

A more confusing view of revelation sees the Scriptures as a witness to divine revelation while denying its final authority. Called neo-orthodoxy, also known as crisis theology or dialectical theology, proponents of this movement, reacting to the humanistic optimism of classical liberalism, have a realistic view of human depravity and sinfulness.[8] They believe that man cannot save himself and must have a saving encounter with the living Christ. Yet while trying to give the Christian faith a biblical reference, the Bible is regarded only as a symbol of God speaking to man, not a part of his Word.

The authors of Scripture are believed to have been inspired in their insight into divine truth, but not inspired in their expression of those ideas in human language. Though the Bible represents man's highest comprehension of that which is divinely inspired, no continuity is recognized between the written Word in the Bible and the living Word in Christ. In their mind special revelation ended with the idea; man was on his own when he put that idea into words.

By this reasoning, the words of Scripture may not always convey the truth. Even the inspired Gospel disclosed in the Bible is not determined by exegeses of the Word itself, but by the Spirit of God in the idea experienced by man. This means that man determines what is to be accepted as revealed truth on the basis of his own enlightenment.

The basic assumption is that God is so completely beyond the bounds of human comprehension that divine truth can never be rationally defined in human concepts. Whereas pure liberalism follows consistently a humanistic philosophy in their denial of the supernatural, this more contemporary approach is inconsistent in that it endeavors to preserve an orthodox view of God while keeping a humanistic view of the Bible. To explain this inconsistency, adherents attempt to divide truth into paradoxes, as if it were always in dialectical tension. The effect is to make the coherent philosophy of liberalism, to use J. I. Packer's words, "incoherent irrationalism."[9]

Such double-talk muddles the truth of the Gospel and frustrates the commission to make it known. God is limited in his rational nature to speak intelligently to his people. Though they exalt the majesty of God by emphasizing his "otherness" in disclosing himself, they actually limit his sovereignty by nullifying his desire and ability to communicate to us in a conceptual way. To insist, as they do, that God could not inspire man to record their insights correctly is to impose on God a human limitation.

However orthodox their assessment of a fallen world, the effect of their view of revelation is to make truth utterly subjective in human experience. By questioning the reality of an established and infallible revelation, what will keep one from believing a lie? While condemning man for his sin, neo-orthodoxy offers him no objective way to distinguish between truth and error. The Gospel may be Good News, but it is still not beyond doubt.

More bewildering, the incarnate Word of God is obscured. Yes, Christ is recognized as being experientially divine, but not necessarily historically so. For example, the testimony of Scripture to his virgin birth or bodily resurrection becomes a matter of opinion. Although these gifted teachers use much the same language as evangelicals, words are typically redefined to mean something different from what the Bible says and the church has traditionally taught. Despite all of the commendable features, neo-orthodoxy produces confusion and uncertainty in evangelism.

### Various Objections Answered

Criticisms of the Bible take many forms and come from different theological perspectives. The issues raised, usually quite sincerely, call for a respectful answer.

> *The objection that evangelicals made the Bible a "paper pope" and give to Scripture an honor belonging to God.* The answer: one honors God by honoring the Word that he himself inspired and is pleased to bless.
>
> *The objection that if God wanted to give man a perfect written revelation, he would have written it in some obvious and permanent way—for example, inscribed on a mountain.* The answer: this would have been in contradiction to God's chosen way of special revelation using human personality through his Spirit to communicate his will. Even the final living Word was expressed in Christ through personality.
>
> *The objection that evangelicals hamstring the freedom of the Spirit by making the Bible an infallible authority.* The answer: the Spirit of God exercises his lordship through the Word, which he inspired and through which he affects God's redemptive purpose.
>
> *The objection that evangelicals destroy the personality of the Bible writers by insisting that God inspired the words of revelation.* The answer: God respected the personal freedom of the inspired writers and permitted them to express his revelation according to their own individual traits,

37

but he saw to it through his Holy Spirit that they selected proper words to present his message correctly.

*The objection that evangelicals need an infallible interpreter of the Word if the Bible is to be regarded as an infallible authority.* The answer: God has made just that provision through the illumination of the Holy Spirit, which he gives to all true seekers after truth in accordance with the rules of interpretation laid down in his Word.

*The objection that evangelicals conflict with science in contending for the inerrancy of the Bible.* The answer: this objection is unproved, though revelation does not rest on the changing conclusions of scientific inquiry. It may be pointed out, too, that often science has confirmed the biblical records. As long as evangelicals stick to the actual text of Scripture, and scientists do not stray from the data of reality, there is no conflict in the facts discovered.[10]

*The objection that evangelicals are anti-intellectual and opposed to scientific inquiry.* The answer: evangelicals have an impassioned desire for truth and welcome honest inquiry. They have everything to gain by exposing their position to the light. What they object to is the superficial and unscientific reasoning of pure humanism.

*The objection that an evangelical view of Scripture tends to engender spiritual pride, a "holier than thou" attitude.* The answer: evangelicals seek only to preserve a commitment to the revealed truth of God. Doubtless many fall below their principle, but the principle itself inculcates true intellectual humility.

*The objection that evangelicals are inconsistent in recognizing the voice of the church in sealing the canon of Scripture while insisting elsewhere experience is no final test of authority.* The answer: the books were accepted into the canon because of their own inherent nature as being divinely inspired, and the church only served to clarify and bear witness to this fact—the church merely said amen to God.

*The objection that evangelicals are schismatic and stand in the way of ecumenical progress.* The answer: consistent evangelicalism, contending as it does for authentic Christian truth, offers the only basis of true catholicity.

One will observe that in every instance, when fairly reviewed, the truth is almost the exact opposite of the criticism. Rather than destroying the case for evangelical scholarship, these criticisms may serve to point out the intrinsic weakness of the opponents' reasoning and perspective.

The Bible has always been the subject of abuse, if not by the derision of its enemies, then by the vacillation of its friends. Yet the Word of God remains unsoiled and immaculate. I am reminded of John Clifford's comparison of the Bible to an anvil.

> I paused last eve beside the blacksmith's door,
> And heard the anvil ring, the vesper's chime,
> And looking in I saw upon the floor
> Old hammers, worn with beating years of time.
> "How many anvils have you had?" said I,
> "To wear and batter all these hammers so?"
> "Just one," he answered. Then with twinkling eye:
> "The anvil wears the hammers out, you know."
> And so, I thought, the anvil of God's Word
> For ages skeptics' blows have beat upon,
> But though the noise of falling blows was heard
> The anvil is unchanged: the hammers gone.[11]

## Summary Applications

*1. Evangelism is the reason for the Bible.*

God wants to save us, and to that end he has given us Scripture, that persons might come to believe in Christ and "have life in his name" (John 20:31; cf. John 5:39; 1 John 5:13). This is the proof of its inspiration and the reason for its life-changing power. Thus whenever any truth of the Bible is fully comprehended, Christ will be seen in it. By preaching only his Word, the evangelist most completely preaches Christ, bringing those who hear to the Savior, whom to know aright is life everlasting (e.g., Acts 2:16–36; 7:1–53; 1 John 5:13; Rev. 19:10).

The power of such preaching comes out in a painting of Martin Luther proclaiming the Word. Standing in a high pulpit, he is holding a Bible in one hand and he is pointing his finger with the other hand. One can see in the picture both the preacher and his audience. But no one in the congregation is looking at the preacher. Rather, following their gaze, there in the corner of the church, you see the unmistakable likeness of Jesus—and every eye is on him. The people are listening to Luther but they are looking at Jesus.[12]

That is our role, whatever form it takes, in order to communicate that the Word accomplishes its mission.

*2. The Bible speaks to the deepest needs of the soul.*

The Bible is given to make us wise for salvation (2 Tim. 3:15)—to "see the salvation of our God" (Isa. 52:10). Consequently much is not revealed because it does not concern our redemption. The Bible, for example, does not answer all the curious questions about creation, how God made the worlds or fixed the stars in space. That would be interesting to know but it does not concern our salvation. Just as the Bible does not go into detail about the beginning of things, it does not explain the details about the end of things. That Jesus will return comes through clearly, but the exact time of his coming is not

39

explained. What matters is that we are ready when he does come. Such is the pattern with many other redemptive facts.

The Bible gets down to where people, not angels, live. After all, a man sinking in the depths of sin does not ask: "Is there a God?" His plea is: "Tell me how one who deserves the judgment of death can find a God of forgiveness!" The power of the Word is its ability to answer such questions.

Nowhere is this more beautifully portrayed than in Christian's journey to Mount Zion in Bunyan's *Pilgrim's Progress*. Through the reading of the Bible, he became greatly distressed and cried out, "What shall I do to be saved?" Thereafter, all along his difficult journey, he appealed to the Book as the guide to his faith. Its promises proved on many occasions the needed encouragement to continue pressing on to the celestial city. The experiences he had, people he met, cities he passed through, milestones along the way—all corresponded to the teaching of his Book.[13] So it is for every person on the way to heaven.

And wherever we may be on the journey, the Book will speak to our soul. Saint Jerome expressed it so well: "The Scriptures are shallow enough for a baby to come and drink without fear of drowning, and deep enough for a theologian to swim in without ever touching bottom."[14]

### 3. The objective authority for the Gospel is the Bible.

The Bible, which is infallible, immutable, and eternal, is the tangible court of appeal.

Faith must rest on some authority. Some persons give this place to reason, the power of deduction and judgment controlled by observable phenomena or experience. This is the authority of theological liberalism and, in a more subtle way, the presupposition on which various forms of neo-orthodoxy rest. The effect is to cloud preaching with doubt, and in the end, either deny the Gospel or else utterly confuse the issues on which salvation depends. Reason can examine doctrine but it cannot make it.

Others make the church authoritative, that is, the consensus of Christians together claiming illumination of the Spirit. This may be associated with Roman Catholicism, which holds that to avoid heresy, the bishops of the church, finally speaking through the bishop of Rome (Pope), can only give a final interpretation of Scripture. Unconsciously, I suspect, all too many Protestants look upon the pronouncements of church councils and authorized church rule books with the same veneration.

While respecting those who differ, it must be said, however, that evangelical, Bible-believing Christians—whether Protestant or Catholic[15]—regard the sacred writings of Scripture as the only objective standard by which to determine the saving Word of God. This is what gave birth to the Protestant Reformation and lies at the root of all evangelical worship.

*4. The Bible gives believers essential unity in doctrine and experience.*

The amazing thing about evangelical Christianity is not its discord but its agreement on the essential facts of the Gospel. We can all, for example, repeat the summation of basic doctrine in the Apostles' Creed.

When persons with differing background and varying degrees of discernment begin to enlarge upon the Gospel, of course, there is real difference of opinion regarding the interpretation and applications of redemptive revelation. The exact nature of the sacraments or modes of church polity are examples. It may be argued by those who hold a particular point of view that their position is indispensable, but when it comes to the rock-bottom essentials of the faith, evangelicals come together around the core of the Gospel. Since lifting up Christ is the supreme purpose of revelation, all believers can join sides in evangelism and discipleship.

The unity of the church does not come by every person's giving assent to Christ in the terms of his or her own experience, except as that experience is grounded in the Scriptures, which is the only absolute way that Christ can be defined. For this reason, persons who deny the deity of Christ cannot be truthfully allied with the historic church since they do not accept the supreme purpose and nature of revelation. Much of the so-called modern ecumenical movement fails precisely at this point. It is impossible to effect unity where there is no common faith in Christ as Savior and Lord. The real division in the church is not between contending interpretations of evangelicals, regrettable as that may be, but between believers and unbelievers of the Word of God.

*5. We should approach Holy Scripture with the respect due its Author.*

"Reverence for the LORD is the foundation of true wisdom" (Ps. 111:10 NLT). The Bible is not to be worshiped (bibliolatry)—it is not divine but it is the Word of God and the means by which he speaks to us.

So, like a letter from home, let us treat it lovingly. Reflecting God's character, it is "pure," "clean," "true, and righteous altogether" (Ps. 19:8–9; cf. 119:1–176). The material universe will someday pass away, but "the word of our God will stand forever" (Isa. 40:8; cf. Matt. 5:18; 24:35). So mighty is his Word that God has decreed it shall never return to him empty, but shall accomplish the purpose for which it was sent (Isa. 55:11). "By myself I have sworn," he says, "from my mouth has gone out in righteousness a word that shall not return: to me every knee shall bow" (Isa. 45:23).

The irresponsible way that some humanists assume omniscience in judging the Bible lacks modesty, to say the least. The Bible is not on trial; we are. Those who seek to discredit the sacred writing bring reproach only on themselves (Deut. 12:32; Prov. 30:6; Rev. 22:19). No one can explain everything in the Bible, of course, but when there is something we don't understand, we would do well to locate the problem in our own finite mind.

With such humility in the presence of divine truth, Sir Walter Scott wrote:

Within this ample volume lies
The mystery of mysteries.
Happiest they of human race
To whom our God has granted grace
To read, to fear, to hope, to pray,
To lift the latch, to force the way;
But better had they ne'er been born
Who read to doubt or read to scorn.[16]

### 6. The Bible calls for a response.

When God speaks, we must do more than listen; we must respond to the message. The creature never has license to ignore the Word of the Lord. Where sin is disclosed, we must confess it; if a command is given, we must act; when we receive instruction in righteousness, there should be grateful acceptance of the teaching. To ignore the Word deliberately displays a spirit of unbelief, which, if not corrected, can hinder further illumination.

Obedience is the demonstration of faith and thus the way of knowing the transforming power of Scripture. By walking in its light, we experience the reality of divine revelation. It is that simple. The blessed are those "who hear the word of God and keep it" (Luke 11:28; cf. Josh. 1:8; Matt. 7:24; John 5:24; 8:31; Rev. 1:3).

### 7. The Bible becomes the instrument of all divine blessing.

The Bible is the means through which the Spirit of God does his work in our lives (Ezek. 37:7; Rom. 1:16; Eph. 6:17). By making clear the Gospel of salvation, it convicts of sin and the need of a Savior (Rom. 3:23; 6:23; Heb. 4:12); it inspires faith (Rom. 10:14–17; 1 John 5:13); it regenerates fallen man (1 Pet. 1:23; 2 Pet. 1:4); it sanctifies and purifies the heart (Ps. 119:9; John 15:3; 17:17; Eph. 5:26; 1 Pet. 1:22); it feeds the soul on the bread of life (Deut. 8:3; Job 23:12; Jer. 15:16; 1 Pet. 2:2), thereby building up one in the holiness of Christ (Acts 20:32); and it gives joy, comfort, and peace forevermore (Pss. 19:8; 119:14, 24; Acts 15:30–31; Rom. 15:4; 1 John 1:4). In short, whatever God the Father accomplishes in redeeming a people for his glory comes through his Spirit-anointed Word written, spoken, and living in Christ.

### 8. Persons who take the Scripture to heart become evangels of the Gospel.

The Bible will not let us be indifferent to the personal activity of God in making known his salvation to a lost world. This, of course, Christ commanded explicitly in the Great Commission to his church (Matt. 28:19–20; Mark 16:15; John 17:18; 20:21; Acts 1:8). But more compelling than the commands of Scripture is the very nature of the Word itself.

What is a word? A word is the expression of someone seeking to make himself known. It is thus inseparable from the personality of the one speaking. Moreover, a word is never silent or static, for the fact that there is communication indicates action.

When this is seen in terms of the Bible, the Word thrusts believers into evangelism. God has spoken—he has personally acted to declare his salvation—and for us to ignore the obligation to make known the Good News would be to repudiate with our lives what we profess with our lips. If we truly believe this Gospel, we should "preach the word" and "do the work of an evangelist" (2 Tim. 4:1–5).

The word *preach* here, and in many other places in the New Testament, comes from a term used in that day to designate a herald of the court. It conveys the picture of a messenger coming into a city, assembling the people in the public square by the blowing of a trumpet, and then with awesome authority, lifting up his voice to read the king's command.[17]

Similarly, we are sent with the Word of God. It is not our responsibility to justify his Word; we are responsible only to make it known. An evangelist is not called to speculate on all the mysteries of the Gospel, nor to discuss the interesting psychological and sociological effects of the message on the audience. God will be his own interpreter. Nor is our assignment to argue the pros and cons of the subject. God needs no defense. And we need not try to impress people with any supposed gifts of rhetoric or knowledge. The power is in the Gospel. Our commission is simply to proclaim with faith and compassion the irrevocable Word of God.

One who has exemplified such preaching in our generation is Billy Graham. However, there was a time in his early ministry when this confidence was missing, and he had to deal with doubts about the Bible's integrity. The struggle came to a head one evening in 1949 when, alone in the mountains of California, he knelt before the open Bible and said: "I surrender my will to the living God revealed in Scripture. . . . Here and now, by faith, I accept the Bible as thy word: I take it all. I take it without reservations. Where there are things I cannot understand, I will reserve judgment until I receive more light."[18]

Within weeks, the Los Angeles Crusade started. There his preaching began to manifest a new power as he quit trying to prove the Scripture and simply declare the truth. Over and over again he heard himself saying, "The Bible says." He said, "I felt as though I was merely a voice through which the Holy Spirit was speaking. Authority created faith. Faith created response."[19]

It was a new discovery for the young evangelist. He found that people were not especially interested in his ideas, nor were they drawn to moving oratory. They were hungry "to hear what God had to say through his Holy Word."[20]

All of us must learn this lesson. Few have the platform of Mr. Graham, but everyone who believes the Bible can bear witness to its message, trusting God to accomplish its purpose.

# 3

# Creation and the Celestial Hosts

"O Lord my God, you are very great! You are clothed with splendor and majesty, covering yourself with light as with a garment" (Ps. 104:1–2). "You have made heaven, the heaven of heavens, with all their host, the earth and all that is in it, the seas and all that is on them" (Neh. 9:6). You "commanded and they were created" (Ps. 148:5). "O Lord, our Lord, how majestic is your name in all the earth" (Ps. 8:1).

The Gospel unfolds around this reality.

## The Handiwork of God

All organic and spiritual substance has its existence only by virtue of God's sovereign will—there is no other biblical explanation for the origin of the cosmos.

### The Trinity in Creation

The creation of "all things" is ascribed to "God, the Father" and the "Lord, Jesus Christ" (1 Cor. 8:6). Moreover, it is said that "they are created" when the Spirit is sent forth (Ps. 104:30; cf. Gen. 1:2; Job 33:4). The activity of the Trinity also comes out in the use of the plural "us," when God made a man in his image (Gen. 1:26).

To see the persons of the Godhead participating together in creation, we might think of the plan conceived by the Father, mediated by the Son, and executed by the Spirit. But the focus is on Christ, as is always true of the Gospel—he is the one seen in the revealing Word. So it is written, "By the word of the Lord the heavens were made, and by the breath of his mouth all their host" (Ps. 33:6). "In the beginning was the Word, and the Word was with God, and the Word was God. He was in the beginning with God. All things were made through him, and without him was not any thing made that was made" (John 1:1–3; cf. Col. 1:15–16; Heb. 1:2).

Beholding the grandeur of his creation amplifies a sense of God's perfection. "O Lord, how manifold are your works! In wisdom have you made them all" (Ps. 104:24). At the same time, we recognize that he who "made the heavens" and "spread out the earth" is the one whose "steadfast love endures forever" (Ps. 136:1–26).

### God's Creative Design

Filling the observer with more wonder, the worlds were made out of nothing except God's sovereign will. He simply decided to do it and did it. "The universe was created by the word of God" (Heb. 11:3). That was enough. The Scripture simply states "God said," and it was done (Gen. 1:3, 6, 9, 11, 14, 20, 24, 26). He spoke it into existence. However one wishes to interpret the Genesis account of creation, the essential fact is that every stage of the process was accompanied by the direct intervention of God.[1] It did not occur by itself.

Prior to creation there was no material existence. The heavens and the earth were not fashioned out of some preexistent substance, nor did the creatures within it evolve out of spontaneous generation. All that exists is the work of God.

Time, too, had its beginning in creation. The eternal God, of course, transcends time, but in creating the world he set in motion a sequence of measured duration in which history will unfold and all creatures will live and move and have their being.

The reason for creation is within God himself. He did not need anything to complement his being, since he was already perfect and complete in his essence. Nor was there anything that existed outside God, so there was nothing external to himself that could influence him. The fact that he created what he pleased evidences only his desire to display his glory to himself.

In all its forms, creation expressed God's perfection. "The heavens declare the glory of God, and the sky above proclaims his handiwork" (Ps. 19:1). He looked on "everything that he had made, and behold, it was very good" (Gen. 1:31).

Yet it must be kept in mind that creation is not a part of God's being or a sort of emanation of his deity. The universe bears the mark of its Designer, to be sure, but he is altogether separate from what he has made. Creation is never to be worshiped.

### To Display His Glory

The end of creation is the praise of the Creator. Only he who made all things is worthy of honor. And this, the Gospel never lets us forget. As God said of his people, "Everyone who is called by my name . . . I created for my glory" (Isa. 43:7). So sang the psalmist, "Let everything that has breath praise the Lord" (Ps. 150:6; cf. Pss. 148–149).

## The Celestial Hosts

God, in his creative plan, made a host of spiritual beings to be his ministering servants.[2] Not a great deal is revealed about this order of creation, for the Bible is not written for the evangelization of angels. However, the celestial beings are brought into the record, for they have a very real influence on the redemption of mankind.

### Origin of the Heavenly Creatures

The time is not specified, but before the creation of humans, God created a vast network of angelic spirits.[3] Immortal beings, their number is said to be "innumerable," and seems to have been determined from the beginning (Heb. 12:22; cf. Deut. 33:2; Dan. 7:10). Unlike humans, they are not made male or female so do not reproduce by generation (Matt. 22:30; cf. Luke 20:34–36).

Indicative of their strength, they are called "mighty ones" (Ps. 103:20) and, compared to us, "greater in might and power" (2 Pet. 2:11).[4] Normally they are invisible to human eyes, though when necessary, they can be seen (Num. 22:31; Luke 2:13) and can even take on a bodily form (Gen. 18:2; Matt. 28:5). Of the appearances recorded in Scripture, however, it is interesting that no angel appears with wings or as a baby.

The celestial beings were ordered in some kind of ascending station or government described as "thrones," "dominions," "rulers," "authorities," and "powers" (Eph. 1:21; Col. 1:16). There are also "cherubim" (Gen. 3:24; Exod. 25:22), and "seraphim" (Isa. 6:2–7), as well as the "living creatures" around the throne of heaven (Ezek. 1:5–14; Rev. 4:6–8). What these heavenly beings do is not elaborated, but they have some significant ministry under the authority of God.

Like everything in the universe, all the heavenly hosts were made to worship and serve their Creator. Enabling this adoring function, they were created with intelligence and freedom to make responsible decisions. Though dependent on God and subservient to him, they are free moral personalities. To assure their fulfillment, they were appointed tasks of devotion to their Lord, in which "obeying the voice of his word" (Ps. 103:20) they would know true happiness. Indeed, this was their experience initially, when the angels, referred to as "sons of God," shouted with joy as God laid the foundation of the earth and "the morning stars sang together" (Job 38:4–7).

### Rebellion in Heaven

All the celestial creations were holy in their original state. But before the temptation of the human beings later created, there must have been a rebellion in heaven with many angels turning against the Lord.

The insurrection seems to have developed out of pride and unwillingness to remain servants. It was a free choice, unprovoked by God. Without giving the details, the Scriptures simply say that they "did not stay within their own position of authority, but left their proper dwelling" (Jude 6). "When they sinned," the wrath of God's holiness was invoked, and the wicked angels were "cast . . . into hell" (2 Pet. 2:4).

Having failed their period of testing, there is no indication that these fallen angels, called demons, can be redeemed.[5] Consigned to the pit, they live, metaphorically speaking, "in eternal chains under gloomy darkness until the judgment of the great day" (Jude 6; cf. 2 Pet. 2:4). Though restricted by God in their bondage, they can operate from their dwelling place of hell in devious ways in the world until the final judgment, when all the forces of evil will be thrown into the "lake of fire" forever (Rev. 20:10).

### The Satanic Empire

The leader of this conspiracy is a spiritual creature called Satan, a personality of great beauty and power in heaven. He gets his significance by being the ultimate opponent to the rightful Lord. Descriptions of the kings of Tyre and Babylon, arrogant rulers on the earth, probably allude to characteristics of Satan, when it is said, "You were an anointed guardian cherub" at God's throne, "from the day you were created, till unrighteousness was found in you" (Ezek. 28:14–15). "Your heart was proud because of your beauty; you corrupted your wisdom for the sake of your splendor," so "I cast you to the ground" (v. 17). "How you are fallen from heaven, O Day Star, son of Dawn!" (Isa. 14:12). "You said in your heart, '. . . I will make myself like the Most High.' But you are brought down to Sheol [hell]" (vv. 13–15).[6] It's interesting that these same pretensions also describe "the man of lawlessness" who will appear in the last days (2 Thess. 2:3). The essence of Satan's sin centers in an attempt to play God—the creature pompously claiming for himself the glory that belongs only to the Creator.

In his treason, Satan comes to embody every attribute of evil. He is anti-God personified. The way he is identified in Scripture reflects his fiendish nature—"the serpent" (Gen. 3:1, 14; 2 Cor. 11:3); "the great dragon" (Rev. 12:9); "the devil," his most common name, which means slanderer (Matt. 4:1; 13:39; 25:41). He is recognized as a "liar" and "murderer" (John 8:44); an afflicter (Job 1:12–19; Luke 13–16); a tempter (1 Chron. 21:1; Mark 1:12–13); a blinder (2 Cor. 4:4); "the deceiver of the whole world" (Rev. 12:9); one who "disguises himself as an angel of light" (2 Cor. 11:14); and one who "prowls around like a roaring lion, seeking someone to devour" (1 Pet. 5:8).

This is our adversary, the "ruler" and god of this world (John 12:31; 14:30; 16:11), "the prince of the power of the air . . . at work in the sons of disobedience" (Eph. 2:2). He, with all his demons, is temporarily permitted by God to exercise tremendous influence across a fallen human society, to such a degree that it can be said "the whole world lies in the power of the evil one" (1 John 5:19).

In opposition to God, he has set up his own kingdom (Luke 11:18), an ingenious fraud, which mimics the social and religious dimensions of the kingdom of Christ. Of course the devil has nothing positive to offer. He cannot create. As the master counterfeiter, he can only pervert and corrupt what God has made.

Satan and the despots at his command will always work to bring disorder and falsehood in the world, relentlessly opposing truth (1 Tim. 4:1). So pervasive is their cunning that demonic activity probably enters into just about everything in our society's disorientation and destructive behavior.

Not just in fostering confusion, evil spirits can afflict the body and mind of people, causing all kinds of debilitation (e.g., Matt. 12:22; Luke 11:14).[7] They can even so dominate a personality that the individual becomes demonized.[8] How one experiences this condition varies.

Since there are both good and evil created beings active in the world, the spirits can be tested to see whether they are from God. Usually a determination can be made by the way they relate to the redemptive work of Christ (1 John 4:1–3). Any spirit that does not confess Jesus is not of God.

One thing is certain: the devilish forces in this world will seek to diminish the glory of God by bringing anguish on the people he loves. By every diabolical scheme of hell, they will try to subvert the Gospel that can release men and women from their bondage.

### The Faithful Angels

Not all the celestial beings entered the rebellion led by Satan. "Myriads of myriads and thousands of thousands" of angels remained steadfast in their created positions of authority and joyfully continued to serve and worship their Lord (Rev. 5:11; cf. Ps. 68:17; Heb. 12:22). Proven faithful in their moral choice, the devotion of these ministering spirits was forever fixed by God. Sealed now in love for their commanding King, these angels behold his face in heaven (Matt. 18:10).

The praises of the Most High seem to flow spontaneously from the angels, who are enraptured with his glory (Ps. 148:2; Rev. 5:11–12; 7:11). The cherubim or seraphim, the white robed elders, and the living creatures have a special role of adoration at the throne in heaven where they are engaged in perpetual worship (Isa. 6:2–3; Rev. 4:8; 11:16).[9]

Often angels appear as the Father's plan of redemption unfolds through the Old Testament. For example, they assist in delivering the law (Acts 7:53). Sometimes they are dispatched to execute judgment on Israel for their disobedience (2 Sam. 24:16–17); at other times they smite their enemies (2 Chron. 32:21). And not surprisingly, they come frequently to rescue God's people during trouble (e.g., Gen. 19:1; Dan. 6:22). As the psalmist said, "The angel of the LORD encamps around those who fear him, and delivers them" (Ps. 34:7).[10]

The angelic hosts are especially prominent in the redemptive mission of Christ. An angel told Mary of her conception of the Son of God through the Holy Spirit (Luke 1:26–35) and gave the same message to Joseph, adding that Jesus would be his name, "for he will save his people from their sins" (Matt. 1:20–21). An angel announced his coming to the shepherds, and then "a multitude of the heavenly host" joined in praising God (Luke 2:8–15). Later Joseph was directed by "an angel of the Lord" to take the child to safety in Egypt (Matt. 2:13). Angels ministered to Jesus after he was tempted in the wilderness (Matt. 4:11); they strengthened him in his agony at Gethsemane (Luke 22:43); they heralded his resurrection (Mark 16:5–7; Luke 24:4; John 20:12); they attended his Ascension (Acts 1:10); and they will come with him in glory when he returns (Matt. 13:41; 16:27; 24:31).

Always interested in the mission of Christ, the angels can be seen ministering in various ways to the saints through the New Testament. Being created spirits, of course, angels are not to be worshiped (Rev. 22:8–9). Only their Creator and Lord is worthy of obeisance.

## Some Mistaken Views

### Atheism

The Bible presents God ruling over what he made, yet he is separate from it. Creation is not God. Persons who see the material universe as the only ultimate reality are atheists. They believe that matter is all there is. Such a view regards man as only a higher form of animal life, with no personality that lives on after death. To them eternal life is irrelevant, so there is no need of salvation. Of course their spiritual nature still exists, and it may come into consciousness, especially in times of crisis. As someone has observed, there are no atheists in foxholes.

### Pantheism

A different turn of materialism may come out in pantheism, where the cosmos is regarded as the only absolute. By making the universe God, it ends up in a form of naturalism, or a disguised atheism. If there is a belief in some kind of a God over creation, he is distantly involved. However viewed, pantheism leads to a depersonalized concept of man. Deliverance from human passions and delusions comes through endless reincarnations of the soul until finally personal identity is completely absorbed in the great "nirvana" or universal being. This theory runs through Hinduism, Buddhism, and most other Eastern and new age religions.

### Dualism

Another disconcerting twist to the biblical teaching on creation is dualism, which holds that matter was coexistent with God. Thus it is believed that there are two distinct ultimate realities in the universe. This other force takes on the quality of evil in contention with God. Such thinking may seem realistic and, in fact, has become quite popular in our *Star Wars* culture, but when pushed back to eternity, it limits God's sovereignty, as well as the unblemished state of matter he made (Gen. 1:31). The meaning of God precludes anything existing in the beginning besides him, nor could the work of his hands be unclean.

### Deism

A more common misunderstanding of God in creation, and perhaps more damaging to the Gospel, comes out of deism. Here the idea is that after forming the universe, God totally abandoned it, leaving the created order to operate without his direction. To be sure, deists have an exalted view of God's transcendence as well as his moral character; but discounting the whole story of God's activity in the Bible, they have no sense of his personal involvement in the world's history. Still, many hold high ethical standards of conduct and even believe that every person will be held accountable by God. The tragedy is that human reason is thought to be sufficient for men to work through all the issues of life. Making the situation more hopeless, they see no need for divine revelation or any supernatural work of grace for salvation.

### Dismissing the Celestial Creatures

Persons with a low view of Scripture usually have little or no place for angels, good or bad, in society. If such beings do exist, they are not regarded as real personalities. The fact that they are frequently mentioned in the Bible is dismissed as poetic or figurative expression, or worse, a carryover of superstition in primitive cultures.

Denial of their existence is most evident in reference to the demonic order, especially Satan. Among liberal churchmen, consistent with humanism, it is just not academically respectable to believe in a personal devil. Often, however, they are so suave in their language that an unsuspecting person may not recognize the heresy. I recall a sermon by Paul Tillich, then one of the world's leading liberal theologians. Commenting on Matthew 6:13, he gave this meaning to "the evil one": "It is the enslaving power which prevents us from fulfilling our human destiny; it is the wall that separates from the eternal life to which we belong, and it is the sickness of our being and that of our world, caused by this separation."[11] Sounds nice, but what he is saying repudiates the teaching of the Bible. Such thinking obscures the deadly conflict with evil in the universe and makes the disorientation of society a mere human tragedy.[12]

Thankfully, the ministry of the good angels is more generally accepted. Even those who have difficulty with the devil may wish to believe in these ministering hosts. Certainly, not to welcome their support would leave anyone more vulnerable to the assaults of "the evil one."

## Summary Applications

*1. The unimaginable design of the created universe compels reverence of the Creator.*

Its expanse is mind-boggling. Just our solar system extends about nine million miles from the sun, and there are a trillion other solar systems. According to the Goddard Space Flight Center at NASA, the ultimate reach of the universe is still unknown, though the farthest edge of a galaxy that we can see is 46.5 billion light-years away.[13] If this seems unbelievable, then realize that just one light-year translates into 6,000,000,000,000 miles.

The figures are just as astounding when one goes in the other direction and tries to imagine the infinitesimal makeup of each particle of created matter. The smallest subatomic unit yet discovered is a quark. Depending on the element, 3 quarks are in 1 proton, up to 118 protons are in 1 atom, and between 2 and 50 atoms are in 1 molecule. Yet most molecules are too small to be seen, even with the most powerful microscopes.[14] To conceptualize this, there are approximately 8,000,000,000,000,000,000,000,000 (21 zeros) molecules in a single cup of water.

Truly the intricacies of the universe, from the farthest star to the minutest quark, are too wonderful for me to comprehend. Yet God spoke it all into existence and gave every star its name (Ps. 147:4). "O LORD, how manifold are your works! In wisdom have you made them all" (Ps. 104:24).

More amazing to me than the handiwork of God's creation, however, is how anyone can seriously examine the structure of the universe and still question the glory of the Creator.

*2. The spiritual component of creation calls for a Gospel that transcends the physical world.*

In fact the spiritual reality of the universe is the most real aspect of it. God is Spirit, and it is his being and character that give meaning and permanence to all that he made.

What the Father wrought by the Spirit and the Word (Pss. 33:6; 104:30) comes into focus in Jesus Christ. By him "all things were created, in heaven and on earth, visible and invisible, whether thrones or dominions or authorities" (Col. 1:16). So it can be said that his Gospel is the most substantial Good News in the universe.

*3. In this present age, we live in conflict with powerful demonic powers.*

These devilish personalities, led by Satan, infiltrate every domain of this fallen world. They may congregate in some areas more than others but they have access to all earthly institutions, including legislative assemblies, the judiciary, and the organized church.

It would be folly to ignore or underestimate the strength and cunning of these evil spirits. They are fallen angels. They are intelligent. Having been around a long time, they know all too well the weakness of human nature.

In their utter selfishness, they relentlessly try to thwart God's plan to save mortal sinners and make them into a new creation of glory. Having sinned away their own opportunity for divine fellowship, they exist in the agonizing knowledge of their own damnation. Their judgment can only awaken bitter memories of condemnation, yet they realize that every human who can be enticed to follow their cause will likewise come under God's judgment. If demons take pleasure in anything, it must be in leading people into their hell.

*4. Nothing will be more fiercely contended by demonic forces than evangelism.*

The devil and his legions know that as the Gospel penetrates his kingdom of evil, men and women held in his clutches of sin can "turn from darkness to light and from the power of Satan to God" (Acts 26:18). So when the liberating seed of the Gospel is spread abroad, the evil one, if he can, "comes and snatches away what has been sown" (Matt. 13:19).

In the same way, when the children of God mingle with other people, offering an occasion for a good testimony, the devil sows among them "sons of the evil one," likened to "weeds," to counteract the worthiness of the Gospel (Matt. 13:38–39). In other cases, the ruler of this world blinds the minds of unbelievers "to keep them from seeing the light of the gospel of the glory of Christ" (2 Cor. 4:4). Whatever the means, we can be sure that the devil will never let up on his opposition.

Ministry involves spirited warfare. Legions of Satan are amassed against "those who keep the commandments of God and hold to the testimony of Jesus" (Rev. 12:17). "We are not fighting against people made of flesh and blood, but against persons without bodies—the evil rulers of the unseen world, those mighty satanic beings and great evil princes of darkness who rule this world" (Eph. 6:12 TLB). There are indications, too, that the battle will become more intense as the end of the age approaches, because the devil "knows that his time is short" (Rev. 12:12).

*5. Knowing the deception and determination of our enemy, we must "put on the whole armor of God" (Eph. 6:11–13).*

While confident of his protecting care, we are to "be watchful" (1 Pet. 5:8), giving "no opportunity to the devil" to gain advantage (Eph. 4:27). The promise is that in resisting the devil, "he will flee from you" (James 4:7). Doubtless, attacks and temptations will reoccur, but through continuing submission to God, the obedient disciple will "be able to stand against the schemes of the devil" (Eph. 6:11). In fact, the very assaults of Satan may serve to drive one more determinedly into the arms of Jesus.

Christians can be victorious over demonic spirits. You do not even have to listen to their recriminations, "for he who is in you is greater than he who is in the world" (1 John 4:4). Evil is not an invincible power. Christ has destroyed "the works of the devil" (1 John 3:8; cf. 2:13–14; Gal. 1:4; Col. 2:15). Satan is a defeated foe (Rev. 12:11). His freedom to ravage the world is limited; he must answer to his conqueror.

Demons do not like to admit it, but they know that Christ is Lord (Mark 1:24; 3:11; John 16:11; James 2:19) and they are subject to his name (Luke 10:17). In that name—the name above every name—Jesus has given his followers authority to cast out demons (Matt. 10:1; Mark 3:14–15; 6:7, 13; 9:38; 16:17–18; Luke 9:1–2; Acts 8:7; 16:16–18; 19:12–17).[15] So let us go triumphantly into the battle, singing with Isaac Watts:

> Should all the hosts of death
> And powers of hell unknown,
> Put their most dreadful forms
> Of rage and mischief on,
> I shall be safe; for Christ displays
> Superior power and guardian grace.[16]

*6. The faithful angels are emissaries of blessing to the saints.*

"Are they not all ministering spirits sent out to serve for the sake of those who are to inherit salvation?" (Heb. 1:14). In all kinds of situations their assistance is called to our attention in Scripture, like carrying messages of comfort and encouragement (e.g., Acts 12:7–9; 27:23–24), effecting deliverance from oppression (e.g., Dan. 10:12–14; Rev. 8:3–5), and assisting in prayer (Dan. 10:12–14; Rev. 8:3–5). Not only do angels help the saints during this life, they have a beautiful ministry at the time of death (Luke 16:22; 1 Thess. 4:16–17).

Whatever the mission on which spiritual beings are sent, they are quite able for the task. After all, they have witnessed the beguiling force of sin that caused the fall of their counterparts in heaven. Not only that, they have seen the struggle of mankind in the battle with spirits of darkness. They know our weaknesses, our trials, our failures. So when God commands his angels to "guard" us, they understand the need (Ps. 91:11; cf. Luke 4:10).

### 7. As heavenly guardians, angels are never far away.

Their presence may not be obvious, but they can still be looking on. In fact, so good is their disguise that sometimes we may entertain one unaware (Heb. 13:2). However, if necessary, they can make their presence known in a recognizable way.

I have not had that experience to my knowledge, but I remember a day at Princeton when my esteemed professor Dr. Emile Cailliet told the class that an angel had earlier appeared to him. He had gone to bed rather distraught because the book he was writing was not coming together. During the night he was awakened by an angel adorned in pure white standing at the bedpost. In a manner he clearly understood, the angel communicated a reassuring message, then vanished. Dr. Cailliet turned over, went to sleep, and the next morning he knew exactly how to finish the book. Not the kind of testimony one normally hears in a seminary classroom, but why not? Visitations of angels occur all through the Bible.

I was not at all surprised when a mother told me that, when her little child died, she heard the angels sing. That was a comfort to her, and though it may not be common, if children have angels that behold the face of the Father in heaven (Matt. 18:10), couldn't they sing when one comes home?

Stories of angelic interaction with God's servants could be multiplied. One such account comes from John G. Patton, a pioneer missionary to the New Hebrides Islands. One night a hostile band of warriors surrounded his mission headquarters, intent on burning down the building and killing Patton and his wife. Having no way of escape, the missionaries prayed all night, asking God for deliverance. When daylight came, they were amazed to see that the attackers were gone.

A year later the chief of the tribe was converted to Christ, and Mr. Patton, remembering the night's ordeal, asked the chief what had kept them from carrying out their plans. Surprised, the chief replied, "Who were all those men you had with you there?" Patton answered, "There were no men there, just my wife and I." But the chief argued that they had seen hundreds of big men in shining guard around the mission station, so they were afraid to attack. Only then did the missionaries realize that God had sent his angels to protect them. The chief agreed that there was no other explanation.[17]

### 8. The angelic host love to be around evangelism.

Oh, how they delight to hear the preaching of the Good News "sent from heaven" (1 Pet. 1:12). Though they can themselves never rise to the position of sonship in the kingdom, nothing thrills them more than to see persons destined to that higher privilege come into their inheritance (Luke 15:10).

I know a man who for many years has gone out in the streets and preached the Gospel, though often only a few people gather to listen. Asked why he keeps going, in view of such little appreciation, he answered: "You do not understand. I'm not here to please the people; I'm here to praise God with the angels."

How wonderful to know that we never lack an audience when Jesus is lifted up (1 Cor. 4:9). Angels will be there with us to join in the praise of God, in this world and in the world to come.

# 4

## Creation of Man and Woman

The celestial hosts, though active in the drama of redemption, are not redemptively addressed in the Gospel. Scripture is concerned with the salvation of creatures made in the image of God. As it is written: "You have made him a little lower than the heavenly beings and crowned him with glory and honor. You have given him dominion over the works of your hands; you have put all things under his feet" (Ps. 8:5–6).

Understanding what this means is basic to evangelism.

### The Apex of Creation

#### A New Kind of Creature

God's creative activity culminated in the making of a man, a being distinct from everything else in the universe.[1] Though made a "little lower" than the angels, in nature he was superior to them in destiny and glory (Heb. 2:7). "The work of creation was not finished till he appeared: all else was preparatory to this final product."[2]

The whole council of the Trinity was involved: "Let us make man in our image, after our likeness" (Gen. 1:26). The words indicate personal participation by the Creator rather than merely a divine fiat. "God created man in his own image, in the image of God he created him" (Gen. 1:27; cf. 5:1–2). To put it a different way, "the Lord God formed the man of dust from the ground and breathed into his nostrils the breath of life, and the man became a living creature" (Gen. 2:7).

Man came into being in a moment of time. Nothing in the record suggests that man evolved in creation from a lower order of life,[3] though he was formed out of "dust," indicating a relationship to the prior created physical earth.

The distinctive aspect of this "living creature" is that God "breathed" into him the "breath of life." He was made a unique self-conscious human being, a real historical person.[4]

### Man and Woman

The generic man was created into two sexes, "male and female." Adam was formed first, then Eve (1 Tim. 2:13). Taken from the side of man (Gen. 2:21),[5] the woman was made a "helper fit for him" (v. 18). As she was brought to Adam, he said, "This at last is bone of my bones and flesh of my flesh" (vv. 22–23). What a beautiful insight to matrimony!

Creating the sexes forms the means for interpersonal relationships in marriage and the family, as well as the reproduction of the human race. In this mutual interdependence, it becomes the basis for a harmonious social structure, and properly functioning, permits unceasing growth in individual and community personhood. Also if we will pursue its spiritual meaning, sexuality offers to humans an ability to understand deeper truths of the mutual giving and receiving within the persons of the Holy Trinity. Oh, the unsearchable wisdom of God's creation!

### Multiplying to the Ends of the Earth

After blessing the first couple, God the Father said to them: "Be fruitful and multiply and fill the earth" (Gen. 1:28).[6] Herein is the mandate to populate the habitable world through reproduction, a commission that will become increasingly clear as the Father's plan to reach the nations unfolds through the Bible. The mandate also is to "subdue" the earth, a charge that has far-reaching cultural and environmental implications for mankind.

To carry out their task, our forebearers were given "dominion" over the natural resources, including "every living thing that moves" (Gen. 1:28; cf. 2:19–20; 9:2–3). Their authority comes through so beautifully in the naming of all the animals and the birds (Gen. 2:19–20). They have control. Nothing is denied them for their happiness in the development of the world.

Fulfilling the mandate, of course, extends the ever-enlarging family of the Father. So he says, "Bring my sons from afar and my daughters from the end of the earth, everyone who is called by my name, whom I created for my glory, whom I formed and made" (Isa. 43:6–7). That is the supreme reason we exist, and in glorifying our Creator, we experience our highest joy.

## Made in the Image of God

The most meaningful aspect of man is his creation in the "image" or "likeness of God" (Gen. 1:26; James 3:9). It is a startling revelation, as Joseph Parker points out:

We have been accustomed to look at the statement so much from the human point that we have forgotten how deeply the divine character itself is implicated. To tell us that all the signboards in Italy were painted by Raphael is simply to dishonor and bitterly humiliate the great artist. We should resent the suggestion that Beethoven or Handel is the author of all the noise that passes under the name of music. Yet we say, God made man! Look at man, and repeat the audacity if you dare! Lying, drunken, selfish man; plotting, scheming, cruel man. . . . Did God make man? Not merely make him in some rough outline way, but made him in the divine image and likeness as an other-self, a limited and shadowed divinity? Verily, then a strange image is God's![7]

Indeed this does present a problem when viewing man's original personhood with that of his present rebellious condition. It is helpful to understand, however, that the "image of God" in man does not mean an identical likeness, but rather something similar in characteristics. In this sense, man represents his Creator, for notwithstanding the loss of his pristine estate, he still bears the similitude of God. Note the following constituent elements of man.

### Self-Conscious Person

Man was made a distinct and unique person. In *self-consciousness*, like God, he knows who he is. Though sharing a common human nature with other people, there is no personality like his. He is one of a kind. It has been called a "person's incommunicable individuality" or "self-possession."[8]

And because of this deep sense of personal identity, he can give himself away. No one can give what is not first of all possessed. This trait of personhood runs through every other aspect of man's divine image and gives meaning to the Gospel appeal for persons to do what they can do—to give themselves to God and develop the full potential of their uniqueness.

### Spiritual Being

Man was made a spiritual creature.[9] It is not necessary to speculate about the constituent elements of human nature. Whether we are composed of matter and spirit[10] or matter, spirit, and soul,[11] the fact is that we have a spiritual component that only God can satisfy.

Man lives in two worlds—the world of matter or the flesh and the world of the spirit. We cannot live by bread alone. For us to deny our spiritual nature and seek to live without God would be a repudiation of our distinctive place in creation; it would be to live on the level of the animals.

So man and woman pray. It is a distinctive characteristic of mankind that can be observed in every culture. Horses do not pray. Dogs do not pray. But people do, for we are made in the image of God, and we need a communion with our Creator to be truly human. In the same way, all people and nations have a built-in inclination to worship. Though too often the worship is misdirected by a perverted concept of God, still there is within the heart of every person a desire for something uncorrupted beyond self that can bring meaning to life.

Evangelism speaks to this inherent yearning of the human spirit. In a profound sense, it calls each of us to our true dignity as a person made in the image of God.

### Immortality

In creation, too, man enters into the timeless dimension of eternity. Derived from God, in whom alone immortality dwells (1 Tim. 6:16), the spiritual being will live forever (Gen. 3:22; Matt. 25:46; Rev. 20:10). The Creator has "set eternity in the hearts of men" (Eccles. 3:11 NIV).

This endless duration of life, of course, is not limited to the soul. The human body also has this quality, and after death in the flesh, most Christians believe some kind of transformed body will exist to provide an enduring vehicle for the spirit to function (1 Cor. 15:43–55).[12]

The reality is that one made in God's likeness will never cease to exist. The material body housing the soul in this present life will decay and return to the dust from which it was made, but the real person—the immortal soul—will never die. A thousand years will pass—and we will still exist. Millennium upon millennium will go by—and we will still exist. At last the sun will cease to shine, the stars will fall from heaven, the earth will be dissolved with fervent heat—and still we will exist. The soul will live on and on somewhere forever.

Evangelism makes one face the future. In countless ways, it impresses on man the unending duration of life and reminds us that a decision regarding the state of our soul must be made now. The question is: where will we spend eternity?

### Intelligence

To give direction to this choice, we were created a rational person. We can gather information, sort out facts, and come to a judgment about the truth. Thus God can say to a man in his image, "Come now, let us reason together" (Isa. 1:18).

By virtue of this mental power, we can receive divine illumination and know the will of God. We can think thoughts after him (Ps. 139:17, 23). Though our finite minds fall immeasurably short of comprehending his infinite majesty and wisdom, yet the knowledge of him to which we can attain is real and trustworthy. Before being infected by sin, man's mind was sharp and fully able to function without confusion. That has changed as a result of the fall, of course, but we still have a mind that can reason.

It is because of this ability to think and to learn that we are responsible for our actions. Evangelism appeals to this capability in man to do the reasonable thing and to follow the truth. By this obedience, through the grace of the Holy Spirit, the believing heart can have certain knowledge of redemption.

### Relational Nature

Though distinct in individuality, no person can be complete within himself or herself. Man was made for reciprocal fellowship. The intercommunion of the three persons within the One Divine Being is the prototype of personhood. Jesus, the God-man, is its perfect expression. Thus the giving and receiving within the Trinity defines the identity of a man created in the image of God.

On the physical level, the relational nature of man becomes obvious in the creation of a man and a woman, both dependent on the other for fellowship and reproductive life. The man finds completeness in relation to the woman, just as the woman finds fulfillment in her sexual opposite. This relationship has its highest expression in marriage, when man and woman can together know the deepest realization of self-giving love.

We come into the world as members of a family. From conception to death, we move through a web of relationships that entwine around our lives. God made us this way—to create societies where people can find in others what they lack in themselves and together build a community producing the Golden Rule. However disappointing these associations may be on the human level, still everyone can find personal fulfillment in spiritual fellowship with God, a relationship reinforced in the communion of the church. Evangelism speaks to this innate need of every man and woman.

### Holiness

Among all the divine characteristics in man's created estate, holiness defines most completely his personhood in God's image.[13] This original condition consisted of an inward awareness of the presence of God, unspoiled by any disposition to displease him. It found realization in a harmonious relationship between the Creator and his creation, especially in marriage where the relational nature of man and woman comes to its most intimate expression. Unselfish love was its essence. Far from a mere passive state free from temptation and responsibility for moral choices, Adam and Eve, until they experienced sin, clearly understood that fellowship with God came through obedience to his Word (Gen. 2:16–17).

Giving vitality and direction to their faithfulness was the Holy Spirit in their lives enabling them to know an intimate communion with God. They walked together in the garden.

Out of this relationship of trust and love, the human race was designed to be fruitful and multiply, until finally the whole earth knew the glory of the Lord. Man and woman through their reproductive power actually entered into the creative work of God, doubtless the most awesome aspect of their divine likeness.

By calling people to holiness, evangelism brings the highest aspirations of the spirit to fulfillment. Had our forebearers continued to walk with God, their uncorrupted created powers doubtless would have developed the full potential of personhood. That it did not work out that way underscores an aspect of man's formation that lies at the root of all his woes. Yet when functioning as God intended, by his grace, it becomes the means for an even more wonderful new creation.

### Freedom to Decide

Man was made with a will to decide his own course in life. Not that he could choose anything he wanted, but he was free to say yes or no to the will of God. The operation of human willfulness, for good or ill, explicates the story of mankind (Jer. 27:13; John 5:40; Acts 5:4; 7:51).

Freedom is a perilous thing, for by its nature it can always be abused. To bestow on man such power, and give him the means to use it at his pleasure, surely involved an incredible trust on the part of God. Of course divine foreknowledge included all human decisions, yet knowing in advance its turn to evil, one may wonder why God still made us this way.

The answer brings us back to the irreducible meaning of personality. Without freedom of will, in addition to his other capacities, man would not truly bear the image of God. He would have been little more than a puppet in the hands of his Maker. Whatever worship man could give to God would not be voluntary; it would not be constrained by love, but rather by some kind of an automated obeisance. To put it simply, the only way that God could accomplish his purpose in creation and be praised for his glory was to make a person like himself who could love. Love is a choice.

So essential is freedom to the development of moral character that God gave man this power though he knew all too well its consequences. Still, if man is to be like God, he must be free to choose his own way. Yes, this gift was terribly misused and brought incalculable suffering on a fallen humanity, but in its use rests the power through grace to turn to God, who has never ceased to love his creation.

Evangelism constantly calls men and women to make this decision—to choose to go with God, and in that resolution of the will, grow in the ever-expanding dimensions of the divine image.

## Some Mistaken Views

### Materialistic Evolution of Mankind

Interpreting the origin of man, of course, can take different paths. One view damaging to the Gospel is naturalistic evolution, often called Darwinism, which sees man emerging out of successive generations of biological organisms through a process of natural selection and the survival of the fittest. The unproved theory debases man's dignity in the image of God. Less offensive is the self-contradictory theory of theistic evolution, which allows that at some point in the natural evolutionary process, God stepped in to make a man.

With this in mind, while looking at creation from the perspective of redemption, let us not fall into the trap of seeing Adam as a mythological individual. Any view that regards him as less than a historical person raises serious problems with the historicity of Christ, the second Adam.

### Sexual Perversion

The wickedness of our fallen world is most graphically portrayed in sexual perversion. This was the dominant characteristic of the Canaanite worship of Baal, a religion so repugnant to God that its practitioners were sentenced to extermination. A holy God cannot endlessly tolerate the desecration of that which was created to reflect the fidelity and purity of his love.

Our sexuality is a sacred gift and must be used for his glory. That is why any breach of a marriage relationship came under judgment, as did prostitution and homosexuality. From the beginning, sexual relations with a person of the same sex, or with an animal, was an abomination to the Lord (Lev. 18:1–30; 20:10–21; Rom. 1:24–27).[14]

Contributing to such unrestrained sexual indulgence is a narcissistic notion of self-gratification, that we have liberty to satisfy our own fleshly instincts as long as no one gets hurt. The tragedy is that such irresponsible individualism does hurt somebody, not just the individual but ultimately the whole of society.

On a broader level, this assumption that people have the right to do whatever they think will make them happy has a beguiling way of justifying both abortion and euthanasia.

### Abuse of the Human Body

Not unrelated to excessive individualism is mistreatment of the body. This may seem trivial but nonetheless it bears on God's gift of life in creation. Just this morning the news reported the death of a young man who overdosed on drugs, and this tragedy repeats itself a thousand times every day around the world. But the problem is not just abdication of illicit drugs. Any harmful substance or debilitating practice injurious to one's health damages what belongs to God. Our bodies are the temple in which the Holy Spirit wants to dwell and thereby should be regarded with respect.

## Summary Applications

Creation touches every aspect of redemption. Some implications, however, immediately come to the fore in evangelism.

*1. Recognize the incalculable worth of every human soul.*
To say that man, even fallen man, bears the image of God staggers the imagination. At the very least it makes us look at people with a sense of wonder.

Jesus taught that every person is of more value than the world. We are spiritual creatures and as immortal beings we shall never die. "What will it profit a man if he gains the whole world and forfeits his soul?" (Matt. 16:26). Reflecting on these words, H. C. Morrison reasoned:

> If Jesus had said, what shall it profit a man if he owned a great palace and lost his soul, we could get an architect to figure the approximate value of a palace, write it down on the back of an envelope, and sometime when a tramp came by asking for a handout, we could give him a sandwich, and then, handing him the envelope, ask him to read the figures on it. And he might read $3,500,000,000; and we could say to him, According to the statement of Jesus Christ, you have under your ragged coat a soul worth more than all that. But that is not what he said. Jesus looked around for something to contrast with souls. Palaces were too small! Cities were not enough; continents were mere trifles. So he took the entire globe, and declared the soul worth more than the whole world.[15]

The next time you look at a man, consider the value of his soul in the sight of God.

As if that is not enough, realize that human destiny is higher than that of the angels. The angelic hosts are ministering servants, but redeemed men and women are destined to eternal sonship. For God's only begotten Son, who condescended to become a man, has lifted us through his merit to partake of his own inheritance.

Above all, a person's value—every person's worth—can be seen only in Jesus Christ. He, finally, in the Father's plan of creation and redemption, is the measure of the worth of a human soul, for our identity is in him.

The loss of all this is what makes sin so tragic. Far more than coming under the judgment of the law, the horror of sin is not mere condemnation, not just going to hell; the tragedy of sin is the loss of what man was made to be—to develop in the image of God, to grow in the likeness of his holy love, to know eternal communion with the blessed Trinity. No wonder Jesus spoke so passionately about the consequences of sin. He knew what it meant to forfeit life—to miss what man was made for.

### 2. We are our brother's keeper.

God made us social creatures, knowing that it was not good for man to live alone (Gen. 2:18). Marriage was God's idea, and from that first union, everyone born into the world has two persons already bonded to him, and likely there are other members of the family to which he or she belongs.

In fact, man in his flesh and blood is related to every other person on earth (Acts 17:26). We are the descendants of the same Adam, and thereby are all members of this extended family. Every single human being in the world, regardless of gender, age, race, national origin, culture, or religion, whether rich or poor, healthy or sick, living in freedom or in the bondage of slavery, no matter how their lives have been ravaged by sin—still in the flesh all are brothers and sisters made in the image of God. Divisions between us, sometimes that may seem immeasurable, nonetheless are artificial and should not obscure our oneness in creation.

Every person deserves equal respect and rights. What God has made, let not man denigrate. Life, liberty, and the pursuit of happiness belong to all bearers of the divine image, including the terminally ill and children yet unborn. When we depreciate the dignity of any member of the human family, we diminish our own.

Finally it comes down to God's love for all people. This lifts the concern for human dignity and social justice to a much higher level. Humanitarian service built only on brotherhood usually falters when the going gets tough. No, it is not just our likeness to each other that constrains us to care for our fellow men and women. It is that God loves them that motivates us. And to be like God—to truly express our divine image—we must love like he loves. Getting the focus on God, not man, gives the Gospel power the world knows not of.

### 3. Cherish the beauty of sexuality.

In human sexual activity, men and women exercise a godlike and divinely given power. Two people together create another without that person's consent, not only to bring him or her into existence, but to nurture the person in the image of God. This is God's work and surely he will hold us responsible for the way this power is used.

However, more came from the creation of the sexes than the reproduction of the human race. Though that was important, the relationship of the man and woman, and the family structure that ensued, brought about a condition that enabled people to enter into a fellowship of mutual giving and receiving that would enable them to approach some understanding of the interpersonal life within God's own Triune Being, dimensions of which we have only begun to dream.

Is it not interesting that the relationships of the home are so prominent in the language of Scripture? God is our Father in heaven. He comforts his people like a mother. We are called the children of God, brothers and sisters in the kingdom. The church is the bride of Christ, married to the Lord. All these terms derive their meaning from the family. Thus experiences within the home influence our ability to understand the Bible and, ultimately, the purpose of God in creation.

God made us this way so that we could know the meaning of love, a love that integrates his own character and overflows in his relationship to mankind—a love that can embrace and permeate the lives of men and women made in his image. Little wonder that heaven can be likened to a loving family at home with God.

### 4. God made us stewards of the earth.

The relationship of God to the material and animal creation is one of ownership. "The earth is the LORD's and the fullness thereof" (Ps. 24:1). Taking care of it, however, was the responsibility of man. Our relationship to the earth, then, is one of stewardship—to work and keep what God had made (Gen. 2:15; cf. Ps. 8:6).

It is an awesome trust. Not only does it involve protecting the world's physical environment, but also it includes utilizing the earth's resources for the good of mankind. It means hard work. And it is not without reward.

Let us never forget, however, that any return belongs to God and it should be held in trust for him. The attempt to assume ownership of the wealth in creation leads to idolatry. Incidentally, basic to the practice of tithing is the acknowledgment of God's ownership of everything on the earth.

### 5. God is abundantly able to supply every need.

It is comforting to know, too, that he who made us continues to nourish his own. Paul put it simply: "My God will meet all your needs according to his glorious riches in Christ Jesus" (Phil. 4:19 NIV). "Nothing is too hard" for him who meted out "the heavens and the earth by [his] great power and by [his] outstretched arm" (Jer. 32:17). Of course, he supplies according to his own purposes, not our indulgences. And since in his infinite knowledge he knows what we need, we can accept what he gives, confident it is for our good. With that assurance we can affirm with David, "The LORD is my shepherd; I shall not want" (Ps. 23:1).

### 6. We are made to live in loving submission to God.

Dependent on our Creator for life, we would be foolish to think we could exist without him. No person is self-originating or self-sustaining. Initially we draw our lives from our mother; then we live from the elements of nature. Without taking into our bodies food, water, and oxygen provided by the Creator, we would soon die. Self-sufficiency simply is a contradiction to our created state.

So we have no recourse but to connect ourselves to him who made us. Thus our place in creation disposes us to trust in God. Pity the self-reliant man who chooses otherwise.

### 7. The Great Commission begins in creation.

God had more in mind than populating the world when he charged our forebearers to multiply. He planned through them ultimately to raise up a people from every tongue and tribe and nation that would "fill the earth" with the glory of God (Gen. 1:28).

The Great Commission articulated clearly by Jesus (Matt. 28:18–20) actually originated in the Garden of Eden. It meant that Adam and Eve would transmit to others their knowledge of the Lord and teach them in turn to do the same, until through the process of multiplication disciples would be made of all nations. Though soon the Commission was forgotten by man, it was never forgotten by God, and through the history of his people it comes again and again to the fore (e.g., Gen. 9:1; 12:1–3). God will not be defeated in his purpose in creation and redemption to make a people for his glory.

*8. Evangelism brings us to join in the praise of God for which we are made.*
The white-robed elders in heaven express appropriately my feelings when they fall down before the throne of God and say, "Worthy are you, our Lord and God, to receive glory and honor and power, for you created all things, and by your will they existed and were created" (Rev. 4:11).

Herein is the purpose of creation. In the familiar words of the shorter catechism, "Man's chief end is to glorify God, and to enjoy him forever."[16] Our fulfillment comes in knowing God's glory, loving him for it, and rejoicing in it; and in this exercise consists God's honor and praise. In this the creature experiences the happiness for which we were made, while exhibiting to God the excellence of his own work, wherein he is pleased.

It is all of God. To use Jonathan Edwards's analogy of sunlight, the beams of glory come from God and are returned to him: "The refulgence shines upon and into the creature, and is reflected back to the luminary."[17] As Charles Wesley sang:

> O all-creating God,
>     At whose supreme decree
> My body rose, a breathing cloud—
>     My soul sprang forth from Thee.
>
> For this Thou hast design'd
>     And formed me man for this—
> To know and love Thyself and find
>     In Thee my endless bliss.[18]

# 5

# Rebellion against God

Aleksandr Solzhenitsyn, who suffered for many years under Communism, recalled that as a child he heard some older people "offer the following explanation for the terrible disasters that had befallen Russia: 'Men have forgotten God; that's why all this has happened.'"

Since then he said, "I have spent well-nigh fifty years working on the history of our revolution. But if I were asked today to formulate as concisely as possible the main cause of the ruinous revolution that swallowed up some sixty million of our people, I could not put it more accurately than to repeat: 'Men have forgotten God; that's why all this has happened.'"[1]

How could people made in the image of God be so forgetful? To understand such degeneracy and shame, let us go back to the beginning and see how it all started.

## Origin of Human Sin

### The Genesis Account

Simplicity is the handmaiden of truth. Nowhere does this seem more apparent than in the Genesis story of the fall (Gen. 3:1–24). No mere allegory, it is a pictorial narrative of facts. The Bible itself never questions its historicity (Job 31:33; John 8:44; 2 Cor. 11:3). There is a large amount of symbolism, however, along with the historical character of the account. Four elements especially possess deep spiritual significance.

The enclosed "garden" in Eden planted by God provided a very special environment for Adam and Eve to live (Gen. 2:8). This paradisiacal setting, completely free from any material impediment, offered to our forebearers unlimited potential for development and happiness.

At the center of the garden was "the tree of life," bearing wondrous fruit, which gave to partakers continued nourishment in divine fellowship (v. 9). It represents the abundant life that persons living in obedience to their Creator and Lord enjoy. Standing as an expression of God's gracious provision for our lives, it was also a beautiful reminder that we are free only within his sovereign will.

Next to this emblem of life was "the tree of the knowledge of good and evil," which bore fruit that Adam and Eve were commanded not to eat (vv. 9, 16–17). They had no knowledge of evil yet in personal experience, but eating the forbidden fruit would bring a knowledge about evil. In their original state, it was enough to understand that living in the garden carried moral obligations, and that disobedience to God had dire consequences they would not want to know.

Finally, there was "the serpent," that mystical creature, "more crafty than any of the wild animals," which Satan used as an instrument in securing the attention of man (Gen. 3:1 NIV).[2] However one may interpret the means of communication, it is important to note that the temptation came from a spiritual being external to man, and the ensuing conversation followed much the same direction seen before in the devil's sin.

### The Temptation

The tempter appears at first as a friend and counselor by taking a keen interest in the relationship Eve had with God. The woman was approached first, though she was with her husband and both were equally involved (Gen. 3:6). Temptation comes down to an individual matter.

In his guise of an advisor, the devil cautiously raised a question in the mind of the creature: "Did God actually say, 'You shall not eat of any tree in the garden'?" (v. 1). Though appearing to be a harmless inquiry, it cast an insinuating doubt on God's veracity.

Having appealed to the creatures' uncertainty, the tempter now approaches his own devious purpose by magnifying the one prohibition of God, while saying nothing about the extensive blessing of man's existence in the garden. All he talked about was the single exception of human license.

Thus prepared by Eve's sympathy, the tempter openly denies God's word. "You will not surely die," the serpent said to the woman (v. 4). Only at this point does the devil call God a liar.

Not only that, the tempter now boldly charges the Lord with being selfish and tyrannical: "For God knows that when you eat of it your eyes will be opened, and you will be like God, knowing good and evil" (v. 5). It's interesting that the despicable nature of Satan and the arrogant sin that caused him to be cast out of heaven is ascribed to God himself. Yet in his cunning the devil makes his accusation, pretending to have the interests of the creature at heart. His temptation was calculated to arouse the same prideful instincts that were the source of his own damnation—to be as smart as God; to know everything, both good and evil; to answer to no one but himself. The devil knew full well this was the most attractive way to entice man, for it was the way he and many angels lost their first estate.

### The Fall

Notice how resistance to sin weakened as temptation progressed. What becomes immediately dangerous is the woman's listening to the serpent. Had she fled from the devil, the whole tragedy would have been avoided.

More foreboding is the willingness of the creature to converse with the tempter and consider the insinuating question respecting the accuracy of God's word. The woman said to the serpent, "We may eat from the trees in the garden; but God said, 'You shall not eat of the tree that is in the midst of the garden.'" To this point she is truthful, but then she adds: "Neither shall you touch it, lest you die" (Gen. 3:3).

Here Eve's restatement of the command is incorrect in two respects. First, in saying that they were told not to eat the fruit and also not to touch it, she suggested a more stringent prohibition than God had actually said (cf. Gen. 2:17). Second, Eve changed the certain consequence of disobedience from "you shall surely die" to "lest you die." A slight change of wording, one might think; nevertheless it indicated how a person wavering in temptation begins to take liberty with the Word of God.

Having begun to tamper with truth, the serpent's accusation of God's harshness seems more plausible to Eve, and she entertains the idea that sin is liberating and self-fulfilling. The woman looked and "saw that the tree was good for food, and that it was a delight to the eyes, and that the tree was to be desired to make one wise" (Gen. 3:6; cf. 1 John 2:16). *Why*, she thought, *it is just like the devil said.*

Captivated by the lure of sin, the woman believed the tempter—"she took of its fruit and ate" (v. 6). Belief always finds expression in action.

Tragically, too, having tasted the fruit, the sinner became a tempter. "She also gave some to her husband who was with her, and he ate" (v. 6). Sin wants company; by its nature it cannot be self-contained.

It is also evident that our forebearers denied responsibility for the act. When God confronted him for his sin, Adam blamed his wife. "The woman whom you gave to be with me, she gave me fruit of the tree, and I ate" (v. 12). In a secondary sense, Adam tried to lay blame on God for giving him such a wife. Eve, on the other hand, blamed the devil: "The serpent deceived me, and I ate" (v. 13). Is it not astounding how creatures try to rationalize away responsibility for their sin?

Eve was deceived by Satan (1 Tim. 2:14), but Adam, who had originally received the command from God, consented to sin with open eyes (Gen. 2:16–17; 3:17). However viewed, their disobedience brought havoc on the human race (Rom. 5:12, 16–19). The sequence of sin in the garden is still unfolding in the lives of men and women across the earth.

### Why Did God Permit It?

In view of the creative purpose of God and his design for mankind, why did he not prevent sin from entering humanity? No answer may be complete, but let it be understood that divine permission in no way can be considered as his desire. True, God did not intervene in sovereign power to stop it, but that would have meant violating the integrity of persons created in his own image.

Realize, too, that God had made every provision to assure the happiness of our first parents. He had placed them in a material environment that offered everything necessary for their well-being. He had given them a mind fully informed of his divine will, so that their decisions could be made with the clearest of conscience. And perfectly free, they had no inward compulsion whatsoever to choose evil. Most of all, they enjoyed an intimate communion with their loving Creator, living in the very presence of God, walking together in the garden. What more could God possibly have done to fortify them to resist the temptation of evil?

We are forced again to the realization that moral character can be developed only by choice. Freedom is necessary to love. If God had not placed the clearly marked prohibition in the garden, created persons would still have been under the necessity of making decisions. Indeed, the tree of knowledge of good and evil was an incredibly simple way of warning our forebearers against wrong choices—a visible and constant witness to our moral obligations to obey the Lord.

God tests people by permitting us to be tempted, but he is not the instrument of temptation. "Each person is tempted when he is lured and enticed by his own desire. Then desire when it is conceived gives birth to sin, and sin when it is fully grown, brings forth death" (James 1:14–15).

Adam and Eve's experience is a deadly story, to be sure, but by not acting to prevent the fall, God, through his permissive will, allows a situation in which ultimately the glory of his grace will be revealed. Obviously for the race to be saved, God will have to take the initiative, for there is nothing in fallen mankind that can bring redemption.

## The Contagion of Sin

Persons choosing self-gratification become enslaved by sin. How this illusion finds expression is variously portrayed in the Bible.

### Blaspheming the Divine Character

Any act or attitude unlike God constitutes sin. Put simply, though made to know God and enjoy him forever, we have all forsaken our true glory and turned to our own way. To use the analogy of Jesus, we are like the prodigal son, who left his father's house and went to a far country where his inheritance was squandered in riotous living. There he lost his once high estate, became destitute, famished in spirit, living like the swine in the mire (Luke 15:11–16).

This picture of willful failure to live as God intends underlies the human tragedy of sin. The word most often used in Scripture describing this condition conveys the idea of "missing the mark," as when a person throws a spear and does not strike the target. In its highest sense, the mark is the character of God—"the goal for the prize of the upward call of God in Christ Jesus" (Phil. 3:14; cf. Matt. 18:15, 21; John 5:14; 8:11, 24, 34). The word implies a moral responsibility for the sin, whether conscious or not. It may refer to the aggregate sins committed, either by an individual or a group. The word *sinner* belongs to this same family.[3] This understanding brings out an often overlooked truth, that the real tragedy of sin is not what we suffer, but what we miss in God's wonderful plan for our lives.

The creature is under judgment because he has perverted what he was meant to be, like salt that has lost its savor (Matt. 5:13), or a tree that does not yield good fruit (Matt. 7:18–19; cf. Luke 13:6–9). The Lord of creation expects us to develop our potential as wise stewards of his trust (Matt. 25:14–30; cf. 18:32–35). Not to do so displays a spirit of rebellion and is an affront to the will of an infinitely loving Father in heaven.

Turning away Christ is the ultimate expression of rebellion, of disbelieving God. One does not have to curse God to show contempt for his love, just reject his Word. "For whatever does not proceed from faith is sin" (Rom. 14:23; cf. John 16:9).

Failing to seek our own good, we also have little sensitivity to the needs of others. We act like the priest and the Levite who passed by the wounded Samaritan (Luke 10:30–37), or the rich man who closed his ears to the beggar's cry at the city gate (Luke 16:19–31; cf. Matt. 18:21–35). Of course, by scorning a fellow human being, we are actually sinning against Christ. "As you did not do it to one of the least of these," Jesus said, "you did not do it to me" (Matt. 25:45).

Ultimately all sin strikes at the character of God. Much like the breach of a marriage contract, it is not so much the breaking of God's law as it is the breaking of his heart. We want our own way. Crazed by conceit, the creature flouts his independence and enthrones himself as the master of his destiny. Such egotism turns into idolatry of self, which becomes most evident in the scorning of God's love as clearly displayed in the Word made flesh in Jesus Christ.

### Defilement of Human Nature

Sin corrupted the life that our forebearers originally enjoyed, leaving humanity both *deprived* of fellowship with God and *depraved* in moral character. This does not mean that there can be no further degree of wickedness in mankind, but rather that the contagion of sin has spread throughout our entire being. The affections are alleviated, the intellect is darkened, and the will is perverted (Eph. 4:18).

The Bible uses very graphic imagery in describing this sinful nature. "The whole head is sick, and the whole heart faint" (Isa. 1:5); sinners "have eyes full of adultery" (2 Pet. 2:14); our "mouth is full of curses and bitterness" (Rom. 3:14); our "throat is an open grave," we use our "tongues to deceive; the venom of asps is under [our] lips" (v. 13); "hearing [we] do not hear, nor do [we] understand" (Matt. 13:13); our "hands are evil devices" (Ps. 26:10); our "feet run to evil, and they make haste to shed blood" (Prov. 1:16); "from the sole of the foot even to the head, there is no soundness in it" (Isa. 1:6); our minds are "defiled" (Titus 1:15); we "have become callous and have given [ourselves] up to sensuality, greedy to practice every kind of impurity" (Eph. 4:19); our flesh "is hostile to God" (Rom. 8:7); utterly "dead in the trespasses and sins" (Eph. 2:1). To put it mildly, we are in bad shape.

It is also obvious that this perversity continues with our permission. By God's forbearance of grace, there is no lack of ability to stop sinning, just the desire. What Adam and Eve did by choice, we do now by nature. As Paul said, "Sold under sin . . . I do not do what I want, but I do the very thing I hate" (Rom. 7:14–15).

### No One Excluded

All of us have inherited this condition. David spoke for mankind when he said, "Behold, I was brought forth in iniquity, and in sin did my mother conceive me" (Ps. 51:5). Personally bequeathed from one generation to the next, "the wicked are estranged from the womb; they go astray from birth, speaking lies" (Ps. 58:3). From the moment one enters into the world, we are inclined to turn to our own way.

It goes back to Adam. "Just as sin came into the world through one man, and death through sin, so death spread to all men" (Rom. 5:12). That is how it started and that is how the whole debacle keeps being repeated, for like our predecessors, "all have sinned and fall short of the glory of God" (Rom. 3:23).

Such is the condition of a fallen race. Individually and collectively, in our natural state, we are "workers of evil" (Luke 13:27). In consequence, mankind is lost in the labyrinth of worldliness and idolatry (Matt. 10:6; 15:24; 18:11; 21:41; Luke 15:4, 6, 8–9, 24, 32; 19:10). No one by his or her own ingenuity can find the way to God. This inherent condition of mankind, called "original sin," distinguishes the Christian faith from all false religions.[4]

### Deliberate and Unintentional Sin

The biblical witness to universal depravity is incontrovertible, and, I might add, keeping abreast of the news today, we find no Christian doctrine is more confirmed by human experience. But are persons responsible for a condition over which they have no choice? The answer to this question brings into focus the nature of moral accountability: "Whoever knows the right thing to do and fails to do it, for him it is sin" (James 4:17). Concerning Adam, we are not condemned for the decision he made, but what he did left such a deep imprint on mankind that everyone inevitably reenacts his original sin. This is why we are responsible. We have all, like Adam, chosen to sin.

Does this mean that we will continue to make wrong decisions? Yes, when responsible for perfectly keeping the law of God, whether realized or not, how can we do otherwise. Unless a distinction is made between deliberate and unconscious sin, we will continue to fall short.

The Reformed tradition especially makes this point. No allowance is made for human infirmities over which we have no control, like ignorance, physical sickness, hereditary handicaps, psychological quirks, going back to childhood, and a lot of other involuntary traits of human nature. Obviously from this perspective, everyone does not measure up to the absolute standard of truth revealed in Jesus Christ, whatever the person's state of grace. To do otherwise would require complete knowledge and no residue of human depravity.

Certainly this view should make us mindful of our shortcomings in the flesh, even as it points us to the endless possibilities of improvement. Also it can help us with humility. We would do well to take a cue from the Westminster Confession and make it a practice to confess every day those unintentional sins committed against the divine Majesty in "thought, word, and deed."[5]

On the other hand, affirming the reality of original sin, many Christians, especially from the Arminian tradition, take the position that no redeemed person has to live in condemnation for known sin (Rom. 8:1). A distinction is made between sins of intent and sins of ignorance or mistakes.[6] An intentional sin may be seen as a wrong choice issuing from an unholy motive. A mistake is a wrong choice issuing from a holy motive; that is, in the will of the perpetrator, there is no conscious desire to disobey God. This does not make the mistaken action any less short of God's perfection, nor does it absolve the sinner from the consequences resulting from the transgression.

But it does allow that the heart is condemned only for deliberate sin, whether in the carnal nature of self-centeredness or in the acts of disobedience that stem from it.[7]

An illustration may help to clarify this distinction. Suppose a friend invited you to go hunting for quail on his farm. So the next morning you go out looking for birds. Suddenly a man appears and accuses you of trespassing. Oh no, you assure him—the owner gave you permission to hunt all over his property. Then, to your surprise, the stranger points to a nearby row of trees and says that marks the place where your friend's property ends. Legally you are guilty, for ignorance is no excuse under the law. Morally, however, you would like to think yourself innocent, since you did not understand the boundary. But suppose on another day you go hunting at your friend's place and, not finding any quail on his farm, you move into that forbidden field. Whether you get caught or not makes no difference. You have deliberately sinned.

Admittedly, the delicate distinction between the involuntary and deliberate aspects of sin may be difficult to apply in practice, especially in sins of omission. Considering our Lord's admonition to pray, for example, when can we say that we have prayed enough? Or can we justify that expenditure for an unnecessary comfort? Can we be sure that every opportunity has been utilized to know what Jesus would do? In this regard slothfulness in seeking the truth can be deceptive. Let us not presume on the grace of God. But in theory, at least, always doing the right thing offers an expedient for believing that an obedient disciple of Christ can go to bed at night with a clear conscience.

## The Judgment on Sin

Sin does not alter God, but it necessarily changes the relation between God and his creation. Any offense against his name inevitably brings judgment.

### The Guilt of Sin

Transgressing God's law leaves the perpetrator with a sense of personal guilt, which can neither be prevented from following sin or removed by the sinner after it has come. Sleeping or waking, working or playing, living or dying, and waking in another world—the person who has committed sin is justly blamed for it. This blame can never be transferred to another except by God and cannot be separated in fact or thought from the sin to which it attaches (Gen. 3:7; Rom. 3:19–20).

Guilt involves both the sense of responsibility for the act of sin and the threatening punishment for it. God made us this way, so that sin naturally brings condemnation and a lashing of remorse heightened by fear of God's judgment. A guilty conscience should bring reasonable persons to repentance (Isa. 6:5; Rom. 1:18–23; 2:15; James 1:13–15).

The consciousness of guilt may be diminished by indifference. Sin not only deceives but also gradually hardens the heart—the conscience becomes calloused and dull the further one goes in resistance to the promptings of the Spirit. More tragically, over time this condition can cause the habitual sinner to feel a false security (Ps. 95:7–10; Isa. 63:17; Rom. 2:5; Heb. 3:8–15). However repressed in this life, the guilt of unforgiveness in sin someday will be fully awakened and will haunt the conscience of the impenitent "forever and ever" (Rev. 20:10; cf. Luke 16:23–26).

### The Punishment of Sin

All sin is punished, whether through the normal and ordinary methods that God has constituted in the universe or by divine decree. A righteous and holy God cannot ignore any insult to his character. He still loves the sinner and desires to bring better things to pass, but his reaction against sin is unalterable disapproval—the wrath of God is evoked (Ezek. 8:18; John 3:36; Rev. 19:15).

The earthly environment of the sinner is penalized by virtue of its proximity to the rebellion. Hence, the created world has come under a curse because it offered a stage for sin to take place (Gen. 3:17–19), and it likewise must be redeemed (Rom. 8:22).

Sin penalizes the whole society since we are all members of the human race. Nations and families suffer as well as individuals—the debilitating effect of one sin is felt across the world (1 Kings 22:52; 2 Chron. 22:3; Jer. 9:14; Amos 2:4; Rom. 2:24).

The personal penalty of sin is death—separation from God (Gen. 2:17; Ezek. 18:4, 20; Rom. 6:23). That human earthly existence did not end immediately after the first sin was due only to God's merciful purpose of redemption.

*Physical death*—the separation of the soul from the body—is the most apparent consequence of sin (Rom. 5:12; 1 Cor. 15:21–22; Heb. 9:27). Though we may try to delay the inevitable, deterioration has already set in.

A less obvious result of sin is *spiritual death*—the separation of the spirit or soul from God. Consequently the bond of union between man and God is broken. The sinner surrenders to the idolatry of self since the absence of the Spirit makes the heart a temple without the true God dwelling within. The flesh now manifests itself as the end of life instead of the glory of God. Self-gratification becomes the ruling obsession of life and is capable of endless development—it grows into "more and more ungodliness" (2 Tim. 2:16). In this sense, it can be said that sin is punished by more sin.

Thankfully, while sin has dominion over a natural person, it does not destroy the potentiality for betterment; that is, sin is within the human will, and thereby, by God's grace, can be turned from evil.

Beyond this earthly life, sin eventuates in *eternal death*—the permanent and irrevocable separation from God. Unless something happens to change the sinner, the penal issues of sin remain forever. Guilt cannot be annihilated any more than the soul of man. Likewise, moral decay has no material limit. All the results of sin, so far as they are spiritual in nature, go on forever. This is "the second death" to those who scorn the love of God (Rev. 20:14; 21:8; cf. 2 Cor. 2:15–16). In this rebellion the sinner is left without the possibility of self-restoration. There is no further opportunity for any helpful influences of divine grace.

The final punishment of sin enacted by God's decree is hell.[8] Actually it was made for the devil and his demons, but those who follow Satan go to his habitation. No one has spoken more clearly about this destiny of the lost than Jesus (Matt. 5:22, 29–30; 10:28; 18:9; 23:15, 33; Mark 9:43, 45, 47; Luke 12:5). His language used to describe it trembles with agony. Only by comparing his word pictures with experience within our mental grasp can we begin to imagine its horror. Jesus called it a place of "torment" (Luke 16:23, 28; cf. Rom. 2:9; Rev. 14:9–11; 20:10) in which "there will be weeping and gnashing of teeth" (Matt. 8:12; 13:42, 50; 22:13; 24:51; 25:30; Luke 13:28). It is a state characterized by "fire" that can neither be ignored nor forgotten—"the hell of fire" (Matt. 18:9), "the fiery furnace" (Matt. 13:42; cf. 13:40), "the eternal fire prepared for the devil and his angels" (Matt. 25:41; cf. Rev. 19:20; 20:10), "where their [devouring] worm does not die and the fire is not quenched" (Mark 9:48). Every vestige of good is gone. The soul is left in the terrifying loneliness of "outer darkness" forever (Matt. 8:12; 22:13; 25:30; cf. Jude 6–7). Although the details are not elaborated, it would be impossible to project an image of hell more dreadful than that portrayed by the Son of God.

### The Measure of Judgment

God's infinite perfection of wisdom and truth precludes any possibility of error in his judgment—"Righteousness and justice are the foundation of his throne" (Ps. 97:2; cf. 89:14; Gen. 18:25; Isa. 11:3; Rom. 2:1–9; 11:33; Rev. 16:5–7; 19:2).

The measure of revealed truth granted to mankind establishes the standard by which we are judged. Allowance is made for varying degrees of privilege, both of opportunity and responsibility. "Everyone to whom much was given, of him much will be required" (Luke 12:48; cf. Matt. 10:14–15; 11:23–24; John 19:11). As to how much knowledge a person may have in making a moral decision, and the content of the transgression, only God knows and can judge.[9]

The heathen Gentiles—those who have never heard of Christ—have the natural law preserved in their conscience and tradition, however obscured and corrupted it may be, to make them accountable. Although the eternal power and divine nature have been revealed to them in creation, "they did not honor him as God or give thanks to him . . . and their foolish hearts were darkened" (Rom. 1:21). "Therefore God gave them up in the lusts of their hearts to impurity . . . because they exchanged the truth about God for a lie and worshiped and served the creature rather than the Creator" (Rom. 1:24–25; cf. 2:12–15).

The Jews have the added instruction of their Holy Scripture, which not only makes clear the standard of holiness under the law, but also points to Christ as the Savior and Messiah (John 5:39–47; 12:48).

Persons who have a knowledge of the Gospel and have rejected the light come under the most severe judgment. "For if we go on sinning deliberately after receiving the knowledge of the truth, there no longer remains a sacrifice for sins, but a fearful expectation of judgment" (Heb. 10:26–27; cf. 6:4–6).

The principle in every case is that the greater degree of privilege brings the greater degree of responsibility before God.[10] Every person must give an exact accounting for every bit of truth received (e.g., Prov. 1:24–31; Jer. 7:12–16; 2 Thess. 2:10–12).

Persons are ultimately judged on the basis of their relationship to Jesus Christ. God judged his Son on the cross for the sins of the world. Thus what we do with Jesus determines our righteousness. The sin that has no forgiveness is to reject God's offer of salvation in Christ (Matt. 12:32; Heb. 6:4–6; 1 John 5:16–17).

## Conflicting Views of Sin and Judgment

God's exacting judgment on human rebellion is not pleasant to contemplate, so, not surprisingly, there have been many attempts through church history to circumvent or at least soften the teaching of Scripture.

### Denial of Depravity

One would think that the mounting tyrannies of war, the endless succession of crimes, the viciousness of greed or lust and hate across the world would make obvious the fallen state of man. And most people acknowledge it. Even many neo-orthodox theologians who question the historic account of Genesis will not deny the sinfulness of mankind.[11]

Yet thoroughly liberal theologians, following in the ancient heresy of Pelagianism, contend that men and women are not inherently prone to evil.[12] People, they believe, are born in the world with the same untainted nature that Adam and Eve possessed before the fall. In their view, everyone can live free from sin by their own power of will, and sin comes down basically to maladjustment. We are simply out of harmony with ourselves, others, and the universe. The malady of human wrongdoing issues from selfishness, with blame resting heavily on our lack of training and our social environment. Cruelty, lying, stealing, sexual perversion, racism, and every other form of wickedness go back to our unfortunate neurophysiological makeup and inferior upbringing.

Since sin comes from the weakness and the debilitating influence of society, it follows that the broken relationship of men and women with God will be resolved when these causes are corrected. Sin, like sickness, is not to be punished but treated. Clean up the environment. Eliminate poverty and disease. Assure that people are well fed and housed. Give everyone first-rate education, emphasizing ethical behavior and morality. Bring justice and honor into government. Then by everyone working together in brotherhood, reinforced by science and technology, the problem of sin can be solved through human ingenuity. And the ever-ascending evolution of the race, we are told, will finally bring about the utopia of personal fulfillment and world peace.[13]

There is just one thing wrong with this prognosis. It is not true, either according to Scripture or human experience. The growing immorality in our world, including the more educationally advanced Western nations, should convince us that the answer lies beyond ourselves. We all want better living conditions for mankind, of course, but merely attacking the deprivation of society does not solve the problem of sin. A businessman's comment seems appropriate here: "Send a man stealing hubcaps to Harvard Business School, and what do you get? A man who steals corporations." The deeper issues of depravity must be dealt with, and only God has that power.

Theological liberalism, with its blindness to human sinfulness, contradicts the premise of the Gospel, that everyone needs a Savior, and hence, reduces evangelism to little more than welfare programs. Taken to its conclusion, the end product does not glorify God, but man.

### Denial of Lostness

Woven into this humanistic thinking is a denial of the eternal consequences of sin. If there is punishment for sin beyond this life, humanists reason, it is remedial, not retributive, and therefore, ultimately, all erring people will be reformed.[14] God's sovereign power, they argue, will finally overcome all resistance to his love, and every creature—even the devil—will be saved.

In fairness to this position, it should be said that the thought of eternal hell for the wicked is painful to accept. Certainly the Christian wishes it were not so. Even convinced of the impossibility of the reprobate gaining entrance into heaven, still as a duty of love, he desires the salvation of all people.

What may be overlooked is that no one has suffered more in contemplating this human calamity than God himself. The cross is his witness. Without destroying man's right to choose, God has done all he can to save men from sin. It is the defiance of this love that makes hell inevitable.

Universalism, with its denial of the eternal consequences of sin, obviously undermines concern for evangelism. If all people will be saved regardless of their rebellion against God, why call sinners to repentance? Does not the preaching of the Gospel become superfluous?

## Annihilationism

Another reaction to hell comes from those who believe that, ultimately, impenitent persons will simply be destroyed; they will cease to exist as a conscious personality. In support of this view, words like *punishment* and *fire* are given a figurative and temporary meaning. Advocates may also point out an inequality between sins committed and eternal retribution. They may have a commendable desire to reach the lost, but their view diminishes the unending horror of sin.[15]

## Summary Applications

The Gospel comes to grips with the basic problem of mankind by bringing sinners to see themselves as they are before God.

*1. Sin is always the result of misdirected human freedom.*

It never has its origin in God or what God originally made. Our first parents were created good. Deliberate perversion of creaturely freedom alone brought on the calamity of sin.

Depravity, however, which all of us inherit from the rebellion of our forefathers, does not itself bring guilt to the soul, but rather it determines the bent of the will to sin. As a result of this proclivity, we all choose to sin.

This choice brings guilt, and here the Gospel places personal blame. We cannot transfer responsibility to someone else or any unfortunate condition—poor living arrangements, bad health, lack of education, a dysfunctional family, or the corporate evil of society.

Granted, in view of God's absolute perfection, we continue to fall short of his glory and will always make mistakes. But from the standpoint of human freedom, through divine grace, we can choose *not* to sin deliberately against the known will of God.

*2. Guilty men and women will always try to belittle sin.*

We are masters at calling transgressions mere indiscretions of the flesh—a trivial misdemeanor, just a misstep. Why make an issue of something so small, we reason. After all, is sin not common to everyone?

How the question is answered will bring out different explanations, and distinctions can be made between the severity of the offense and whether it was intentional or unconscious. Some sins are greater than others in terms of their results and abomination, to be sure (e.g., John 19:11; Matt. 5:19; cf. Ezek. 8:6–15). But still sin is sin.

The sin of Adam may be considered a little thing—just eating from a forbidden tree. But God did not consider it such. Just that one transgression was enough to plunge the whole human race into hell. Adam's sin, typifying all sin, represented and embodied a crime of infinite blasphemy. It was gross infidelity that Adam believed the devil rather than God; it was unabashed arrogance in thinking that God had denied him that which was necessary for his happiness; it was prodigious pride in wanting to take the place of God; it was, in effect, setting up the creature as lord and sovereign of the universe. This idolatrous act of man, this unmitigated refusal to obey God, this presumptuous attitude of the creature assuming the power of his Creator, this haughty, egotistical, self-exalting rebellion against Almighty God is expressed in every conscious, voluntary sin committed by mankind.

*3. Anything that mars the communion of the creature with God must be seen as sin.*

This sense of broken relationship with a loving God has special meaning in our postmodern culture, which is so experience oriented. The words of Susanna Wesley to her son John were aptly spoken: "Whatever weakens your reason, impairs the tenderness of your conscience, obscures your sense of God, or takes off your relish for spiritual things, that to you is sin."[16] Taking her admonition to heart should help us all weigh every decision carefully.

*4. Sin creates the illusion that human beings are self-sufficient.*

In our modern period of history, this view is represented by the philosopher Descartes. Trying to find a fixed point from which he could build a natural system and find surety in life, he finally reasoned, "I think, therefore I am." With this conclusion, modern man begins everything, not from a point of reference outside himself, but from inside himself. Whatever reference there is to God, if at all, is purely secondary. However sophisticated the pretense, moderns act from the premise that we can get along without God.

Nowhere is this satanic deception more eloquently expressed than by William Ernest Henley in his poem "Invictus." After thanking "whatever gods may be," he boasts of his "unconquerable soul" in the face of adversity. Then with "unbowed" head, he defiantly cries, "I am the master of my fate, the captain of my soul."[17] What a pathetic picture of a man who acknowledges no authority beyond himself.

*5. Sin is never so beguiling as when clothed in the guise of religion.*

It was the self-righteous Israelites, you recall, who were most often derided by the prophets of God, and among them no group was more spiritually blind than the sanctimonious priests and Levites.

We dare not forget, too, that next to Judas, Jesus singled out the Pharisees for his strongest denunciations. These highly regarded men went through all the external demands of the law, but God's love was not in it. They were not condemned for their piety but for their hypocrisy—pretending to be something they were not (Matt. 6:2, 5–6; 7:5; 15:7; 16:3; 22:18; 23:13–29; 24:51; Mark

7:6; Luke 6:42; 11:44; 12:56; 13:15). So complete was their deception that they considered everyone but themselves sinners (Matt. 9:11; 11:19; Mark 2:16; Luke 5:30; 15:1; 19:7; John 9:16, 24).

The irony is that the moralistic Jews failed to take sin seriously. Though careful to avoid certain obvious forms of wickedness, like murder and adultery, they ignored the underlying pride and lust that found expression in more subdued, but no less real, forms of perversion (Matt. 5:21–22). In their preoccupation with performance, even grading sins as to which were of less consequence than others, they simply did not reckon with the inner corruption of human nature. "For from within," Jesus said, "out of the heart of man, come evil thoughts . . . and they defile a person" (Mark 7:21–23).

No wonder the Pharisees were offended by this teaching. The good reputation they had worked so hard to achieve was seen by Jesus as a display of vanity. Even their philanthropic generosity in building memorials to venerate the prophets was a cover-up for their iniquity (Matt. 23:29–32). They were like those very whitewashed tombs, glistening with beauty on the outside but full of putrefaction within (vv. 27–28).

I cannot forget the conclusion of John Bunyan's dream in *Pilgrim's Progress*, when he realized that there was a door to hell even from the gates of heaven.[18] What a sobering thought!

### 6. The cross of Christ brings the penalty of sin into focus.

There we see the certainty of judgment when God laid on his Son the iniquity of us all. The giving of his life unto death in our place brings the world to account.

It can be said that we interface with judgment in three dimensions of time, all of which center in our response to the revelation of God's love at Calvary. There is the *past* judgment of our sin when Jesus died in our place. As we confront that fact, we are brought to a *present* judgment. What will we do with Jesus? That choice made by persons now will ultimately decide our *future* judgment on the last day.

### 7. Sin leads to disillusionment in the end.

The consciousness of remorse for sin usually becomes more intense through the years of unfulfilled dreams. This can be seen often in the lives of celebrities who have lived for their own glory. I think of Elvis Presley. After his last show in Las Vegas, at age forty-four, he was asked by a newspaper reporter, "Elvis, when you started out you said you wanted three things out of life: to be rich . . . to be famous . . . to be happy. Are you happy?" The king of rock and roll replied, "No, I'm not happy. I'm lonely as hell."[19]

Remember Marilyn Monroe, the sex symbol of her day who reveled in the adulation of her fans? Finally coming to realize the meaninglessness of it all, reflecting on her career, she confessed to a reporter, "Fame will go by, and so long. . . . I've always known it was fickle."[20]

Not long after, when she died alone, a bottle of sleeping pills was found by her bed and her lifeless hand clutching the telephone. A reporter under the Hollywood dateline wrote a newspaper epitaph for her: "She was thirty-six, childless, obviously wretched about her fading career—and an apparent suicide."[21]

One can only wonder why we trifle with habits and lifestyles that can lead only to self-destruction. Sin always has a payday.

God has so constituted things that sin brings retribution. The human body suffers and ultimately dies for it. The conscience of the sinner is condemned, causing inward remorse and shame. Other people suffer for it—loved ones, friends—and eventually all of society bears its consequences. But finally, and most decisively, the living soul of the person is damned forever. Sin reaps its harvest. The Gospel thunders this inescapable conclusion: "Be sure your sin will find you out" (Num. 32:23).

### 8. The hell awaiting impenitent sinners must invoke concern.

Nothing quite so contradicts compassion as indifference to the lostness of mankind. An atheist expressed it when he wrote:

> Did I firmly believe, as millions say they do, that the knowledge and practice in this life influences destiny in another. . . . I would esteem one soul gained for heaven worth a life of suffering. Earthly consequences should never stay my hand, nor seal my lips. . . . I would strive to look upon eternity above and on the immortal souls around me, soon to be everlasting happy or everlasting miserable. I would go forth to the world and preach it in season and out of season and my text would be "what shall it profit a man if he gain the world and lose his soul?"[22]

Would that we could have a burden for a perishing world! Not that we would become morbid in its contemplation, least of all insensitive to the feelings of persons who do not share our faith. No one can think of hell and be judgmental, for we know that except for the grace of God we would be as those without hope.

But realizing the impending doom of the unsaved, we must reach out to them with the Word of life, "Warning everyone and teaching everyone with all wisdom" (Col. 1:28).

Reflecting on this admonition of the apostle Paul, Bishop Francis Asbury expressed his apprehension that many who had been taught the Gospel were now "negligent" in sounding its warning. Then, as if exhorting himself, he wrote in his journal:

> Tell this rebellious generation they are already condemned, and will be shortly damned; preach to them like Moses from Mount Sinai and Ebal, like David— "The wicked shall be turned to hell, and all the nations that forget God"; like Isaiah—"who amongst you shall dwell with everlasting fire?" . . . pronounce

the eight woes uttered by the Son of God near the close of his ministry, and ask with him—"Ye serpents, ye generation of vipers, how can you escape the damnation of hell?" Preach as if you had seen heaven and its celestial inhabitants and had hovered over the bottomless pit and beheld the tortures and heard the groans of the damned.[23]

Such preaching may run counter to our culture but the burden it expresses dare not be ignored.

*9. Yet, out of the despair of sin's consequences, God works to show the glory of the Gospel.*

The rebellion of man, and the judgment it brings on, does not defeat God's plan to make a people to display his character. Ah, yes, sin invokes his wrath, but the miseries of sin can bring a reasonable person, convicted by the Spirit of truth, to call on the name of the Lord. The cry for salvation is usually born out of despair.

When every other recourse for help is gone, the Gospel comes as our only hope. It is the amazing news—incredible to the world, but still the glorious truth—that God has actively intervened to save a fallen creation by taking on himself the judgment of our sin. All of grace—nothing earned, nothing deserved—it is simply the mercy of God reaching down to save a sin-bent, hell-bound people.

Our task is to make known what God has done—what he alone could do—to redeem poor lost sinners through the cross of Jesus Christ. With this mission, I can hear the pleas of John Wesley: "Give me one hundred preachers who fear nothing but sin and desire nothing but God, and I care not a straw whether they be clergymen or laymen. Such alone will shake the gates of hell and set up the kingdom of heaven upon earth."[24]

# 6

# The Son of God

The story is told of a little girl whose father was serving overseas. One day as she looked at his photograph, in a burst of longing, she cried, "Oh, Daddy, I wish you would come out of the frame and talk to me."

That is what God did when he came into human history in the person of Jesus Christ. He stepped out of the frame and entered into our lives, clothed in a suit of flesh—"the Word became flesh and dwelt among us" (John 1:14).

## The Gospel Incarnate

### The Human Unveiling of God[1]

Christ is the second person of the Holy Trinity, yet distinct from the Father and the Holy Spirit (Matt. 28:19; 2 Cor. 13:14). He was always God, preexistent and eternal (John 1:1–3; 8:56–58; Phil. 2:6–8), equal with the Father in glory and power (Matt. 28:18; John 10:30–38; 17:5; Rom. 9:5; 1 Cor. 1:24; Eph. 1:21–22; Phil. 3:21; Col. 1:17; 2:9; Heb. 1:3). He is the manifestation of the Godhead, so that whenever God expresses himself in action, the person recognized is Christ (John 14:9; 16:5). When viewed as the Word, he is God disclosing himself (John 1:1, 14; 1 John 1:1; 5:7–9; Rev. 19:13); when viewed as the Son, he is the object of God's expressed love for himself (Matt. 3:17; 17:5; Luke 1:35; John 1:34; 3:18; 5:31–32, 37; 9:35; 10:36; 11:27; 1 John 5:9).

The whole Godhead was not incarnate in Christ, but only the second person of the Trinity. Of course, since the essence of the Godhead exists in each of the three persons, as Father, Son, and the Holy Spirit, we may say that, when the Son became incarnate, there dwelt in him all the fullness of the Godhead bodily.

### Divine and Human Nature

Christ in the incarnation is one personality with two natures. By way of differentiation, the person of Christ is he who does the acting; the nature of Christ is that by which the actions are done. To put it in our language, the person says who we are; the nature says what we are.

The Son possessed the divine nature in its fullest sense. The second person of the Trinity did not cease to be God when he became man. That is, the incarnation was not a form of transmutation in which Christ relinquished for a time his divine essence, not even in his death on the cross. Christ was always God.

Yet he had a human nature in every sense of humanity so he could be called the Son of Man. Christ was no illusion or angelic spirit. He had a real human body. As such, he was born, suffered, died, and was buried (e.g., Matt. 4:2; 27:33–36; John 4:6; 19:29). He had not just a body but a real human soul (e.g., Matt. 26:38; John 12:27). Furthermore, Jesus had a real human will, so that what he did and said issued from consent of his volition as a man.

### The God-Man

The two natures of Christ are united in a common self. Saint Chrysostom, the Greek church father, aptly acknowledged the obvious:

> I know Christ was hungry, and I know that with two loaves he fed five thousand men. I know Christ was thirsty, and I know Christ turned water into wine. I know Christ was carried in a ship, and I know Christ walked on the water. I know Christ died, and I know Christ raised the dead. I know Christ was set before Pilate, and I know Christ sits with the Father. And truly, some of these I ascribe to the human, others to the divine nature, for by reason of this he is said to be both together.[2]

The human and the divine natures of Christ each retain their respective properties and functions, without either alteration of essence or interference with the other. As to how this was done, Luther suggested intercommunication between the human and the divine. Reformed theologians, however, objected, saying that the human nature could never have fully contained the divine, and vice versa, and suggested a connecting link, such as gifts of the Spirit between the human and the divine natures. Whichever view one holds, it still remains a mystery.

The possession of two different natures does not involve a double personality, but rather emphasizes the essential unity of his person. The union of God was not with a human person, but with a human nature; that is, God did not possess a man who had already developed a personality. Rather, the human nature that Christ acquired received its personality by virtue of its union with him. The varying modes of consciousness may pass quickly from the divine to the human, but the person is always the same.

To boil it down, Christ in the incarnation became the God-man. He is not God apart from man, nor man apart from God, but he is God and man united in one perfect union of eternal consciousness. As such he continues to reign as the exalted head of the "new man" (Eph. 2:15; 4:15; Col. 2:19) and the redeemed human organism of his body, the church (1 Cor. 12:12, 27; Eph. 1:23). Thus, through his incarnation and his subsequent triumph over sin and death, he has lifted true humanity to its intended glory in the Father (John 17:5). Indeed, in this sense, only Christ can be considered as the perfect man.

### Begotten through the Holy Spirit

Christ was incarnated in flesh by the Holy Spirit. The creating third person of the Trinity planted the seed of God in the womb of the Virgin Mary, so that she conceived and brought forth in time the Son of God (Matt. 1:20, 23; Luke 1:35; John 1:14; Rom. 1:3; Gal. 4:4). The Gospel of Matthew mentions the virgin birth of Christ as the fulfillment of prophecy, while Luke regards it as the fundamental fact of historical revelation. This truth has been violently assailed by unbelievers, but those who deny it involve themselves in far greater difficulties than those who freely admit its miraculous nature.

Though admittedly a mystery, it is consistent with the work of the Holy Spirit. He had always been the divine agent, enabling persons to do God's appointed service (e.g., Gen. 41:38; Exod. 31:3; 35:31; Num. 11:17, 25–30). So would he not be involved in this most supreme demonstration of his redemptive purpose? Moreover, the Spirit created the worlds as well as life in the beginning by the council of the Holy Trinity (Gen. 1:2; 2:7; Job 26:13; 33:4; Ps. 104:30). It would be expected, then, that the same energizing power of God created the living personality of God's own Son.

Christ thus conceived was born without any sin. Had he been generated in the ordinary manner of men, he would have inherited the depravity of the race. In this connection, it is interesting to recall that the transmission of sin was through Adam as the federal head of the race and not his wife. Eve simply became "the mother of all living" (Gen. 3:20). Since Jesus had no earthly father, his life was pure from the beginning.

God could speak of Christ as his "begotten" Son (Heb. 1:5–6; cf. John 1:14; 3:16). Only a direct lineal descendant could be perfectly represented in this way (e.g., 2 Sam. 7:12–14; 1 Chron. 22:7–10). As his only Son, Christ's relationship with the Father was intimately direct and personal.

## Human Godliness Displayed

The conduct of Christ was the visible demonstration of the way a perfect person should live before God and man. Vividly portrayed, no one can mistake the revelation.

### He Became a Servant

The incarnate Son renounced his own rights. "Though he was in the form of God, did not count equality with God a thing to be grasped, but made himself nothing, taking the form of a servant, being born in the likeness of men" (Phil. 2:6–7). Such a display of humility would have been impossible for anyone but God—it represented so completely the renunciation of self. Christ continued to show the same spirit through his life, as was finally evidenced by his submissive death on the cross. What happened on Calvary was already evident at the manger in Bethlehem.

Jesus had every power to rise above his servitude, as was sometimes demonstrated in his miracles. Still, he chose to live in subjection to his assumed human bondage. He grew in wisdom and stature as a man growing normally in physical and mental development (Luke 2:40, 52). Like other people, he experienced hunger (Luke 4:2), poverty (Luke 9:58), and weariness (Luke 8:23; John 4:6). He knew what it was to labor all day in a carpenter shop. The workload would have been especially hard, for probably his earthly father, Joseph, died while Jesus was still in his teens,[3] leaving him as the eldest son the major responsibility for taking care of his mother along with the younger brothers and sisters (Matt. 12:46; Mark 6:3). Jesus knew sorrow and the toils involved in raising a fatherless family.

### Authentic Humanity

Let us not forget, too, that as a man, Jesus was tempted by sin (Matt. 4:1–11; Luke 4:13; Heb. 4:15). His temptation, like that of the first Adam, did not come from within but from without. What he was confronted with, however, far exceeded anything that any other human has ever had to face, including Satan's offer to rule the world. He resisted every suggestion of wrong, thus experiencing in the ultimate sense the real force of temptation. Though it was impossible for him to sin, his testing was every bit as real as ours. In fact, because he never yielded to the allurements of sin, as have all of us, he is the only man who has ever been tempted to the uttermost.

Consider, too, the observance of accepted human disciplines throughout his life. As a babe he was circumcised (Luke 2:21) and later baptized like other participants in the ministry of John (Matt. 3:13–17). He attended synagogue and temple services and observed the Jewish feast days. His discipline of personal prayer constantly shines through the Gospels as well as his use of the

Holy Scriptures.[4] These spiritual exercises, so conspicuous in the daily routine of Jesus, certainly call to our attention how a person made in the image of God should live.

His humanness can be seen in the way Jesus lovingly identified with the lot of mankind. "He came to his own" (John 1:11). The fact that the people did not receive him caused heartbreak but it never erased his sense of oneness with them. He wept when he saw their suffering (e.g., John 11:36–37), and moved with compassion, he sought to help the unfortunate multitudes about him (e.g., Matt. 9:36; Mark 1:41; Luke 7:13). It did not matter what the conditions were in which he found them—poor, sick, demon possessed, publican, or Pharisee—he loved them all and wanted to help them (e.g., Luke 13:34; 19:41–44; 23:34).

### Total Obedience to God

Jesus committed all to his life's purpose. Fully sensitive to the will of God the Father, he knew what he was sent to do and he set himself to do it. He was on business for God (Luke 2:49); he "came not to be served but to serve, and to give his life as a ransom for many" (Matt. 20:28; Mark 10:45). This was his reason for being in the world, apart from which his life had no meaning, and he would not be deterred from fulfilling his mission (e.g., Luke 4:4; 19:10; John 4:34).

This dedication to the purpose for which he was commissioned by God the Father exemplifies the kind of commitment he expects of his followers when later they are sent out to do his work. His consecration for us becomes the model for the sanctification of his church (John 17:18–19; cf. 10:36).

The capstone of it all was his obedience unto death. His chosen way of servitude was never easy, not just because of the physical suffering he endured; more painful was the daily realization of the horrible destiny awaiting the masses of people blinded by sin.

He knew they were aimlessly wandering through life, like lost sheep on their present course headed for certain destruction (Matt. 9:36). That the world hated him was no surprise (John 15:18), though it added to his heartbreak. Truly, as the prophet Isaiah had said, "he was despised and rejected by men; a man of sorrows, and acquainted with grief" (Isa. 53:3). No one else shared the burden with him, not even his closest disciples, but Jesus bore it willingly in obedience to the Father's will.

The humanity of Christ is nowhere more vividly seen than in Gethsemane. There, overwhelmed with sorrow, Jesus saw the Father holding a cup before him. It expressed in some mysterious way the intense anguish awaiting him. In his human frailty he asked that the cup might be taken away. No normal man wants to suffer. Though he prayed earnestly for deliverance, he realized at last there was no other way for his task to be completed, and he drank the cup to its dregs, hurling it forth in victory (Matt. 26:36–46; Mark 14:32–42; Luke 22:39–46).

Jesus lived in obedience; he died in obedience. His sufferings as a man were only the means of teaching him more about obedience (Heb. 5:8). In this sense the cross displays a life totally given to the will of God. Jesus always did those things that the Father commanded (John 8:28, 55; 14:31; 17:4), thereby permitting God to perfect his purpose in human flesh.

What a contrast to the life of Adam! Yet it was this very obedience of Christ, the second Adam, that made his life a worthy and perfect renewal of humanity (Rom. 5:19; Heb. 10:6–7).

## Prophet, Priest, and King

Classical theologians like to think of Christ fulfilling three offices of ministry, which met mankind at every area of need.

### As Prophet

Christ pronounced the counsel of God, thereby dispelling the ignorant schemes of mankind. As Prophet, he was the channel through which light came into a world of darkness. Jesus, in this role, was the consummation of a long line of Hebrew prophets through which God had spoken across the ages (Deut. 18:15, 18; Heb. 1:1–2), the last being John the Baptist (John 1:30; 3:30). The definite prophetic authority by which he spoke replaced "Thus says the Lord" with "Truly, I say to you" (e.g., Matt. 18:3; John 5:24). Not surprisingly, it was said of him, "No one ever spoke like this man!" (John 7:46), "for he taught them as one who had authority, and not as the scribes" (Mark 1:22). Moreover, he confirmed his work with mighty signs and wonders, such as had accompanied the beginnings of new epochs in the previous history of Israel (e.g., Mark 1:27; John 3:2).

Christ's prophetic office continues through his chosen people (Num. 11:29), and in particular, the gifts of ministry in the church (1 Cor. 12:28; 14:29; Eph. 4:11), "until we all attain to the unity of the faith and of the knowledge of the Son of God, to mature manhood, to the measure of the stature of the fullness of Christ" (v. 13).

### As Priest

Jesus offered sacrifices for God, thereby effecting reconciliation and deliverance for his people. "He is the mediator of a new covenant" (Heb. 9:15; 12:24), "and there is one mediator between God and men, the man Christ Jesus" (1 Tim. 2:5).

Functioning in the capacity of priest, Jesus's ministry was of the order of Melchizedek, a king of righteousness and peace, "having neither beginning of days nor end of life," to whom Abraham offered tithes (Heb. 7:3; cf. 6:20). Vastly superior to the Aaronic, temporal priesthood, constantly changing through bodily descent, Christ is "a priest forever" (Heb. 7:21; cf. Gen. 14:18–20; Ps. 110:4).

As both our priest and the sacrifice, he offered himself to God. And having finished the work assigned to him by the Father, his sacrifice is complete "once for all" (Heb. 10:10; cf. John 19:30).

Though his atoning sacrifice ended at Calvary, he continues his mediation of the New Covenant as our great High Priest in heaven (Heb. 8:6; 9:11; 12:24). There at the throne of God, he intercedes for his people (Rom. 8:34; Heb. 7:25), enabling all who come to him to have access to salvation full and free (John 10:9; Rom. 5:2; Eph. 2:18; 3:12; Heb. 10:19–22).

### As King

Christ rules the kingdom of God, thereby perfecting God's will in the affairs of men and nations. Appropriately called "the blessed and only Sovereign, the King of kings and Lord of lords" (1 Tim. 6:15), "the Almighty," (Rev. 15:3), he embodies in himself the reality of the kingdom (Luke 17:21). He was the fulfillment of all the messianic promises relating to the kingdom. Though rejected by the nation of Israel, in him the Davidic line of the throne has eternal validity (Ps. 8:5–6; Matt. 21:42; John 9:35–38).

He reigns, too, as the Lord of the church. Seen this way, the kingdom has already come; it is present now in the hearts of his people (Matt. 4:17; 13:24–47; 18:23; Col. 1:13; 3:1–4). He is also the coming King of Glory who will return in power to establish his eternal kingdom at the end of time (Matt. 13:39, 49; Mark 9:1; Luke 9:11). In this future sense, his royal office is in abeyance, but a kingdom is promised when all his enemies shall be made his footstool (Luke 1:32–33; 1 Cor. 15:25; Heb. 1:8–9, 13; Rev. 11:15). This is the heavenly kingdom assured his people as a reward and an inheritance (Matt. 5:10–12; 7:21; 8:11; 13:43; 25:46; Luke 12:32).

## Differing Perspectives on Christ

Views of Christ contrary to the Gospel are plentiful, though when examined carefully, they generally fall into one of the following categories.

### Denial of Christ's Divinity

Theories that relegate Christ to the position of a mere man deny the incarnation of God in the person of Jesus. Classical theological liberalism takes this humanistic approach. Christ is regarded as a great teacher, perhaps the greatest teacher who ever lived, and in fact the very best expression of God, but still a man.

This view, of course, destroys any real reason to worship Christ, since man is forbidden to worship anyone but God. While popular today in various ecclesiastical councils and seminaries, the view actually is not new. It reflects some of the ancient heresies of the Greco-Roman world, such as Arianism, which were so firmly repudiated by the church fathers in the Creeds of Nicea (AD 325), Constantinople (AD 381), and Athanasius (AD 449).

### Denial of Christ's Humanity

On the other extreme, theories that regard Christ only as God deny the incarnation of man. This philosophic approach contends that Christ did not possess true humanity, either denying the reality of his human body or his human soul. Such a view, of course, if carried over into the practical realm of Christ's life, destroys any likeness he had with genuine human temptation, suffering, death, and finally the resurrection.

Basic to this false premise is the idea that matter as such is evil, and therefore Christ could not have actually possessed it. While not fashionable anymore, such views in one way or another were expressed in such ancient heresies as Gnosticism, Docetism, and Appolinarianism.

### Confounding His Divine and Human Nature

More common today are theories that accept the spiritual incarnation of Christ, but not necessarily in any generic sense. The biblical account of the virgin conception is either denied or dismissed as irrelevant, along with Christ's blood atonement and bodily resurrection. Adherents to this position worship a heavenly Christ revealed by the Holy Spirit, but they are not greatly concerned with the details of his life in the flesh. Invariably the emphasis is on an experience of Christ through a personal encounter of faith. When one seeks to clarify who Christ is and what he did, the whole experience becomes vague.

Following their irrational thinking, historical events are considered as only symbols of the truth. Yet to the degree these divines evade the real-time facts associated with the incarnate Christ, to that extent they are tragically inconsistent in reckoning with reality. For this reason, their whole system of thought is basically incoherent. In trying to recast the incarnation in modern terms, they have simply restated many of the old liberal and philosophic heresies. This position can only produce confusion and uncertainty in evangelism, and where forced to its conclusion, it can destroy any validity for the Gospel of Christ.

### Is Christ the Only Savior?

The crucial issue in the world of evangelism—one that has increasingly come to the fore in our generation—is whether Christ is the only Savior.[5] Proponents of pluralism answer in the negative. Consistent with their liberal theological presuppositions, they believe that there are many ways to salvation and that Jesus is only one of them. Rejecting the revelation of God in Scripture and treating the claims of Christ with typical humanistic unbelief, they contend that any authentic quest for ultimate reality and spiritual fulfillment is acceptable. In this view, finally it makes no difference what one believes about Jesus Christ.[6] Such a view, of course, destroys any reason for evangelism.

Rejecting pluralism, yet wanting to soften the exclusivist claims of Christ, some Christians respond to the question, Is Jesus the only Savior? with a qualified, Yes, but . . . On the one hand, this inclusive group affirms that no one can be saved apart from Christ, but at the same time, they hold that one does not have to explicitly know about Christ to receive salvation. A distinction is made between the historical facts of Christ's redeeming work and the epistemological necessity of hearing the Gospel and believing on Christ.[7] This dubious position, while not denying the Gospel, enlarges the scope of salvation to include devout persons of other religions who are sincerely living uprightly according to the light they have. This concept comes dangerously close to relativism and salvation by good works, and if pushed, moves in the direction of pluralism.

## Summary Applications

*1. The Christ that we know is the Christ of the Bible.*

The course of Christ's life is foretold from old.[8] Tracing these prophecies in the Old Testament and their fulfillment in the New Testament is a fascinating study.[9] It encourages faith and even fills the skeptic with wonder.[10]

What is also evident, all through the Bible in symbolism, typology, prophecy, and actual personal appearance, is that Jesus is the theme of Scripture. Every book of the Bible in some way depicts the Savior.

Of course, because of the brief scope of Holy Writ, only a few things about Christ could be recorded. If everything had been set forth that could be said, as John noted, "the world itself could not contain the books that would be written" (John 21:25).

*2. The validity of the Gospel rests on the uniqueness of Jesus Christ.*

If he were not the incarnate person of God in the flesh, then our faith would be in vain; but because he is the Son of God, then all he said and did has eternal significance. We must be clear at this point. Jesus did not start out to save the world as a man, and by virtue of his godly life become the Son of God. Jesus came to the earth as God, and through the miraculous conception effected by the Holy Spirit in the Virgin Mary, he became the incarnate God-man. In other words, he did not become Redeemer in order to be the Son of God, but he came as the Son of God to be the Redeemer.

The notion popular in some religious circles that Jesus was merely a great moral and spiritual teacher is, to use the words of C. S. Lewis, "patronizing nonsense." For Christ to make the claims he did, "he would either be a lunatic on the level with a man who says he's a poached egg—or else he would be the devil of hell; you must take your choice. Either this was, and is, the Son of God, or else a madman or something worse. You can shut him up for a demon; or you can fall at his feet and call him Lord and God."[11]

However repulsive this conclusion may seem, it is consistent with the exclusive witness of the apostolic church, which boldly declared: "Jesus is Lord" (Rom. 10:9), and "There is no other name under heaven given among men by which we must be saved" (Acts 4:12).

Dr. Radhakrishnan, the Hindu philosopher who became president of India, was once asked if it was arrogant for Christians to affirm with Christ that he was the light of the world. "Is that not a subtle form of exalting ourselves, as if to say 'We only have the light'?" The distinguished statesman paused and after long thought replied, "Yes, but the Christian has no choice. This is what your Scriptures say: you cannot say less. You are saved from arrogance when you say it in the spirit of Jesus Christ."[12]

### 3. Jesus perfectly reveals the character of the Father.

Until the incarnate God clothed himself in human personality, how could we see him in our image?

The story is told of a farmer who had become cynical in his faith and could not joyfully celebrate Christmas. One cold winter night he heard a thumping sound against the kitchen window. It was followed by another, then another. Going to the window to investigate, he saw huddled in the snow a flock of shivering sparrows. They had been caught in the storm and in a desperate search for warmth had tried to fly through the window.

*I can't let those poor creatures freeze out there*, he thought. So bundling up he trudged through the snow to open the barn door for the birds to find shelter. He turned on the lights and sprinkled some grain near the door. But the birds did not come in. He tried scaring them into the barn by walking behind them and waving his arms, which only caused the birds to scatter in every direction. They could not understand that he was trying to help.

Dejected, the farmer returned to his house and watched the doomed sparrows through the window. Suddenly the thought came to him: if I could only become a bird—one of them—then I could show them the way to safety. At that moment, he heard the sound of the church bell in the distance announcing the Christmas service, and in that moment, he understood the meaning of the incarnation.

A man becoming a bird is nothing compared to the Sovereign of the universe becoming a man. Yet great as is the distance between us, there was no other way by which a shivering humanity, lying helpless in this cold world, could ever know the way to salvation.[13]

*4. The incarnation enabled God to fully experience human suffering.*

If Jesus were to feel our sorrows and finally bear the anguish of our sin, then he had to be like us. Previous to becoming flesh, the Logos, or Word, could not completely enter into the pangs of human emotions, but after the incarnation he could personally "sympathize with our weaknesses," and in such a state Christ now reigns eternally (Heb. 4:15).

Persons who have suffered most are those most able to serve this hurting world. James Damien was such a man. For many years he was a medical missionary among the lepers on the island of Molokai in Hawaii. The stricken people he served grew to love him dearly. One day while preparing his bath, making for himself a cup of tea, some boiling water spilled on his bare foot. He sprang back, then a quick throb of horror gripped him—he did not feel any sensation. The doctor knew all too well what this meant.

That day as he went to chapel to lead the community in worship, he opened the service in a different way. Usually he began his sermon with the words, "My brethren . . ." but this morning he began with the words, "We lepers . . ."[14] Subsequently, we are told, Damien entered into his ministry with the greatest zeal and joy, and "acted as though the coming of his disease was something to be welcomed, in as much as it removed the final barrier between him and his people."

In an infinitely greater measure, Jesus identified with us, bearing in his pure spirit the marks of our corruption. He went through every torment, every temptation that a man can suffer, that he might be able to minister perfectly to humanity.

*5. The incarnation brings into focus true humanity.*

As Pascal so pungently wrote, "Not only do we know God by Jesus Christ alone, but we know ourselves only by Jesus Christ."[15] Seeing the beauty of his life, we recognize how ugly we are. Yet at the same time, we see what we want to be like. Thus Christ's perfect life restores a vision of man in God's created image—what we were meant to be—and prophesies of the estate that we can aspire to attain.

Why would anyone not want to know him, the dearest lover of every human soul?

> No voice can sing, no heart can frame
> Nor can the memory find
> A sweeter sound than Jesus' name
> The Savior of mankind.[16]

*6. The incarnation shows how God works to transform our lives.*

In a different sense, yet not unconnected, the incarnate life of Christ through the supernatural intervention of the Holy Spirit foreshadows not only the need for a new birth, but also God's method of effecting it. Truly, if there had been anything inherent in man that could have saved him, God would have utilized it in his incarnation. The fact that Christ bypassed the natural means of generation and was born by direct agency of the Holy Spirit upon the virgin proves the depravity of mankind. Human nature must undergo transformation. Moreover, the change comes through the Holy Spirit's directly working in one's life. In the spiritual sense of the new birth, this is exactly what happens. Entrance into the redemptive life of God comes through the Spirit's agency.

### 7. Jesus Christ in his person meets any and every need of mankind.

As Prophet he gives knowledge of God, as Priest he brings us to God, and as King he reigns over us as sovereign. His threefold office sets the redeemed free in the three powers of our utmost being—the understanding, the feelings, and the will. Enlightenment, holiness, and security thus become the believer's experience in Christ.

### 8. The magnetism of the Gospel is Jesus Christ.

When he is lifted up he draws one to God. Everything about his life captivates the imagination.

He was born in a stable, the child of a peasant. He grew up in an obscure village, where he worked as a carpenter until he was thirty. Then for three years he became an itinerant preacher. He did none of the things that usually accompany greatness. He never went to college nor wrote a book. He accumulated no wealth nor held a public office. He never traveled more than one hundred and fifty miles from the place where he was born. Though loved by the poor and oppressed, religious leaders derided him as a friend of sinners and publicans. He was only thirty-three when they arrested him, put him through a mock trial, then nailed him to a cross between two thieves. While he was dying, his executioners cast lots for his garment, the only possession he had on earth. When he died, his body was laid in a borrowed tomb.

Twenty centuries have come and gone, and today he is the central figure of the human race. All the armies that ever marched, all the parliaments that ever sat, all the kings that ever reigned—put together—have not affected the life of people on this earth as much as that one solitary man.[17]

### 9. The ultimate purpose of Christ's life was evangelism.

He threw off the robes of glory and became flesh for no other purpose than to save perishing men and women. To use his words, he came "to save the world" (John 12:47); "to seek and to save the lost" (Luke 19:10); "not . . . to call the righteous but sinners to repentance" (Luke 5:32); "that they may have life and have it abundantly" (John 10:10); "and to give his life as a ransom for many" (Matt. 20:28). Everything about his incarnation realistically expresses the ceaseless love of God for a lost world.

The fact that God gave his Son for us surely allows us no escape from giving ourselves. This is our clear mission. John Wesley said it well: "You have only one point to attend to—Immanuel, God with us; to secure that single point—Christ in us, the hope of glory! What is all besides in comparison to that? O let it engage your whole soul. Yet a little while and all the rest will pass away like a shadow."[18]

# 7

# The Death of Christ

A missionary told of a boy who appeared at a mission hospital in Kenya with a gaping wound on his foot. He had accidentally injured himself while cutting grass far out in the jungle, and part of his heel was cut off. Without waiting to inform anyone of the mishap, he set out cross-country to find the mission station where he knew medical help was available. Every time his little foot touched the sandy earth, it left a faint trace of blood. The journey was long and difficult, but at last he arrived.

After a time, the boy's mother appeared. The doctors were surprised that she found the way. There were no well-defined trails, and she had never made the trip before. "How did you do it?" she was asked.

The woman, overjoyed to be with her child, replied, "Oh, it was easy. I just followed the blood!"

In a much more profound sense, that is how we come to Jesus. We just follow his footprints. They are easy to find, for each one is stained with blood.[1]

## Saved by the Blood

### A Common Ingredient of Life

In seeking to show how sinful people can be redeemed, God clothes his Word in concepts with which creatures can easily identify. The most significant of these is the blood. Altogether this word is used 460 times in the Bible, and if related terms would be counted, like *cross, altar, sacrifice, offering, priesthood, covenant,* and many others, there would be few pages of Scripture that do not have reference to the blood. It is the scarlet thread that weaves the whole scope of revelation into one harmonious witness to the Gospel of salvation.

This substance is so closely related to the mystery of life and death that naturally it becomes a symbol of religious expression. From time immemorial, people from every culture of the world have used blood to speak those unutterable feelings of the soul all of us know.[2]

Since the heart is the center of the blood circulatory system, it becomes the epitome of life. The term is used this way hundreds of times in Scripture to designate the total human personality (e.g., Ezek. 11:19; Joel 2:13; Matt. 15:19; Rom. 10:10).

### Sacrificial Blood

Sacrifice brings the spiritual significance of the blood into focus. Life was returned to God in the shedding of blood; not in the sense that life was released from the flesh, but rather that life was brought to an end. Properly observed, the offering was a voluntary surrender of that which was most precious to man in the earnest desire to establish communion with God. As such, it expressed the highest devotion of which a person was capable. In the shed blood life was poured out unto death—nothing more could one give, yet nothing less could God accept.

The act of worship was represented through the sacrifice of an innocent animal, substituted for the worshipers. Whatever kind of animal was used, it had to be a male "without defect or blemish" (Lev. 22:21 NIV).

Having selected a fitting substitute, the individual brought it to the door of the tabernacle. Then the one making the sacrifice placed his hands on the head of the offering, indicating a transference of life. It was as though the one making the sacrifice was being offered to God. In certain public sacrifices for the people, the "elders," as representatives of the congregation, laid on hands (Lev. 4:15). On the Day of Atonement the High Priest laid on hands for the nation (Lev. 16:21).

Taking the life of the substituting animal was a vivid display of divine judgment on sin. At the same time, it witnessed to the inviolable nature of God's holiness. Nothing that is corrupted can live in his presence.

For the worshiper, the shed blood expressed his sorrow and repentance for sin, while also conveying his complete surrender to God. Moreover, resting on the altar, the blood declared an unqualified trust in God's Word. The act of obedience in giving the sacrifice evidenced this faith. Thus, for example, when Moses sprinkled the blood of the covenant, it was altogether fitting that the people cry out, "All the words that the LORD has spoken we will do" (Exod. 24:3–8).

### A Witness of Love

The whole validity of the offering in God's sight, of course, was in the sincerity with which one's identity with the blood was intended. Where the sacrifice was desecrated by making it a mere ceremony, as was often the case in Israel, the people were severely punished by God. True sacrifice never could be fulfilled by external rites—it was only an object lesson of an inward and spiritual experience.

As a spiritual act, sacrifice was an offering of love—a demonstration of the quality of moral holiness that cannot be put into words. The blood on the altar, when the offerer was fully conscious of its meaning, represented a choice of complete abandonment to God, and thereby expressed a perfectly holy desire. As such, this desire was without sin. It was this fact, and this fact alone, that made the blood acceptable in God's sight.

What is equally precious is that the blood on the altar represented God's reception of the sacrifice, and therefore a perfect expression of his love to man. It was the witness of his grace whereby God disclosed his merciful purpose to save his people. Though God was altogether holy and separate from sinners, and though his justice demanded that all uncleanness be separated from his presence, the shed blood on his altar made known that he still loved his creation. It said that at any cost he wanted to restore union with that life that he made. Hence, the Sovereign Lord was willing, even seeking, to be reconciled in a way whereby his integrity could be preserved. The blood offered on his altar was that way—the way that his love could be demonstrated in justice and holiness.

### One with God

The shed blood restored communion with God. Spiritually understood, it was literally a blood transfusion of life. Life relinquished in the shedding of blood becomes life provided through the blood.

In its most elemental sense, the blood covered sin from God's view and, hence, held back his wrath. This idea is embodied in the root form of the word *atonement* in the Old Testament. The word occurs this way when describing the covering or "pitch" used to hold back the waters about the ark of Noah (Gen. 6:14). The idea is actually introduced in the first sacrifice of an innocent animal when God made "garments of skins" in the garden to cover the nakedness of Adam and Eve so they could appear in his presence (Gen. 3:21).

By covering the sin that separated them, the blood effected reconciliation of God and man so that now they could have fellowship in peace. The term *mercy seat*, the place where God met together with man, is derived from the word for "atonement cover," which actually means at-one-ment with God (Exod. 35:12; 39:35; Lev. 16:14–15; Heb. 9:5).

### Symbol Becomes Reality

When Jesus came into the world, he said to the Father: "Sacrifices and offerings you have not desired, but a body have you prepared for me. . . . I have come to do your will, O God" (Heb. 10:5–7). It was not the slaughter of beasts that pleased God. The Father wanted a life to be lived before him in perfect obedience. Only the blood of such an offering could fulfill the intent of true sacrifice.

Thus Jesus clothed himself with a "body" to do the will of God. Through the miraculous conception of the Holy Spirit in the womb of the virgin, the eternal Word became "flesh and blood" (Heb. 2:14). With our identity, he bore our sorrows and carried our grief, being tempted in every respect as we are. Yet, unlike the priests of old who offered up sacrifices daily for their sin (as well as for the sins of the people), Jesus had no sin. So as one blameless under the law, he could offer himself as a perfect sacrifice.

All that had been represented for millennia in the Old Testament sacrifices, thus, came to fruition at Calvary. As his blood ran down the cross, forming a red pool at his feet, Christ's mission on earth was accomplished. The cry from the cross, "It is finished!" were the most thrilling words ever heard by men or angels. It was a mighty echo from the councils of eternity when this moment was planned. All that happened before and all that has happened since derives its meaning from what happened there when Jesus gave his blood for us. In making provision for the world to be saved, his work was finished. A perfect atonement was made for the human race, once and for all.

Identifying with his blood by faith, we appropriate the saving reality of his death. Jesus says: "Whoever feeds on my flesh and drinks my blood has eternal life" (John 6:54). But the question might be asked: Why did he invite us to drink his blood? Was not drinking of blood directly forbidden by the law?

The answer brings immediately into focus the ultimate spiritual meaning of the blood—a truth faintly seen in every sacrifice but only fully disclosed at the cross of Christ. To drink of his blood is to take into our heart the life-renewing power of his Spirit. Only he who was to die as our perfect sacrifice could give us the privilege of union with himself.

Testifying to this new life, the Bible tells us that through his own blood Christ has entered the sanctuary not made with hands "to appear in the presence of God on our behalf" (Heb. 9:24). Here the blood takes on its highest meaning. We are left utterly breathless in wonder. Though the details are not explained, the death of Christ has dimensions reaching into eternity. For like the resurrected body of our Lord, his blood remains incorruptible, and in its true spiritual substance will always appear in heaven as witness to God's everlasting covenant.

It is there now before the throne. It will be there forever—the remembrance of his unspeakable gift and the revelation of his unchanging Word.

## More Biblical Concepts[3]

### The Covenant Kept

The blood of the cross bore witness to God's faithfulness to his covenant[4] of grace. He had promised to save a people for his glory, beginning in the

Garden of Eden (Gen. 2:8–9), and that purpose was reaffirmed again and again through the history of Israel (Gen. 12:1–2; 17:2; Exod. 19:5–8; Num. 25:12–13; 2 Sam. 23:5).

In all these covenants that progressively unfold God's gracious design for his people, there is the anticipation of something better—not clearly disclosed—but always promised as their inheritance. Sometimes the prophets spoke of it as a "new covenant," when God would write his law in their heart (Jer. 31:33–34; cf. 2 Sam. 23:5; Heb. 8:10). The fulfillment of this promise is seen in the Messiah: the branch of righteousness growing out of David (Jer. 33:14–16, 20–22), who will bring salvation "unto the end of the earth" (Isa. 49:6 KJV).

In the Old Testament world it was customary to seal agreements in some kind of bloodletting ritual.[5] It's interesting that the Hebrew word for covenant, used nearly three hundred times in the Bible, probably comes from a word meaning "to cut." The blood that was drawn expressed a commitment unto death, and thereby witnessed to the inviolable nature of the promise.

Among primitive people this quality was dramatized by the shedding of blood in some kind of ceremonial testimony. For example, if two persons wanted to enter into a friendship pact, they might cut the palms of their hands so that the blood freely flowed. Then they would clasp their palms, much like we shake hands today. The intermingling of the blood bound their lives together in an undying witness to solidarity. Doubtless this custom was in the mind of the prophet when he said, "Behold, I have engraved you on the palms of my hands" (Isa. 49:16).

In the same sense of covenanting, if a person wanted to impress a congregation of people with the veracity of his word, he might cut his forearm in their presence. Then lifting it up toward God, he would make his statement. As the blood ran down his arm, the symbol of his strength, it bore witness that what he said with his lips he would support with his life. Very likely this was in the thinking of Isaiah when he wrote: "The Lord has sworn by his right hand and by his mighty arm" (Isa. 62:8). The practice even today of lifting up the arm when taking an oath, as in a court of justice, may trace back to this ancient custom of swearing by one's blood.

However it might be expressed, blood is inherent in the concept of a covenant—a solemn pact binding the parties to do what they say. In a much deeper way, this pledge was seen in all the blood sacrifices in Jewish altars for thousands of years. Though the children of the covenant did not keep their part of the agreement and were often punished for their unfaithfulness, God still loved them and remembered his merciful promise of redemption sealed in blood (Zech. 9:9–12; Luke 1:72).

In the New Testament the word for covenant takes on the meaning of the last will and testament that is inoperative until after the testator's death. It is the legal sense of the term as used in the Roman world and which is still reflected in our law today. This idea is developed particularly in the epistle to the Hebrews, where Christ is called the "mediator of a new covenant," and by means after death we might "receive the promised eternal inheritance—now that he has died as a ransom to set them free from the sins committed under the first covenant" (Heb. 9:15–16 NIV; cf. 8:6; 12:24).

That which all symbol and rite, all inspired prophecy, all yearning of life through the age had anticipated came to its glorious climax at Calvary. Jesus had said that the new covenant would be given in his blood (Matt. 26:28; Mark 14:23; Luke 22:20), and now the promise was fulfilled. The blood of the cross bore witness.

It was as though God lifted his holy arm and proclaimed to the ends of the earth: "I have kept the covenant of love" (Deut. 7:9, 12; 1 Kings 8:23; Neh. 1:5; 9:32; Dan. 9:4). I so loved the world that I have given my one and only Son to die for you, "that whoever believes in him shall not perish but have eternal life" (John 3:16).

### An Offering to God

One of the most beautiful descriptions of Calvary is Christ giving "himself up for us, a fragrant offering and sacrifice to God" (Eph. 5:2). It is a free and voluntary gift issuing from his love. The picture here is that of the High Priest of heaven entering the Most Holy Place and offering for us his own blood on the altar of God.

A priest serves as a mediator between God and man. Under the old law, persons serving in this capacity were specially consecrated for the task, and those so dedicated could then offer sacrifice (Heb. 5:1; 7:22–28). Still, because of their sinfulness, they had to offer sacrifices for their own sin, as well as for the sins of others. Moreover, their priesthood was only temporary, since death prevented them from continuing in office (Heb. 7:11–23).

But the sinless Christ needed no ritualistic symbol of purity to qualify him for the priesthood, nor would his ministry ever be terminated by death. For as a priest forever, after the order of the King of heaven and as the promised Lamb without spot or blemish, he offered himself to God as our perfect sacrifice. Not as a service to be repeated every year, as the priests of old, "but now he has appeared once for all at the end of the ages to do away with sin" (Heb. 9:26 NIV).

Therefore, "he is able to save to the uttermost those who draw near to God through him, since he always lives to make intercession for them" (Heb. 7:25). What a Savior!

### Propitiation Effected

Closely associated with the atonement[6] of Christ is "propitiation through faith in his blood" (Rom. 3:25 KJV). It refers to the provision made for God to show mercy to a sinner. Sin repudiates God and necessarily invokes his judgment. Something must be done to remove his divine wrath.

In pagan religions, propitiation usually had reference to what people could do to appease the offended deity—as if their god could be bribed by some offering. But for the Testaments of Scripture, it is God who takes the initiative in removing his wrath. A gift is offered, but it is God who offers it in Christ. He gives his blood. The gift is pleasing to the Lord because it discloses his own glory in that he sacrifices his life for the creature of his love.

This changes the whole nature of our salvation. God is seen as both the subject and the object of propitiation. His wrath is removed, not because we do something, but because he did something. From beginning to end, it is a display of his sovereign grace.

God hates evil but he loves mankind. His love blazes against that which would destroy his beloved—a love so pure that it would not let us go, even while we were yet sinners. Such love can be known only in Christ. "In this is love, not that we have loved God, but that he loved us and sent his Son to be the propitiation for our sins" (1 John 4:10; cf. 2:2).

The word for *propitiation* can literally be translated "mercy seat" (Heb. 9:5; cf. Exod. 25:17; 31:7; 35:12; 37:6; Lev. 16:2, 13). This probably refers to the place above the ark of the covenant in the Holy of Holies where the blood of the atoning sacrifice was sprinkled. It was here that the Shekinah glory came down and filled the inner chamber with the presence of God.

The mercy seat covered the tablets of the covenant (Heb. 9:4; cf. Exod. 25:21). It was a perpetual reminder that salvation had not yet come in the flesh. Hence, the mercy seat was hidden from the people's physical sight in the holiest of all places. Yet they could see it by faith, and in that manner they entered in with the High Priest when he approached the mercy seat with blood.

In contrast to the old law, Christ's offering at the cross was not hidden from the view of the people. Rather he was set forth openly as a public spectacle "to be a propitiation" for us (Rom. 3:25 KJV). The blood of Calvary now boldly invites whosoever will to come and meet with God at the place where we are accepted in the beloved.

### Redeemed

*Redemption* is another term often related to the atonement. The word means to buy back or to loose. As applied to us, it signifies the loosing of the bonds of a prisoner, setting him free. Commonly, in Jesus's day, the term referred to the amount required to purchase the life of a slave; or in a slightly different rendering, it might be used in the context of ransom, where a sum of money was supplied as the condition for release.

The purchase price of our redemption was the blood of Christ (Eph. 1:7; Col. 1:14). His death became our ransom from sin (Matt. 20:28; 1 Tim. 2:6).

An incident during the tumultuous era of the Civil War in nineteenth-century America brings out this concept. While law and order was at a minimum, a band of organized outlaws in the Southwest called Quantrill's Raiders would sweep down on an unsuspecting community on the frontier to rob, pillage, burn, and then ride away before help could come. The situation became so desperate that some people in Kansas formed a militia to search out the desperadoes. They had orders to execute without delay any of the raiders that could be found.

Not long afterward, a group of these men were captured. A long trench was dug; they were lined up, hands and legs tied and eyes covered. The firing squad was forming. Suddenly a young man rushed out of the underbrush, crying out, "Wait! Wait!" Covered by the guns of the firing squad, he approached the officer in command. Pointing to a man who was waiting to be shot, he said, "Let that man go free. He has a wife and four children and is needed at home. Let me take his place. I am guilty."

It was an extraordinary appeal, but the stranger insisted that it not be denied. After a long consultation, the officer decided to grant the request. They cut the ropes and released the condemned man. The volunteer was put in his place and fell dead before the firing squad.

Later the redeemed man came back to the awful scene of death, uncovered the grave, and found the body of his friend. He put it on the back of a mule and took it to a little cemetery near Kansas City, where he was given a proper burial. There he erected a memorial stone on which were inscribed the words, "He took my place. He died for me."[7]

In a more profound way, this is what happened when Jesus died at Calvary. He took our place. We were those sold to sin, under the sentence of death. But with God's incredible love, Jesus came forward and offered himself as our Redeemer. We are not redeemed "with perishable things such as silver or gold, but with the precious blood of Christ, a lamb without blemish or spot" (1 Pet. 1:18–19; cf. Heb. 9:12).

### A New Relationship

The blood of Christ enables us to have a totally new relationship with God. Both our relations to him and his attitude toward us changed. He is always the same, but the way he looks at us is different.

One way of describing it is through justification. Christ is represented as accepting our judgment by taking on himself the wrath of the law. It was as though he assumed our legal liability when he suffered the consequences of our sin. By identifying with his blood, we thus can be forgiven (Rom. 5:9).

The concept of reconciliation, closely related to atonement, is another way to get at this truth. The idea is to bring together two parties that are separated. The sin that kept us apart from God is now removed. By "making peace by the blood of his cross," we who were once enemies of God, alienated in our mind by wicked works, have been brought back as his friends (Col. 1:20).

The same idea comes out in bringing the Gentile world to God. Without Christ we were all "foreigners to the covenants of the promise, without hope" (Eph. 2:12 NIV). But now in the Savior we who formerly "were far away have been brought near through the blood of Christ. For he himself is our peace, who has made the two one and has destroyed the barrier, the dividing wall" (vv. 13–14 NIV). By his death, the whole system of Jewish laws has been eliminated, so that in him there is no longer Jew or Gentile. He has gathered us all up in himself as one new person.

### Cleansing from Sin

More than effecting a new relationship with God, the atonement made possible an inner transformation of character. One way the Bible expresses it is by cleansing or purifying the heart (1 John 1:7). The guilt and pollution of sin are washed away by the blood (Rev. 1:5; 7:14).

An illustration of this principle is the old Levitical ritual for cleansing persons who had been contaminated by exposure to death. A red heifer without spot was sacrificed outside the camp (Num. 19:1–22). The blood was taken by the High Priest and sprinkled seven times toward the sanctuary, after which the whole animal was burned. When the offering had been consumed by fire, the ashes were mixed with pure water, a hyssop dipped into the solution, and the unclean persons sprinkled. Upon washing themselves in water, their defilement was removed.

This ceremonial rite, observed by some people every time there was a death in Israel, was in the thinking of the author of Hebrews when he wrote:

> If the sprinkling of defiled persons with the blood of goats and bulls and with the ashes of a heifer sanctifies for the purification of the flesh, how much more shall the blood of Christ, who through the eternal Spirit offered himself without blemish to God, purify your conscience from dead works.
>
> Hebrews 9:13–14 RSV

Here the whole person is cleansed from sin's defilement by the blood-applying ministry of the Holy Spirit. Our hearts are cleansed from a guilty conscience and our bodies "washed with pure water" (Heb. 10:22). Sanctification comes by virtue of the atoning blood of Christ (Heb. 13:12; 1 Pet. 1:2).

### Made Ministering Servants

We must not overlook, too, that the cleansing effect of the blood is to enable us to "serve the living God" (Heb. 9:14; cf. 2 Tim. 2:21). Christ "has freed us from our sins by his blood and made us a kingdom, priests to his God and Father" (Rev. 1:5–6). The washing and the ministering go together. The result of cleansing continues on into heaven, for those who "have washed their robes and made them white in the blood of the Lamb" are seen "before the throne of God, and serve him day and night in his temple" (Rev. 7:14–15).

Think of what this means to our prayer life. The blood that was offered by Christ for us binds us to his intercessory ministry for the world. Here we enter most completely into the heart of our Savior's love.

It was the custom in biblical days for the Israelites to bow in prayer outside the sanctuary while incense was placed by the priest on the burning coals at the golden altar (Luke 1:8–10). The fire that burned the incense was taken from the brazen altar where a sacrifice was offered. Thus their prayers mingled with the ascending cloud of smoke in a beautiful expression of faith and dependence on the blood.

This is still the case. In the symbolism of the temple in Revelation, heaven has a golden altar on which incense is offered with the prayers of the saints (Rev. 8:3–4; cf. 5:8). We can assume from this mystical figure that the fire, which lifts the incense, is taken from the altar where Christ gave his blood. It is here as our will is consumed with his that prayer has its ultimate purpose.

## Essential Aspects of the Atonement

Through the ages, theologians, and their views restated by church councils, have formulated various explanations of Christ's work at the cross. These statements seek to provide a rationale for the atonement, but no theory captures the full meaning of a truth so vast. Even the apostle Paul, when reflecting on Christ's love—the heartbeat of the doctrine—confessed that it "surpasses knowledge" (Eph. 3:19).

To attempt to treat even some of these theories would go beyond the scope of this study. That task I must leave to others.[8] My purpose here is best served by sorting out essential ingredients of any evangelical approach, which taken together give insight into what happened at Calvary.

### Christus Victor

One theme running through explanations of the atonement, sometimes called the "dramatic" or "ransom" view, emphasizes the victory of Christ over the principalities of evil, freeing them from the tyranny of Satan.[9] By his death, Christ destroyed "the one who has the power of death, that is, the devil" (Heb. 2:14; cf. 1 John 3:8). "And having disarmed the powers and authorities, he made a public spectacle of them, triumphing over them by the cross" (Col. 2:15).

Contrary to popular opinion, some suggest that the devil did not want Christ to die. Does not this appear to be the point of Jesus's rebuke to Peter when the apostle objected to the Lord's announcement of his impending death? "Get behind me, Satan," Jesus said. "You are a hindrance to me. For you are not setting your mind on the things of God, but on the things of man" (Matt. 16:23; Mark 8:33). The assumption is that the devil knew the Scriptures well enough to understand that the bondage in which he held the world would be broken by the Messiah's sacrifice.[10] How easy it is for us, like Peter, to think that God's plan of redemption from sin can avoid the cross.

But grasping the completeness of the finished work of Christ, and uniting with his defeat of Satan, we can "overcome" the onslaughts of the demonic world (Rev. 12:11; cf. John 12:31; 16:11). We do not even have to listen to the accusations of the evil one. For "now have come the salvation and the power and the kingdom of our God, and the authority of his Christ" (Rev. 12:10 NIV). The kingdom of the world ruled by Satan "has become the kingdom of our Lord and of his Christ" (Rev. 11:15; cf. Luke 10:18). Jesus reigns on the throne (Matt. 28:18). By his power, whatever comes, we are "more than conquerors" (Rom. 8:37).

### Perfect Obedience

Giving eternal meaning to the death of Christ was the intrinsic value of his outpoured life. The perfect "lamb" of sacrifice who was "sent" to do the will of God was obedient unto death (John 1:36; 4:34; Phil. 2:8; 1 Pet. 1:19). For the first time in human history, there was one among us whose life met every ethical demand of the divine law. Moreover, within the Trinity the Father experienced in the suffering of his Son the infinitude of perfect love.

Jesus sets before us an example of incarnate holiness, a submission to God that defines what every person should aspire to attain—his selfless devotion, his loyalty to deity, his faithfulness to truth, his unwavering love that will not give up on a lost world. What a display of saintliness lived out on earth! There are no depths in our lives to which he has not already gone to bear our burdens and carry our grief. Viewing Christ's giving of himself from this perspective surely brings powerful motivation for mankind to be reconciled to a God like that. By the same token, his obedience to the Father becomes a tremendous influence on our moral behavior, just as it challenges us to greater dedication.[11]

Affirming this truth, though, must not obscure other essential aspects of the atonement, as liberal theologies tend to do.[12] We are not redeemed by following the example and teaching of Jesus. However earnest the effort, we still fall far short of the perfect obedience required under the law of God. Such noble endeavor has appeal, to be sure, but by itself circumvents the blood; it would be something like a self-atonement through human initiative, and the end result would be to glorify man, not God.

Still, no theory of the atonement can be complete without recognizing the exemplary life and work of Christ. How can anyone behold such love and not be moved to fall at his feet?

### Directed to God

The force of Christ's sacrifice was not toward man but to God. More than exerting influence on a fallen race to change our way, the real change wrought at the cross was in the heart of the Father. Something happened there that forever changed his relationship to the world. Love within the Holy Trinity had triumphed over sin and the devil. God could now look on his creation in the embrace of his Son.[13]

Making possible this new reality was the satisfaction of God's honor and authority through the suffering and death of his Son. The holiness of God demands that sin be expiated. Jesus accepted that judgment in our place, bearing in his body the wrath of the law. By identity with him, we appear before God adorned in his righteousness, "to the praise of his glorious grace, which he has freely given us in the One he loves" (Eph. 1:6 NIV).

Implicit in this transference of identity is the idea of substitution—"Christ suffered once for sins," the just for the unjust, that he might bring us to God (1 Pet. 3:18). To put it another way, "God made him who had no sin to be sin for us, so that in him we might become the righteousness of God" (2 Cor. 5:21 NIV; cf. Gal. 1:4; Eph. 1:7). Among those who take a governmental approach, Christ's death is not seen as bearing the actual penalty of sin, but rather as a substitute for the penalty.[14]

Some reject the vicarious element of the atonement on the grounds that it would be immoral for God to lay on an innocent man the condemnation of another. The argument might have validity if the innocent one were an unwilling victim; but it could never apply to Jesus who joyfully came to do the will of God and was determined that nothing would prevent his accomplishing that purpose (Matt. 20:28; John 12:27; 15:10; Heb. 10:1–4). Should not the infinitely holy God, if he pleased, be free to take to himself the doom of those his love would save?

The answer finally brings one to realize a love within the Trinity so perfect that Christ can speak of his death as making known the glory of God (John 17:1–5, 22–26). It is a display of sovereign grace, as Charles Wesley sang:

> 'Tis Mercy all, immense and free
> For, O my God, it found out me.[15]

Though we cannot explain it, of this we are sure: God demonstrated his love for us in that "while we were still sinners, Christ died for us" (Rom. 5:8).

### Universal but Limited

Everyone was represented in Jesus's offering. He is likened to the second Adam in solidarity with the race: "For as by the one man's disobedience the many were made sinners, so by the one man's obedience the many will be made righteous" (Rom. 5:19; cf. 1 Cor. 15:22). Since "in Adam all die" (1 Cor. 15:22), "much more will those who receive the abundance of grace and the free gift of righteousness reign in life through the one man Jesus Christ" (Rom. 5:17).

In Christ's representation of mankind, the scope of his sacrifice is universal. "God so loved the world" that he gave his Son (John 3:16); he "desires all people to be saved and to come to the knowledge of the truth" (1 Tim. 2:4); "the grace of God has appeared, bringing salvation for all people" (Titus 2:11); the Lord does not want "that any should perish, but that all should reach repentance" (2 Pet. 3:9); "in Christ God was reconciling the world to himself" (2 Cor. 5:19); "he is the atoning sacrifice for our sins, and not only ours but also for the sins of the whole world" (1 John 2:2 NIV).

That Jesus died for the world seems clear, but whether everyone can benefit from it has been a subject of contention in the church through the ages. Basically Arminians believe that the atonement extends to all people who ever lived and therefore, through God's grace, everyone can be saved. On the other hand, Reformed theologians argue that Christ died for everyone but that does not mean that he paid the penalty for everyone. The Gospel is offered to all but only the elect will be moved by God to accept it.[16] What appears to be an irreconcilable contradiction, however, need not be an impediment to evangelism.

Whether Arminian or Reformed, the Gospel must be received by faith for the atonement of Christ to be efficacious. "To all who did receive him, who believed in his name, he gave the right to become children of God" (John 1:12). So in either system of thought, the Gospel is freely offered to every person, and whosoever will may come to Christ. Only those who respond to the invitation will be saved, and in that response their election is known, whether Arminian or Calvinist. Without evangelism neither system of theology has any practical value.

## Summary Applications

*1. The blood of the human race ultimately flows into and out from the cross of Christ.*

Every drop of blood in the veins of mankind from the beginning of time speaks of the life of God's Son poured out for us. Apart from this indisputable fact of history, our lives would have no value or destiny. Let this come to mind every time you see blood flowing from a wound.

*2. The cross resonates in the eternal consciousness of God.*

Calvary simply bore witness to God's set purpose and foreknowledge (Acts 2:23). In the mind of God, Christ was slain before "the foundation of the world" (Rev. 13:8). That is why he could show mercy to people under the curse of sin following human rebellion in the Garden of Eden.

### 3. *The cross makes clear the reasons for Christ's incarnation.*

He was born to die for the world. His life from childhood to maturity demonstrated a sinless personality so that he could be offered as a perfect sacrifice, "a lamb without blemish or spot" (1 Pet. 1:19). The great events of his life, including his circumcision as an infant, his baptism by John, his temptation in the wilderness, and his transfiguration on the mountain, all had meaning for his redemptive mission. Similarly his resurrection from the grave, his ascension to heaven, his reign at the throne, and his coming again have eternal significance because that same triumphant Savior once died for our sins.

Not surprisingly, many of the religious elite who watched Jesus die mocked him. "He saved others; he cannot save himself" (Matt. 27:42; Mark 15:31). How like the thinking of self-righteous worldlings! What they failed to understand was that Jesus had not come into the world to save himself; he was sent to save us and he would not be denied the reason for his incarnation.

### 4. *The cross vividly unmasks the awfulness of sin.*

No death could be more shameful in the eyes of the world. Only the foulest of criminals and slaves—persons with no standing in society—could be subjected to such an ignominious demise. Among the Jews such a death implied a curse (Deut. 21:23; Gal. 3:13).

The torture of the cross was so terrible that the Romans had to fashion a new term to describe its pain, the word from which our word *excruciating* is derived. Normally in that day the condemned man was stripped naked, his garments falling to the executioners as their booty for the ordeal. Then the victim was thrust across the heavy wooden crossbeams with outstretched arms and his hands were nailed fast to either end by long spikes hammered through the palms or wrists. Thereafter the cross with its quivering load was hoisted on the upright, and usually supported by a peg or notch in the lower cross. The feet, like the hands, were nailed to the upright by a single spike transfixing both. And then the bleeding victim hung in agony, gasping for breath, lingering on sometimes for days.

In the case of Jesus, because of the approaching Sabbath, the Jews asked Pilate to hasten his death by ordering the soldiers to break his legs. But they found that Jesus was already dead, so instead of breaking his legs, they pierced his side with a spear, "bringing a sudden flow of blood and water" (John 19:31–37 NIV). His suffering was so intense, particularly his anguish over the rejection by the people he came to save, that he died from a broken heart.[17]

From the standpoint of his human nature, however, greater than the physical agony of death was the sense of being separated from God. Recall that as the hours of his suffering lengthened, while darkness hung over the land, Jesus cried: "My God, my God, why have you forsaken me?" (Mark 15:34). His cry of dereliction voices a profound theological question to be sure. How could God be disconnected from himself? The answer lies in distinguishing between the two natures of Christ, it being only his human nature that was separated in death (this was the nature he assumed in the incarnation). Though it still remains a mystery, this much is clear—Christ in his dying moments experienced as a perfect man the realization of being utterly alone, forsaken by the Father in heaven. This is the spiritual essence of hell—the ultimate horror of sin.

### 5. *The cross bears witness to the certainty of judgment.*

It is the final evidence that full satisfaction will be made for sin. God cannot ignore the rebellion of creatures who scorn his sovereignty. Justice demands that his name be vindicated. Thus when Christ took on himself our identity, he accepted the sentence of our death.

God spared not the "angels when they sinned" (2 Pet. 2:4). God did not spare his own chosen people of Israel, "the natural branches," when they sinned (Rom. 11:21). One might think, however, that an exception would be made for Jesus, the perfect man. But when he became one with us, God "did not spare his own Son" in judgment (Rom. 8:32).

### 6. *The cross brings into glorious focus the love of God.*

Of course, every moment in the incarnate life of Jesus manifested that love, but the cross was the climactic revelation, the unveiling of what is eternal in the Holy Trinity. "This is how we know what love is: Jesus Christ laid down his life for us" (1 John 3:16 NIV). We can possibly understand someone dying for a righteous man, but God demonstrated his love toward us "while we were still sinners" (Rom. 5:8). Though such love "surpasses knowledge" (Eph. 3:19), no effort brings more joy to the soul than an attempt to make it known.

Just as at the cross, this love can be demonstrated better than explained. A story told by D. James Kennedy, reported to have happened in 1937, is an illustration.[18] He told of John Griffith, a gatekeeper of a bridge that crossed the Mississippi.

> One day his eight-year-old-son, Greg, came to see where Daddy worked. The boy was wide-eyed with excitement as his dad showed him how the huge bridge went up to let boats go by on the river and then lowered so that trains could pass over.
>
> At twelve o'clock the father had put up the bridge since no trains were due for a while. Then they went out together a couple hundred feet on the catwalk to the observation deck and sat down. Mr. Griffith told his boy about the faraway lands that some of the ships were going to visit. The boy was entranced. The time whirled by.
>
> Suddenly they were drawn back to reality by the shrieking of a distant train whistle. John Griffith quickly looked at his watch. He saw that it was time for the 107, the Memphis Express with 400 passengers, to be rushing across that bridge in just a few minutes. He knew he just had time. Telling his son to stay where he was, he leapt to his feet, jumped to the catwalk, ran back, climbed the

ladder to the central room, went in and put his hand on the lever that controlled the bridge. He looked up and down the river to see if any boats were coming.

Then he saw something which terrified him. His boy had tried to follow him to the central room, and had fallen into the huge pit that housed the gears that operated the massive drawbridge. His son's left leg was caught between the two main gears. The father knew that if he pushed that lever his son would be ground in the midst of tons of grinding steel. His eyes filled with tears of panic. What could he do?

He saw a rope there in the control room. He could rush down the ladder to the catwalk, tie off the rope, lower himself down, extricate his son, climb back up the rope, run back to the central room and lower the bridge. No sooner had his mind done that exercise than he knew there was not time. He would never make it. There were 400 people in that train. He heard the whistle again, now startlingly closer. He could hear the clicking of the locomotive wheels on the track.

He knew what had to be done. Burying his head in his arms, he pushed the gear forward. The great bridge slowly lowered into place just as the express train roared across.

The father lifted his tear-smeared face and looked into the flashing windows of the train as it sped by. He could see people reading papers, sipping tea, enjoying the comforts of the ride. Nobody looked at him. Nobody heard his cries. Nobody realized what it had cost for the train to cross the bridge.

But when persons on that train later learned what happened at the bridge to assure their safe passage, can you imagine anyone not being moved by the father's sacrifice? The analogy is inadequate, of course, but in some sense that is how we begin to feel when coming to understand what happened at Calvary.

### 7. The cross precipitates a crisis of personal decision.

Realizing that the Son of God died in our place brings every convicted sinner to a moment of truth. No longer can anyone pretend that it does not matter what we do with Christ. Whether we like it or not, we must respond to his love.

Having been born and raised in Texas, I am reminded of those 182 patriots in 1836 who fought for their liberty at the Alamo, an old Spanish Mission in San Antonio. Surrounded by the Mexican Army, numbering several thousand soldiers, for thirteen days the Texans were under attack. One day during a lull in the bombardment, William B. Travis, the commander, called his men together and explained their hopeless military position. The only way to save themselves would be to surrender. However, there was the possibility that at night individuals might be able to slip through the enemy lines and he would understand if some of them chose to leave. Unsheathing his sword, placing its point to the earth, Travis walked in front of his battle-weary men until a line was drawn on the sand. Then in a voice trembling with emotion, he said, "Those prepared to give their lives in freedom's cause, come over to me."[19]

Without hesitation every man, save one, crossed the line. James Bowie, too sick to walk, asked that he be carried over on his cot.

In the early predawn of March 6, with bugles sounding the dreaded "Dequello" (no quarter to the defenders), columns of Mexican soldiers attacked from all directions. The Texans fought off the first attack and the second, but the third assault breached the north wall, and the Mexican troops poured into the Alamo compound. In furious hand-to-hand combat, the Texans fought until every soldier had bathed the earth with his blood. That is why the cry "Remember the Alamo" became the cry of Texas's independence. The line had been drawn, and now every person who lived in the territory had to choose which side they were on—to stand with Texas or with Mexico. Neutrality was not an option.

In an infinitely greater way, God has drawn a line across the conscience of humanity. He has taken an old rugged cross, firmly planted in the earth, and out of its almighty love comes the Gospel invitation—to come to Christ or to go with the world. We cannot have it both ways.

*8. The decision made at the cross allows no compromise.*

One dies on the cross. Crucifixion may be a slow and sacrificial death, but it is certain. When we come to Christ, comprehension of the cross in all its implications is limited, to be sure, but there should be no reservation in the desire to accept all that is understood. Deeper dimensions of what it means to take up the cross will become clearer as we follow Jesus. Isaac Watts expressed it well in his hymn:

> When I survey the wondrous cross
>   On which the Prince of Glory died,
> My richest gain I count but loss,
>   And pour contempt on all my pride.
>
> Were the whole realm of nature mine,
>   That were a present far too small;
> Love so amazing, so divine,
>   Demands my soul, my life, my all.[20]

*9. The cross will always be an offense to the world.*

There is no way the Gospel of the cross can be made compatible with the egotistical wisdom of a fallen race (Gal. 5:11). It throws human reckonings of achievement into confusion by showing the absurdity of earning salvation through good works. Persons infatuated with their own morality naturally will look on the cross as a "stumbling block"; while others who view religion only in terms of beautiful ideals will regard the cross as "foolishness" (1 Cor. 1:25). We might as well face it. Proud unrepentant worldlings resent the testimony of the blood against their self-sufficiency.

*10. But thanks be to God, persons who come to the end of all their spiritual resources—who realize that they are utterly lost and undone—will hear of the shed blood of Christ with tears of joy and shouts of praise.*

This is the Gospel! When our hearts are broken, and mercy is our only hope, then the cross is seen as the wisdom and the power and the glory of God.

There is a legend of a rich man seeking entry into heaven. As he stood at the gate, an angel asked him to give the password. The finely dressed gentleman replied, "I have contributed generously to the church. My virtues are beyond dispute. Everywhere I am respected among men. Surely, I have earned a place in heaven."

But the angel answered, "That is not the password. You cannot enter." As the famous benefactor was turned away, another man of distinguished appearance knocked on heaven's door. Challenged by the angel to give the password, he replied, "I have served the Lord as a minister of the cloth. I have performed great works of righteousness in his name. Renowned institutions have honored me with their highest degrees. I deserve heaven's favor."

But the angel answered, "That is not the password. You do not know the King."

No sooner was the man cast out than an old woman approached the gate. Her body was bowed from many years of toil. But there was a twinkle in her eye and a shine on her face. Asked by the angel to give the password, she lifted her hands and started to sing: "The blood, the blood, is all my plea. Hallelujah! It cleanseth me. Hallelujah! It cleanseth me."

Immediately the gates of pearl swung open and, as the dear spirit entered into the celestial city, the choirs of heaven joined in singing her song.

The theology of this old story may be oversimplified, but the point cannot be missed. When all is said and done, our only claim to heaven is the blood of Jesus Christ. Here is the password into the presence of God:

> Just as I am without one plea,
> But that Thy blood was shed for me,
> And that thou bidd'st me come to Thee,
> O Lamb of God, I come, I come![21]

# 8

# The Triumph of Christ

There is a story that news of the Battle of Waterloo was brought by sailing ship to the south coast of England. From there the tidings were relayed by the semaphore to London, and the semaphore on the Winchester Cathedral began to repeat it. Letter by letter, it spelled out W-E-L-L-I-N-G-T-O-N D-E-F-E-A-T-E-D. Just then a heavy fog settled down and blanketed from sight the semaphore's signal. It appeared that the battle was lost and gloom spread over the land.

Later the fog lifted and the semaphore respondent was able to read the full message. It read: WELLINGTON DEFEATED THE ENEMY. What a difference it made! Sorrow turned into rejoicing and songs of victory now rang through the streets.

In a similar way the world received the message of the cross. It seemed that Jesus was defeated. Hell was jubilant. Disillusionment gripped the hearts of the disciples, who "had hoped that he was the one to redeem Israel" (Luke 24:21).

But God's message was not complete. Not until early on the morning of the third day was the news received in full, as the angel announced that Jesus had left the grave; he was alive.

## The Resurrection

Visualize the scene. After the crucifixion the blood-drained body of Jesus had been taken down from the cross. His friends had wrapped the corpse in a linen shroud with preservative spices, as was the burial custom among the Jews.

The body was laid in a tomb in Joseph's garden, after which a large stone was rolled against the entrance (Mark 15:37–46; Luke 23:46–55; John 19:33–40). To make sure that no one would disturb the tomb, at the insistence of the chief priests and Pharisees, Pilate had ordered that a contingent of Roman soldiers guard the tomb, and said, "Go, make it as secure as you can" (Matt. 27:65).

### He Descended into Hades

The body lay in the grave for three days. What Jesus did during that time is not clear, though many believe, following the Apostles' Creed, that "he descended into hell."

Support for this may be found in the Pentecost sermon, when, referring to David (Ps. 16:10), Peter says that the soul of the Holy One will not be abandoned to Hades (Acts 2:27, 31; cf. Rev. 1:18). To this might be added the statement in Ephesians 4:9 that he "descended into the lower parts of the earth." If Ephesians 4:8 and 1 Peter 3:19 and 4:6 are associated with this period, it is thought that Christ preached the Gospel to "the spirits in prison" and released those who had been in bondage. This reference to the dead may relate to persons who had died under the Old Testament dispensation, and who were awaiting deliverance into paradise; or it might allude to the reprobate, even the fallen angels. Information provided about this descent in Scripture is limited and can be interpreted many ways, so I think it best to make any conclusion tentative.[1]

As for the phrase "descended into hell," it is not found in the earliest versions of the Apostles' Creed. When it does appear about AD 390 (some three centuries after its first use), the words were understood to mean that Christ "descended into the grave." Not until the middle of the seventh century was its present form delineating hell incorporated into the Creed, apparently intending to explain what Christ did following his burial.[2] Actually, the visit to hell, in my mind, does not add any necessary component to the redemptive work of Christ, nor would its omission from the Creed affect negatively any vital Christian doctrines.

It may be well to note that the word for "hell" used in the Creed as well as the Scriptural portion does not refer to a place of punishment. That would have been expressed by the Greek term *gehenna*; rather the word is *Hades*, which like its Old Testament equivalent, *Sheol*, simply represents the place of those who have departed this life, both the righteous and the unrighteous. To think of Christ going to hell, then, does not necessarily indicate further suffering.

However, many of the fathers of the church, as well as Reformed theologians like John Calvin, have taught that after his death on the cross Jesus actually had to endure the pangs of God's vengeance in hell to fully appease his wrath.[3] From the standpoint of our human comfort, as the Heidelberg Catechism reasons, when we are going through great temptation, it is reassuring to know that Christ by "his inexpressible anguish, pains, and horrors, which he suffered in his soul on the cross and before, has redeemed me from the anguish and torment of hell."[4]

But why would Christ need to endure more torment? Was not the atonement finished "once for all" at Calvary (Rom. 6:10; Heb. 7:27)? I can see where the entrance of Christ into the realm of the dead would assure that his identity with mankind was complete, and that his appearance to the dead gave witness that what he had accomplished on the cross extended to all people who ever lived. But if it was essential that he join them in the grave, it was not the last excruciating experience of his humiliation but rather the beginning of his triumphant exaltation, a descent to announce his resurrection.

### His Conquest of Death

Whatever Christ did after his death, it is certain that his body did not stay in the grave. On the third day, when Mary Magdalene, Mary the mother of James, and Salome came to the tomb to anoint his body, the large stone at the entrance had been rolled away by an angel, who was still present. He told the astonished ladies: "Do not be alarmed. You seek Jesus of Nazareth, who was crucified. He has risen; he is not here. See the place where they laid him" (Mark 16:6; cf. Matt. 28:1–8; Luke 24:6).

The soldiers who had been guarding the tomb, trembling with fear, had fled into the city and reported to the chief priests what had happened. Trying to deal with the problem, the priests gave the guards "hush money" and told them to broadcast that the disciples of Jesus had stolen his body away during the night while they were asleep (Matt. 28:4, 11–15).

Yet despite the libel made use of by the Sanhedrin priests, the world could not discount the fact that there was an open grave in Joseph's garden. The great stone at its door was rolled away (Matt. 28:1–4; Mark 16:2–4; John 20:1). Inside the sepulchre the linen cloth wrapped around the body of Jesus rested in a sunken heap. The napkin covering his head was folded at the place where the Lord lay (Luke 24:12; John 20:5–7).

If someone had stolen the body by night, as the frantic rulers claimed, why had the burial garments been so carefully preserved? The tomb showed no evidence of disorder. I cannot imagine that the disciples stole the body and then later deliberately died for a faith that was based on the resurrection. People do not die for what they know is a lie.

Then who did take the body? Surely not the temple priests, else they could have produced the mummified remains to forever discredit the testimony of the disciples. No one resorts to abuse and persecution when in possession of evidence to prove their point.

And certainly we cannot believe that the Roman guards stole the body, knowing that such an act of disobedience was punished by death. But if they had, who could have prompted them to do it? No, however viewed, the only reasonable explanation was given by the angel: "He is not here; he has risen!"[5]

### A Multitude of Witnesses

So astounding is the fact of Jesus's resurrection that at first many of the disciples could scarcely believe it (Matt. 28:17; Mark 16:13–14; Luke 24:13–32, 36–43; John 20:19–31). Understanding their dismay, Jesus made it a point to personally come to them. He appeared to Mary Magdalene in the garden on Easter morning (Mark 16:9; John 20:15–18). He spoke to the women on the way to the tomb and bid them hurry to tell the disciples that he was risen (Matt. 28:9–10). The same day he walked with two disciples on the road to Emmaus, then sat at their table and broke bread with them before disappearing from their sight (Luke 24:13–32). Jesus appeared to Peter and had a private interview in his room (Luke 24:34; 1 Cor. 15:5). He met with the eleven disciples on the evening of that first Easter day, showing them the nail prints in his hands and feet (Mark 16:14; Luke 24:36–43; John 20:19–25). Again the next Sunday he appeared to the whole apostolic company; this time Thomas was present and given opportunity to thrust his hand into the wound of his Lord's side (John 20:26–29).

On the shore of Tiberias, Jesus manifested himself to the disciples while they were fishing and later had breakfast with them beside the sea (John 21:1–14). At an appointed meeting on the mountain, he spoke to more than five hundred followers, at which time he bid them go and make disciples of all nations (Matt. 28:16–20; Mark 16:15–18; 1 Cor. 15:6). Jesus appeared to his half brother James (1 Cor. 15:7). Finally, he met with the disciples at Bethany before ascending up into the clouds of heaven (Mark 16:19–20; Luke 24:50–53; Acts 1:9–12) to take his place at the throne of God, from which he shall come again in like manner as he went.

On many different occasions, in various parts of the country, appearing to hundreds of people from all walks of life, Jesus Christ was seen in his resurrection glory. It was no illusion—no wishful thinking; those eyewitnesses saw a real person—they talked with him, they ate together, they touched him with their hands (1 John 1:1). Though his glorified body no longer was bound by the limitations of the flesh and could assume whatever form necessary for communication, clearly the same Jesus who was crucified had risen from the grave.

Following his resurrection, over a period of forty days, Jesus gave his disciples "convincing proof that he was alive" (Acts 1:3 NIV). It appears that he was staying with his disciples (v. 4 NIV),[6] so these times of fellowship afforded many opportunities for Jesus to open their understanding of Scripture (Luke 24:44–47; John 21:1–23). We are told that particularly he spoke to them about the kingdom of God, a subject in which clearly they needed more instruction (Acts 1:3, 6–9).

On one occasion as they were staying together (v. 4), he told them "not to depart from Jerusalem, but to wait for the promise of the Father" which he had told them about concerning the baptism of the Holy Spirit (vv. 4–5), after which they would be "clothed with power from on high" (Luke 24:49; cf. Acts 1:8). It was also during this time that Jesus gave his disciples the Great Commission, assuring them of his presence with them to the end of the age (Matt. 28:16–20; Mark 16:15–18).

## The Ascension

Having given the disciples their marching orders, Jesus led them out to Bethany, not far from Jerusalem, "and lifting up his hands he blessed them" (Luke 24:50). "While he blessed them" (v. 51), as his disciples "were looking on, he was lifted up" (Acts 1:9; cf. Mark 16:19), "carried up into heaven" (Luke 24:51), "and a cloud took him out of their" view (Acts 1:9).

What a sight that must have been—to see Jesus ascend into the heavens before their eyes! No mirage. Nothing speculative about this. That crowd of witnesses actually saw their Lord, master over the law of gravity, slowly rise above the earth until hidden by a cloud.

"While they were gazing into heaven as he went, behold, two men stood by them in white robes" (v. 10). These were angelic messengers appearing here in the most natural way for communication. "Men of Galilee," they said, "why do you stand looking into heaven? This Jesus, who was taken up from you into heaven, will come in the same way as you saw him go into heaven" (v. 11; Luke 24:51).

With this promise of the Lord's return, overwhelmed with wonder, the disciples went back to Jerusalem "with great joy" and then were continuously in the temple praising God (vv. 52–53).

The ascension marked the closure of Christ's earthly incarnate work and made clear that he was assuming a new heavenly ministry. He was not resurrected to die again, but to live eternally as Lord of the universe.[7] Had he not ascended, we might have wondered where he went.

## His Reign in Heaven

Entering the realms above, Jesus "sat down at the right hand of God" (Mark 16:19; cf. 1 Tim. 3:16). This seating of Christ at the throne is often referred to as "the heavenly session," the description taken from a word that originally carried the idea of sitting down when a task is finished. It had been prophesied that the Messiah would sit at the right hand of God after his enemies were vanquished (Ps. 110:1). So, having completed his redemptive mission, "after making purification for sins, he sat down at the right hand of the Majesty on high" (Heb. 1:3). Then "having received from the Father the promise," he poured out the Holy Spirit on his waiting church (Acts 2:33). Sitting at God's right hand indicates the place of honor and glory to which Christ has ascended—the exalted place he had with the Father before "the world existed" (John 17:5).

His praise never ends in heaven; the angels along with the white-robed elders and seraphim are continually declaring, "Worthy is the Lamb who was slain, to receive power and wealth and wisdom and might and honor and glory and blessing" (Rev. 5:12). They are joined by every creature ever made, saying, "To him who sits on the throne and to the Lamb be blessing and honor and glory and might forever and ever" (v. 13; 7:9–12).

In this exalted state Christ has assumed a mediative ministry "in the presence of God on our behalf" (Heb. 9:24). He is spoken of as a "forerunner" representing his people on earth, "having become a high priest forever" (Heb. 6:20).

In his heavenly session, Christ has been given supreme jurisdiction over the universe, "far above all rule and authority and power and dominion, and above every name that is named" (Eph. 1:21), he will reign in undisputed sovereignty until "he has put all his enemies under his feet" (1 Cor. 15:25).

## Conflicting Views

Not surprisingly, many persons who honor Christ do not accept his bodily resurrection and ascent into heaven. Basically these unfortunate views fall into two categories—complete denial and spiritualizing the fact—the first being more easily recognized.

### Complete Denial

Naturalists and liberal theologians reject outright Christ's victory over the grave. In their thinking, the physical elements of his body are still buried somewhere on the earth. Consistent with this position is denial of the inspired Scripture, with its witness to the incarnation of Christ and the blood atonement. To them, anything miraculous is contrary to reason. Typical of their school is Rudolf Bultmann, who bluntly says, "A historical fact that involves resurrection from the dead is utterly inconceivable."[8]

As to how they try to account for the evidence to the resurrection, on no subject has humanistic ingenuity been more exercised. Some contend that the body was stolen as the soldiers were paid to say. If the scam was not perpetrated by the disciples, then they might make Joseph of Arimathea or a Roman official the culprit, though their explanation how the conspirators got by with it becomes more unbelievable than the miracle.

Others surmise that Jesus was not dead when laid in the tomb—he had only swooned on the cross. Recovering his strength in the grave, they say, he pushed aside the stone and walked away. Later, it is claimed, he died after fooling all the disciples about his death and resurrection. Why hundreds of his loyal followers would then give their life for him is not explained.

Then there is the theory that the women on Easter morning went to the wrong tomb. Later it is said that John and Peter made the same mistake, even after seeing the burial cloths of the Lord's body where he lay.

Another theory, just as far-fetched, proposes that the disciples only imagined that they saw Jesus after the resurrection. The idea is that they wanted to believe so much that they all convinced themselves of its reality—a supreme example of the power of positive thinking.

To explain the twisted logic of these and other attempts to refute the resurrection, and to show their fallacy, lies beyond the scope of this work. Others have done that, and for those wanting to pursue it, there are ample resources.[9] My purpose here is to point out that unbelief struggles in the face of the resurrection evidence. One has to determine to ignore the evidence of Scripture and history to reject it. Denying the bodily resurrection, of course, rules out the visible ascension of Christ and his bodily return.

### Spiritualizing the Fact

A more subtle, if not illusive, approach regards the resurrection as an experiential reality, but not as a historical fact. Christ rose only spiritually to those that believed in him. In such a view, the resurrection becomes visionary—it lacks the objectivity of substance. Most neo-orthodox theologians generally take this direction.

As to the physical body of Christ that was placed in the tomb, they would say that, having fulfilled its purpose, it was no longer able to restrain the mighty force of God, which wanted freedom. Hence, his body was dissolved and became spirit in the tomb, perhaps in the way matter becomes energy in a nuclear explosion.

The resurrection is looked on as a revelation or symbol of eternal truth. It shows that good will triumph over evil and that the Spirit of Christ lives—his teachings are alive. That part of man worthy of immortality survives death, and the resurrection is the promise of a new life in Christ.

This may sound very nice, for these scholars use much of the same terminology as evangelicals. But in their thinking, the actual body of Christ did not rise from the grave. When pressed to explain, they would say that the resurrection, as any miracle, is not subject to historical proof. It can only be experienced, which makes the reality entirely subjective.

Proponents of this ideology, in contradiction to pure liberal theologians, have an appreciation for spiritual revelation and divine mystery. Yet validating miracles only by experience, and diminishing the factual documentation of miracles in history, their views cloud evangelism with doubt and, pressed to a conclusion, can destroy any credibility of the Gospel.

## Summary Applications

*1. The resurrection proves that God's Word is true.*

God had said through the prophets that the Messiah would die for the sins of the world, yet he would not be abandoned to the grave, for on the third day he would be raised up (Ps. 16:10; Isa. 53:8–10; cf. Matt. 12:39–40). Likewise Jesus said on numerous occasions that the Son of Man would be rejected by the chief priests and scribes, that he would be killed, and that he would rise again on the third day (e.g., Matt. 16:21; Mark 8:31; Luke 9:22; John 2:19–22). God keeps his promises.

This note rang through the preaching of the apostolic church. Take the sermon of Peter at Pentecost as an example. "Men of Israel," he said, "hear these words: Jesus of Nazareth . . . delivered up according to the definite plan and foreknowledge of God, you crucified and killed by the hands of lawless men. God raised him up, loosing the pangs of death, because it was not possible for him to be held by it" (Acts 2:22–24; cf. Acts 3:18). Then after quoting from David's prophecy, Peter concluded: "He foresaw and spoke about the resurrection of the Christ, that he was not abandoned to Hades. . . . This Jesus God raised up, and of that we all are witnesses" (Acts 2:31–32; cf. 3:18).

Similarly Paul testified: "I delivered to you as of first importance . . . that Christ died for our sins in accordance with the Scriptures, that he was buried, that he was raised on the third day in accordance with the Scriptures" (1 Cor. 15:3–4). It was all foretold in the Bible. The resurrection confirms the Word of God.

*2. The claims of Christ's lordship rest on historic fact.*

He "was declared to be the Son of God in power . . . by his resurrection from the dead" (Rom. 1:4). It happened in time and space, like any other event that could be reported in the news media. Contrasted with the virgin conception of Jesus, which was concealed in the womb of Mary, the resurrection body of Christ was seen in public.

True, what the world regards as inviolable laws of nature seem to have been defied. Yet to those who must have objective evidence to believe, there are no observable dictions of science more confirmed by reasonable testimony. Hundreds of people in various places and at different times over a period of nearly seven weeks actually saw the resurrected Lord—they gazed on his face; they had dinner with him; they walked with him along the roads of Judah. To have them all tell their story before an impartial jury could not be dismissed as fancy in a courtroom of law today.[10]

There were some, of course, who doubted what they heard. For example, Thomas, who was not present when Jesus first appeared to the disciples, said, "Unless I see the nail marks . . . and put my hand into his side, I will not believe it" (John 20:25 NIV). Jesus understood the problem and sought out the sincere doubter. "Put your finger here; see my hands," he said. "Reach out your hand and put it into my side. Stop doubting and believe!" Whereupon, the convinced man, now overwhelmed with the reality, cried: "My Lord and my God" (vv. 27–28 NIV).[11] From the observable data, there was no other conclusion.

Unfortunately, many people remain skeptical in face of the facts. In various and devious ways, they have diluted the biblical reality into some kind of a mystical experience, or worse, a myth.

Yet the victory of Jesus over death cannot be removed from history. It is not a symbol of something else that can only be perceived by the imagination. That Jesus is Lord, evidenced by his bodily resurrection and ascension, is fact, and on this reality, the Christian faith rests. The apostle Paul put it bluntly, "If Christ has not been raised, your faith is futile and you are still in your sins" (1 Cor. 15:17).

The historicity of Christ's resurrection gives credibility to every other aspect of his life and work. Once this crowning event is accepted, we are in a position to believe unto salvation. For the promise is, "If you confess with your mouth that Jesus is Lord [the first creed of the church] and believe in your heart that God raised him from the dead, you will be saved" (Rom. 10:9; cf. 1 Cor. 12:3).

### 3. The resurrection makes one confront the issues of Christ's death.

The cross now becomes a baffling problem to the world. For when one dies, who has power to come back from the grave? In all honesty, we must ask, why did he die in the first place?

To these unavoidable questions, the Bible gives only one answer: Jesus "was delivered up for our trespasses and raised for our justification" (Rom. 4:25).

The resurrection was the confirmation of God's approval for his Son's completed mission of redemption. And because of that acceptance, we, who were dead in trespasses and sin, can be made alive with Christ "by grace" (Eph. 2:5).

Persons who reject what Christ did must still give account, because God "has fixed a day on which he will judge the world in righteousness by a man whom he has appointed; and of this he has given assurance to all by raising him from the dead" (Acts 17:31). Not a frequent subject for an Easter sermon, but nonetheless, the cross cannot be ignored. The resurrection established the certainty of a day of judgment.

### 4. Christ's triumph proves God's power to change lives.

That "power toward us who believe," Paul said, is like "his great might that he worked in Christ when he raised him from the dead and seated him at his right hand in the heavenly places" (Eph. 1:19–20). To put it in Peter's words, we have been "born again to a living hope through the resurrection of Jesus Christ from the dead" (1 Pet. 1:3).

In this light, we see the ultimate meaning of rising with Christ into newness of life. Our old calculations of what is possible and impossible become obsolete. The power that raised Christ from the grave surely can take human personality and re-create it according to its true purpose.

The social planner can point to a derelict on skid row and say, "Let me clean up his environment and I will put a new coat on that man's back." But the evangelist can say, "Let that man experience the resurrection power of God, and I will put a new man in that coat." This is the Gospel. "If anyone is in Christ, he is a new creation. The old has passed away; behold the new has come" (2 Cor. 5:17).

Because Jesus lives, there is no person beyond the reach of God's grace—no life too wasted for him to save, no sin too great for him to cleanse, no burden too heavy for him to bear.

Moreover, the same power that raised Christ from the dead is available for every believer to live victoriously. So, birthed in the resurrection is the promise of God's transforming work in sanctification.

*5. The ascension established the basis for the present ministry of the Holy Spirit.*

Before God chose to pour out his Spirit on all flesh, he wanted the glory of his Son to be fully revealed. Hence, Jesus had told his disciples, "It is to your advantage that I go away, for if I do not go away, the Helper will not come to you. But if I go, I will send him to you" (John 16:7).

The ascension, thus, made possible the bestowal of the Spirit's power, glorifying Christ in the ministry of the church and the promised gifts of God (John 16:8–14; Eph. 4:10–14). As Peter said at Pentecost, "Being therefore exalted at the right hand of God, and having received from the Father the promise of the Holy Spirit, he has poured out this that you yourselves are seeing and hearing" (Acts 2:33).

*6. Christ's ascension and heavenly reign give believers indescribable confidence in prayer.*

Because Christ is now at the right hand of the throne, "we have an advocate with the Father, Jesus Christ the righteous" (1 John 2:1). As our High Priest (Heb. 6:20), "he is able to save to the uttermost those who draw near to God through him, since he always lives to make intercession for them" (Heb. 7:25; cf. Rom. 8:34).

What comfort this brings—to realize that we have a mediator in heaven who knows all about our weakness and failures, who understands perfectly the deep yearnings of our soul. So, "let us draw near with a true heart in full assurance of faith" (Heb. 10:22), "that we may receive mercy and find grace to help in time of need" (Heb. 4:16).

Frequently some dear friend will tell me that I am remembered in prayer. That means much to me, for it is the greatest gift a person can give to another. But to know that there is one person praying for me—a friend closer than a brother, one who loved me unto death, who pleads for me at the right hand of God—the very thought brings tears to my eyes. Such is the reality of prayer—real prayer when the soul is in communion with Christ at the throne of heaven.

### 7. Christianity is a living faith.

Other world religions have their prophets, but they all died and remain buried in an earthly tomb.[12] Jesus is alive!

What a powerful stimulus this fact gives to our seeking assurance of eternal life. Talleyrand was perceptive when asked by Lépeaux how to popularize a new religion that would appeal to people. The bishop of the French Revolution thought for a moment, then replied: "I would recommend that you be crucified and then rise again the third day."

Who can dispute the bishop's perception? There is something about the resurrection that the human spirit reaches out to embrace. Even the skeptics may pause to wonder—and to pray—that it be true. Here is the one place in history where the aspirations of the soul cannot be suppressed.

However people may discount the creeds and rituals of the church, the world can never completely ignore the testimony of men and women who have experienced the living Savior. Their changed lives bear witness. The old Gospel song expresses the reality well: "You ask me how I know he lives. He lives within my heart."[13]

### 8. The resurrection shows what is to come for the followers of Christ.

Jesus's glorified body is "the firstfruits of those who have fallen asleep" (1 Cor. 15:20). "God raised the Lord and will also raise us up by his power" (1 Cor. 6:14). Jesus had said, "I am the resurrection and the life. Whoever believes in me, though he die, yet shall he live, and everyone who lives and believes in me shall never die" (John 11:25–26).

What the transformed body will be like is not explained in the Bible, except that it will be like the glorified body of our Lord, when he was raised from the dead (Rom. 8:11; cf. 6:5; John 5:21). Just as we have the likeness of an earthly person, so shall we bear the likeness of the man from heaven. "When the perishable puts on the imperishable, and the mortal puts on immortality, then shall come to pass the saying that is written: 'Death is swallowed up in victory'" (1 Cor. 15:54).

No more can death ensnare the souls of men and women. Its gloom is gone! Its strength is done! God has rent the bars in twain and loosed the prisoners from the grave. Death is only the entrance into eternal life.

### 9. The Savior King in heaven will someday return in the clouds of glory.

Christ's victory over death was but the prelude to assuming his exalted state. As he went into the heavens, his ascension foreshadowed the way Christians who are alive on earth when he comes will "be caught up together" with the saints returning with him "to meet the Lord in the air, and so we will always be with the Lord" (1 Thess. 4:17).

This is "our blessed hope, the appearing of the glory of our great God and Savior Jesus Christ" (Titus 2:13). It makes us walk on tiptoes. Knowing that our Lord will return, we look to the eastern skies with joyous anticipation. The King is coming.

*10. Christ's absolute authority over the universe assures the completion of God's purpose in the world.*

For "through the resurrection," Jesus Christ "has gone into heaven and is at the right hand of God, with angels, authorities, and powers having been subjected to him" (1 Pet. 3:21–22).

We can now begin to understand the full significance of the cosmic Christ. Not only were all things created through him, but he still upholds all things by the word of his power. All the realms of human endeavor exist and have their endurance only in reference to his ownership. There is not one thing in the entire universe that does not come under his dominion. Nothing can finally defeat his purposes nor diminish his glory. He is Lord!

Reaffirming this truth, Jesus assured his disciples: "All authority in heaven and on earth has been given to me" (Matt. 28:18). This is the way the Great Commission begins, and in that confidence, whatever the difficulties, the church goes forth in triumph.

It reminds me of an incident in the life of Rev. E. P. Scott, a pioneer missionary to the tribes of northern India. On one of his journeys to an unreached area, he came upon a savage band on a war expedition. They seized him and pointed their long spears at his heart.

Feeling utterly helpless, not knowing what else to do, he drew out the violin he carried with him and began to play and sing in the native language: "All hail the power of Jesus' name."

As the music and words of the song rang out, he closed his eyes, expecting death at any moment. But when nothing happened, even after the third stanza, he opened his eyes and was amazed to see that the spears had fallen from the hands of his captors. Tears filled their eyes.

They begged him to tell them of that name—the name above every name, the only name under heaven given among men whereby we must be saved. So he went home with them and for several years labored among them, winning many to Christ.[14]

I see in this experience a parable of the victorious church. Faithful servants who bring the good tiding may not always be delivered from the spears of the enemy. Nevertheless, the triumph of Christ proves that his Gospel will someday prevail to the ends of the earth, and he shall be crowned Lord of all—"His kingdoms stretch from shore to shore till time shall wane and be no more."[15]

126

# 9

# The Holy Spirit

"You will receive power when the Holy Spirit comes upon you, and you will be my witnesses" (Acts 1:8). These words of Christ reverberated in their minds as they watched him ascend into the heavens. In the flesh, he would no longer be with them. Yet after sending them into the world to disciple the nations, he said, "I am with you always, to the end of the age" (Matt. 28:20).

## The Executor of the Trinity

### A Neglected Teaching

To understand these words, it is necessary to see the role of the Holy Spirit in the present ministry of Christ. Strangely, though, he is often overlooked.

I am reminded of a British pastor who was quizzing his class on the Apostles' Creed. Each boy was to repeat a phrase of the creed. The first began, "I believe in God, the Father Almighty, maker of heaven and earth."

The second said, "I believe in Jesus Christ, his only Son, our Lord."

The recitation proceeded smoothly until it fell silent at one spot. The minister looked up from his notes to see what caused the silence. One of the scholars spoke up, "I am sorry, sir, but the boy who believed in the Holy Spirit is absent today."[1]

Some people in the church, I am afraid, are absent when it comes to the teaching in the Bible about the Holy Spirit.

### The Presence of God

As already noted, when considering the character of God, everything ascribed to deity is associated with the Spirit. He is called "the Spirit of God" (Rom. 15:19), has the attributes of God (Ps. 139:7), and is worshiped as God (Heb. 9:14). He is God in action, through whom all that God does in the world is accomplished.

Emphasizing his place in the Trinity, the name Spirit is coupled with Father and Son in the baptismal formula (Matt. 28:19), as well as in the benediction (2 Cor. 13:14). Moreover, his work in redemption and glory attests to his equality in creative power.

### The Spirit Is a Person

Personal names and pronouns relate to the Spirit.[2] Likewise, personal acts are ascribed to him, such as speaking (Acts 1:16), teaching (1 Cor. 12:29), comforting (Acts 9:31), guiding (Rom. 8:14), working (1 Cor. 12:11), giving (Heb. 2:4), and worshiping (John 4:23–24). As a person, too, he can be tested (Acts 5:9), lied to (Acts 5:3), quenched (1 Thess. 5:19), grieved (Eph. 4:30), resisted (Acts 7:51), and blasphemed (Matt. 12:31–32).

Above all, one can have communion with the Spirit in prayer and ministry. Ultimately the whole realm of personal salvation falls within his operation.

### The Third Person of the Godhead

The Holy Spirit completes the revelation of God, unveiling the glory of Christ, who in turn glorifies the Father (John 17:1–5). Jesus told his disciples, "When the Helper comes, whom I will send to you from the Father, the Spirit of truth, who proceeds from the Father, he will bear witness about me" (John 15:26).[3] As God the Helper, the Spirit derives his being from the self-giving love of the Father and the Son, in which the unified personality of God has expression in three distinct ways.

Again we are overwhelmed with the limits of our human ability to comprehend the inner being of God. Yet it can be observed that God acts in his Spirit. What the Father plans, and the Son reveals, the Spirit effects. Within the Godhead, the Spirit completes the personality of the Father and the Son; outside of God, in the world and in mankind, he communicates the divine will. Though the three persons of the Godhead are equal in glory and superiority, when acting in power, the Holy Spirit comes into prominence.

## The Spirit in the Old Testament

### Forming the Cosmos

We are introduced to the work of the Holy Spirit in the creation of the universe, when it is said: "The Spirit of God was hovering over the face of the waters" (Gen. 1:2). To put it in the words of the psalmist, "By his breath [Spirit] the skies became fair" (Job 26:13 NIV).[4] The Father conceived the design, it was manifested through the Son, and the Spirit executed the divine word.

### Creating Human Life

By the same power, "the LORD God formed the man of dust from the ground and breathed into his nostrils the breath of life, and the man became a living creature" (Gen. 2:7). As Job expressed it, "The Spirit of God has made me, and the breath of the Almighty gives me life" (Job 33:4).

Not only in the origin of life, but in the presentation and substance of his creatures, the Spirit is the link between God and his created people. All through the Old Testament, he is present in their "midst" to "instruct" and "lead" (Neh. 9:20; Isa. 63:11; Hag. 2:5). Whatever communion God had with persons was through the Holy Spirit.

When divine fellowship is broken through human disobedience, the Spirit strives with the rebellious soul, seeking reconciliation with the creature of his love. Such conviction of the sinner evidences God's desire for restoration. Hence, the repentant David prayed, "Cast me not away from your presence, and take not your Holy Spirit from me" (Ps. 51:11). Tragically, however, more often than not, "stiff-necked" transgressors will not heed the gracious appeals of God, and choose "to resist the Holy Spirit" (Acts 7:51; cf. Gen. 6:3; Ps. 139:7; Isa. 30:1; 63:10).

### Making a Holy People

God always seeks communion with his people, but the Old Testament does not develop the Spirit's work through indwelling believers. That inward transformational power will come into prominence after the atoning work of the Messiah is completed and the era of a new covenant begins. Yearning for that day, Moses wished that "the LORD would put his Spirit" in all his people (Num. 11:29). Looking to this time, Ezekiel envisioned God cleansing his people from their uncleanness, removing "the heart of stone" from their flesh. "I will give you a new heart," God said, "and a new spirit I will put within you" (Ezek. 36:25–27; cf. Isa. 32:15–17). Although this inner working of the Spirit seems apparent in the lives of a few persons living under the old covenant, attention centers on their leadership roles while doing the work of God.

### Persons Prepared for Service

Whatever degree of spiritual experience one may have known in the Old Testament, chosen persons were enabled by the Spirit to do God's work. Joseph was such a person during his sojourn in Egypt (Gen. 41:38), just as the Spirit inspired Moses's leadership in the wilderness, as well as the seventy men who assisted him in bearing the burdens of Israel (Num. 11:17, 24–25, 29). Through the same power, others were qualified to serve as craftsmen in the building and furnishing of the tabernacle (Exod. 28:3; 31:3–5; 35:31–35).

Another specially endowed leader was Joshua, who was "full of the spirit of wisdom" (Deut. 34:9; cf. Num. 27:18).

Some of the judges were equipped for their roles by the Spirit—Othniel (Judg. 3:9–10), Gideon (Judg. 6:34), Jephthah (Judg. 11:29), and Samson (Judg. 13:24–25; 14:6, 19; 15:14). These men were far from model saints, but for a particular time and purpose, they were used by God to deliver his people from their enemies. Similarly, King Saul was empowered for leadership, and for a season, he was "turned into another man" (1 Sam. 10:6). Tragically he later grievously sinned against God. However, at the same time "the Spirit of the Lord departed from Saul" (1 Sam. 16:14), "the Spirit of the LORD rushed upon David from that day forward" (1 Sam. 16:13). These men of old were not always faithful to their trust, yet insofar as they fulfilled God's calling, it was the third person of the Holy Trinity who gave them strength and wisdom.

The prophets probably illustrate this ministry of the Spirit most completely. In the flesh these spokesmen were no different from other men, but on certain occasions the Spirit would come on them and so activate their perception and quicken their ability to communicate that they could declare accurately the message of the Lord (2 Sam. 23:1–2; Ezek. 3:12, 14; 8:3; 11:1, 5, 24; 43:5; Mic. 3:8; cf. Matt. 22:43; Mark 12:36; Acts 1:24–26; 28:25). Our whole doctrine of biblical inspiration rests ultimately on the fact that men of God spoke as they were borne along by the Holy Spirit (2 Pet. 1:21; cf. 2 Tim. 3:16).

In all these ministries through the Old Testament, the necessary component for service was the power of God's personal enablement. His work cannot be done in the energy of the flesh. Only as human resources are under his control can his work be done. It is "not by might, nor by power, but by my Spirit, says the LORD of Hosts" (Zech. 4:6).

## Jesus and the Spirit

### Incarnation of the Son

The unfolding drama of redemption through the Old Testament focuses on the promised Messiah. He who was foreshadowed in the priestly offerings, typified in mighty acts of deliverance, and proclaimed in prophetic word would someday dwell with his people in person.[5]

As foretold, a virgin would conceive by the Holy Spirit and bear a Son who would be called Immanuel—"God with us" (Isa. 7:14; Matt. 1:20–23). On this branch growing out of the root of David, the Spirit of the Lord would rest without measure (Isa. 11:1–2), and through him a Messianic age was to dawn when the Spirit would be poured out on all flesh (Isa. 32:15; Ezek. 39:29; Joel 2:28–29; Zech. 12:10).

That Christ should come through the Spirit's agency is thus quite predictable. Though his incarnation was physically different in nature from anything that had happened before, it preserved the continuity of God's agelong redemptive program. The Spirit who had been working faithfully for millennia through chosen vessels, at special times, in limited degrees, now brought forth the Man of God in absolute and permanent fullness.

### The Spirit without Measure

What was so prominent in Christ's birth received new stress as he began his public ministry thirty years later. Anticipating his work, while distinguishing it from his own, John the Baptist announced that Jesus would baptize with the Holy Spirit and with fire (Matt. 3:11; Mark 1:8; Luke 3:16).[6] These words, pregnant with visions of the divine presence and power, indicated the kind of ministry he would have. As John later observed, "For he whom God has sent utters the words of God, for he gives the Spirit without measure" (John 3:34).

When Jesus appeared at the River Jordan to be baptized by John, the prophet hesitated to oblige, knowing that he was unworthy even to loose Christ's shoes. But Jesus insisted, explaining that submission to this act was necessary to fulfill all righteousness. Then, after Jesus had demonstrated obedience to the Father's will, the Holy Spirit descended on him, and a voice spoke from heaven saying, "This is my beloved Son, with whom I am well pleased" (Matt. 3:13–17; Mark 1:9–11; Luke 3:21–23; cf. John 1:32–34). What a beautiful affirmation of the Spirit! Publically the seal of divine approval rested on Jesus, but more personally, inwardly, there was the full assurance of that living bond of union he sustained with the Father.

Thereafter Jesus, "full of the Holy Spirit," left the scene of John's revival, and "was led by the Spirit in the wilderness" (Luke 4:1; cf. Mark 1:12) "to be tempted by the devil" (Matt. 4:1). The Spirit's direction in this supernatural confrontation may be appreciated when the principle at issue emerges. The devil, in three tempting ways, asked Christ to compromise the spiritual character of his mission by conforming to the popular expectations of the world. Jesus was not to be deceived. He would not demean the kingdom of God by adapting the methods of the flesh to attain it. Supported by Scripture, he commanded Satan to depart (vv. 2–11; Luke 4:2–13). Though the testing would be repeated later in other forms, the spiritual nature of his ministry was firmly established.

### Ministering in the Spirit

Ready now to launch his public ministry, "Jesus returned in the power of the Spirit to Galilee" (Luke 4:14). So mighty was his work that soon his fame spread across the country, and he was "glorified by all" (v. 15; cf. Matt. 4:17; Mark 1:14–15).

Lest someone miss the source of his ministry, at the first invitation to speak in his home synagogue in Nazareth, Jesus stood up and read from the scroll of Isaiah: "The Spirit of the Lord is upon me, because he has anointed me to proclaim good news to the poor. He has sent me to proclaim liberty to the captives and recovering of sight to the blind, to set at liberty those who are oppressed, to proclaim the year of the Lord's favor" (Luke 4:18–19; cf. Isa. 61:1–2). Having finished reading the passage, he rolled up the parchment, gave it back to the attendant, then sat down and announced to the startled congregation, "Today this Scripture has been fulfilled in your hearing" (Luke 4:21).

He wanted everyone to know that what he did and said were not in the strength of man; it was in the power of the Holy Spirit.[7] Nothing about his ministry could be explained in naturalistic terms. This was quite shocking to most Jews of his day, for they commonly believed that the Spirit's activity in the world had ceased and would not return until the end of the age.[8] Thus by associating his work with the Spirit, Jesus was saying that God was moving again among his people. It was an end to an era of alienation and the beginning of a time of grace.

Those who rejected Christ, of course, were unwilling to accept his claims regarding the Spirit. To do so would require a recognition of his messianic mission. So they had to account for his supernatural power some other way. On one occasion, following the healing of a demoniac, Jesus was accused by the Pharisees of being in league with the devil. Pointing out how ludicrous their reasoning was, he answered: "And if I cast out demons by Beelzebul, by whom do your sons cast them out? Therefore they will be your judges. But if it is by the Spirit of God that I cast out demons, then the kingdom of God has come upon you" (Matt. 12:27–28; cf. Luke 4:19–20). Jesus was simply underscoring again the true source of his ministry. By closing their hearts to this fact, the unbelieving Jews were in danger of committing an unpardonable sin—they were blaspheming the Holy Spirit (Matt. 12:31–32; Mark 3:28–29; cf. Luke 11:14–26).[9]

The point is that the Spirit was ever present in the Son to make his life a revelation of God, both in deed and word. Thus imbued with the Spirit, Jesus went about doing good, healing and teaching and preaching, and training some disciples to carry on his work. Finally, as the sin offering for the world, "through the eternal Spirit [he] offered himself without blemish to God" as a sacrifice at Calvary (Heb. 9:14). His atoning work then finished, by the same mighty power, he was raised from the dead (Rom. 8:11) and "declared to be the Son of God" (Rom. 1:4).

### His Continuing Presence

Jesus called him "another Helper," indicating that the Spirit would have a ministry with the disciples much like his own (John 14:16).[10] He was not comparing himself with some vague, impersonal energy in the universe, but with a person—one who in the unseen realm would be as real among them as was Jesus when they walked the trails of Galilee. This was no makeshift substitute, but the promise of the real presence of their Lord.

Just as Jesus had led them when they were together, now the Spirit would guide them. He would answer their questions (John 16:13); he would teach them what they needed to learn (John 14:26); he would help them pray (John 14:12–13; 16:23–24); he would show them things to come (John 16:13); he would give them words to speak (Matt. 10:19–20; Mark 13:11; Luke 12:12); and by his strength, they would do the very work of Christ, even greater works than these (John 14:12). In short, the Spirit would take Christ's place among them (John 15:26; 16:14–15).

The ultimate purpose of all the Spirit's work is to lift up the Son. "He will glorify me," Jesus said, "for he will take what is mine and declare it to you" (John 16:14; cf. 14:26). The Spirit never points to himself. Christ is the visible Word, the speaking self, the person in whom the Father may be known. But we see Christ only through the ministry of the Holy Spirit (1 John 4:2).

Of course the Spirit had already been with the disciples in their association with the Savior, but in a more intimate way, he was now to glorify Christ in and through their lives. Until Jesus had finished his work on earth and was exalted at the right hand of God (John 7:39), this could not be realized. Only after he assumed his kingly reign on the throne could the Spirit be released in power on the church.[11]

## The Spirit in the Church

### The Pentecostal Outpouring

Jesus charged his disciples to return to Jerusalem and tarry until they were endued with power (Luke 24:49; Acts 15:8). He who had been Christ's strength had to become real within them. Unless they were possessed by his living presence, their lives would be forlorn of joy and peace, and the ministry of their Lord would never thrill their souls.

The promise began to unfold at Pentecost. As the disciples were assembled in the upper room, "suddenly there came from heaven a sound like a mighty rushing wind, and it filled the entire house where they were sitting" (Acts 2:2). The wind, symbolizing the strength of the Spirit, came first to the house of God, from whence it would sweep across the earth with life-giving power. Then there appeared to them "tongues as of fire," a flame resting on the head of each person (v. 3). The distribution of the sacred fire pointed to the truth that the Spirit had come to dwell, not with a few officers of the society, but with all who would obey him and everyone who would minister in the manner to which they were called. Descriptive, too, of their witness-bearing appointment, they "began to speak in other tongues as the Spirit gave them utterance" (v. 4), going out among the people in the city declaring what God had done.

The enduring miracle, however, was not in the outward phenomenon associated with the initial outpouring, but in the inward realization of the exalted Christ that came to those "filled with the Holy Spirit" (v. 4). To the church it was proof that Jesus was reigning in heaven. "Having received from the Father the promise of the Holy Spirit," Peter explained, "he has poured out this" (v. 33; cf. Luke 24:49).

Pentecost was the culminating act in an agelong process of the divine into the human. Now Jesus as the eternal Presence became the enthroned Sovereign in the hearts of his people. A new era of the kingdom had begun in Spirit-filled witnesses. The Gospel had become life and power within them.

## Acts of the Spirit

The full significance of what Pentecost meant becomes increasingly apparent. With obvious intent, in Acts the whole early church movement is attributed to the Spirit's activity. More than fifty times he is specifically mentioned, more than in any other book of the Bible. So prominent is the Spirit in the narrative that the book has been properly called "The Acts of the Holy Spirit."

It is by his power that the disciples witness for Christ with boldness (Acts 1:8; 2:4; 4:8, 31; 5:32; 6:10; 13:9; 19:6), and through his enablement, persons were equipped for ministry (Acts 2:17–18; 4:8; 6:3, 5; 9:17; 11:28; 19:6; 20:28; 21:4–11). Joy and comfort in the Spirit came to faithful servants of the Lord (Acts 7:55; 8:8; 9:31; 11:24; 13:52; 20:32). He gives direction through the inspired Scripture (Acts 1:2, 16; 28:25), and Spirit-equipped persons sensitive to his voice receive special guidance in crucial situations (Acts 8:29, 39; 10:19; 11:12, 15; 13:2, 4; 16:6–7; 21:4, 11). Not only does he help in making decisions, the Spirit confirms truth to the hearts of the brethren (Acts 5:32; 15:8, 28).

His leadership role is noted in matters of church discipline and administration (Acts 5:3, 9; 6:3, 5; 7:51; 15:28; 20:28). Attention is given to the Spirit in the breakthrough of the Gospel to the Samaritans (Acts 8:15, 17–19), then the Gentiles at Caesarea (Acts 10:19, 44–45, 47; 11:12, 15–16; 15:8). He is instrumental in sending out the first missionaries at Antioch (Acts 13:2, 4) and assists in various ways all through the expansion of the church to the uttermost parts of the earth (Acts 13:9, 52; 16:6–7; 19:2, 6; 20:23, 28; 21:4; 28:25).

The work of the Spirit in the Acts typifies what can be seen also in other books of the New Testament. Unmistakably, the amazing growth of the church was the demonstration of the Holy Spirit. Whenever God moves in power to accomplish his purposes, the divine Paraclete does the work.

## Personal Experience

The action centers not on dynamic programs or campaigns but on persons prepared by the Spirit for the Master's use. Descriptions of the modes of endowment are variable. Sometimes the Spirit is depicted as a gift or described as giver; at other times he is received. These terms look to the divine source of the graceful impartation and the realization of the promise in experience. Intertwined with these expressions, the Spirit is represented as being "poured out," "falling," or "coming" on people. Also used is the ceremonial idea of "baptizing," which identifies the experience with the message of John and the teachings of Jesus, while "anointing" of the Spirit relates to the power to accomplish an appointed task.

Most characteristic of the terms used in reference to the Pentecostal experience is "filled with the Spirit." Used ten times, in a variety of situations, the figure conveys the idea of a person being pervaded by the Spirit's power and influence (Acts 2:4; 4:8, 31; 6:3, 5; 7:55; 9:17; 11:24; 13:9, 52). However understood, this was the norm of Christian experience in the New Testament. When members of the church were not living in this fullness, they were exhorted to do so (Eph. 5:18).

What these and other descriptions of the personal spiritual experience mean will be considered later. Suffice it to say now, to use the words of Jesus, "It is the Spirit who gives life; the flesh is no help at all" (John 6:63; cf. 2 Cor. 3:6). Not only infusing the life of Christ into believers, the Spirit continues to nourish the new saints, bringing forth fruits of holiness and transforming them into the character of their Lord "from one degree of glory to another" (2 Cor. 3:18). And someday, completing his creative work in God's people, he will change even our mortal flesh into a body like the glorified body of our Lord in the resurrection (Rom. 8:11).[12]

## Summary Applications

*1. God acts in the world by his Spirit.*

Everything that God does upholding the universe falls within the Holy Spirit's jurisdiction. In a special sense, however, he works within history to accomplish God's redemptive purpose, administering grace and effecting the salvation of his people. Evangelism becomes operative through God the Holy Spirit. And since he has all power, no person or situation is beyond redemption. The reverse is also true. Without the Spirit's enablement, there can be no Christian life or witness.

*2. The Spirit makes the Word of God come alive.*

He who inspired the Scriptures breathes life into them, enabling them to accomplish the purpose for which they were written: that persons "may believe that Jesus is the Christ, the Son of God" and "have life in his name" (John 20:31).

This is why biblical exposition should be the centerpiece of every sermon. The power of the sermon is not in the preacher, but in the Word. Hopefully the message can be structured and presented in such a way that the scriptural truth comes through clearly. But even if delivered poorly, let no one underestimate what the Spirit-empowered Word itself can do.

I recall an incident in the ministry of George Whitefield. A group of scoffers, who called themselves the "Hell-fire Club," were making fun of the preacher. A man of the group, named Thorpe, began mimicking to his cronies the sermon of Whitefield, almost repeating it word for word, when he himself was so pierced with conviction that he sat down and was converted on the spot.[13]

What makes the Word of God powerful is the Savior whom it reveals, the Word living among us. He is the magnet of the Spirit drawing persons to God, whether it be through a person, group Bible study, personal testimony, or simply the Christlike example of a godly life. That is how his ministry can be recognized. Any spirit that does not glorify the incarnate Word is not of God (1 John 4:3). By the same criteria, the way Christ comes out in our witness will largely determine its effectiveness.

As the Holy Spirit lifts up the Holy One, and Jesus is seen as the unveiling of God in our midst, the world becomes aware of its perverse nature (John 16:8–9). Persons are convicted of their sin through unbelief. They recognize in Christ's completed work of redemption the only way one can appear righteous before a holy God. Moreover, the world's standard of truth is shown to be utterly in error. Jesus, condemned by the world, is seen exalted in heaven; whereas the prince of this earth, the devil, is cast down.

What a load this takes off the shoulder of an evangelist! We do not have to convince anyone of the Gospel. That is the Spirit's work. Our responsibility is simply to bear testimony to the truth. And in spite of the world's blindness and indifference, the Spirit of God will penetrate the darkness of sin and prod sinners to seek the Savior.

This is sometimes spoken of as the second witness—the inner voice of the Spirit bearing witness to the outward voice of the speaker. It is this voice of God within the heart that verifies the truthfulness of the spoken word.

### 3. The Spirit extends the invitation.

Having brought one to understand the Gospel, the Spirit invites a response. He is the person of the Trinity drawing people to God (John 6:44), and this includes the whole scope of personal redemption. Appropriately, then, the Bible closes with the invitation: "The Spirit and the Bride say, 'Come!' And let the one who hears say, 'Come.' And let the one who is thirsty come; let the one who desires take the water of life without price" (Rev. 22:17; cf. Isa. 55:1; John 7:37).

A word of caution, however, is in order. No one comes to Christ any time they feel like it, as if we can initiate our salvation. That would be presumption. We can come only when invited, and the Spirit alone has that prerogative.

136

*4. Trifling with the Spirit is dangerous.*

He may not always strive with sinners (Gen. 6:3). The time came in Noah's day when his patience was exhausted with that rebellious generation, and the door of opportunity was closed.

In respect to the claims of Christ, the Spirit has no obligation to continue pleading with worldlings who "go on sinning deliberately after receiving the knowledge of the truth," for spurning the Son of God, they have "outraged the Spirit of grace" (Heb. 10:26–29). Such strong language surely is a warning against treating the Spirit lightly.

After all, the Spirit is a person, and like any personality, he has feelings. He can be grieved by the indifferent way we disregard his instruction (Eph. 4:25–32; 1 Thess. 5:19).

Yet in pointing out our un-Christlike behavior, conviction of the Spirit can be seen as an invitation to move on to higher ground. God wants something better for us. Best of all, he will lead us on the way (Rom. 8:14).

This comes out so beautifully in the voice of the Spirit to the seven churches in Revelation (Rev. 2:1–3:22). In the last invitation, Christ is depicted standing at the door of a wealthy, quite contented congregation in Laodicea. "I know your works," he says, "you are neither cold nor hot" (Rev. 3:15). Then he condemns them for their pompous lukewarmness, saying that they make him sick in his stomach. At the same time, he tells them: "Those whom I love, I reprove and discipline, so be zealous and repent" (v. 19).

Then, using this church as an illustration, he makes a general application to us all. "Behold I stand at the door and knock. If anyone hears my voice and opens the door, I will come in to him and eat with him, and he with me" (v. 20).

An artist has portrayed this scene in a striking painting. Jesus is seen knocking, but the door remains closed. In fact, it looks like the door has not been opened for a long time, for a vine is growing over one corner.

A little boy, noticing the picture, asked his mother, "Why don't they open the door and let him in?"

She thought for a moment, then said, "I suppose it's because they live too far back in the house and don't hear him knocking." May this not be true of us.

*5. The Spirit is sovereign in the church.*

When Jesus had completed his work on earth and returned to sit on the throne of heaven, his Spirit came and "sat" or "rested" on the heads of the assembled disciples in the upper room (Acts 2:3 KJV; cf. Mark 16:19; Heb. 1:3).

The symbolism is quite striking. When in the presence of royalty, people stand; the king sits. This figure beautifully underscores the transition of authority that has taken place. The Spirit had taken over. He was now in charge of Christ's earthly body, representing the presence and power of him who now reigns in heaven.

### 6. The Spirit enables us to pray.

Prayer is communion with the Spirit, as he takes a worshiper into the life of the Triune God (Jude 20). When we cannot see the way ahead, and do not know how to express our thoughts, "the Spirit helps us in our weakness," interceding for us "with groanings too deep for words" (Rom. 8:26). Even better, the Spirit prays for the saints "according to the will of God" (v. 27).

The Spirit, thus, is the one who really does the praying. Our part is to let the Spirit have his way. He is ever seeking to conform us to the character of Christ thereby enabling us to pray in his name (John 14:13; 16:24). The measure of the Spirit's presence in our lives is the measure of the effectual prayer.

### 7. The outpouring of the Spirit at Pentecost ushered in the age of the harvest.

The day of gathering had come. Everything needed to provide salvation for the world had been done. The initial workers for the harvest had been trained. The power from on high had come on them. A mighty harvest was waiting.

The fruit-bearing ministry of the church was symbolized in the celebration of Pentecost. The Jewish feast was a time when the firstfruits of the grain harvest were brought to the temple as a thank offering to God. For the Christians, though, it marked the firstfruits of a great ingathering of souls.

Immediately the "greater works" that Jesus had said his followers would produce become evident (John 14:12). Beginning when Peter preached the Gospel to crowds at Jerusalem, about three thousand were converted. That is more than Jesus could count as believers in three years of active ministry. After that, the outreach accelerated daily, until within a generation the Gospel penetrated large segments of the civilized world, and the work was going forward unabated when the book of Acts closed (Acts 28:31). In fact, Acts really has no conclusion, for we are still living in that harvest age of the Spirit, and it will continue until the children of the new covenant are gathered from every tongue, tribe, and nation to praise the Lamb forever.

### 8. The coming of the Holy Spirit fulfills the promise of the Great Commission.

Having given the command, Jesus told his disciples: "I am with you always, to the end of the age" (Matt. 28:20). This was not a promise to be realized when they got to heaven; it was the assurance of the present reality they were to experience while going forth to make disciples.

His return to the Father would not disrupt their fellowship. Actually his going away and exaltation in heaven were for their own good. While he was with them in the flesh, they saw little need to rely on his Spirit. In his absence, however, they would come to understand the secret of their Lord's constant communion with the Father. Out of necessity, they would learn to live in the Spirit and thereby know the continued presence of Christ. For the Spirit is not limited by time and space, as was Jesus in his earthly body, and hence, they could always be together.

This is why the Great Commission will be fulfilled. The one who sends the church, the Lord of glory, who has "all authority in heaven and on earth" (v. 18), goes with us. And by his Spirit the disciples are "clothed with power from on high" (Luke 24:49).

To the degree that we permit the Spirit to enthrone Christ in our lives, we can expect to do his bidding. Without the energizing power of God, we are as useless as lightbulbs without electricity. Make no mistake about it, making disciples is the Spirit's work. Being a supernatural ministry, it cannot be engineered by man. Human effort can organize campaigns, publish literature, raise budgets, build edifices, earn degrees, and even civilize nations, but only God can breathe into a soul the breath of life. The secret of evangelism is here, living in the presence of Jesus, the indwelling of the Holy Spirit.

# 10

## The Grace of God

The Holy Spirit activates God's redemptive purposes in the world by dispensing grace. What this means goes so far beyond human capability that its contemplation can only fill one with wonder. The words of John Newton, the slave ship captain who came to Christ, aptly express my feeling.

> Amazing Grace! How sweet the sound!
> That saved a wretch like me.
> I once was lost, but now am found,
> Was blind but now I see.[1]

Wrapped up in this old hymn is the defining reality of the Christian faith. And the more we contemplate its meaning, the more amazing grace seems.

### Love That Will Not Let Us Go

#### Unmerited Favor

Grace, within the context of the Gospel, is the free gift of a merciful God. Though mankind was made to glorify our Creator and to enjoy his fellowship, we have all turned to our own way, scorning his love, blaspheming his name, and we have brought on ourselves the just sentence of death. Humankind deserves nothing but hell. The Lord of the universe owes us nothing. Yet the judgment of sin we deserve, God has accepted for us in his Son. In reality, he has given us the opposite of what we deserve and has not given us what we do deserve.

Amazing indeed! God has not dealt with us on the basis of our worth, but rather on the basis of our need. Utterly without any means to earn divine favor, bankrupt of any merit, we could never do for ourselves what he does for us. Neither given because of good deeds, nor denied because of misdeeds, grace comes without charge (Acts 8:20; Rom. 4:4; Eph. 2:8); it is "the gift of God, not a result of works, so that no one may boast" (Eph. 2:8–9; cf. Rom. 3:24; 2 Tim. 1:9).

Grace stands in contradiction to every human effort to justify ourselves before God. It excludes any pretense of self-achieved righteousness.

### God Alone Its Source

The reason for grace lies within the nature of God's goodness and infinite compassion. "Every good gift and every perfect gift is from above, coming down from the Father of lights" (James 1:17). To put it in the words of the prophet John: "A person cannot receive even one thing unless it is given him from heaven" (John 3:27; cf. 1 Cor. 4:7).

The way God restrains his wrath, showing mercy to undeserving people, can be explained only within the infinitude of his long-suffering love (Isa. 54:4–10). Grace displays God's character. As he said to the rebellious house of Israel, "It is not for your sake . . . that I am about to act, but for the sake of my holy name, which you have profaned. . . . 'The nations will know that I am the LORD,' declares the Lord God, 'when through you I vindicate my holiness before their eyes'" (Ezek. 36:22–23).

### Disclosed in Christ

Grace centers finally in the redemptive life and work of Jesus Christ.[2] Though only those who receive him as Savior experience his salvation, the whole world benefited from his atonement (John 3:16), which had been determined "before the ages began" (2 Tim. 1:9). Had it not been for God taking on himself the sin of humanity from "the foundation of the world" (Eph. 1:4), civilization could have ended after the fall. That God did not destroy the rebellious world but rather has sought, at incredible cost, the restoration of a degenerate mankind evidences undeserved mercy.

To live by grace is to live by the mind of Christ. He is our righteousness, holiness, and redemption. Any good thing about us is not in ourselves but outside us in Christ whose life comes into the redeemed through the transforming power of the Holy Spirit.

The full disclosure of God's goodness comes in Jesus, who manifests in himself "the riches of his grace, which he lavished upon us, in all wisdom and insight making known to us the mystery of his will" (Eph. 1:7–9). Grace, like everything else in the character of God, becomes manifest in the incarnate Word.

## Common Grace

God's beneficence to the world, often called common grace, extends to every aspect of human existence. To sinner and saint alike, "the Lord is good to all, and his mercy is over all that he has made" (Ps. 145:9; cf. vv. 13, 17). Apart from his love for the world, no one could survive, for we are all dependent on the resources he freely provides for daily sustenance, even the oxygen we breathe.[3]

The very preservation of the created world witnesses to his grace. God causes the sun to "rise on the evil and the good, and sends rain on the just and on the unjust" (Matt. 5:45). Through no virtue of our own, the earth brings forth "fruitful seasons," satisfying people "with food and gladness" (Acts 14:17). We can see God's goodness in the grandeur of nature, filling the natural world with splendor. Many appropriate this gift and bring forth beautiful works of art and music.

In the realm of human affairs, grace restrains the destructive inclinations of a depraved society, so that evil does not produce its full effect. As Job was told, "If [God] should set his heart to it and gather to himself his spirit and his breath, all flesh would perish together, and man would return to dust" (Job 34:14–15). Unregenerate mankind is so corrupted that without divine assistance civil institutions could not function. The diabolical designs of Satan are held back by a gracious God (1 Tim. 1:9; cf. 1 Sam. 16:14; 2 Kings 19:27; 2 Thess. 2:6).

Sinful people thus can live together in peace and harmony by his kindness. There could be no goodwill and mutual respect among people, even within the family, without God's forbearance of our perversity. For the same reason, governments, with their laws and judicial systems, could not operate. "There is no authority except from God, and those that exist have been instituted by God" (Rom. 13:1). So we are instructed to pray "for kings and all who are in high positions" (1 Tim. 2:2). They serve with God's blessing to deter the potential for wickedness in a fallen race, and thereby promote the well-being of society. Of course any human enterprise can be misdirected and turned to evil. Let it be remembered, too, that God's restraining activity can be withdrawn and man given over entirely to the reprobate mind (Rom. 1:24, 26).

In the same gracious concern for our happiness, notwithstanding human depravity, God has given persons an innate sense of decency, so that we want to do the right thing. From this goodness comes works of charity and unselfish acts of heroism.

A newscast today from the war zone in Iraq brought an illustration. The reporter was interviewing American soldiers waiting in line to give blood at a medical station. Earlier in the day a skirmish with insurgents resulted in a number of severe casualties on both sides. An urgent call from the doctors for blood donors had brought in these volunteers. Turning to one of the young men, the reporter told the soldier that his blood likely would go to save the life of his enemy. "Does that make any difference to you?" he asked. "No," said the soldier, "he is a human being."

Such unassuming kindness reflects something about the character of God. And when seen, it lifts one to nobler thoughts and actions. I recall an incident told by Dr. Wilfred Grenfell while he was a resident physician at a hospital in England. Late one night when he was on duty, a woman terribly burned was rushed into the emergency room. Her burns were so extensive that it was immediately apparent that she could not survive. Her husband had come home drunk and in a rage had thrown a burning paraffin lamp over her that had caught her dress on fire.

When the police arrived, they brought with them the half-sobered husband. The magistrate leaned over the bed and insisted that the patient tell the police exactly what had happened so that charges could be filed. He tried to impress on her the importance of telling the truth since she would soon die.

The woman turned her face from side to side, avoiding looking at her husband who stood at the foot of the bed, a savage, degraded-looking creature. Finally, her eyes came to rest on his hands and slowly rose to his eyes. The look of suffering disappeared from her face, and in its place there came one of tenderness and love. Then she looked back to the magistrate and said in a quiet, clear voice, "Sir, it was all an accident," and with a shadow of a smile still on her face, she snuggled down in the pillow and died.[4]

It was a Godlike act, one that exemplified the heights to which human beings can rise by his grace. Such acts make us glad and call forth praise. Yet admirable as they are, they are not able to earn us our salvation.

## Saving Grace

### Must Be Received

Only the saving grace of God administered by the Holy Spirit can fill the vacuum in the heart of man. Seeking to satisfy this yearning of the soul, people through the ages have devised a multiplicity of religious exercises. Yet, blinded by sin, these human efforts incorporate the same criteria for receiving divine favor by which they give honor to others—they have to earn it. That is the way the world operates. The idea of God giving his blessing freely, unconditionally, and without merit—because he has already been fully satisfied—is a concept utterly foreign to persons struggling to achieve salvation. Considering their ceaseless effort, one would think that the message of grace would be good news indeed.

Why, then, does not everyone readily embrace it? Many people, of course, have not heard the Gospel, and "how are they to hear without someone preaching" to them (Rom. 10:14)? Certainly, getting the message of grace to them is a high priority in Christian ministry. Still, the heathen are not "without excuse," for what could be known about God through his "invisible attributes" in natural creation, they rejected "in their thinking, and their foolish hearts were darkened" (Rom. 1:19–23).

More puzzling, however, is the rejection of people who have heard the Gospel, perhaps have heard it numerous times, yet who do not believe. Assuming that they do understand the invitation of God's grace, how can you explain their continuing obstinacy and hardness of heart? What excuse do they have for dismissing their Savior?

There is no excuse, for everyone who sincerely comes to Christ will not be turned away (John 6:37). The promise is that all who call upon "the name of the Lord will be saved" (Rom. 10:13). Responding to the Gospel is finally a personal decision every person makes for themselves. No religious system can take away that responsibility and privilege.

### Irresistible to the Elect

Though it is every person's responsibility to receive God's grace, there are different ways that theologians have in explaining people's varying responses to the Gospel invitation. Reformed theologians contend that some persons will be constrained by God to believe in Christ, while others will not. Common grace, they point out, can bring one to the point of decision, but only those previously chosen by God will have saving grace.

This election was determined before "the foundation of the world" (Eph. 1:4). And those God "foreknew he also predestined to be conformed to the image of his Son. . . . And those whom he predestined he also called, and those whom he called he also justified" (Rom. 8:29–30).

Certainly God has the right to do whatever he pleases. This is very evident in the way he chose Abraham to raise up a posterity for himself. In the same way, through no merit of his own, Jacob was chosen over Esau, "in order that God's purpose of election might continue" (Rom. 9:11). Within Israel, too, there was a distinction between "the elect" who obtained God's blessing, "but the rest were hardened" (Rom. 11:7).

Further support for this divine election can be seen when Paul writes to the Thessalonians, telling his beloved brethren that they were chosen from the beginning to be saved (1 Thess. 1:4; 2 Thess. 2:13). Likewise, writing to Timothy, he reminds him of God "who saved us and called us to a holy calling, not because of our works but because of his own purpose and grace, which he gave us in Christ Jesus before the ages began" (2 Tim. 1:9).

Therefore, it is reasoned, those who were elected in Christ, and "called according to his purpose" (Rom. 8:28), will be saved. They cannot do otherwise. The grace that is freely bestowed on those chosen ones is irresistible, since God is sovereign and he cannot be defeated in his purpose.

As to those who refuse the Gospel call, they lack the motivation to respond. They have a common grace by which the Holy Spirit makes known God's will to all people, but they do not have sufficient grace to overcome their own fallen nature to believe and be saved.

This view underscores the divine initiative in making a people for his glory. For the chosen ones, it gives reason to magnify the Lord, while at the same time, a deep feeling of loss and regret for those not so blessed. There is no joy in contemplating the separation of the reprobate. Certainly nothing in this truth can cause the elect to boast. Yet even in the sadness of seeing others unmoved to seek the Savior, there may be some comfort in realizing that in the last analysis we cannot change the heart of anyone. Finally, God alone is able.

### Prevenient Grace

Differing from Calvinism, those of the Arminian persuasion hold that grace extends to everyone the ability to believe. Just as no support is found to limit the atonement of Christ, so there is no reason to limit saving grace. As Wesley put it, "There is no man, unless he has quenched the Spirit, that is devoid of the grace of God. . . . It is more properly called preventing grace."[5]

The term *prevenient* comes from two Latin words that mean "to come before."[6] Used theologically, it refers to the operation of God's grace in the heart before one comes to Christ. This preparatory grace is comprehensive, including any movement of man toward God, and involves illuminating divine truth, conviction of sin, call to repentance, and the exercise of saving faith. Yielded to, these gracious impulses increase; when stifled, they tend to diminish. All these promptings of the Spirit imply some awakening of spiritual life, some beginning of deliverance from a heart of stone.

Paul reminds us: "Work out your own salvation with fear and trembling." But he added, "for it is God who works in you, both to will and to work for his great pleasure" (Phil. 2:12–13). Too easily we miss the point that it is God who enables us to work out our salvation.

Our responsibility is to respond to the workings of grace in our heart. Some speak of it as cooperation between man and the Spirit. Though God always works for the welfare of the world, and "desires all people to be saved and to come to the knowledge of the truth" (1 Tim. 2:4), he respects the freedom given to every person to choose his or her own destiny.

Prevenient grace prepares one to believe the Gospel, but it cannot make the decision for us. Contrary to Reformed teaching, grace sufficient to believe on the Lord for salvation is not irresistible. Though salvation has been procured for mankind through the blood of Christ, that does not assure human concurrence with God's will.

The ministry of the Spirit lifting up the claims of Christ can be ignored. Grace can be resisted. Paul appealed to the Corinthians "not to receive the grace of God in vain" (2 Cor. 6:1). He did not want, he said, to "nullify the grace of God" (Gal. 2:21).

145

As to the election from time immemorial, Arminians understand this divine choice to refer to persons who believe in Christ. The elect, then, are those who respond to the Gospel call. Those persons were foreknown before the worlds were made, and "whom he foreknew he also predestined to be conformed to the image of his Son" (Rom. 8:29). So it is believed that divine foreknowledge determines the divine decrees.

Persons who refuse to come to Christ are those who do not utilize their privilege of grace. They have prevenient grace sufficient to believe the Gospel but do not take advantage of that opportunity. Those who do respond to the Gospel call, of course, recognize that God has done it all. The fact that they receive the invitation is no indication of special merit, for even the acceptance by faith in the finished work of Christ is of grace (Eph. 2:8).

## Distorted Views of Grace

Grace is so contrary to the natural human instinct toward self-gratification that it can be easily misrepresented.

### Lure of Humanism

Failure to keep every move toward God within the boundaries of sovereign grace may lead to humanism, the exaltation of man as opposed to the glory of God. Fallen human nature, being what it is, wants to take some credit for what looks commendable, which of course includes salvation. After all, we reason, have not our noble efforts deserved God's favor?

This is the direction of theological liberalism within Christianity. That we are totally without merit seems repugnant. Yes, we are not perfect, but, humanists reason, good deeds make up for what we lack. The fallacy is that we have no merit to start with. The pernicious idea latent in humanism is that God needs our assistance in redemption.

Such reasoning often comes out in theological debates within the church. It's interesting that, when the discipline of the Methodist Episcopal Church was renewed at the General Conference of 1804, one preacher moved to strike out the word *preventing* from an article and insert in its place the word *assisting*. Superintendent Thomas Coke, having waited impatiently for the man to finish, rose to his feet and at the top of his voice exclaimed, "Where am I? In a Methodist Conference? I thought so, but have we turned Pelagian? Do we think that we can get along in our natural depravity with a little assistance without preventing grace?" He insisted that the proposed amendment would ruin the intent of the article, which, as it stands, asserts the utter inability of anyone to do anything toward personal salvation except as God's grace through Christ comes before. "Brethren," he cried, "do not change the word. I would go to the stake, yes, to the stake, for that word, as soon as any word in the

Bible."[7] Coke won his point, for the word was not changed, and, furthermore, it remains the same today. Unfortunately, I am afraid many Methodists, despite the stated position of their church, have adopted the Pelagian idea that people have to assist God in working out their salvation.

If for one moment persons think that they have anything positive to do with their salvation, other than simple faith that God has acted to manifest his own glory, then it is nothing more than a scheme of salvation by human works.

## Trap of Legalism

Related to the self-inflating effort of humanism, but with a different attraction, is the appeal of moralism in fostering a Christian lifestyle. The effort now centers in rigidly observing respectable norms of behavior and set religious rituals, things to do and not to do to demonstrate spirituality and incur divine favor—going to church and prayer meetings, reading the Bible every day, helping at the homeless shelter, and limitless other good things, all the while being careful to avoid any activity offensive to the culture, like going to the track or watching certain movies. Doubtless these good disciplines are practiced with the best of intentions, and so strengthen moral and spiritual resolve, but they are not meritorious for salvation. If virtuous living is thought to deserve God's saving grace, one can slip into a subtle form of works-righteousness.

This pitfall lies in the path of sincere believers all along the way to heaven. Both liberals and conservatives can fall into it. Let us not be so foolish. Paul admonished the church: "After beginning with the Spirit, are you now trying to attain your goal by human effort?" (Gal. 3:3 NIV; cf. 5:2–4).

Conforming to man-made regulations has a way of indulging our prideful, sinful nature and can easily turn into a Pharisaic self-righteousness, giving meticulous care to external rites of piety while neglecting "justice and the love of God" (Luke 11:42). Such an attitude not only contradicts the nature of true holiness, but also destroys any opportunity to give the watching world a positive witness to the Gospel of grace.

## The Deception of Antinomianism[8]

Avoiding the trap of legalism, however, does not release one from keeping the law of God. We are not saved by "works of the law" (Gal. 2:16), to be sure, for Christ has freed us from its curse "by becoming a curse for us" (Gal. 3:13; cf. 5:1; Eph. 2:15). But the demands of the law have not changed, for it expresses God's moral character. "The law of the LORD is perfect" (Ps. 19:7); it is "holy and righteous and good" (Rom. 7:12), and always stands as a guide for conduct.

What has changed for the saved is the motivation to obey. No longer do we keep the law to earn merit. "The love of Christ controls us" (2 Cor. 5:14). Gratitude for his immeasurable and unspeakable gift of love compels obedience. As Jerry Bridges so aptly expresses it: "We obey God's law, not to be loved, but because we are loved."[9]

This is a much greater motivation than a mere sense of duty. "Love is the fulfilling of the law" (Rom. 13:10; cf. 1 John 5:3). Obedience is simply demonstrating devotion to Christ, as he said, "If you love me, you will keep my commandments" (John 14:15); "whoever has my commandments and keeps them, he it is who loves me" (v. 21; cf. vv. 23–24).

Redeemed sinners who imagine that they are free to live as they please must reckon with Christ's words. He presents himself to us as the measure of the law, no longer written in stone, but incarnate in his own perfect life and work. He made clear that all who love him will obey his commands.

An area where this obligation has particular urgency is evangelism. The church has been charged by Christ to go and "make disciples of all nations," and we have no recourse but to obey (Matt. 28:19; cf. Mark 16:15; Acts 1:8). Too easily we have ignored this command, even within evangelical circles. Some devout ministers may still be like the eighteenth-century churchman who responded to William Carey's request for missionary service, "Young man, sit down. When God pleases to convert the heathen, he will do it without your aid or mine."[10] Whatever our theological position, we cannot transfer our Christian duty to someone else, nor can we make God's predetermination of the elect an excuse for not seeking to bring the Gospel to the ends of the earth.

## Summary Applications

*1. Grace is more easily imagined than explained.*

So great is the wonder of grace that church creeds describing it invariably lack personality. But we can picture it in our minds.

Some years ago I heard a story that helped me visualize its beauty. No doubt the narrative lacks factual basis, but the message that comes through is real.[11]

A haggard man occupied a seat on the 10:15 train out of Chicago. His unshaven face, slumped shoulders, and worn-out shoes made him an object of pity. A few people turned to look at him, but he was unaware of their glances because he was reliving his life.

His mind had gone back nearly twenty years to when he was a boy who lived in a little red brick house next to the railroad track—the place where the train would soon be passing. Many times he had stood on the porch and watched the trains go past. It was strange how well he could remember those days—and the pansies his mom had planted along the walk, and the swing his dad had made for him in the front yard, and the path where he learned to ride his bike.

The warmth of those thoughts hurt him, and he shrugged impatiently as his memory traveled on another ten years. The bike had been exchanged for a motorcycle, and after a while he began to come home less often. He had a job by then and plenty of friends. The pubs were a lot more fun than being with Mom and Dad. He did not really want to remember those years, or the day when his gambling debts piled up, and he had gone home meaning to ask for money. But why ask? He knew where his mom and dad kept their savings; and later when they were out in the garden, it was easy to help himself to what he wanted.

That was the last time he had seen them. He had not wanted to go home after that. He had gone abroad and never communicated with his parents to tell them where he was. They knew nothing about the derelict he had become, the years of wandering, nor the prison sentence for his crime. But locked in his cell at night, as the moonlight moved across the wall, he used to wonder what had happened to them.

When he had served his time, he would love to see them again. Would they let him come home? But what right had he to impose himself on them? He had only brought disgrace to the family. Could they ever reconcile the convicted felon he had become with the boy they had loved and who so bitterly disappointed them?

A few days before being set free, he summoned his courage and wrote them a letter telling of his longing to see them again. Though very short, it took hours to write. He told them that he would be on the morning train that went by their house, and if they would have it in their hearts to let him come home, he would get off at the station. The letter ended with these words: "I know that I do not deserve your love and I don't want to bring more heartbreak to you, but if you can somehow forgive me, hang a white handkerchief in the window of my old bedroom. If I see it when the train goes by, I will get off at the station. But if not, I will go on my way."

Now the time had come. The little red brick house was just around the bend. The disheveled man had pulled down his window to see more clearly. As the train rounded the turn, he peered nervously out the window and looked—and looked—and there hanging in his old bedroom window was a white handkerchief. And every other window in the house was hung with white—white pillowcases, white tablecloths—white sheets filled the clothesline, and white muslin curtains trailed across the roof from the attic window. Every wall of the house gleamed with white in the morning sun. And there, affixed to the fence beside the railroad track was a big sign emblazoned with big letters:

WELCOME HOME
WE ARE AT THE STATION WAITING FOR YOU

*2. Grace fills life with gratitude.*

Considering our fallen nature, whatever commendable thing that comes to us is undeserved. Even what may appear as good works are really gifts of grace in disguise. Commenting on Deuteronomy 8:17 and the accumulation of worldly goods, Martin Luther wrote that these things are "simply blessings of God, sometimes through our efforts, sometimes without our efforts, but never from our efforts and always given out of his free mercy."[12]

There is grace for everything: grace to come and grace to go, grace to speak and grace to keep silent, grace to mourn and grace to dance, grace to weep and grace to laugh, grace to pack and grace to unpack, grace to be sick and grace to heal, grace to plant and grace to harvest, grace to tear down and grace to build up, grace to love and grace to hate, grace to live and grace to die. From beginning to end, life becomes a rhapsody of grace. Even the desire for grace comes by grace.

What a new outlook this gives to our daily toil! We see things through a new lens—one that helps filter out false pride and bring more clearly into focus the reality that all we are and all that we hope to be is because of the mercies of God.

Not only does this awareness motivate obedience to Christ, but it also arrests attention in the world. Again to quote Martin Luther: "A law giver insists with threats and penalties; a preacher of grace lures and incites with divine goodness and compassion shown to us; for he wants no unwilling works and reluctant services, he wants joyful and delightful services of God."[13]

*3. Grace separates Christianity from other world religions.*

Philip Yancey tells about a conference on comparative religions in England where scholars were debating the uniqueness of the Christian faith. In different teachings it was noted that other religions had accounts of their gods coming to earth in human form. Some had claims of their leaders returning from death. The discussion was going at a lively pace when C. S. Lewis walked in the room and asked what they were talking about. Told that they were trying to decide the uniqueness of the Christian religion, Lewis replied, "Oh, that's easy. It's grace."[14]

After further discussion, the experts agreed with him. From a practical standpoint, I expect they were right. However, in fairness, when grace is seen in the atonement, Judaism could be an exception.[15] Unfortunately, this truth has been generally lost by moralistic Jews seeking to earn God's favor by keeping the law.

Grace by its nature does not resonate well with the prescriptions for salvation contrived by men striving to justify themselves by works. Islam has the Five Pillars to help the faithful have more good deeds than bad deeds on the day of judgment. Hindus, bound by the law of karma, struggle through the cycle of birth, death, and many rebirths and lifetimes, until eventually they attain the desired unconsciousness. Similarly, Buddhism offers nirvana to its zealots through self-reliance and following the eightfold path. Confucianism wants to actualize human goodness by teaching people to behave in accordance with cultural norms. Zoroastrianism, Jainism, Shintoism, Taoism, Mormonism, and many other religious systems could be added to the list, including the contemporary New Age movement.[16] They all have their peculiarities and distinctive rituals—but they have one thing in common—they seek to earn favor with God and man by what they do.

In this sense, Christianity spells religion differently, as Bill Hybels likes to point out.[17] The other religions spell it "Do," whereas persons who put their faith in the completed work of Christ spell it "Done."

### 4. No one is beyond the reach of grace.

God's unmerited love embraces the world, and all who come to him may drink at the same fountain of eternal life. It may be that one has completely quenched the inviting Spirit, but we do not have that information. Nor do we have advanced knowledge of the chosen ones. Evangelism will identify who the elect are. From our perspective, we always operate on the premise that everyone can be saved. There are no hopeless cases.

When sharing the Gospel with unbelievers, it is not uncommon to hear one say that their sin is too huge, their life too messed up for God to redeem. But how can that idea be supported in Scripture? The Bible says that "where sin increased, grace abounded all the more" (Rom. 5:20). Is anything too hard for God?

Look at some of the disgraceful people in Scripture, whom God not only transformed but used in mighty ways to show his glory. Take that rascal, Judah, who had an affair with his son's wife (Gen. 38:1–30), yet in God's mercy he became the chosen one through whom the posterity of Abraham was passed down to us, and even Jesus is called the "Lion of the tribe of Judah" (Rev. 5:5). Think of Rahab, the harlot who showed compassion to the spies at Jericho (Josh. 6:20–25) and later by God's grace appears in the lineage of Christ (Matt. 1:5) and is listed among the stalwarts of faith (Heb. 11:31). Or consider David, guilty of adultery (2 Sam. 11:1–27) yet forgiven (Psalm 51) to reign over the kingdom of Israel. Turning to the New Testament, immediately Peter comes to mind, a man who three times openly denied his Lord (John 18:15–27) yet becomes the leader of the church. Then look at Paul, who, under divine inspiration, felt himself to be the biggest sinner of all (1 Tim. 1:15). That statement certainly offers encouragement to those persons who, because of their sin, have thought themselves beyond hope of salvation.

### 5. Grace should be accepted when offered.

The work of Christ for us having already been completed, nothing that we do can make grace more acceptable. Waiting does not make the gift more attractive or relevant. Remember, too, that it can be withdrawn, if God pleases. Let us, then, not presume on God's mercy. "For he says, 'In a favorable time I listened to you, and in a day of salvation I have helped you. Behold, now is the favorable time; behold, now is the day of salvation'" (2 Cor. 6:2).

### 6. There is limitless sufficiency.

Since grace is available and free, we dare not limit the possibilities of sainthood. The overflowing resources of grace know no bounds. Whatever the need,

God "is able to make all grace abound to you, so that having all sufficiency in all things at all times, you may abound in every good work" (2 Cor. 9:8). The promise is all inclusive, so let us not restrict what God wants to do.

What he starts he plans to finish. God enables the believer to "grow in the grace and knowledge" of Christ (2 Pet. 3:18), "being transformed . . . from one degree of glory to another" (2 Cor. 3:18). The Spirit's ministry in the Christian never ends. There is always more to learn and appropriate from the "riches of his grace" (Eph. 1:7).

I sometimes marvel at the way we impose on the infinities of grace our paltry anticipations, as if God cannot work outside the confines of our traditional box. This impoverished mind-set becomes particularly obvious when we come to the outworking of sanctification in our lives. Do we really believe that "the God of all grace" (1 Pet. 5:10) can satisfy the deepest longings of our soul?

The beautiful reality of grace unfolds day by day in Christian discipleship. It becomes powerfully evident in times of adversity, as Paul learned when encountering the harassment of Satan, which seemed like a "thorn" in the flesh. Though he asked to be delivered from the trial, God assured him, "My grace is sufficient for you" (2 Cor. 12:9). That is enough, for however difficult the circumstances, "God will supply every need . . . according to his riches in glory in Christ Jesus" (Phil. 4:19).

When the Reverend J. W. Fletcher of Madely was asked by Lord North if there was anything he could give him in return for his service to his country, the saintly pastor sent back word: "He was sensible of the minister's kindness, but he only wanted one thing, which he could not give him, and that was more grace."[18]

Yes, that is all we need.

> When we have exhausted our store of endurance;
> > When our strength has failed ere the day is half done;
> When we reach the end of our hoarded resources;
> > Our father's full giving is only begun.
> His love has no limit, his grace knows no measure.
> > His power no boundary known unto men
> For out of his infinite riches in Jesus
> > He giveth and giveth and giveth again.[19]

### 7. Grace levels the playing field.

All saints are sinners saved by grace, so no one can boast except in Christ. We share equally in the gift of salvation. Differences that appear—race, sex, culture, nationality, education, recognition in society—all fade into the background when we gather at the cross.

And I should add that this community of saving grace pertains to differences in theology. Charles Simeon, a strong Calvinist, tells about a conversation he had one day with John Wesley. It progressed like this:

| Simeon: | Sir, I understand that you are called an Arminian, and therefore I suppose we care to draw daggers. But before I consent to begin the combat, with your permission, I will ask you a few questions. Pray, sir, do you feel yourself a depraved creature, so depraved that you would never have thought of turning to God, if God had not first put it into your heart? |
|---|---|
| Wesley: | Yes, I do indeed. |
| Simeon: | And do you utterly despair of recommending yourself to God by anything you can do, and look for salvation solely through the blood and righteousness of Christ? |
| Wesley: | Yes, solely through Christ. |
| Simeon: | But, sir, supposing you were at first saved by Christ, are you not somehow or other to save yourself afterwards by your own works? |
| Wesley: | No, I must be saved by Christ from first to last. |
| Simeon: | Allowing, then, that you were first turned by the grace of God, are you not in some way or other to keep yourself by your own power? |
| Wesley: | No. |
| Simeon: | What then, are you to be upheld every hour and every moment by God, as much as an infant in its mother's arms? |
| Wesley: | Yes, altogether. |
| Simeon: | And is all your hope in the grace and mercy of God to preserve you unto his heavenly kingdom? |
| Wesley: | Yes, I have no hope but in him. |
| Simeon: | Then Sir, with your leave, I will put up my daggers again; for this is all my Calvinism; this is my election, my justification by faith, my final perseverance: it is in my substance all that I hold, and therefore, if you please, instead of searching out terms and phrases to be a ground of contention between us, we will cordially unite in those things wherein we agree.[20] |

8. *The church will never cease to celebrate the grace of God.*

Grace grows sweeter with the years. We have been "raised up" and "seated" with Christ in heavenly places "so that in the coming ages he might show the immeasurable riches of his grace in kindness toward us" (Eph. 2:5–7). There is no end to it. The old converted slave ship captain had it right:

> When we've been there ten thousand years,
>    Bright shining as the sun,
> We've no less days to sing his praise
>    Than when we first begun.[21]

153

# 11

## Coming to Christ

The good news of God's grace calls for a response. Jesus proclaimed, "The time is fulfilled, and the kingdom of God is at hand; repent and believe in the gospel" (Mark 1:15). Both repentance and faith issue from grace and are essential to salvation. However, they differ in this respect: faith in Christ is the sole condition for entering the kingdom of God, while repentance is the condition for saving faith.[1]

### Turning from Sin

*Repentance* means a change of mind and purpose. It is a strong word, implying moral action and resolution of amendment affecting one's total personality. Knowing the impending doom awaiting sinners, whether they be notorious felons or respectable religious gentry, Jesus made clear: "Unless you repent, you will all likewise perish" (Luke 13:2–3). His words echo a refrain that reverberates through the Bible (e.g., Ezek. 18:30; Joel 2:13; Matt. 3:2; Mark 6:12; Acts 17:30; Rev. 2:5). There was a note of urgency in his voice, for the day of mercy was coming to an end (Matt. 5:24–26; 22:1–14; 25:1–13; Luke 13:16–18; 14:16–24).

Akin to repentance is the idea of conversion, meaning to turn around and go in a new direction. Without this change of heart, or as Jesus said, "Unless you turn and become like children," no one can "enter the kingdom of heaven" (Matt. 18:3).[2] So let us see how it unfolds.

### Conviction of Truth

The Holy Spirit initiates the process by making persons aware of the Gospel. So darkened is the mind of worldlings that apart from his illumination, we could not discern the depths of our depravity, much less the unmerited mercies of God (1 Cor. 2:4, 14; 1 Thess. 1:5). Even the fact that we can comprehend the Gospel evidences divine grace (Acts 5:31; 11:8; Rom. 2:4).[3]

The primary means by which the Spirit brings this conviction is the living Word of God, "sharper than any two-edged sword, piercing to the division of soul and of spirit . . . discerning the thoughts and intentions of the heart" (Heb. 4:12).

Though the Bible is the most authoritative source of truth, the Spirit can bring conviction through any number of other means (1 Thess. 1:5). Often he speaks through the counsel of Christian loved ones and friends or through our reading a book, seeing a display of power in nature, or meditating on some providence of deliverance. Usually these varied influences accumulate over a period of time, one experience building on another. As the awareness of need dawns on the consciousness, one begins to feel a discomforting awareness of spiritual truth.

The way it manifests itself will be different with every person. For some, like the prodigal who took his father's inheritance and went away to a far country to spend "all he had . . . in reckless living," conversion came in the realization of a wasted life and "squandered" opportunity for happiness. When he realized what a fool he had been and that he was "no longer worthy to be called" his father's son, he wanted to go home (Luke 15:11–20).

Others may feel the pangs of conviction, like the publican who saw himself condemned by the moral law of God. Contrasted to the self-righteous Pharisee, who prided himself on his good behavior, the tax collector knew all too well that he had woefully fallen short of God's holiness. So great was the anguish of his soul that he "would not even lift up his eyes to heaven, but beat his breast, saying, 'God, be merciful to me, a sinner'" (Luke 18:9–14).

To Saul of Tarsus, conviction began in seeing the faith of devout Christians he was persecuting. It came to a head on the Damascus Road when suddenly he was confronted by the living Christ in a blinding vision (Acts 9:1–9; 22:3–11; 26:1–18). The reality of the encounter awakened in him a history of misdirected religious zeal, and he knew that his whole concept of earning God's favor was wrong. The enormity of his error, sincere as it was, he would never forget.

However slow and eventful conviction develops, it comes to fruition finally at the cross. There the Spirit brings one to see eternal love disclosed in Christ, bearing in his body God's judgment on our sin. More than a historical fact, it becomes a very personal, awesome realization that Jesus died for me.

## A Broken and Contrite Spirit

In anguish of soul, under conviction, we know that we are guilty. Whatever may have been the form of our transgression, our sin has found us out (Num. 32:23).

It is not a pleasant sight. When Job finally came to see himself before God, he cried: "I had heard of you by the hearing of the ear, but now my eye sees you; therefore I despise myself, and repent in dust and ashes" (Job 42:5–6).

Likewise, David, when found out for his adultery and murder, utterly shattered and disgraced, could only pray: "Have mercy on me, O God . . . I know my transgressions, and my sin is ever before me." Because of the gravity of his sin, no relief could come by offering a sacrifice, else, he "would give it." He could only appeal directly to God, knowing that his "broken and contrite heart" would not be despised (Ps. 51:1–17; cf. Isa. 6:5).

God heard that prayer, for from David came the assurance, "The LORD is near to the brokenhearted and saves the crushed in spirit" (Ps. 34:18; cf. Isa. 57:15). One so broken is not far from the kingdom. "God opposes the proud, but gives grace to the humble" (James 4:6).

Yet repentance is not to be confused with merely feeling sorry for our sin. Judas felt remorse for betraying Christ, but his regret did not bring him to God, but to suicide. "We should hate our sins, not ourselves," Billy Graham points out. "Hate your false ways, hate your vain thoughts, hate your evil passions, hate your lying, hate your covetousness, hate your greed, but do not hate yourself. Self-hatred leads to self-destruction, and it is wrong to destroy that which was created in God's image."[4] Godly sorrow, however, "produces a repentance that leads to salvation without regret, whereas worldly grief produces death" (2 Cor. 7:10).

## Confession of Sin

Contrite in spirit, the repentant sinner pours out his soul to God. "I will confess my transgressions to the LORD," the psalmist said, "and you forgave the iniquity of my sin" (Ps. 32:5). The promise is: "He who confesses and forsakes [sin] will obtain mercy" (Prov. 28:13; cf. Lev. 5:5; 26:40–42). To put it in the words of John, "If we confess our sins, he is faithful and just to forgive us our sins and to cleanse us from all unrighteousness" (1 John 1:9).[5]

The word *confess* means "to agree with or to line up with the truth." It is a common word for making a legal contract. The concept broadens to declare what we believe and takes on this idea in the confessions of the early church.

In regard to sin, confession admits to the fact as specifically as we know our offense. Nothing is covered up. Repentance is complete or it is not repentance. A repentant person is not like the man who sent a tax payment with a note, saying, "If I can't sleep tonight, I will send in the rest tomorrow."

There is honest acceptance of responsibility for the sin. We do not blame it on someone else. We do not transfer guilt to our fallen society. We do not excuse it on the basis of our weakness or ignorance. We do not justify the act through rationalization. We do not minimize it as being of no consequence. We do not compensate for the sin by doing something to make up for it. No, we acknowledge the truth and flat out confess our guilt, ask for forgiveness, and resolve not to repeat the sin again.

Confession is not mere misgivings and regret over sins; it expresses a desire to follow a new path of righteousness. No longer does the penitent heart want to gratify its old lusts of the flesh. Jesus expected the rich young ruler to give up the worship of mammon (Matt. 19:21; Mark 10:21; Luke 18:22); the self-righteous lawyer to abandon his pride (Luke 10:25, 37); the adulterous woman to go and sin no more (John 8:11; cf. 5:14).

### Making Things Right

As we turn from the old patterns, our repentance leads to restitution, our genuine desire, insofar as may be possible, to correct the wrong caused others by the sin. This willingness to repair sin's damage was modeled in the law of Moses. It stated, for example: "If a man causes a field or vineyard to be grazed over, or lets his beast loose and it feeds in another's field, he shall make restitution from the best in his own field and in his own vineyard" (Exod. 22:5). In other situations, restitution may require payment of bad debts, return of stolen property, and apology for gossip and wrong deeds (Exod. 22:1–5; Num. 5:5–10).

In the case of sexual indulgence, "if a man seduces a virgin who is not [engaged to be married] and lies with her, he shall give the bride-price for her and make her his wife" (a shotgun wedding). "If her father utterly refuses to give her to him, he shall pay money equal to the bride-price for virgins" (Exod. 22:16–17). Other examples of required restitution come out in the Old Testament wisdom literature (e.g., Prov. 6:31), the prophets (e.g., Ezek. 33:14–16), and the historical narratives (Neh. 5:1–13).

Significantly, before a trespass offering could be offered to God and atonement made, the law meticulously spelled out the necessary restitution. It was only after this was done that the guilty person was entitled to offer his sacrifice and receive forgiveness (Lev. 6:1–7).

Jesus's Sermon on the Mount reflects on this practice when speaking about a man who brings a gift to the altar and there remembers that a brother has something against him. "First," he said, "be reconciled to your brother, and then come and offer your gift" (Matt. 5:23–24; cf. James 5:4). When we know that others have been hurt by our sin, we would do well to follow the example of Zacchaeus and do "anything" to restore broken relationships (Luke 19:1–10).

This becomes very evident in days of great revival when hearts are tendered by the Holy Spirit. I remember such a time at Asbury College in 1970 when the Spirit's presence was so heavy that for eight days and nights classes had to be dismissed as contrite students and faculty sought the Lord. Confessions at the altar overflowed in countless initiatives of reconciliation, reuniting estranged family members, putting back together broken marriages, and healing racial divisions. Seeking to correct a general disregard for the city's needs (not unusual in a college town), some students went out and cleaned up a long neglected garbage dump on the edge of town; while another group went to the city hall, borrowed brooms, and went through the streets sweeping the gutters. Probably, though, the most obvious change of heart came in a new concern for evangelism as people left the altar to tell their story of deliverance by a mighty Savior.[6] This is the kind of repentance that makes the world take note that there has been a change of heart.

### Continuing Penitence

What is most assuring, though often forgotten, is that true repentance results in a lasting change. Persons who have started to follow Christ do not want to look back. Elements of the initial act of repentance—conviction, brokenness, confession, and restitution—characterize this ongoing state of penitence.

One has a whole new attitude toward the world and its attractions. As natural men, we were spiritually blind, but now we see truth in a new light. Things we once loved, now we hate; and things we once hated, now we love. The old chains of darkness have been broken, and in all sincerity, as we know our heart, we determine to go out of the sin business.

This continuing state must be distinguished from penance, which is the idea that voluntary acts of suffering and good works lessen the consequence of sin. Penance is a sacrament of the Roman Catholic Church, stressing the virtue of godly sorrow. Devoutly observed, it is believed that the sacrament assists in sanctification and will shorten the period of purgatory after death. Penance, however, does not necessarily result in a change of character, nor does it absolve one from the haunting sense of guilt.

### If One Does Not Repent

Tragically, the call to repent can be resisted (Acts 7:51). God does not repent for us. Putting away sin is a human responsibility. The Spirit may continue his appeals, for God is long-suffering, not wishing that any should perish, and that all should reach repentance. But we should not presume on his patience.

In his mercy, God may speak in more violent ways. For example, natural calamities, defeats in battle, and sickness unto death were often means of getting people's attention in the Old Testament, though, unfortunately, usually people "refused to take correction" (Jer. 5:3; cf. Amos 4:6–13).[7]

If in distress, they would "confess their iniquity," and "their uncircumcised heart is humbled and they make amends for their iniquity," then God would again remember the covenant he had made with their forefathers and bless them (Lev. 26:40–45). However, he said, "If you will not listen to me," then "I will set my face against you," and your sorrows will increase. "If in spite of this" the people still continue to go on their own way, "then," God said, "I will discipline you again sevenfold for your sins" (vv. 14–22). Repeated refusals to repent would accelerate the judgments that would come on Israel until their land would be devastated, the people utterly decimated, subjected to unspeakable horrors, and at last, carried away into captivity as slaves and scattered among the nations (vv. 23–39). That is exactly what happened. So reads the tragic story of rebellion in the Old Testament.

In the New Testament the persistent rejection of God's Word brings the same forebodings of disaster. Further conviction of the redeeming truth will be less easily recognized, and the heart "hardened by the deceitfulness of sin" (Heb. 3:13; cf. Rom. 2:5). In time, the conscience can become completely insensitive to the distinctions between right and wrong, and sinners give "themselves up to sensuality, greedy to practice every kind of impurity" (Eph. 4:19; cf. Rom. 1:24, 26, 28; 1 Tim. 4:2).

Ultimately complete perversion of the human spirit is expressed in the rejection of Jesus Christ as Lord and Savior—the ultimate blasphemy of the Holy Spirit, who from the beginning has sought to draw a fallen race to God through the Son (Matt. 12:31–32; Mark 3:29; Luke 12:10–12; Heb. 12:25). The scorning of his love, so perfectly revealed at the cross, closes the door to salvation, for apart from the blood of Christ, there is no way one can be forgiven. This stubborn, persistent, and final unwillingness to receive forgiveness is the unpardonable sin.

## Faith

Repentance turns the heart to receive the gift of salvation, but it is faith in Christ that saves (Mark 1:15). "Truly, truly," Jesus said, "whoever hears my word and believes him who sent me has eternal life. He does not come into judgment, but has passed from death to life" (John 5:24). But what is faith?

### Common Faith

What may not be realized at first is that everyone lives by faith. Life requires acceptance of the unseen as real and trustworthy. Such trust makes possible the human experience. To deny that we live by faith would be, in effect, to deny the possibility of life.

Take the daily sustenance of our physical body as an example. You eat what is set before you at a café without even checking to see if it is safe.

Amazing! Why, the food could be contaminated, even poisonous. Yet that possibility never enters your mind because of an implicit trust in those who prepared it.

Perhaps a more extraordinary faith comes in driving a car on a busy highway. Only a few feet separate you from a head-on collision with the car passing on the other side of the road. Though you have no idea who that other driver is, still you drive, oblivious to your precarious situation. You must have an incredible amount of faith in those strangers who speed by you. Yet without that trust, you could never drive a car. And in a thousand other ways every day you act on the necessity of believing in what you cannot see.

Of course, your trust can be wrong. The food, though appearing delectable, may make you sick, just as you may get hit by the supposedly safe driver on the road. That is why there are government agencies to test the purity of food served in restaurants, and for the same reason, vigorous tests are mandated for persons licensed to drive a car.

Safeguards are needed to give assurance to faith. They serve to point out mistaken trust, while also justifying what is believed. Valid faith must be relevant to demonstrated faith. It can be proved but not invented. In matters great and small, intelligent belief has as its object that which is worthy of trust. Far from being a blind leap into the unknown, it is a commitment to reasonable certainty.

Such trust involves our whole being. Nothing can be held back once the decision is made. There may be a place for hesitancy, even doubt, in coming to faith, but when one truly believes, everything is laid on the line. Faith, by its nature, has to be complete. And what we believe, we act on.

The story is often told of the high-wire artist who announced that he would walk across Niagara Falls pushing a wheelbarrow on a cable stretched across the chasm. "Do you believe I can do it?" he asked the crowd gathered to watch. One hand went up. "Alright," he said, "now you get in the wheelbarrow."[8]

Faith is getting in the wheelbarrow—committing to the object of our trust, letting our weight down on it. Unfortunately, the practice of our faith often falls behind its profession. Not what we say but what we do indicates what we believe. It may be wrong and unjustified by reason. Nevertheless, right or wrong, we will live out what we believe. Life in all its varied dimensions comes down finally to faith.

### Saving Faith

What weaves life together every day in the physical world comes over into the more meaningful spiritual realm of reality. Whether realized or not, the necessary steps for experiencing eternal life in Christ have already been learned. The spirit of grace simply applies the components of common faith to their intended end in salvation.

The process begins in the unsettling awareness of our human perversity, intensified by disillusionment with human efforts to bring personal fulfillment and happiness. Feeling a growing loneliness and insecurity in the world, under conviction of the Spirit, we come to recognize our lostness. Unless help comes from outside of self, there is no hope for salvation.

Realism, awakened by grace, looks for "the things that are unseen" (2 Cor. 4:18) and calls for faith in a supernatural Savior, the One who created the universe by the word of his power (Heb. 11:3). "Whoever would draw near to God must believe that he exists and that he rewards those who seek him" (v. 6). Out of this necessity comes the reality: "Faith is being sure of what we hope for and certain of what we do not see" (v. 1 NIV).

### Authority for Belief

The reasonableness of saving faith rests on the trustworthiness of divine revelation. "Faith comes from hearing, and hearing through the word of Christ" (Rom. 10:17). The Spirit-inspired Scriptures were given for this purpose to supply a credible authority for truth—"so that you may believe that Jesus is the Christ, the Son of God, and that by believing you may have life in his name" (John 20:31; cf. 5:24; 17:20; 2 Thess. 2:13; 1 John 5:13).

To the written Word of God can be added the supporting testimony of the church across two thousand years. Confirming this witness would be the personal experience of the redeemed today. Ask anyone who truly has believed to see its certainty.

### Focus on Christ

Faith looks to Jesus Christ alone for salvation—he is the object of faith that saves. Paul summed it up to the Philippian jailer: "Believe in the Lord Jesus, and you will be saved, you and your household" (Acts 16:31).[9]

This was the simplicity of the Gospel proclaimed by the New Testament church, that by Christ "everyone who believes is freed from everything from which you could not be freed by the law of Moses" (Acts 13:38–39; cf. Rom. 4:3). Again and again the message is sounded forth, and all "who believed in his name, he gave the right to become children of God" (John 1:12). "Whoever believes in me, though he die," Jesus said, "yet shall he live, and everyone who lives and believes in me shall never die." Then he asks, "Do you believe this?" (John 11:25–26; cf. vv. 45). The issue is simple—those who believe Christ will live; those who do not will die in their sin (John 8:24).

Belief in Christ means a firm reliance on his Word (Luke 24:25; John 2:22; 3:36; 5:46; 8:40; 20:29, 31) and the appropriation of his power (Mark 5:28; John 2:11; 4:50; 12:46; 20:27, 29).[10] It rests on the conviction, full of joyful trust, that Jesus is the Messiah, the divinely appointed Author of eternal salvation in the kingdom of God,[11] affirming the historic events of his life, death, and resurrection. Jesus has done it all. We contribute nothing toward salvation. Even our faith is a gift of God (Eph. 2:8–9).

Get it clear, though. Saving faith is not anchored in the mere credibility of Christ's work, but in him who did it; not faith in the blessings that Christ gives, but in him who is our life; not faith in our prayer for salvation, but in him who answers. And, must it be said, it is not faith in faith, but faith in Jesus Christ, the object of saving faith, who is all and in all. In his arms the believer rests secure. Martin Luther expresses it well: "Faith is a living, daring confidence in God's grace, so sure and so certain that a man would stake his life upon it a thousand times."[12]

This faith embraces its object (John 11:27; 20:31). Jesus does not ask us to believe a creed, but to believe a person. He says, "Come to me . . . and I will give you rest. Take my yoke upon you, and learn from me" (Matt. 11:28–29). This is the beauty of Christian faith. Jesus offers us himself, as he said, "If anyone thirsts, let him come to me and drink" (John 7:37); "whoever comes to me I will never cast out" (John 6:37).

To believe in Christ is to come to him (John 5:40; 6:35, 37, 40, 47, 65; 7:37), to receive him (John 1:12; 5:43), to love him supremely (John 8:42; 13:34; 14:28; 15:12; 16:27).

### Personal Relationship

Belief in Christ always has to become personal to save. More than the recognition that God was in Christ reconciling the world to himself, it is the overwhelming realization that he "loved me and gave himself for me" (Gal. 2:20). Faith in the blood of Christ offered to God on my behalf means just that, that it is accepted as my own. Similarly, the eternal life Christ gives is made my own by that same trust in his finished work.

John Wesley describes it well as he tells about listening to a layman read from Martin Luther's *Preface to the Book of Romans*. "While he was describing the change that God works in the heart through faith in Christ, I felt my heart strangely warmed. I felt I did trust in Christ, Christ alone for my salvation; and an assurance was given me, that he had taken away my sins, even mine, and saved me from the law of sin and death."[13]

The description of his experience, as well as the struggles leading up to it, indicate that it was for Wesley an evangelical conversion.[14] Others will express their coming to faith differently, of course, but that sense of personalizing what Christ accomplished is the liberating reality for all.

### Obedient Commitment

This faith, under the influence of the Holy Spirit, finds expression in action.[15] It is a commitment of life, incorporating the whole personality of the believer. The mind, the emotions, and the will all coalesce in full, unreserved trust in the Savior.[16]

The living demonstration of this faith becomes evident in obedience to his Word. "Come, follow me," is his invitation (Mark 10:21; Luke 18:22; cf. Matt. 4:19; 9:9; Mark 1:17; 2:14; Luke 5:27; John 1:43). Following Christ is the continuing expression of faith, just as it is the witness of our love. "Whoever has my commandments and keeps them," Jesus says, "he it is who loves me" (John 14:21; cf. vv. 23–24; 15:10).

In this pledge of love is the surrender of all that we know of ourselves to all that we know of Christ.[17] Though scarcely comprehended in the beginning, at least in its practical applications there is wholehearted resolve to obey the will of God. Jesus made it clear: "If anyone would come after me, let him deny himself and take up his cross and follow me" (Matt. 16:24–26; Luke 9:23–25). The implications of what this means will continue to unfold throughout our lives, in this world and the world to come.

### Growing Faith

Faith grows with obedience as the Spirit of God continues to lead into new dimensions of truth. Incomplete knowledge, or course, does not mean the believer is any less sincere. A child can fully trust Christ for salvation, yet have a very limited understanding of doctrine. Thankfully, God is not finished with any of us.

There are degrees of faith. Paul exhorted the Roman church to welcome the "weak in faith" (Rom. 14:1). The saints at Corinth he characterized as "infants in Christ," not able to digest solid spiritual food (1 Cor. 3:1–3). On a higher level, the zealous Christians at Thessalonica were an "example to all the believers in Macedonia and in Achaia" (1 Thess. 1:7) and were still "growing abundantly" (2 Thess. 1:3), though Paul prayed that God would supply what was "lacking in [their] faith" (1 Thess. 3:10).

The disciples struggled with what Jesus called their "little faith" (Matt. 6:30; 17:20). Certainly they had much more to learn about the sacrificial lifestyle of Christ.[18] Even their comprehension of the atonement was clouded by their upbringing and incomplete understanding of Scripture.[19]

Yet Jesus patiently endured their human failings because, in spite of their shortcomings, with the exception of the traitor, they were willing to follow him. That is the crucial issue. It is not what we know, but who we obey. Jesus is the one who commands.

Persons who will practice all the truth that he gives will never stop growing in faith.[20] And knowing how little we have yet experienced in the infinite reaches of God's love and power, like the disciples, we too should pray to the Lord, "increase our faith" (Luke 17:5).

## Common Misconceptions

### Circumventing Biblical Authority

Without the directives of Scripture, subjective human experience and reason determine what to believe. This danger, inherent in liberal theology, opens the door to almost any kind of aberration, and in its most extreme form, eliminates any need for salvation at all.

Even among neo-orthodox believers, some look on faith as a leap into the unknown, thereby obscuring the objectivity and finality of God's saving Word in Christ. Such well-intentioned efforts result in undue emphasis on feelings and can lead to excessive emotionalism or radical mysticism.

Once the Bible is relegated to merely an advisory role in salvation, humans can set their own rules. The tendency is either to take away all boundaries or to add new ones that more narrowly define the playing field. Where it all ends is left to the discretion of the players, not the one who wrote the rulebook.

### Presuming on Grace

Repentance and faith require an act of the will, yet not without divine assistance. Persons thinking from a humanistic perspective tend to rule out the enabling grace of God. To them repentance is basically a necessary correction from a bad situation. As to saving faith, if it may be thought of in a redemptive sense, it amounts to an exercise in realizing human potential.

Associated with the expressions of remorse and moral improvement may be an assortment of spiritual disciplines and religious rituals, sometimes involving mortification of the flesh—all intended to relieve a burden of guilt and bring a more satisfying life. With it, too, may come ministries of humanitarian compassion with gratifying benefits to society.

Sincere and commendable as these efforts may be, however, without coming to Christ in the humility of grace, they are still self-gratifying. Salvation is made a human achievement. We must not forget that true repentance makes us confess that we have no rights before Christ and true faith affirms that he alone is worthy of our lives.

### Divorcing Faith from Life

Perhaps the most common misconception of saving faith comes in living out commitment. What we say may be perfectly correct, but our profession is not translated into daily practice. "Many believed" in the mighty works of Christ and acclaimed him as a great teacher, but their hearts were not in it—their acceptance was merely an assent to a historical fact—but "Jesus on his part did not entrust himself to them" (John 2:23–24; cf. 6:65–66; 12:13–19).

This kind of faith seems prevalent in many churches and Christian schools. Doctrinal correctness is affirmed in their founding documents and official public statements, but all too often, the profession does not carry over into practice. How easy it is to separate intellectual orthodoxy from personal integrity!

Despite pronouncements to the contrary, this fabrication of faith becomes apparent in the absence of obedience to the Word of God, a failure especially obvious in the disregard for evangelism and discipleship. Mere lip service to the truth of the Gospel does not produce committed followers of Christ.

Needless to say, the problem is not limited to any theological position or church denomination, whether orthodox or liberal. In fact, I suspect that most of us would do well to take an honest look at our lifestyle and ask ourselves: am I living by what I believe? We may not live up to our profession but we will all live by what we believe.

## Summary Applications

### 1. Hearing the Word brings conviction.

God will not let what he has said return to him void. The Spirit sees to that. Whenever Christ is lifted up, men and women will be "cut to the heart" (Acts 2:37), for "the word of God is living and active, sharper than any two-edged sword" (Heb. 4:12). We cannot convince anyone of the Gospel. Our part is to bear witness to the truth. God will effect the response.

### 2. Convicted persons see themselves naked before God.

No one can get away from the searching Spirit, who reads our lives like an open book, discerning the thoughts and intentions of the heart, and "all are naked and exposed to the eyes of him to whom we must give account" (Heb. 4:13). Quite a discomforting realization to those who have something to hide! No sinner likes to be exposed.

It has been this way ever since Adam and Eve "hid themselves from the presence of the LORD God among the trees of the garden" (Gen. 3:8). "Where are you?" God asked—the first question in the Bible (v. 9). No wonder they were afraid.

The lame excuse they gave for not wanting to be seen betrays their underlying sense of guilt. That their sin would escape the knowledge of an all-knowing God is ridiculous, of course. But their attempt to hide from truth about themselves still characterizes sinners. You will see it expressed in the multitudinous ways people today try to stay away from the church and biblical teaching.

Rather than avoiding these gracious means for conviction of truth, which is always for our good, we should earnestly seek to learn where we fall short. In this desire, we need to continually pray: "Search me, O God, and know my heart! Try me and know my thoughts! And see if there be any grievous way in me, and lead me in the way everlasting" (Ps. 139:23–24).

### 3. Repentance begins conversion.

Conversion can be thought of as the beginning of a journey, turning from sin and turning to Christ. To use the analogy of Jesus, it is leaving the broad way of the world and entering the narrow gate of eternal life (Matt. 7:13–14). The turning is definite. Though the precise time and place of the change may not always be identified, the new direction is certain.

It is this clear sense of forsaking all known sin that characterizes repentance. However incomplete one's understanding may be, there is no desire to go on living in rebellion against God. Repentance is a fresh start.

When the Spirit brings new conviction in the process of sanctification, the penitent should quickly respond, own up to the truth in confession, make any amends necessary, and move on with Christ. Where there is this ongoing walking in the light God gives, no follower of Christ ever needs to go to bed at night with a guilty conscience (Rom. 8:1–2; 1 John 1:7).

Let it be clear, however, that repentance is not meritorious. In fact, it renounces all human merit. Though repentance is necessary, trusting in Christ alone brings salvation. And faith, like repentance, if genuine, should continue throughout life. If this biblical truth were practiced, a spirit of revival would always flow through our churches.

### 4. Saving faith is resting in the arms of Jesus.

Jesus held a little child in his arms to characterize one who turns and believes on him (Matt. 18:3; cf. 19:14). What a beautiful illustration of uncomplicated trust!

I remember so well seeing this displayed in my two young daughters when I would come home after a day's work. As soon as they saw me coming down the street, they would throw down their tricycles and, running and squealing with joy, they would jump up into my waiting arms. There was no fidgeting; they had no thought of my dropping them, no anxiety at all, but with absolute trust they just relaxed in my love, resting in my arms. Saving faith is like that when we come to Jesus.

John G. Patton, missionary to the New Hebrides, when translating the Gospel of John into the native language, could not locate a word for "believe," so instead he used a term meaning "resting one's whole weight upon." Perfect! That is what faith is—turning loose every other support of life and resting our whole being on the person of Jesus Christ.[21] Try inserting this description for "believes" in John 3:16.

### 5. Faith brings spiritual reality into personal experience.

The unseen reality of the Spirit is always present but it becomes visible to the heart of faith (Heb. 11:1). In this sense, faith delivers one from the illusion that only the material universe is real and opens the door to the eternal world that shall never pass away. The presence of the living Christ by faith can become more real than breathing.

This actualizing of the promise of salvation is not dependent on dogma or the scientific method for proof. God's Word is the evidence. The old Gospel song says it well: "Standing on the promises that cannot fail . . . by the living word of God I shall prevail."[22] Faith takes God's Word as a promise of fulfillment.

Paul cites Abraham's faith as an example. While Sarah was barren, God told Abraham that he would have a son, though all empirical reason seemed to indicate the contrary. Yet the old patriarch did not stagger at the promise of God, "being fully persuaded" that God would do what he said (Rom. 4:21 NIV). To use an unforgettable sermon of H. C. Morrison as an illustration, when Abraham received the promise, he went out immediately and bought a baby buggy.[23]

However, every dimension of reality that can be known is consistent with faith. Reason tries to make sense out of the historical experience of mankind as a whole, but it recognizes that there is always more undiscovered truth. By careful observation, too, reason helps us see the untrustworthiness of our human gods and prods an honest person to seek something more. Usually faith is born out of this struggle. Reason can point to the necessity of a Savior, but it takes faith to experience the reality.

### 6. Faith is faithful.

God calls us to live by faith. It is a life he wants, a life that he can transform and work through to show his glory, just as he did with Abraham. Abraham obeyed the call to "go out" with God: "By faith he went to live in the land of promise" (Heb. 11:8–9).

Living what we believe will be manifest in our deeds. The call of Christ is to follow him, which means to keep going wherever he leads and to do whatever he asks. Once committed, an obedient disciple has no desire to turn back (e.g., Luke 9:62). It is faith all the way "from faith to faith, as it is written, 'The righteous shall live by faith'" (Rom. 1:17; cf. Heb. 4:2).

From this unswerving trust in Christ comes the strength to live a godly life and to bring forth works of righteousness. For we are his workmanship, "created . . . for good works . . . that we should walk in them" (Eph. 2:10). "Faith by itself," James tells us, "if it does not have works is dead" (James 2:17, 26)—it is as useless as no faith at all.

Yet there is no notion that these works of faith earn merit. If valid, they are motivated by the love of Christ implanted in the heart by the Holy Spirit and simply express our gratitude to God for his unspeakable gift.

### 7. Faith appropriates the resources of divine omnipotence.

Grace flows out of the goodness of God but it also issues from his sovereign power. And as Jesus often reminded his fainthearted disciples, "nothing is impossible" for God (Matt. 17:20; 19:26; Mark 10:27; Luke 1:37; 18:27).

Trying to grasp the dimensions of this reality staggers our imagination. We are dealing here with the power that rolled out the heavens and set the stars in place. This is the force at work in redemption. Only our lack of faith will curtail what God can do. When put in the context of new creation in Christ, we dare not ever use the word *impossible*.

A Scotsman clinging to a piece of floating debris in the freezing waters of the Atlantic after the sinking of the *Titanic* heard a voice cry out, "Believe on the Lord Jesus Christ, and thou shalt be saved." The message came from John Harper, also a passenger on the ship who had sought refuge on a piece of wreckage. As the waves washed over both men, the reply came back, "No, I am not saved." So again, Harper shouted the promise, "Believe on the Lord Jesus Christ and thou shalt be saved," before losing his grip on the wood and sinking into the sea. The other man was rescued and later said, "There alone in the night with two miles of water under me, I trusted Christ as my Savior."[24]

We do not know all that went through the mind of that lost soul when he heard the Gospel—how complete was his understanding, how conviction had been working in his life—but whatever the circumstances we know that it was believing on Christ that day that brought salvation. It may seem too simple, too miraculous, but that is the Gospel.

### 8. Repentance and faith meet at Calvary.

The ultimate choice every person must make is climaxed at the cross. There we see in the bleeding Savior the consequences of our sin and, at the same time, behold the revelation of God's grace. Facing this reality we must make a decision.

This comes into bold relief in the response of the two criminals crucified on either side of the Savior (Matt. 27:38; Mark 15:27; Luke 23:32–43).[25] Possibly, until this day, neither had ever seen Jesus. Their impression of him was largely formed by his manner at that time. We might think they would show sympathy, since they were under the same sentence. However, in their case, death was a just penalty for their deeds.

One of the outlaws, railing in his bitterness, asked Jesus, "Are you not the Christ?" He had heard this said in the mocking of the people standing around. So he raised the question himself and then ordered, "Save yourself and us!"

If what they said about Christ were true, the felon demanded that Jesus do what was expected by the world. He did not affirm any faith in Jesus, nor did he show any remorse for his sin. His only thought was for his own physical deliverance. Even for this he cast complete responsibility on God. After all, he reasoned, if Jesus is powerful and loving, let him stop all this agony. And in his proud impenitence, like a wounded animal, he gritted his teeth and bore his anguish alone.

As time passed, though, something began to happen in the heart of the other criminal. Sensing the tragedy of what was taking place, he took the side of Jesus and defended him against the taunts of his fellow outlaw. "Do you not fear God, since you are under the same sentence of condemnation? . . . We are receiving the due reward of our deeds; but this man has done nothing wrong." Then with a broken and contrite spirit, he said, "Jesus, remember me when you come into your kingdom" (Luke 23:39–42).

The dying man did not request deliverance from the sentence of death, which he recognized as just. Nor did he have any idea that his Lord would escape death, innocent of sin though he is. He knew they would all die. There is honest realism here. But he believed that Jesus had a kingdom beyond the grave. Though it was unexplained, veiled in mystery, he knew that there was going to be a resurrection. And in that spiritual anticipation, he asked to be remembered by the King in his coming glory.

Jesus did not reply to the thief who rejected him, which would have added to his suffering further condemnation. He had not come to condemn the world but to save it. The embittered man was left with his own decision. But to the repentant thief who turned to the Savior in faith, there was given the assurance that on that very day they would go to Paradise together.

What a contrast in the attitudes of the two men! In the beginning they shared the same hostility to Jesus but, as they watched him suffer, their responses were completely different.

In some way, one or the other of those two criminals speaks for us all. In the beginning, we are the same—all guilty, all under the judgment of death, all brought to confront Christ on the cross, and all having to make a decision. It is our response, like theirs, that makes all the difference. We must repent and believe the Gospel (Mark 1:15).

# 12.

# The New Life

More than the creation of the cosmos, the remaking of a fallen human being into the image of Christ displays the magnificence of God's grace and power as nothing else. In the ages to come the redeemed will never cease to marvel.

When faith lays hold of saving grace, something wonderful happens. The convert receives pardon from all past sin, release from death into eternal life, and is accepted into the family of God. It is a spiritual miracle. This transformation can be summed up in three basic concepts: justification, regeneration, and adoption.

## Justification

The doctrine of justification, or as it is affirmed in the Reformation motif, *sola fide* (justification by faith alone), lies at the heart of the Christian Gospel.

### Sovereign Act of Pardon

Normally the words *justify* and *justification* have a forensic reference, closely related to the idea of trial and judgment. That is, one is justified when the demands of the law have been fully satisfied. However, the word may be understood in different ways.

In one sense the word *justified* may describe someone who is just on his own merits and against whom no accusation can be made (e.g., Rom. 2:13). Or it may designate one who is charged with a crime but, after the trial, is found innocent (e.g., Deut. 25:1). But how could this apply to us? No one is inherently righteous. We have all turned to our own way, transgressing the moral requirements of the law. Individually and collectively mankind has come under the just condemnation of sin and death. Obviously from any standpoint of merit or innocence, we cannot be justified before God.

Only in the Gospel sense of pardon can this term apply to sinners. Simply by his own sovereign will, God forgives our sin for the sake of his Son who died in our place. In this figure, Jesus is seen as the one altogether lovely, taking on himself the judgment of a fallen race.

The law's penalty is not circumvented; rather it is upheld, for Christ has paid the debt we owed. As our representative, he assumed our legal liability when he suffered the consequences of our sin. The Father "made him to be sin who knew no sin, so that in him we might become the righteousness of God" (2 Cor. 5:21; cf. Rom. 5:18; Gal. 3:13).

### Accounted Righteous by Faith

*Imputation* or *reckoning* are terms used to describe the way Christ's merit and character are ascribed to the repentant sinner. The words mean that the righteousness by which we are justified is not our own; it is his and is accounted to the believers entirely by God's Word of grace. One might say, justification is God's response to our "faith in Jesus" (Rom. 3:26). Abraham's belief when God promised him a son is the classic illustration: "His faith was 'counted to him as righteousness'" (Rom. 4:22; cf. 4:3, 9). But it was not "for his sake alone, but for ours also. It will be counted to us who believe in him who raised from the dead Jesus our Lord . . . for our justification" (vv. 23–25; cf. Gen. 15:6; Gal. 3:16; James 2:23).

Let it be clear, however, that while faith is the medium through which we have access to God, it has no personal merit. Faith comes as a gift of God "so that no one may boast" (Eph. 2:9).

For this same reason, good works have nothing to do initially with salvation, though works should follow saving faith. Jesus said, "Not everyone who says to me, 'Lord, Lord,' will enter the kingdom of heaven, but the one who does the will of my Father who is in heaven" (Matt. 7:21; cf. Luke 9:62). Paul tells the Philippian saints: "Continue to work out your salvation with fear and trembling," while reminding them that it is God who works in them "to act according to his good purpose" (Phil. 2:12–13 NIV).[1]

### The New Relationship

Identification with the perfected work of Christ establishes for the believer a completely new relationship with God. Both our relation to him and his attitude toward us is changed through the cross. God's nature is not changed;

he is forever the same. But the way he looks at us is different—he sees us as we are in Christ (Rom. 3:24–26; 1 Cor. 1:30).

Thus the justified person stands before God free of all sin. Sins of the past are canceled by the forbearance of divine grace. "There is therefore now no condemnation for those who are in Christ Jesus" (Rom. 8:1). No charge of sin can be brought against them (v. 33). For through Christ "everyone who believes is freed from everything from which you could not be freed by the law of Moses" (Acts 13:39).

As a result, "justified by faith, we have peace with God through our Lord Jesus Christ," who gives us access "into this grace in which we stand, and we rejoice in hope of the glory of God" (Rom. 5:1–2; cf. Rom. 8:30; Titus 3:7).

### Living Justified

The justifying act of God, instantaneous upon faith in Christ, introduces one into a state of righteousness. Justification is not a long, drawn-out process whereby the believer becomes increasingly free from sin through gradual infusion of divine grace; rather the justified person, by present and continuing faith in the completed work of Christ, lives all the time accepted by God. But something else happens, distinct from justification.

## Regeneration

The outward declaration of God, absolving the believer from the penal evils of sin and establishing a right relationship with God, is accompanied by an inward renovation of the fallen human nature. There begins a change in moral character. Put another way, justification relates to what God does *for* us; regeneration refers to what God does *in* us through the re-creative power of the Holy Spirit.

### Participating in the Divine Nature

The "precious and very great promises," now activated by faith, come alive, "so that through them you may become partakers of the divine nature" (2 Pet. 1:4; cf. Heb. 12:10). Much about this transformation remains a mystery, but it is clear that "the Father of lights" through "the word of truth" brings forth "a kind of firstfruits" of the life to come (James 1:18). The God who loved us, even when we were dead in our trespasses, has "made us alive together with Christ" (Eph. 2:5; cf. Col. 2:13).[2]

Jesus describes this new life to the Pharisee Nicodemus as being "born again" (John 3:3, 7). "That which is born of the flesh is flesh, and that which is born of the Spirit is spirit" (v. 6). He is not talking about moral improvement, but a totally new quality of life wrought by the Holy Spirit. Just as a person is born into the physical world through natural birth, there must be an equally definite beginning of the spiritual life. So picking up on this analogy, John says, "Everyone who believes that Jesus is the Christ has been born of God" (1 John 5:1). Or to use Peter's words to the church, "You have been born again, not of perishable seed but of imperishable, through the living and abiding word of God" (1 Pet. 1:23).

### A New Creation

Beginning anew in Christ, "you have put off the old self with its practices and have put on the new self, which is being renewed in knowledge after the image of its creator" (Col. 3:9–10). As God intended in the beginning, this new self is "created after the likeness of God in true righteousness and holiness" (Eph. 4:24). It is like starting all over again, with new motivation and resolve to fulfill your destiny. This does not mean that God destroyed your personhood and ability or that your human nature is absorbed into the divine. Rather he takes your natural powers and, by his Spirit, bends them to their true created purpose.

### Indwelt by Christ's Spirit

The Spirit's creative work brings forth Christlikeness (Eph. 2:10). You begin to live and move and have your being in him. Illustrating this relationship, Jesus said, "I am the vine; you are the branches. Whoever abides in me and I in him, he it is that bears much fruit, for apart from me you can do nothing" (John 15:5). Emphasizing how central this truth is to the Gospel, the New Testament speaks of the believer being "in Christ" 146 times.[3] So real is this mystical union that Paul could say, "It is no longer I who live, but Christ who lives in me" (Gal. 2:20). Life is permeated by the indwelling Spirit of the Son of God.

This Christlikeness can be seen in three personal dimensions. The upward expression is manifest in worship (e.g., John 17:4; cf. 13:31). An obsession to magnify the Lord becomes the end of your aspirations—the controlling purpose of life. "So, whether you eat or drink, or whatever you do," you want to "do all to the glory of God" (1 Cor. 10:31).

Internally the characteristics of Christ's character start to flow through your life. They are called "fruit of the Spirit"—"love, joy, peace, patience, kindness, goodness, faithfulness, gentleness, self-control" (Gal. 5:22–23; cf. Rom. 7:4; 8:5; Eph. 5:9; Col. 3:12–17). Renewed by the Spirit, the soul embraces and delights in the holiness of God. Increasingly the mind, the emotions, and the will act in conformity to the divine will. Obedience becomes a joy. Spiritual perceptions are heightened, and a whole new system of values begins to fall into place.

There is also an outward evidence of Christlikeness. A concern for people who do not know the Savior emerges, resulting in evangelism and world missions (Acts

8:4). Likewise, love overflows within the church, energizing the desire to "bear one another's burdens, and so fulfill the law of Christ" (Gal. 6:2). The new sense of belonging to God and to each other brings out another aspect of salvation.

## Adoption

Declared righteous by virtue of faith in Christ, and made spiritually new, the believer at the same time becomes a member of the King of heaven's family. Though distinct from justification and regeneration, adoption here refers to a restored relationship with the Father and the privileges of divine sonship.[4]

### Children of God

All who have "received" Christ, "who believed in his name, he gave the right to become children of God, who were born, not of blood nor of the will of the flesh nor of the will of man, but of God" (John 1:12–13). "See what kind of love the Father has given to us, that we should be called children of God; and so we are" (1 John 3:1). "For in Christ Jesus you are all sons of God, through faith" (Gal. 3:26). "God sent forth his Son, born of woman, born under the law, to redeem those who were under the law, so that we might receive adoption as sons" (Gal. 4:4–5). "I will be a father to you," God says, "and you shall be sons and daughters to me" (2 Cor. 6:18).[5]

Because we are sons, completing the operation of the Holy Trinity, "God has sent the Spirit of his Son into our hearts, crying, 'Abba! Father!'" (Gal. 4:6; cf. Rom. 8:15). To address God in this manner underscores the endearing relationship of father and son. *Abba* is a term expressing an affectionate filial relationship and might be translated "daddy."

What a beautiful way to think of God! He is not some distant power, some impersonal cosmic force. He is our "Father in heaven" (Matt. 6:9).[6] He knows all about us. He understands us better than we do ourselves. He cares for us with parental love and delights to give good things to his children (Matt. 7:11).

### Incorporated into God's Family

Being a child of God, we are related to all the other family members. Universal in scope, all persons—past, present, and future—who put their faith in Christ, share this spiritual birthright. We bow our "knees before the Father, from whom every family in heaven and on earth is named" (Eph. 3:14–15).

### Receiving the Son's Inheritance

As children, you become "heirs—heirs of God and fellow heirs with Christ" (Rom. 8:17; cf. Gal. 4:6). Though adopted, the Father gives you the same inheritance rights as his own son. Think of it! "All things are yours," for "you are Christ's, and Christ is God's" (1 Cor. 3:21–23).

Incredible! Yet it is "your Father's good pleasure to give you the kingdom" (Luke 12:32). Being "born again," you have come into a living hope "to an inheritance that is imperishable, undefiled, and unfading, kept in heaven for you" (2 Cor. 4:17; 1 Pet. 1:3–4).

### The Father's Likeness

Perhaps most blessed about this relationship, children grow up, and in maturing, unless hindered, reflect the character of their Father. His holiness, his love, his goodness, and every other aspect of his moral nature begin to show through members of his family. Though still far from the goal to which we aspire, and the example of Christ set before us, we dare not disregard our responsibility to live as "children of God without blemish," and to "shine as lights in the world" (Phil. 2:15; cf. Matt. 5:16).

## Doctrinal Distinctives

It's not surprising that church theologians interpret differently the way one receives this new life in Christ. Among those who take seriously the great creeds of Christendom, the issue is not primarily about the divine initiative in saving grace, but how faith makes one righteous.

### Traditional Roman Catholic Teaching

Roman Catholic doctrine asserts that salvation is by grace alone through faith, and faith works itself out through deeds of love. Justification begins with the infusion of supernatural grace at baptism, which has the effect of nullifying inherent sin. Catholics allow no human merit initially in receiving salvation.

The difference with Protestantism comes in the way justification is understood. The Roman church teaches that the baptized Christian is progressively made righteous as faith finds expression in freely chosen actions proceeding from God's grace.[7] Good works do not justify, but when one comes to Christ by faith, meritorious works are made possible and receive a reward by increasing the response of the Christian to the grace of God.

Thus, from this perspective, justification is not viewed as a completed work upon faith in Christ but rather an ongoing process through life. The believer gradually becomes more justified in proportion to his or her merit and obedience to God. So it might be said that one is saved by faith but justified by works. The teaching and sacraments of the church become very important in cultivating holiness. As to justification, according to the Council of Trent, it is "sanctifying and renewing of the inner man."[8] In practice, then, justification and ongoing sanctification go together. One becomes more righteous through growth in sainthood.

### Protestant Thought

While agreeing with the Roman Catholics that the initial act of salvation comes by grace alone through faith, traditionally Protestants do not see faith contingent on something else. We are saved by faith alone in Christ alone. By this it is meant that nothing can be added to faith to make ourselves more acceptable to God. Generally Protestants see a clear distinction between justification and sanctification, contending that the act of making one righteous is complete. At the moment of true repentance and faith, wherever one may be in progress toward sainthood, the person stands before God free from the guilt of sin.

However, there is an interesting difference between Reformed and Arminian theologians concerning the origin of saving grace. Calvinists, following their view of eternal degrees, hold that the soul is "passive with respect to that act of the Holy Spirit whereby it is regenerated."[9] Because human beings are so totally corrupt, it is believed, only after the heart is awakened by God's exertion of creation power can the person exercise saving faith (Ezek. 36:26–27; John 6:44–45; 1 Cor. 2:14; 3:11). According to this position, a form of regeneration precedes justification, though in point of fact it may be concomitant. This perspective stresses that the empowering call comes apart from human initiative but it may also allow room for carelessness on the part of those who are not inclined to repent and believe the Gospel.

Calvinism emphasizes that the righteousness of Christ is imputed to the believer, who now appears before God with the identity of the Savior (Rom. 3:21–22; 1 Cor. 1:30; Phil. 3:9). It is not that faith has virtue because of some inherent goodness, but that it is the means by which one can rest entirely on the merit of the Lord.[10]

Contrasted to this thinking, Arminians hold that it is faith that is imputed for righteousness (Rom. 3:24–25; 4:3, 22, 24; 10:4). Such faith has no personal merit; rather it is the divine gift of prevenient grace. Since grace is entirely initiated by God, the difference with Reformed theology at this point is not human inability to believe, but rather the ability of everyone by grace to have saving faith.

As to works of righteousness, whether Reformed or Arminian, we must not minimize the obligation to keep God's moral law. "Faith by itself, if it does not have works, is dead" (James 2:17; cf. Matt. 25:34–46; Gal. 5:6). Even those, like Luther, who had a hard time with this passage, still contend for faith expressing itself in obedience to the Word of God.[11] That we live entirely by grace in no way implies liberty to sin. Something is wrong with any concept of justification that does not result in holiness.

## Common Problems

Misunderstanding of the transformed life in Christ takes many forms. These wrong conceptions, though sincere, are no less harmful.

### Counterfeiting Its Nature

One perversion, widely accepted, relegates Christianity to human sophistication—a well-integrated personality. Respectability, social maturity, raising a nice family, having a multitude of friends, community leadership, and a host of other noble characteristics are certainly commendable, but these qualities are no evidence of spiritual rebirth.

Covering over an inner rebellion, unbelievers often adopt some kind of moralism to hide the true state of their heart. A person may claim to live by the Golden Rule yet harbor hatred toward God. In fact, by subtly soothing a guilty conscience, ethical pride can actually be a deeper form of self-deception than outright vice. Tragically, such duplicity may be concealed in religious piety. We have only to think of the hypocritical Pharisees to recognize the danger (e.g., Matt. 3:7–8; Luke 8:9–14).

Equally misleading can be public identity with the Christian faith. One can assent to the truth of the Gospel without believing it. Such pretense is the more beguiling when clothed in academic regalia. I can only imagine how many young people have been adversely influenced by teachers in religious institutions who do not live the message they profess.

By way of caution, however, persons who know whom they believe must recognize that others can experience regeneration in a different way. Authentic relationship in Christ is not dependent on any prescribed manifestation attended by signs. Demonstrative wonders may accompany conversion but they should not be confused with the reality. Most Christians experience membership in the family of God much like we do in our homes. There is a quiet confidence in the Father's embrace, reciprocal love, and trust giving to the soul a beautiful sense of peace.

### False Ways of Attainment

How one enters the kingdom also can be mistaken. Circumventing the supernatural work of the Holy Spirit, many people with a naturalistic perspective believe the transformation results from human ingenuity. Education especially is the big thing—understanding ourselves and our place in the world. Social progress also plays a part—better housing, good health care, improved working conditions, and financial security. All these factors are beneficial, of course, but can never regenerate the soul.

Others with a religious orientation emphasize participation in church rituals and sacraments. Unquestionably these duties assist godly development and, when entered into by faith, become means of grace, but their observance is only as life changing as the spiritual reality that they represent.

Taking the misunderstanding even further, some devout persons seek re-creation in Christ through self-denial—subduing the flesh, refusing any physical comfort, afflicting punishment on the body. Such practices imply the false idea that the body is evil, and though well intended, reflect a cruel form of trying to earn God's favor through human effort.

### Uncertain Completion

Another problem can arise regarding the time when justification takes place. Persons who fuse the act of God declaring a believer righteous with the continuing work of the Holy Spirit making one holy may hesitate to see themselves fully justified, until the process of sanctification is complete. This can tend to forestall present assurance of salvation, and even obscure the prior necessity of full repentance and faith by which one receives the new birth.

On the other hand, persons are misled who do not recognize that the act of justification enrolls the believer in the school of sanctification. Failure to see this ongoing work of the Holy Spirit stymies Christian growth in character transformation as well as good works, and if not corrected, can lead to antinomianism. Both dangers should be avoided.

## Summary Applications

*1. The new birth is the highest privilege of mankind.*

No greater miracle can happen to a human being. It is like starting all over again, a "new creation" (2 Cor. 5:17). The old physical creation of the world will someday pass away, but the new spiritual creation does not end. Life takes on a reinvigorated quality, which will unfold throughout eternity. No achievement in this world can be compared to it.

Illustrative of the Christian's new sense of values, Malcolm Muggeridge, the famous British news correspondent, playwright, and novelist, after his conversion, wrote:

> I may, I suppose, regard myself or pass for being a relatively successful man. People occasionally stare at me in the streets. That's fame. I can fairly easily earn enough to qualify for admission to the higher slopes of the Internal Revenue—that's success. Furnished with money and a little fame, even the elderly may partake of trendy diversions—that's pleasure. It might happen once in a while that something I said or wrote was sufficiently heeded for me to persuade myself that it represented a serious impact on our time—that's fulfillment. Yet I say to you—and beg you to believe me—multiply these tiny triumphs by a

million, put all of them together, and they are nothing—less than nothing, a positive impediment—measured against the draught of that living water Christ offers to the spiritually thirsty, irrespective of who or what they are.[12]

### 2. Like any miracle, this new life cannot be fully explained.

"How great . . . are the riches of the glory of this mystery, which is Christ in you" (Col. 1:27). One does not have to understand what is hidden in order to know the reality. Jesus used the analogy of the wind to illustrate the phenomenon. "The wind blows where it wishes, and you hear its sound, but you do not know where it comes from or where it goes. So it is with everyone who is born of the Spirit" (John 3:8).

Since the reality is variously experienced, let us avoid trying to impose a preconceived pattern on someone else. God suits the regenerating Spirit's ministry to the uniqueness of each person. One's personality, family, education, environment, culture, and many other factors preclude the sameness of spiritual expression.

### 3. Yet the beginning of the new life is decisive.

There is a process by which the Spirit of God draws one to Christ and there is the development in the Christian life after the new birth, but there is a time when the person passes from death unto life (John 5:24). Whether the precise moment can be identified or not, it happens. Not being able to identify the exact time of conversion does not nullify the definiteness. The reality is all that matters.

### 4. One comes to Christ with childlike humility.

Holding a young child, Jesus said, "Unless you turn and become like children, you will never enter the kingdom of heaven" (Matt. 18:3). Further elaborating, he said, "Whoever humbles himself like this child is the greatest in the kingdom" (v. 4; cf. Mark 10:15; Luke 18:17; 1 Pet. 2:2).

The characteristic particularly noted here is humility, a quality of spirit free from pride and arrogance. A baby expresses complete submission to the person in whose arms he rests. The child is utterly dependent on others for sustenance of life, though he has done nothing to deserve such loving care. In his helplessness, all he can do is trust that someone will meet his need. What a beautiful example, also, of the way a grown-up, in the realm of the Spirit, exercises faith to receive the grace of God.

Unfortunately, in the natural world, an attitude of hostility soon develops as a child grows, and the latent selfishness of inbred sin becomes apparent. An "age of accountability" comes as the child reaches adulthood and the meaning of personal responsibility for sin is understood. At this point the adult through humility in repentance and faith must turn to Christ and receive the gift of salvation. Fortunate is the person who travels this road early, before the debilitating effects of sin accumulate to fill life with regret. For the one who thinks himself self-sufficient, to reverse course gets more difficult with time. It is a humbling thing for an adult to become like a child and admit the need for a Savior, but there is no other way to enter the kingdom.

This childlike attribute remains with the children of God through this life and into eternity. How else could we continue to learn and grow in the grace and knowledge of the Lord (Matt. 11:25; cf. 1 Cor. 1:26–27)?

### 5. Regeneration authenticates Christian ministry.

Exhibit number one to the power of the Gospel to save is the transformed life of the minister. Dr. Charles Berry, an eminent English preacher, has told how he had to struggle in coming to a personal experience of Christ.[13] When he began his ministry, he said, like many other persons with humanistic training, he looked on Jesus more as a great moral teacher than a divine Savior; he saw Christianity essentially as living a good life.

During his first pastorate, late one night, a poorly dressed Lancashire girl came to him in his study. "Are you a minister?" she asked. Getting an affirmative answer, she went on anxiously, "You must come with me quickly. I want you to get my mother in."

Imagining that it was a case of some drunken woman out on the street, Berry said, "Why? Go get a policeman."

"Oh, no," said the girl, "my mother is dying, and you must come with me and get her in—to heaven."

Not wanting to turn her away, the young minister dressed and followed her through the lonely streets on a journey of more than a mile. Led finally into the woman's room, he knelt down beside her bed and began to describe the kindness of Jesus, explaining that he had come to show us how to live unselfishly. Suddenly the desperate woman cut him off. "Mister," she said, "that's no use for the likes of me. I'm a sinner. I've lived my life. Can't you tell me of someone who can have mercy on me and save my poor soul?"

"I stood there," said Dr. Berry, "in the presence of that dying woman, and I had nothing to tell her. In order to bring something to that dear woman, I leapt back to my mother's knee, to my cradle faith, and told her of the Christ who was able to save."

Tears began running over the cheeks of the eager woman. "Now you are getting at it," she said. "Now you are helping me."

And the famed preacher, concluding the story, said, "I want you to know that I got her in, and praise be to God, I got in myself."

Isn't that wonderful? A repentant young preacher and a dying old woman going into the kingdom together. And the way they went in is the same for us all. Until we make this journey to the cross, any work we do for Christ becomes artificial and unconvincing.

*6. Receiving Christ changes the believer's focus.*

When you commit yourself to Christ, he gives identity to your experience. "United with him" (Rom. 6:5), the significance of his life gives meaning to yours. In fact the union is so complete that you are called by his name—"Christian" (Acts 11:26; 26:28; 1 Pet. 4:16).

It can be likened to what happens at a marriage when the bride takes the name of her husband. Her highest joy and fulfillment is found in him. Have you noticed the bride's countenance when she comes down the aisle at the wedding? Of course, everyone turns to behold her beauty. But the bride's gaze is fixed on her husband, who is waiting to receive her to himself.

So it is with you, coming to Christ. Others will look at you and, hopefully, notice the changes in your life. And that is good. But you—oh, you are not looking at them—you are absorbed only in the wonder of your Lord and the glory of his love.

That is the focus of a life in Christ. It is all about him. So keep your eyes focused on Jesus. He is your reason to rejoice, the fulfillment of all you want to become. Martin Luther expressed it well: "Seek yourself only in Christ and not in yourself; then you will find yourself in him eternally."[14]

*7. Life in Christ is always growing.*

Coming to Christ is only the beginning. God never forecloses on his grace (1 Pet. 3:18). Whatever you have experienced this far, there is more ahead. The way goes through many trials and disappointments; sometimes the sufferings will seem overwhelming. But God "is able to keep you from stumbling and to present you blameless before the presence of his glory with great joy" (Jude 24). "He who began a good work in you will bring it to completion at the day of Jesus Christ" (Phil. 1:6).

Even in heaven I expect there will be no end to growth in the Christian life. God wants us "to comprehend with all the saints what is the breadth and length and height and depth, and to know the love of Christ that surpasses knowledge" (Eph. 3:18–19).

*8. Everything that Christ has given the believer is already your possession by promise.*

Live in this realization. Consider just some of the benefits that are yours now. You are united with the Holy Trinity, "in God the Father, and the Lord Jesus Christ" (1 Thess. 1:1); and "he who is joined to the Lord becomes one spirit with him" (1 Cor. 6:17) "if in fact the Spirit of God dwells in you" (Rom. 8:9).

You are foreknown and predestined by God, "for those whom he foreknew he also predestined to be conformed to the image of his Son" (v. 29; cf. Eph. 1:5, 11).

You are "God's elect" (Rom. 8:33; 1 Pet. 1:1); his "chosen ones, holy and beloved" (Col. 3:12); "rejected by men but in the sight of God chosen and precious" (1 Pet. 2:4); "a chosen race, a royal priesthood, a holy nation, a people for his own possession" (v. 9).

You are "called to the one hope that belongs to your call" (Eph. 4:4); "called to freedom" (Gal. 5:13); "called according to his purpose" (Rom. 8:28); and "those whom he called he also justified, and those whom he justified he also glorified" (v. 30).

You are "reconciled to God" (Rom. 5:10). Though once "alienated and hostile in mind, doing evil deeds, he has now reconciled in his body of flesh by his death, in order to present you holy and blameless and above reproach before him" (Col. 1:21–22). "All this is from God, who through Christ reconciled us to himself" (2 Cor. 5:18).

You "have access in one Spirit to the Father" (Eph. 2:18), having "obtained access by faith" (Rom. 5:2), and can "with confidence draw near to the throne of grace" (Heb. 4:16; cf. 10:19–20).

You are "saved" (Titus 3:5), "forgiven . . . all [your] trespasses" (Col. 2:13). "And you are clean" (John 13:10), "cleansed" (Eph. 5:26), "washed . . . in the blood of the Lamb" (Rev. 7:14). Christ is made your "wisdom . . . righteousness . . . sanctification and redemption" (1 Cor. 1:30). Indeed, he "has perfected for all time those who are being sanctified" (Heb. 10:14).

You are "delivered . . . from the domain of darkness and transferred . . . to the kingdom of [God's] beloved Son" (Col. 1:13). "Therefore," there is "no condemnation" (Rom. 8:1); you are set "free in Christ Jesus from the law of sin and death" (v. 2).

You are one of "God's children" (1 John 3:2), "and if children, then heirs— heirs of God and fellow heirs with Christ" (Rom. 8:17), qualified "to share in the inheritance of the saints in light" (Col. 1:12; cf. 1 Thess. 5:5); "an inheritance that is imperishable, undefiled, and unfading, kept in heaven for you" (1 Pet. 1:4; cf. Eph. 1:14). In fact your name is already "written in heaven" (Luke 10:20), where you have "citizenship" (Phil. 3:20), with all "the saints and members of the household of God" (Eph. 2:19).

And there is much more—much more salvation (Rom. 5:9–10; Phil. 2:12); much more of "the riches of his glorious inheritance in the saints, and what is the immeasurable greatness of his power toward us who believe" (Eph. 1:18–19). The half has not been told (John 21:25). "No eye has seen, nor ear heard, nor the heart of man imagined, what God has prepared for those who love him" (1 Cor. 2:9).

Summing it up in one sweeping statement, God "has blessed [you] in Christ with every spiritual blessing in the heavenly places, even as he chose [you] in him before the foundation of the world" (Eph. 1:3–4). What more can be said, for "all things are yours . . . and you are Christ's, and Christ is God's" (1 Cor. 3:21–23).

Does not just the thought bring a smile to your face? Think of your new situation this way, as imagined by Raymond Ortlund: A homeless person who lives on the street in a cardboard box receives a message that his long-forgotten uncle has died and has left him a million dollars in his will. The check is on the way. As the man stands there in his ragged clothes, a smile spreads over his face. He realizes that everything about his life has changed. He looks around at his old, dirty, dilapidated shelter and thinks, *I can live in this old box a few more days. No big deal, I'm a millionaire. The check is on the way.*[15]

In an infinitely greater way this is how a redeemed sinner feels after receiving the gift of salvation. Whatever our circumstances, we have received all the riches of Christ. The benefits of that bequest are transforming our lives, and the wonder of it grows sweeter every day. Oh that we could communicate the beauty of this life to a lost world. That is the challenge of evangelism.

# 13

## Sanctification

Off the coast of Scotland lies a little island where Christianity first took root in the nation. To accommodate the many tourists who want to make the trip across the bay to visit the historic site, there is a rental shop on the mainland where transportation can be obtained. Over the door of the small building, emblazoned in bold letters, is the signboard: "Visit the Holy Isle Where the Saints Have Trod." Then, more to the point, underneath are the words, "We Can Take You."[1]

In a much more profound sense, those last words express what the church is about—taking people where the saints have trod. In practical terms, this means bringing men and women into the ever-expanding reaches of sainthood. Personal holiness lies at the heart of God's strategy of world evangelization.

### Holiness to the Lord

#### A Holy People

It has been said, "Show me your gods, and I will show you your people." It is true. If, for example, people worshiped a warlike god like Jupiter, as did the Romans, we would expect them to live brutal lives. That was the kind of god they worshiped.

Or if people worshiped a god of sensual indulgence, as did many of the Ephesians who worshiped the goddess Diana, we would expect the people to live sexually immoral lives. That was the kind of god they worshiped. People never rise above their god.

But the God we worship, the God and Father of our Lord Jesus Christ, is holy. The word means "separate from anything unclean or evil." Holiness is his essential nature. So it follows that because he is holy, he expects his people to live holy lives. "You shall be holy, for I am holy" (1 Pet. 1:16; cf. Lev. 11:44). A loving Father always wants the best for his children. This was in the mind of God "before the foundation of the world" when he chose us in Christ "that we should be holy and blameless before him" (Eph. 1:4).

To this end in the fullness of time Christ "appeared to take away sins" (1 John 3:5), "to redeem us from all lawlessness and to purify for himself a people for his own possession" (Titus 2:14; cf. John 8:34–36).

All through the Bible, the call is to holiness, and "whoever disregards this, disregards not man but God, who gives his Holy Spirit" (1 Thess. 4:8).

By this same Spirit, God is preparing for his people a "holy city" (Rev. 21:2), where "nothing unclean will ever enter it" (v. 27). And when the day of Christ's appearing comes, "everyone who thus hopes in him purifies himself as he is pure" (1 John 3:3).

### Sainthood

It's not surprising, then, that Christians are called "saints" or "holy ones" (Acts 9:13, 32, 41; 26:10; Rom. 1:7; 1 Cor. 1:2; 2 Cor. 1:1; Eph. 1:1; Phil. 1:1).[2] The term comes from a root meaning "to set apart," which in its moral reference takes on the idea of separation from anything defiled. A saint is a person set apart from the world and owned by God. There is no reason to reserve the word for persons who have exhibited extraordinary godliness, supported by miraculous works.

Holiness is simply living as a normal human being—the kind of life that God intends for every person. A good way to think of it is that holiness is spiritual health.

Sainthood begins when through repentance and saving faith a justified sinner comes into union with Christ through the regenerating Holy Spirit. The old corrupted self is laid aside and a new self is put on, "created after the likeness of God in true righteousness and holiness" (Eph. 4:24).

To the extent that the heart is controlled by the Holy Spirit, the mind, the emotions, and the will, moved by love, act in obedience to the divine will. Spiritual perceptions are heightened, along with an increasing awareness of eternal values. That which brings glory to God is seen as the chief end of humankind.

### Christlikeness

The holy life all centers in Christ, whom the Spirit exalts within the believing heart. He "is all, and in all" (Col. 3:11). There is a mystical union so real that Christ can be said to live in us and we in him (John 15:4; cf. 14:20; Gal. 2:20; Col. 1:27; 3:4). "Beholding the glory of the Lord, [we] are being transformed into the same image from one degree of glory to another. For this comes from the Lord who is the Spirit" (2 Cor. 3:18).

Sanctification is this process of being conformed to the Son of God.[3] It means that the Holy Spirit is working within the believer's heart, setting apart a people for himself, leaving the print of Christ's character on them.

Like any surgical operation, the undertaking is not without struggle. There are times of suffering and pain. As understanding of God's will enlarges, misdirected areas of present experience must be brought into obedience to the Lord. A pesky disposition of selfishness, asserting one's own way, may not yield easily to the lordship of Christ, but it too must be nailed to the cross.

### Purity of Desire

Let no one imagine that sanctity frees us from the impairments of our mortal bodies. The debilitating effects of the fall are still very much in evidence, including sickness, disease, and eventually, physical death.

More troublesome, saints have to contend with their own ignorance. Though learning more of God can correct some areas of our darkened intelligence, despite these noble efforts, we are going to make some poor judgments. Holy people are still fallible in knowledge. Sainthood does not bring immunity from life's problems, any more than it delivers from temptation and the ever-present freedom to sin willfully.

Yet, notwithstanding our many shortcomings and the inevitable consequences resulting from them, obedient saints can live victoriously when the intention of the heart is to please God. Holiness in this world is not distinguished by perfection of performance but by purity of desire.

### Love Governing Life

An experience with my son years ago illustrates what I mean. It was a hot day at the end of the harvest season. Jim, who was no more than four years of age, saw me in the backyard working in my garden, and it occurred to him that I might be thirsty. So he pulled up a chair to the kitchen sink, found a dirty glass, and filled it with warm water from the faucet.

The next thing I knew I heard my name called. As I turned around, there was my son coming across the garden holding the smudgy glass of warm water and saying, "Daddy, I thought you were thirsty, so I brought you a drink." And as he held up the glass, a smile stretched across his face from one ear to the other.

I might have thought, *Couldn't he do better than that? Why, that is not cold water; that's not even pure water.* And I would have been right. But when I looked at his face, I had to say that was pure love. He was doing the best he knew to please his daddy.

In a similar way, this is how every believer should live in devotion to Christ. Though we continually make errors in judgment and fall woefully short of our desire to be like Christ, still in our hearts we can do the best we know to please him. Yes, we will make mistakes and sometimes stumble and fall, but as best we know how, we can love God with all our heart, with all our soul, with all our mind, and love others as ourselves (Matt. 22:37–40).

This is holiness in practice. It fulfills "all the Law and the Prophets" (Matt. 22:40; cf. Rom. 13:8–10). It is the bond of perfection and the way that saints should live every day.

## Sin in Believers

### Freedom to Sin

The question might be asked, Does this mean that a Christian can live without sin? Before an answer can be given, however, we need to define terms (see chapter 5). Suffice it to say, if holiness is freedom from all un-Christlike thought, word, or deed, as perceived in the Reformed tradition, I doubt that state is attainable in this world.[4] This is even more obvious if our human nature with its infirmities is not distinguished from willful selfishness. When sin is understood as any deviation from the absolute holiness of God, whether realized or not, everyone comes short of the glory of God.

The only sense in which such perfection could be allowed is from the vantage point of heaven, where, because of identity with Christ by faith, God imputes to saints the righteousness of his Son. Complete experiential sanctification, however, must await the day of the restoration of all things when believers are delivered from a corrupted body in glorification.

Though believers are made new in Christ, they still must "put to death the deeds of the body" (Rom. 8:13) and kill what is "earthly" in them (Col. 3:5). Among those traits are "immorality, impurity, passion, evil desire, and covetousness, which is idolatry . . . anger, wrath, malice, slander, and obscene talk" and lying (vv. 5, 8, 9).

This fleshly mind is "hostile to God, for it does not submit to God's law" (Rom. 8:7; cf. 7:14; 1 Cor. 3:1–3). It is likened to "old leaven," which spreads "malice and evil" through the whole lump (1 Cor. 5:7, 8). In another context Christians are cautioned against a "root of bitterness," which can spring up to cause them trouble and defile others (Heb. 12:15).

Paul is speaking to the saints (Rom. 1:7; Col. 1:2), and his warnings here and throughout his letters make us keenly aware that we must continue to resist attacks of Satan and the weaknesses of the flesh. The deceitful pleasures of the world are always near to entice the careless to sin. The sanctified are still free moral beings and therefore can make choices in contradiction to the will of God.

### Overcoming Sin

Obviously, persons who see no difference between unconscious expressions of sin and intentional disobedience cannot think of a saint's conduct perfectly conforming to the character of Christ. Still, this view need not diminish a desire to follow Christ. When one disobeys, of course, the sin must be confessed and forsaken. Though in Reformed thought no distinction is made between transgressions and the deeper root of rebellion within the heart, still the tendency to sin can be repressed or counterbalanced by relying on grace and obedience in the Spirit. Partaking of Christ's nature progresses in sanctification until at last believers are taken in death and glorified.

Within this tradition, the "deeper life," or Keswick movement, teaches that by abandonment of all known sin and complete yielding to the Holy Spirit, one can have an endowment of power to live victoriously and to serve God more effectively. Generally this deeper experience is thought to come subsequent to regeneration and is maintained by daily abiding in Christ.[5]

More definitive is the classical Wesleyan emphasis on "entire sanctification," as the compound word in 1 Thessalonians 5:23 may be translated. It points to a particular moment in the developing life of grace when a saint comes to grips with inbred carnality sapping spiritual vitality.[6] Human infirmities have to be endured, but the self-centeredness exists by a person's consent and, like any volitional perversion, can be confessed and cleansed.[7] When this disposition to sin is dealt with, the Holy Spirit fills the soul with a deep sense of the divine presence and an earnest desire to serve, which Wesleyans call a perfection of love.[8]

Other traditions have their own way of describing this state of grace—complete consecration, the rest of faith, baptism by or with the Holy Spirit, full salvation, or something else that fits more naturally their theological framework. However defined, it does not mean a perfection of behavior or attainment.

### Pressing On to Higher Ground

Overcoming conscious sin is a daily task. In the ongoing experience of holiness, all kinds of frustrations and disappointments will come up. Some of these problems will occasion very real spiritual battles, but in meeting them, the fully consecrated saint can draw on the strength of a heart fully yielded to the will of God.

This commitment must be constantly renewed, else the victory over sin can be lost, though thankfully, regained. For this reason, it would be better not to think of cleansing and filling of the Spirit primarily as a crisis, but as a life. The life is made up of a series of decisions, and how each is made will determine the blessedness of holiness.

Corrections will be called for as we follow Christ. Renouncing our own rights and taking up his cross has implications in prayer and ministry of which we may have only faint comprehensions now, but the Spirit will point them out as we seek his guidance.

Thankfully, there is no foreclosure on progress. Whatever has been experienced thus far, there is more to learn. As the character of Christ is more fully understood and faith enlarges to embrace it, there will be unceasing expansion in the Spirit's fullness, even as life lengthens into the timeless dimensions of eternity.

The goal is nothing less than the very perfection of our Lord. The apostle expressed it well: "Not that I . . . am already perfect, but . . . straining forward to what lies ahead, I press on toward the goal for the prize of the upward call of God in Christ Jesus." Then he added, "Let those of us who are mature [same word as for *perfect*] think this way" (Phil. 3:12–15).

Such sainthood should characterize every Christian. Pressing on toward "the goal for the prize of the upward call of God," the closer we get to the heavenly city, the more we will long to see the beauty of holiness in the face of Jesus Christ.

In view of the mercies of God, Paul wrote to the saints at Rome: "I appeal to you . . . to make a decisive dedication of your bodies . . . as a living sacrifice, holy (devoted, consecrated) and well pleasing to God, which is your reasonable (rational, intelligent) service and spiritual worship" (Rom. 12:1 AMP).

Should we ever want to do less?


## Problem Areas

### Sanctified Stagnation

Probably no aspect of Christian life precipitates more misunderstanding among sincere believers than sanctification. One of the most glaring problems is failure of a newborn saint to "go on to maturity" (Heb. 6:1). Though sins were done away with at the cross and the believer is given the righteousness of Christ, this does not close down the Spirit's work. The convert is but a babe in faith and must grow up in the Lord. But while sanctification is God's part in facilitating the spiritual process, it requires loving parental care on the part of the church.

Without this development in holiness the young believer's growth will languish in atrophy for lack of nourishment. Such neglect is deadening to evangelism, for it cuts the nerve of vital Christian witness and arrests any fruitful service for the kingdom.

Initial sanctification must be seen as enrollment in Christ's school of discipleship. There is no end to learning. In the process we will increasingly learn how far short we actually have fallen from God's holiness. What once we regarded as only fleshly weaknesses will be recognized as presumptuous sins. Neglect of duty and opportunities for service will become apparent. More troubling than wrong actions will be our reactions, especially when offended and rejected. That old debilitating, self-serving instinct will also come to light. And mediocrity, though generally the norm of contemporary Christianity, will be seen as utterly repugnant to God.

Thankfully, though, following Christ we learn increasingly more about the potential of grace, and the possibilities of sainthood. Failure of the church to appropriate these available resources for fulfilling the Great Commission is our most grievous sin.

### Sanctification through Works

Believers must strive for perfection but never think that the goal can be reached in their strength. Saints are not self-made. The Holy Spirit imparts holiness to believers as a gift of God. Never earned by anything we do, it comes by faith alone in Jesus Christ.

I have heard it said by some that one is justified by faith but sanctified by faith plus works. The inference is that something more than grace is required for sainthood, particularly the sacraments of the church and meritorious works. Certainly, these good things are helpful, even commanded, but they cannot add to what Christ has already accomplished. External deeds and rituals may be means of expressing faith in the finished work of Christ, but their value is in what they are intended to represent.

This principle follows through in every human effort to achieve sainthood—church faithfulness, observance of baptism and the Lord's Supper, washing the feet of the saints, giving of alms, caring for widows and orphans, ministerial service, disciplines of self-denial and ascension. To this can be added social activism and humanitarian charity. All good works are to be admired but are not sufficient to make a saint.

Probably one of the most misleading avenues to sanctification comes out in the modern human potential and pastoral psychology movement where the objective is self-fulfillment. If not kept within the context of the Gospel, counseling takes the place of confession, and holiness is confused with health-fulness and emotional stability.

Let it be clear, good works are essential; the more the better. Without them civilization could not long endure. But holiness is not of this world, nor can it be engineered by man. It is the work of God.

### "Holier than Thou"

One may avoid the danger of stagnation and works righteousness in sanctification and still be overcome by self-conceit. I suspect that the most subtle misrepresentation of Christian holiness takes the guise of spiritual pride. Like the Pharisees in Jesus's day, such persons have an unbecoming air of righteousness superiority. Though wholly hidden from the perpetrator, it is picked up by others, and nothing brings more disdain from the watching world.

What God did at Calvary cannot be forgotten by saints. Its remembrance still brings tears of penitence. If there is anything of good report in their lives, it is all because of Jesus. They are bold to speak of his goodness, but not of their own.

More revealing, their humility is so unassuming they are not even aware of it. When Jesus described those who were commended by God for their acts of compassion, the righteous answered: "Lord, when did we see you hungry and feed you . . . thirsty and give you drink . . . a stranger and welcome you . . . naked and clothe you . . . sick or in prison and visit you?" (Matt. 25:31–40).

What a beautiful picture of holiness! I suspect that the more saints grow in Christlikeness the more unconscious they are of their own achievements. At best, they see themselves as unprofitable servants.

## Summary Applications

*1. Sin is a contradiction to the Christian life.*
Addressing the children of God, John wrote:

You know that [Christ] appeared to take away sins, and in him there is no sin. No one who abides in him keeps on sinning; . . . whoever makes a practice of sinning is of the devil. . . . The reason the Son of God appeared was to destroy the works of the devil. No one born of God makes a practice of sinning, for God's seed abides in him, and he cannot keep on sinning because he has been born of God.

1 John 3:5–9

These are strong words. Clearly, habitual sinning flies in the face of God's atoning love in the sacrifice of his Son. How sin is understood, of course, becomes crucial, and that is why considerable attention has been given to this subject. But however defined, sin must be dealt with in sanctification.

*2. Every saint can live victoriously in Christ.*
Although theological definitions of sanctification will differ, what finally matters is not our definitions of doctrine, but our personal trust and obedience to the living Son of God. Catholic or Protestant, Reformed or Arminian, the condition for joyous salvation is simple faith in the finished work of Jesus Christ. In terms of consecration, this means offering all that we know of ourselves to our loving Lord. Such commitment begins at conversion and continues throughout life as we walk "not after the flesh, but after the Spirit" (Rom. 8:1 KJV).

Why, then, would any Christian live in defeat and condemnation?

Hannah Whitall Smith tells about a man who was traveling along the road, bending under a heavy burden, when a wagon overtook him. The driver kindly offered to help him on his journey. He happily accepted the offer, got into the wagon, but when seated continued to bend beneath his load, which he still held on his shoulders. "Why don't you lay down your burden," asked the kindhearted driver. "Oh!" replied the man, "I feel that it is almost too much to ask you to carry me and I could not think of letting you carry my burden too!"[9]

Is not this like many of us, still bending under the heavy burden of a troubled heart, while all the while God invites us to cast our cares on him?

A tragedy of the Christian journey is to refuse to maintain the condition for a victorious life—to keep up-to-date in confession of all known sin, to be wholly consecrated to God, and by faith in the provisions of his grace, to follow the Spirit of Christ where he leads.

### 3. Self-centeredness must die.

Other transgressions of the law may be more easily recognized, but our selfishness is also sin. "If anyone would come after me," Jesus said, "let him deny himself and take up his cross and follow me" (Mark 8:34; cf. Matt. 10:38–39). Paul speaks of this as being "crucified with Christ" (Gal. 2:20). "Those who belong to Christ Jesus," he says, "have crucified the flesh with its passions and desires" (Gal. 5:24).

By way of clarification, love of God does not negate love of self. Indeed, love of self becomes joyous for the saints because they belong to Christ.[10] However, if love for self and others seeks fulfillment apart from God's love, it breeds endless discontent and more sin.[11]

This tendency of the uncrucified flesh, ever lurking in the shadows of disobedience, will arise stealthily to take control. Consent to its leavening influence may be so gradual and refined as to be unnoticed at first, and when it is detected, likely it will seem normal. After all, do we not need times to relax and enjoy the pleasures of the world? Do we always have to bear the cross of Christ? Why should we have to bring the Great Commission into every aspect of our lifestyle?

Such questions may seem innocent enough, but carnality has a beguiling way of turning our response into self-indulgence. All too easily we pamper ourselves under the pretense of God's blessing, failing to measure our lives by the pattern of Christ. This inclination is but the flesh lusting against the spirit, traits of the "old man" underlying the attitudes seen in the classical seven deadly sins—lust, envy, anger, pride, gluttony, avarice, sloth.[12] However we may try to ignore the deeper problem of self-preoccupation, it is there to frustrate, if not defeat, the victorious life.

Holiness is an exacting standard, and as the values of Christ's kingdom become clearer, the more we will identify with the publican when he cried,

"Lord, have mercy on me!" Quibbling over hairstyles and forms of dress will not be the issue. But when seeing ourselves with more Christlikeness, I suspect that we will become far more sensitive to such areas as worldliness, materialism, prayerlessness, disregard of the oppressed, and indifference to the lost multitudes that have never heard the Gospel.

Here we must be utterly honest with ourselves, and with God's help, relentlessly seek day by day to bring our lives into conformity with his holiness.[13] If we try to trim the corners and excuse a few favorite shortcomings, carnality reigns in our hearts. As long as this condition exists, we diminish the blessing holiness can be to others.

### 4. Holiness manifests the fruit of the Spirit, rather than particular gifts.

The Holy Spirit does bestow special gifts to persons, as will be discussed later when considering the church, but sanctification centers attention on the Giver. The holiness of the Spirit characterizes his fruit—"love, joy, peace, patience, kindness, goodness, faithfulness, gentleness, self-control" (Gal. 5:22–23; cf. Eph. 4:2). All these qualities, of which love is the summation, shine forth in the Son of God, whom the Spirit always glorifies.

Gifts of the Spirit are important but they are not the main attraction of holiness. Keep the focus on Jesus.

### 5. Love gives itself away.

The impartation of holiness, received as a divine gift, cannot be self-contained. Just as God gave himself away in his love for the world, so the experience of that love in Christ becomes self-giving. To keep it would in effect deny its presence, while giving it away is evidence of its possession.[14]

Holy men and women of God will be involved some way in pouring out their lives in service for Christ. The form of ministry will vary with each person and find expression through one's particular giftedness, but holy love is the motivation that empowers it.

I remember kneeling beside a lonely grave in a little village in the jungles of the Congo, where lay the physical remains of Burley Law, a missionary pilot. For many years he ministered in the remote areas of the country—taking critically ill patients to medical clinics, delivering food supplies to villages in times of famine, and in many other ways coming to help in crises. When not flying, like any missionary, he would pitch in to help whenever needed. All over that part of the land, he was known and loved for his joyful servant heart.

One day he was killed while trying to rescue some friends who were in grave danger during an insurrection in the country. The marauding rebels saw his light plane coming in, and when he landed, they rushed out of the bushes and shot him. Efforts of his friends to save his life were in vain.

His body was laid to rest there in a clearing near the village. Though surrounded by jungle growth, the grave is easily found, for leading to it is a well-worn path trod by the natives that he loved. There, carved in a memorial stone, are the words of Jesus: "Greater love has no man than this, that he lay down his life for a friend."

### 6. Holiness makes evangelism believable.

Love-filled lives verify the claims of the Gospel. Worldlings can see that the persons who bear the name of Christ are different. There is a graciousness about their lifestyle. Obedience is joyful. Even amid sufferings, when ridiculed and oppressed, the bitterness of the world does not keep the saints from praising God from whom all blessings flow.

Such a life creates a mystery; it is so uncharacteristic of a fallen race, and those most observing, just like the church-watchers of the apostolic era, have to admit the believers have been "with Jesus" (Acts 4:13).

### 7. Holiness is God's strategy to reach the world.

The great commandment to love finds expression in the Great Commission. It can be seen in the beginning when Adam and Eve were told to multiply and fill the earth (Gen. 1:28). The commission was boldly announced when Abraham was called to separate himself from the old haunts of sin and go to a new land of promise (Gen. 12:1–3; cf. Heb. 11:8–10).

To this end God chose Israel to be his witness among the nations, so that people, beholding their holy manner of life, would want to follow their God (Pss. 2:8; 46:10; Isa. 55:4–5; Jer. 10:7; Zech. 8:23).

When the Jews succumbed to the sensual culture about them, the Lord sent his Messiah-Son to raise up a new Israel, a holy nation, through which Jesus's life was a witness to the world (Gen. 49:10; Isa. 49:6; 53:11–12; Dan. 7:13–14; Zech. 9:10). The Spirit is now fashioning the church in his image in order to show the glory of God to the nations.

### 8. World evangelism depends on the sanctification of the church.

When carnal barriers to the flow of the Spirit come down, saints take seriously the mission of the cross. This was brought out clearly in the high priestly prayer of Jesus, when he prayed to the Father: "As you sent me into the world, so I have sent them into the world. And for their sake I consecrate myself, that they also may be sanctified in truth" (John 17:18–19). In Jesus's case, this setting apart of himself to God was not necessary to effect cleansing, since he was always pure; nor was it necessary to receive power, since Jesus already had all power in heaven and earth. Rather his sanctification, as the context reveals, was a commitment to the task for which he was "sent . . . into the world," and in dedication to that purpose, he continually gave his life "for their sake."

His sanctification, then, was not for the purpose of benefiting himself, but it was for his disciples, that they might "be sanctified in truth." For Jesus that mission for which he was sent would end on the cross in a few hours. There his redemptive work was finished. For the disciples, their sanctification would also involve a cross—not that they had to do something to atone for their sin, but that they needed to die to themselves in commitment to the mission of making known the completed work of Christ. Through their witness, and in turn the witness of those they discipled, Jesus visualized how the world would come to believe in him (John 17:19–21).

The fruitfulness of his ministry—indeed, the fulfillment of his whole incarnate life, death, and resurrection—depended on their faithfulness to this mission. Had they remained as they were, self-centered and unconcerned for the lost, the world would never have known the Gospel, and we would be without hope today.

It is this dimension of holiness that is so essential to world evangelism. Without such self-giving sainthood, cleansing from sin and empowerment for victorious living would seem to revolve around a selfish purpose and thereby repudiate the very thing from which we are delivered. The Spirit's work within the heart is not to gratify the desire for personal blessing, but to make us "useful to the Master and prepared to do any good work" (2 Tim. 2:21 NIV). Jesus said that "when the Holy Spirit has come upon you," then "you will be my witnesses" to the world (Acts 1:8). We cannot take that which God has redeemed for his glory and divert it to our own ends.

The prayer of Christ for his church began to be answered at Pentecost. To a remarkable degree those apostolic Christians left the upper room with a new sense of ministry. No longer preoccupied with their own interests, those Spirit-intoxicated disciples could not ignore the needs of humanity about them or keep silent about the Gospel. The love of Jesus infused into their hearts by the Holy Spirit constrained them to reach out in compassion to a dying world (Rom. 5:5; 2 Cor. 5:14). Nothing could stop them—not the anger of mobs or the irritation of daily trials—but as rivers borne along with a mighty rushing sound at flood tide, they go on their way praising God.

Living in the fullness of the Holy Spirit is still our privilege today. "For the promise is for you and for your children and for all who are far off" (Acts 2:39). Here is the power to become what God has called us to be. To the degree that we take his Word to heart and make Christ Lord of our lives, we can expect to do his work.

### 9. The church must hear and understand the message of holiness.

In view of the inexhaustible blessings of this life of divine grace, we would think that the body of saints would constantly herald its promise. Yet strangely, this does not seem generally to be the case. Not that the doctrine is denied; it is just that other things seem to be more urgent, and the church, under the illusion of relevance, tends to accept the world's agenda of concerns. Inevitably, more mundane and humanitarian interests take precedence over the demanding claims of the lordship of Christ and obedience to his last command to his church.

The late Alan Redpath, beloved pastor of the Chicago Moody Church, was on target when he said: "Failure to preach the entire message, which includes not only forgiveness of sin but deliverance from the power of the sin principle, has produced a generation of independent evangelical Christians who simply have not progressed with God, and who do not grow."[15]

Or to put it in the words of Frank Colquhoun, "Christians," generally speaking, "are living on the right side of Easter, but on the wrong side of Pentecost."[16]

Bound up with this confusion may be an inordinate fear of offending people content with the status quo, who liken the way of the cross to fanaticism. But if making disciples of Christ is indeed a militant movement, like any advancing army, the flanks of the church will always be vulnerable to aberrations. Let us be careful, however, that in our desire to be removed from these perceived excuses, we do not become defensive and divert our energy from the attack. Whatever the misrepresentations and criticisms that may come, the church must not be intimidated into fighting a holding action.

Our call is not to hold the fort but to storm the heights. Anytime we become more concerned with our self-preservation than with proclamation, we have lost our advantage in the mission of Christ. True holiness needs no defense; it will vindicate itself when seen in its own beauty and power.

### 10. Lord, make me a holy man.

The saintly Scottish pastor Robert Murray McCheyne once wrote: "My people's greatest need is my personal holiness." He was right. The greatest gift any person can give to those people who look to him or her for leadership is a wholly sanctified life.

I will never forget the closing service of the World Congress on Evangelism at the Kongresshalle in Berlin, West Germany, in 1966. Billy Graham was speaking on the need in Christian work for "a gentleness and a kindness and a love and a forgiveness and a compassion that will mark us different from the world." He said, "The Christian minister is a holy man."[17] Then to illustrate his point, he told the story of the conversion of H. C. Morrison, founder of Asbury Theological Seminary. He described a day many years earlier when Morrison was working on a farm, cultivating corn. Looking down the road, he saw an old Methodist circuit rider riding by on his horse. The young plowman had seen the preacher before and he knew him to be a holy man. As he watched the saint go by, he felt the power of his godly presence way out there in the field. Such a conviction for sin came over Morrison that, fearful for his soul, he dropped on his knees and there between the corn rows, alone, he made a resolve to give his life to God.

Concluding the story, setting an example before us all, Billy Graham earnestly prayed, "Oh, God, make me a holy man—a holy man."[18]

This is my prayer too, for it expresses my greatest need and desire.

# 14

## Perseverance of the Saints

The great scientist Sir Michael Faraday was asked as he was dying: "What speculations do you have about life after death?"

"Speculations," he replied in astonishment. "I know nothing about speculations! I'm resting on certainties." Then from memory he quoted, "I know whom I have believed, and am persuaded that he is able to keep that which I have committed unto him against that day" (2 Tim. 1:12 KJV).[1]

### Assurance of Salvation

#### Promise to All

God wants every person to have confidence his or her sins are forgiven and to know for certain he or she belongs to Christ. Could anything less be ascribed to a God of infinite love? To know his conforming ownership is the only way that Christian experience can be stabilized amid the difficulties, the suffering, even the loneliness of death in this world. Without this assurance of present communion with God, one could not enjoy a positive life of prayer (Heb. 10:22). And as for evangelism, how could a testimony to salvation be convincing to anyone else if the witness himself is not sure of it (1 John 1:3)? People already have enough doubt of their own and are not attracted to more unbelief.

An incident in the experience of Queen Victoria comes to mind. She had heard a sermon that left her wondering if one could be absolutely sure in this life of eternal salvation. So she asked her chaplain, and he replied that such assurance was not possible.

This was published in the *Court News* and it caught the eye of a minister of the Gospel, John Townsend. After reading of the queen's question and the answer received, he prayed much about the matter, then sent a letter to the queen.

> To her gracious Majesty, our beloved Queen Victoria . . . from one of her most humble subjects: with trembling hands, but heart-filled love, and because I know that we can be absolutely sure now of our eternal life in the house that Jesus went to prepare, may I ask your Most Gracious Majesty to read the following passages of scripture: John 3:16; Romans 10:9–10? These passages prove there is full assurance of salvation by faith in our Lord Jesus Christ for those who believe and accept his finished work. I sign myself your servant for Jesus' sake, John Townsend.

In about a fortnight he received an envelope containing the following letter:

> To John Townsend: Your letter of recent date received and in reply would state that I have carefully and prayerfully read the following portions of Scripture referred to. I believe in a finished work of Christ for me, and trust by God's grace to meet you in that home of which he said, "I go to prepare a place for you" (signed) Victoria Guelph.[2]

### What Is Assurance?

Whether one is an earthly monarch or simple peasant, eternal life does not depend on rank in society or religious ceremony but entirely on the merits of him who purchased us with his own blood. Assurance of salvation is the knowledge of belonging to God, the consciousness of sonship, a sureness maintained by faith in the integrity of Jesus Christ (Rom. 8:15; Gal. 4:6).

The assurance rests on the testimony of God's Word, which can be called the objective witness (John 5:24; 1 John 1:1–3). Within the human spirit the Holy Spirit witnesses to the truth of the Word believed, authenticating membership in God's family (Rom. 8:16; 2 Cor. 5:5; Eph. 1:13–14; 1 John 4:13; 5:13).

Further confirming the reality of salvation is the fruit of the Spirit in the believer's life (Matt. 7:16; Gal. 5:22–23). Assurance and fruitfulness, thus, issue from a vital relationship with Christ, like a branch growing from a vine. "I am the vine," Jesus said, "you are the branches. Whoever abides in me and I in him, he it is that bears much fruit" (John 15:5; cf. vv. 1–17).

### Keeping the Law

Abiding in Christ finds expression in obedience to the word of Christ summed up in the law of God (Matt. 22:36–40; cf. Mark 10:19–21). "If you keep my commandments," Jesus said, "you will abide in my love" (John 15:10).

The law serves as a practical guide for the people of God. Of course it must be understood in the context of its purpose. What might be called the ceremonial law, prescribing such practices as sacrifices and feasts, has fulfilled its function and is no longer binding. The judicial law, which deals with matters like divorce or making restitution, is obligatory only as it speaks of the moral law. But the moral law of God seen in such statements as the Ten Commandments or the Sermon on the Mount is forever the same, for it reveals the unchangeable character of our Lord.

The law of God comes into its ultimate focus in Jesus Christ. He is the personality of the moral law disclosed in our likeness. Therefore he becomes our rule of conduct in every area of life.

When all is said, love fulfills the law, for it assures obedience. "If you love me," Jesus said, "you will keep my commandments" (John 14:15; cf. vv. 21, 23; 1 John 2:5). And in keeping his commandments, we abide in his love (John 15:9–10). Amazing! A Christian falls head over heels in love with the law. Even more wonderful is that God writes the law on the heart, "even upon [our] innermost thoughts and understanding" (Heb. 8:10 AMP).

### Guaranteed Possession

Following Christ brings an inward sense of security. Love casts out all fear (1 John 4:18). "Whoever keeps his word, in him truly the love of God is perfected. By this we may know that we are in him" (1 John 2:5).

The certainty of this relationship with Christ, which comes through the Spirit, is likened to a seal placed on a contract validating ownership. Those who have believed in Christ are "sealed with the promised Holy Spirit, who is the guarantee of our inheritance until we acquire possession of it, to the praise of his glory" (Eph. 1:13–14). Elsewhere Paul speaks of this seal of the Spirit as God's "security deposit" on the fulfillment of his promise (2 Cor. 1:22 AMP).

In Romans 8 what begins with the assurance of no condemnation to those in Christ Jesus (vv. 1–2) concludes with the assurance of no separation from him: "neither death nor life, nor angels nor rulers, nor things present nor things to come, nor powers, nor height nor depth, nor anything else in all creation, will be able to separate us from the love of God in Christ Jesus our Lord" (vv. 37–39). Now that's security!

### Christians Can Backslide

What is called backsliding results from unfaithfulness to Christ, or as someone has said, backsliding comes through slack abiding, meaning it is a willful act of disregarding the will of God. Having begun in the Spirit, one turns aside and again starts to walk in the flesh (Gal. 6:1; 1 John 1:8–9). This can happen to the best of people. Remember how even Peter in his weakness three times denied his Lord (Mark 14:66–72; cf. Matt. 26:34–35).

The path of obedience leads through many dangers in this fallen world. Jesus told his disciples that "temptations to sin are sure to come" (Luke 17:1; cf. Matt. 18:7). The devil and his legions of darkness can be expected to challenge every forward movement of God's people. With this in mind, Paul wrote the believers at Corinth: "I am afraid that as the serpent deceived Eve by his cunning, your thoughts will be led astray from a sincere and pure devotion to Christ" (2 Cor. 11:3; cf. 2 Cor. 2:11; 1 Thess. 3:5).

Temptation begins with a suggestion of evil, which if not resisted, becomes more attractive as the idea is entertained. Sin emerges when we consent to the evil thought, whether or not it issues in an act of rebellion (Prov. 1:16; 4:14).

Knowing our human weakness, remembering the admonition of our Lord, we should pray to avoid temptation (Matt. 6:13; 26:41; Mark 14:38; Luke 22:40, 46). Though God is not responsible for these trials—"he himself tempts no one" (James 1:13)—he will not permit anyone to be tempted more than our ability to endure (1 Cor. 10:13). Because our Lord has been through it all, in ways more devious than our own, yet never having sinned, we can be sure that "he is able to help those who are being tempted" (Heb. 2:18; cf. 2 Pet. 2:9).

To repel the attacks of Satan, we are told to "take up the whole armor of God . . . and having done all, to stand firm" (Eph. 6:13). "Resist the devil, and he will flee from you" (James 4:7). There is no hint that overcoming temptation will be easy, but "blessed is the man who remains steadfast under trial, for when he has stood the test he will receive the crown of life" (James 1:12). Indeed, James would "count it all joy" (v. 2) when meeting these testings, for in conquering them comes the sweet assurance of God's faithfulness.

But if we yield to sin, inevitably we will backslide. Disobedience breaks fellowship with Christ (1 John 1:6–7). By not walking in his light, the joyous sense of his presence loses its freshness, and eventually, if not corrected, impacts assurance of salvation. Now the question must be asked, Does the loss of fellowship also mean the loss of a relationship with the Savior?

## Security of Believers

Evangelical interpretations of security, with many variations, answer differently the question of the saint's perseverance.[3] Basically they come down to two options: unconditional security and conditional security.

### Unconditional Security

The classical Reformed position holds that the truly converted will be kept secure in their faith by the power of God until the end of their lives. Fellowship with Christ can be lost and often is, but never a relationship.[4] A person once born of the Spirit is forever a child of God. To accept the possibility of a saint losing salvation would be tantamount to denying the sufficiency of Christ's completed work.

Among the many Scriptures cited in support is Jesus's teaching that "everyone who looks on the Son and believes in him should have eternal life, and I will raise him up on the last day" (John 6:40), that he "should lose nothing of all given" to him by God (v. 39). Another reference speaks of his sheep who follow him: "I give them eternal life, and they will never perish, and no one will snatch them out of my hand" (John 10:27–30). Other passages that speak of faith assuring eternal life are John 3:16, 18; 5:24; 6:47, 39–46; 17:9–24; 1 John 5:13). To these words could be added any number of other Scriptures that emphasize God's keeping power to those who believe in Christ (e.g., Job 19:25–26; Eccles. 3:14; Rom. 4:5–6; 8:29–39; 11:29; 1 Cor. 12:13; 2 Cor. 5:17, 21; Eph. 1:4–5; Phil. 1:6; 4:3; 2 Tim. 4:18; 1 Pet. 1:5, 7, 9, 21; 5:9; 2 Pet. 1:1, 5).

Where fellowship with Christ is broken by disobedience, of course, the believer will be chastened by the Holy Spirit, who is grieved when we do not walk in the light (Eph. 4:30). God is always seeking to bring the wayward back to himself. And, thankfully, penitence restores fellowship.

But what happens if one does not repent? Can a believer go on and on in deliberate sin, with no sense of remorse or regret, and still regard himself a child of God?

To this question different answers may be given. The most reasonable is that the person was never saved in the first place. Though one may make a profession of faith, and even display an exemplary moral lifestyle, the individual is a hypocrite. Genuine Christians simply do not live habitually in sin, arrogantly ignoring the pleas of God's Spirit to repent. Unbroken fellowship with Christ identifies true believers.

Another view, less exacting, holds that a Christian may completely backslide and remain resistant to the Spirit, yet God will bring the elect back to repentance before death. However, insofar as one lives out of fellowship with Christ, assurance may be delayed until the time of restoration.

A more difficult position to maintain within the tradition allows that a converted person who becomes unfaithful can never fall completely away from grace (2 Tim. 2:13). It is believed that salvation is a gift of God that cannot be revoked (Rom. 11:29). The renegade will be sorely chastened by the Spirit and suffer the loss of rewards in heaven (1 Cor. 3:12–15) but cannot lose salvation.[5] Such a view offers security to persons who remain unrepentant and have no semblance of fellowship with Christ.

### Conditional Security

Representing a different perspective, the classical Arminian view holds that eternal security is conditional on continuing faith in Christ. Fellowship with Christ is lost through disobedience (inactive faith), but contrary to Calvinism, a saving relationship can be lost, but only by unconfessed sin, culminating in apostasy.[6]

Support for this position is also abundant, often citing the same Scripture as Reformed theologians. In the case of John 6:38–40, for example, it is pointed out that the use of the present tense in the word *believe* in this and other relevant passages emphasizes a present and continuing action. Similarly, the sheep passage, which says that they shall never perish, also says, "they follow" Christ, indicating a continuing obedience (John 10:27–29).[7]

Scriptures that underscore the dire consequences of unfaithfulness could also be multiplied (e.g., Ezek. 32:32; Gal. 5:19–21; 2 Pet. 3:7; Rev. 3:3). Much is made of the "if" passages, which indicate that security depends on character (e.g., John 8:51; 15:6, 10, 14; 1 Cor. 15:2; Col. 1:21–23; Heb. 3:6, 14). The texts in Hebrews that speak of the judgments that come to those who deliberately go on sinning after receiving the gift of Christ are especially significant to Arminians (Heb. 6:4–6; 10:26–29). Why would there be such strong warnings against falling away if it was impossible?[8]

Though Calvinists and Arminians differ on the ultimate perseverance of all true believers, there can be consensus on backsliding. Disobedience breaks fellowship with Christ, and the erring child of God, convicted of sin by the Holy Spirit, knows that fellowship can be restored only through penitence.

If the backslider does not repent, and resolutely continues to live in rebellion against God, probably the person was never truly converted, though it is possible that at one time he was a believer. Regardless of his former state, however, unbelief expressed in disobedience drains fellowship with Christ of its vitality, which then clouds assurance of a relationship.

The question might be raised as to when this loss of assurance happens. A few Arminians believe that the least misstep causes one to lose salvation—any overt sin after conversion results in loss of a saving relationship. This position makes no distinction between sins of consent to evil and denial of Christ. Hence, continual unconfessed sin amounts to apostasy. This viewpoint may give strong incentive for diligence in holiness, but it can also make security seem "momentary."[9]

A much preferred position, and more generally held, is that deliberate sin breaks fellowship with Christ, but the relationship can be lost only by apostasy. The progression of sin in disobedience is distinguished from the ultimate end of sin, the denial of Christ as Lord and Savior. It is unlikely that a true believer would ever come to this point, but if it does occur, many Arminians hold that there would be no opportunity for restoration. Defiant disregard of "the blood of the covenant" can lead to that tragic consequence where there "no longer remains a sacrifice for sins, but a fearful expectation of judgment, and a fury of fire" (Heb. 10:26–27, 29).[10] "If anyone does not abide in me," Jesus said, "he is thrown away like a branch and withers; and the branches are gathered, thrown into the fire, and burned" (John 15:6).

## Common Ground

In fairness to both sides of the evangelical spectrum, whether Reformed or Arminian, we can come together around the essential truth of the Gospel invitation. Only those persons who respond to the Spirit's call and come to Christ in true repentance and faith receive the gift of salvation. It is all of God, initiated by divine grace.

When believers do not practice their faith through obedience, and become backslidden, they must repent and restore their first love. Those who persevere in faith to the end die in the assurance of salvation. All true believers have eternal life in Christ.

Neither position has any practical relevance without evangelism. For until a person hears the Gospel and believes in the Son of God, there is no way to be saved. Moreover, no one can enjoy security as a believer without following the Lord. Though there will be mishaps along the way, the saints—those who trust themselves to Christ—abide in eternal security.

Let us then appreciate each other. Charles Spurgeon, the beloved preacher of London, put it well:

> It seems to me that the path of truth is to believe them both; to hold firmly that salvation is by grace, and to hold with equal firmness that the ruin of any man is wholly and entirely his own fault; to maintain the sovereignty of God, and to hold the responsibility of man also; to believe in the free agency of both God and man; neither to dishonor God by making him a lackey to his creature's will, nor on the other hand, to rid man of all responsibility by making him to be a mere log or a machine.[11]

His counsel was to let the Bible speak for itself. Then as a parting word, he added:

> I trust you never desire that any text might be amended so as to read a little more Calvinist or a little more like the teaching of Arminius. Always stand to it that your creed must bend to the Bible, and not the Bible to your creed, and dare to be a little inconsistent with yourselves, if need be, sooner than be inconsistent with God's revealed truth.[12]

## Problem Areas

### Careless Behavior among Believers

Persons are sadly mistaken who use security in Christ as an excuse for living in sin. While not associated only with perseverance of the born-again, it often comes out in this doctrine.[13] Nothing could be more misleading. In fact, where professing saints seem to show no regard for the law of God, there is good reason to assume that they have no saving relationship with Christ. Even among those who allow that such persons may be saved, there still will be an accounting on judgment day. What should characterize persons eternally secure is an attitude of penitence, whenever convicted of sin by the Holy Spirit. Saints persevering in faith have already pledged to repent when made aware of their transgression.

Regrettably, however, there are those with a Christian identity who do not appear to know the Lord. Paul speaks of "false brethren" (Gal. 2:4 KJV) and servants of Satan who "disguise themselves as servants of righteousness" (2 Cor. 11:15). When thinking of sin in the context of perseverance, it is well to recall the words of Jesus: "Not everyone who says to me, 'Lord, Lord,' will enter the kingdom of heaven, but the one who does the will of my Father" (Matt. 7:21–22).

### Despair of Persevering

That the saints can die to faith may raise undue anxiety in the minds of persons struggling with the decision to follow Christ. For the unconverted, the goal may seem too distant and the bar too high. They need assurance that what God begins, he will finish, and whatever comes, his grace is sufficient to complete the journey (Phil. 1:6).

But those who are already on the way may also have some doubts. The problem often comes out among backsliders who stumble and fall in their walk with Christ, and repeated failures lead to feelings of hopelessness. The convicted may get to the point where they no longer feel worthy of God's forgiveness and are prone to give up. Thomas Oden thinks "that more sinners are destroyed by despair than presumption. Many who once fought in spiritual combat," he says, "now no longer strive, feeling victory impossible to attain."[14]

Christians who believe salvation can be lost by any conscious sin especially have trouble stabilizing their experience. These devout believers may have an unnecessarily oversensitive conscience, but if there is true guilt, they need reassurance of God's faithfulness, that he is quick to forgive the penitent who call on him, and that without delay.

### The Nonelect Presumption

A caution is in order when celebrating the doctrine of the saint's perseverance. Persons who have no assurance of salvation may negatively assume that they are not among the elect. This is poor reasoning. The only way that one can come to that conclusion is by not coming to Christ. For a person to blame God for their unbelief is self-deception. The promise is clear that "whoever" believes in the Son of God will be saved. It is nonsense, bordering on blasphemy, for a person to claim that he can live in sin because he has no other choice.

## Summary Applications

*1. That one can be sure of salvation startles the skepticism of our relativistic society.*

It is shocking enough for self-indulgent worldlings to be told that one must be converted to Christ to enter the kingdom of heaven, but to go on and say that one can be certain of entering heaven seems unimaginable. For many people today, nothing is certain, least of all an experience with God.

For example, Gandhi reflects this attitude in his aversion to converting others to the Christian faith. "But aren't you the biggest converter of all?" he was asked. "Aren't you trying to convert the British Empire to your views?"

"Oh," said Gandhi in reply, "that is quite true for in the realm of the political and social and economic we can be sufficiently certain to convert, but in the realm of religion there is not sufficient certainty to convert anybody."[15]

Doubtless many would agree with Gandhi. Yet notwithstanding their suspicion about certainty, that is precisely the promise of the Gospel to all who come to Christ, and without this assurance, evangelism could be dismissed as irrelevant by a world that has lost its way.

*2. Personal assurance of salvation is a present reality.*

A person can have all the traditional credentials of Christianity, and by astute reasoning prove the truthfulness of the Gospel, yet be unsure of conversion to Christ without the Spirit witnessing through the Word to the reality. In fact, for all he knows, he could still be lost.

The issue of security finally comes to how saving faith is understood, since it is agreed that all believers are eternally secure. Can faith (freely enabled by grace) be revoked by a person no longer choosing to believe? That is, does freedom of the will no longer operate once a decision to follow Christ has been made?

The use of the Greek present tense verb generally in the New Testament when speaking of salvation implies a present and continuing action. For example, John 3:16 literally translates "whoever continues to believe" in the Son of God has eternal life. It is the fact that the believer has faith now that gives assurance, not that somewhere in the past a decision was made for Christ. In no way does this discredit that previous high moment in one's experience where there was a clear sense of conversion, for certainly there is a beginning to saving faith, but the continuing reality of that experience is what verifies a saving relationship with Christ.

Here all of us must ask ourselves: do I have confidence that if I were to die tonight, by God's grace, through the merits of Jesus Christ alone, I know I would go to heaven?

Bishop Butler, one of the most famous leaders of the Church of England in the eighteenth century, as he was dying, told his chaplain: "Though I have endeavored to avoid sin, and to please God, I am still afraid to die." The chaplain said, "My Lord, you have forgotten that Jesus Christ is a Savior." "True," said the bishop, "but how shall I know that he is Savior for me?" "My Lord," replied the chaplain, "it is written, him that cometh to me I will in no wise cast out." "True," said the dying prelate, "and I am surprised that though I have read that Scripture I suppose a thousand times over, I never felt its virtue till this moment. And now I die happy."

Thankfully, he died in assurance of salvation, but what a tragedy that for scores of years he lived with no certainty.[16]

### 3. Anyone who lacks assurance needs counsel.

When a sincere seeker does not have confidence of being in Christ, something is obviously lacking, and the counselor needs to find out why. Often the problem comes down to ignorance, simply not understanding that assurance is promised by God in his Word. Some believers, solid in their faith, may think it would be presumptuous to claim certainty of salvation in this life, believing that no one can be sure they are the elect until persevering unto death. It would be well to point this believer to 1 John 5:11–13. Ask him to read it, then tell you what it says. Other verses that could be read in the same way are Job 19:25–26; Romans 8:16; 2 Corinthians 5:5–8; and Hebrews 10:22–23.

I remember years ago staying at a hotel in Germany where I noticed on my first night that shoes were placed outside the doors of the other rooms on the hall. I realized that the occupiers of those rooms were setting out their shoes to be picked up by a porter during the night, and the next morning their shoes would be outside their door brightly shined. Later when they checked out of the hotel, a hefty charge for the service would be added to their bill.

The next day I commented that I had never been in a place like that before where it seemed everybody but me got their shoes shined at night. "Well, why don't you do it too?" my friend asked. I explained that I could not afford the luxury. In dismay, my friend replied, "Man, don't you know in this hotel that's part of the service provided free to all guests? You are paying for it whether you get your shoes shined or not."

Some Christians, I am afraid, are just like that when it comes to assurance. Ignorance of God's Word deprives them of what is already theirs by promise.

More common than not understanding the provision, however, is confusion about what assurance means. Many persons get it mixed up with intense emotional feeling or extraordinary signs, and because that does not happen, they wonder if their faith is real. In this case, it would be well again to call their attention to the quiet witness of the Spirit, as promised in Scripture (e.g., Rom. 8:16).

Another reason for uncertainty could be that the believer is backslidden. Christians not walking in the light are always in the dark. To help such a person, find out when fellowship with Christ was lost, identify the problem, and deal with the issue. Likely temptations to fall away will occur again at the same point of failure, so help strengthen the believer to overcome that weakness. Included in the counsel will be the discipline of prayer, getting into the Word, meeting with fellow believers, and active involvement in church activities.

Of course one lacking assurance may not ever have been converted. The man or woman appears to be a Christian, perhaps even holding a place of prominence in the church, but either by ignorance or stubbornness, has never met the conditions for salvation. When this is discovered, the counselor has a wonderful opportunity to explain the Gospel and point the person to the Savior.

*4. Let the redeemed of the Lord say so.*

An assured Christian should not be ashamed to bear testimony to his or her faith. How the witness comes forth depends on the situation, but every believer should be ready, as the Spirit prompts, to say a word for Jesus.

I remember a girl at Asbury College who was reading her Bible while going to Cincinnati, Ohio, on a bus. The man next to her asked what she was reading. It precipitated a very natural opportunity to give her testimony.

When the college coed told the man about her love for the Word and spoke about God's plan of redemption, the listener became so impressed that he wanted a friend to hear her story. So they switched seats, and the girl proceeded again to tell her testimony. Before she was finished, the elderly gentleman in front turned around and asked her to speak louder for he was having difficulty hearing every word. By this time the woman across the aisle was interested. So the youth asked, "Would you like for me to speak so that everyone could hear?" They nodded. Accordingly, she stood up behind the driver's seat and gave her witness to all the passengers. She was just concluding when the bus pulled into the Cincinnati terminal. But before opening the door, the driver turned to the girl and asked, "Young lady, do you have anything else to say?" To which the student responded, "All I want to say is hallelujah!"[17]

I doubt if it will ever happen to you like that, but there is a lesson in this for us all. Let our lives be so noticeably different from the world that it creates a mystery, and observing people become curious to know the reason why. In this way, our witness becomes a response to their interest, not an imposition of our will.

*5. Resisting temptation requires continuing spiritual alertness.*

Knowing that in this age of darkness, Christians will always be assaulted by powerful forces of evil, we dare not underestimate the cunning of our enemy. The devil has been around long enough to know where we are most vulnerable.

I remember hearing the late Bishop Fulton Sheen reflect on the seasons of life when temptation has its greatest attraction: in youth, he said, it centers on lust; at middle age, it is power; and in senior years, the temptation revolves around avarice. I suspect he was right. But whatever the focus of temptation, we can be sure that the devil will attack at our weakest point.

To overcome, we can resist either through sheer willpower or by filling our mind with such heavenly delights that the temptation has no appeal: the one sometimes effective, the other always successful. Using a classical illustration, Daniel Steele recounts that in Greek mythology near the coast of Italy was an island where Sirens sitting on the beach would sing so charmingly that seamen in ships passing by would be lured to shore, only to be destroyed on the rocks. Knowing the allurement of their songs, Ulysses filled the ears of his crew with wax and lashed himself to the mast while his ship passed through the deadly waters. By this determination they escaped.

However, when Jason and his companions sailed by this island, he told Orpheus to strike his lyre. He played so beautifully and sang so sweetly that the music of the Sirens seemed harsh discord. Such is the better way to resist temptation. The joy of a Spirit-filled life surpasses anything the world can offer. To use Dr. Steele's words: "When all heaven is warbling in the believer's ear, the whispers of the tempter grate upon the purified sensibilities as saw-filing rasps the nerves."[18]

### 6. Persevering saints need shepherding care.

The hard part of evangelism comes in looking after those who have begun to follow Jesus. Newborn babes in Christ must be nurtured by spiritual guardians, like a mother and father taking care of their own children (1 Thess. 2:8, 11). Just as in the physical world, the young saints must have food and shelter and guidance, and above all, lots of love. Without such attention it is doubtful they would survive.

As seen in the analogy of Jesus, people are like sheep who need a shepherd to lead them. Not only does he watch over them while they graze in the field, but at the end of the day, he leads them into the fold; then to assure that they will not be molested by marauders at night, he makes his bed at the entrance. The shepherd will lay his life down for the sheep (John 10:11, 15).

The shepherd knows his sheep. They listen for his voice and come when he calls. Sheep who do not obey receive discipline. I am told that when a sheep repeatedly disobeys, and ignoring warning, wanders into harm's way, the shepherd will deliberately break one of its legs, "ensuring that the warning the sheep failed to hear with its ears would now be felt in its bones. And by having been carried awhile, it would learn that the hands that discipline are also the hands that protect."[19]

Persons who know the Lord are told to "shepherd the flock of God that is among you" (1 Pet. 5:2). We must be especially sensitive to the immature sheep that are prone to wander away. Samuel Shoemaker in his "Apologia for My Life" tells how we stand by the door not only to help people on the outside find their way to Christ, but also to encourage those who have come in to stay when they get afraid and would like to run away.

Somebody must stand by the door to tell them that they are spoiled for the old life. Once taste God, and nothing but God will do any more. Somebody must be watching for the frightened who seek to sneak out just where they came in, to tell them how much better it is inside. So, for them, too, I stand by the door.[20]

All of us need to be such doorkeepers.

### 7. *Perseverance puts faith to the test.*

The call to follow Christ brings forth faith, but it is overcoming roadblocks on the journey that prove its mettle. "Consider it pure joy, my brothers, whenever you face trials of many kinds," James said, "because you know that the testing of your faith develops perseverance." Then he added: "Perseverance must finish its work so that you may be mature and complete, not lacking anything" (James 1:2–4 NIV; cf. 1 Pet. 4:12–13).

Every testing brings another opportunity to prove God's faithfulness and grow in the likeness of Christ, who found his fulfillment in doing the will of the Father who sent him (John 17:4). But it is not always easy.

I remember the story of how the ancient Arabs trained Arabian steeds for the king's stables. Their equestrian trainer carried a whistle, and the horses were taught to stop all activity and come to the trainer whenever they heard the whistle sound. Complete obedience was required.

Toward the end of the training, the horses were not fed for five days, and for three days they were denied water to drink. On the last day, troughs of grain and water were placed about one hundred yards from the corral. Then suddenly the corral door would be sprung open, and the surprised horses would gallop toward the troughs. But when they were about twenty-five yards from them, the trainer standing off to the side would blow the whistle.

Everything about the horse would tighten. A choice had to be made! Go to the troughs or go to the trainer? If the horse went to the waiting troughs to gratify hunger and thirst, thus disobeying the call of its trainer, that horse failed the test. If the horse resisted its own fleshly instincts and went to the trainer, it qualified for the king's service and would then be allowed to go to the troughs.[21]

In less dramatic ways, but no less real, every follower of Christ on the way to heaven makes choices as faith is tested every day. Let us remember in that moment God is faithful to the saints and on the other side of the testing awaits the joy of victory.

### 8. *Live in the confidence of everlasting life.*

Eternal life is the birthright of every child of God, who in receiving Christ by faith has "passed from death to life" (John 5:24). Life in Christ is unending because he is eternal. What is called eternal security is simply a by-product of that relationship.

That saints persevere emphasizes the keeping power of God for all who believe (John 6:39–40; Phil. 1:6; 2 Tim. 1:12; 4:18). Since the righteous "live by faith" (Rom. 1:17), the completion of the journey is assured from the beginning. John summed it up:

> This is the testimony, that God gave us eternal life, and this life is in his Son. Whoever has the Son has life; whoever does not have the Son of God does not have life. I write these things to you who believe in the name of the Son of God that you may know that you have eternal life.
>
> 1 John 5:11–13

For worldlings aimlessly stumbling along in fear of the darkness, the Gospel speaks to that longing in their soul for certainty of salvation. And for those who have found that pearl of great price, eternal life, there is reason to celebrate. You have begun to explore the riches of Christ, and the end is not yet.

# 15

# The Church and Her Ministry

Christ is making a church to display his glory—a communion of saints to enjoy him forever. The old hymn expresses it well: "From heaven he came and sought her to be his holy bride; and with his blood he bought her, and for her life he died."[1]

## Nature of the Church

### The Body of Christ

Every person born of the Spirit—past, present, and future—belongs to this "people for [God's] own possession" (1 Pet. 2:9; cf. Titus 2:14), purchased by "the precious blood of Christ" (1 Pet. 1:19). In a real sense, the church is God's trophy of grace, displaying to himself the magnificence of his holiness and power.

Many graphic metaphors are used in Scripture to describe this new creation, each conveying some aspect of the Lord's relationship to his people. In one category the church is "the Bride" of Christ, emphasizing his relationship of love with his beloved (Rev. 21:9; cf. 2 Cor. 11:2; Eph. 5:21–23). In another analogy, the church is "a royal priesthood" (1 Pet. 2:9), serving under Christ as mediator between God and man (Heb. 8:1; Rev. 1:6). As a "kingdom of priests," she constitutes a "holy nation," reflecting the character of her Lord (Exod. 19:6; 1 Pet. 2:9).

From a pastoral perspective, the church is the "flock" of the Great Shepherd who watches over his sheep (Acts 20:28; cf. John 10:1–16). Applying this all-inclusive fellowship to construction, the church is "God's building" (1 Cor. 3:9), "built on the foundation of the apostles and prophets, Christ Jesus himself being the cornerstone, in whom the whole structure, being joined together, grows into a holy temple in the Lord" (Eph. 2:20–21).

A metaphor especially meaningful to me speaks of the church as the body of Christ. Seen in the picture of marriage, "The two shall become one flesh" (Eph. 5:31). Christ is the head, and we are the members of "his body, the fullness of him who fills all in all" (Eph. 1:22–23; cf. Col. 1:18). "Rooted and built up in him" (Col. 2:7), every believer stands in direct relationship to the head.

Consider what this means to the care of the body, "for no one ever hated his own flesh, but nourishes and cherishes it," just as Christ does the church (Eph. 5:29). It behooves us, then, to follow obediently his leadership, from whom the whole body "grows with a growth that is from God" (Col. 2:19), until we mature in the stature of our Lord (Eph. 4:13).

### Unity of the Body

In fellowship with Christ, members of his body are also members of one another. All Christians have a mystical union with every other believer. Within this oneness, of course, there is diversity of theological perspectives, worship styles, church government, cultural patterns, and any number of other disparities that obscure "the unity of the Spirit" (Eph. 4:3). But we should not be so enamored with our own ecclesiastical distinctives that we disown other members of the universal church that are not like us. We need each other.

A church on the Island of Jersey in the English Channel beautifully illustrates this truth. The walls of the church are built from stones contributed by people of the congregation, each person bringing at least one stone. The master builder used them all, whatever their shape or weight, large or small; even some pebbles that mothers placed in the hands of their babes are there. The old building has weathered many a storm for several centuries and stands today as a symbol of the way every person in the church "like living stones are being built up as a spiritual house" (1 Pet. 2:5).

Since all of us belong to the same family of faith, let us "bear one another's burdens, and so fulfill the law of Christ" (Gal. 6:2). "If one member suffers, all suffer together; if one member is honored, all rejoice together" (1 Cor. 12:26).

The solidarity encompasses the whole spectrum of our spiritual well-being. "Therefore," James said, "confess your sins to one another, and pray for one another, that you may be healed" (James 5:16). What implications this has for discipleship! And it surely pertains to those in the church who are backslidden. "My brothers, if anyone among you wanders from the truth and someone brings him back, let him know that whoever brings back a sinner from his wandering will save his soul from death" (vv. 19–20).

### Called Out from the World

The word *church* comes from a Greek word, *ecclesia*, meaning "called out." It takes its cue from the Old Testament term sometimes used to describe an assembly of people gathered to hear the word of God (Deut. 4:10). In this broad sense, the New Testament can speak of the people of Israel as a congregation (Acts 7:38; Heb. 2:12). We can understand why the gathering of believers today would be known by this name, for in hearing the Word of God and responding to it, the church is formed—called out from the world to serve the Lord.

Christians, thus, become a pilgrim people, living as strangers in an alien land. They march to a different drummer. Though remaining in the world, they are not of it (John 17:14, 16; 18:36). Their "citizenship is in heaven" (Phil. 3:20).

The church may be likened to a boat on a lake. The boat is in the lake but not like the lake in which it sails. Only because it is separate from the lake can it be useful. So it is with the church. Though a community involved in society, only as the church is unlike the world in her life can she fulfill her purpose. As soon as the church becomes like the world in her character and conduct, she loses any usefulness.[2]

### Community of the King

When "born again," one enters "the kingdom of God" (John 3:3, 5)—the reign of God is in the hearts of his people. Whether or not the kingdom is separate from the church is academic.[3] What matters is that the kingdom is present whenever Christ is loved and served (Matt. 18:3). It is "not a matter of eating and drinking but of righteousness and peace and joy in the Holy Spirit" (Rom. 14:17).

Jesus announced that the kingdom was at hand (Matt. 4:17, 23; Mark 1:15; Luke 4:43). In setting forth this truth, he focused a theme that runs through the whole of Scripture. That which had been given in covenant, embodied in the law, typified in Israel's government, and envisioned by the prophets was personified in his life and work. In his mind the kingdom had come and was coming. What Oscar Cullman called the "already" and "not yet" both existed in him.[4]

As the community of the King, living under the lordship of Christ, the church is custodian of the Gospel and holds the keys to the kingdom (Matt. 16:19). Doing the will of God on earth as it is in heaven (Matt. 6:10), she displays in her holy lifestyle something of the character of the world to come, awaiting the day when finally the Gospel will reach all nations and the kingdom comes to fruition at the end of time.

## The Church in Ministry

### *Proclaiming the Word of God*

An experience as a young preacher still lingers in my mind. I was one of two speakers that year at the Delanco Camp Meeting in New Jersey. The other preacher was an elderly man, who before beginning his sermons always laid his big railroad watch on the pulpit, indicating that he was going to stop on time.

On this evening he had gotten a slow start and had scarcely moved past his introduction when he glanced at his watch, and rather apologetically mentioned that he had only about twenty minutes left. Picking up the pace of his sermon, he went on for another ten minutes before looking at his watch and commenting that he was cognizant of the time. He was really getting into his message when again he looked at his watch and exclaimed, "My goodness, I've just got five minutes left!" Then he proceeded to preach faster and harder, when suddenly he saw his watch and cried, "Oh, I've only got two more minutes!"

By this time everyone in the tabernacle was getting nervous, and an old man in the back, unable to restrain his exasperation, hollered out: "Don't mind the clock; give us the Word!"

Well, despite the circumstances that day, what the old man said was on the mark. We must give out the Word. The church is gathered around the Holy Scripture, which gives her birth and continues to nourish her growth in the character of Christ (Rom. 10:17; 2 Tim. 3:15–17).

### *A Worshiping People*

God dwells in the midst of his praises, so ministry of the church centers in worship—the adoring response of a person to the grandeur of God's holiness and love. While it presupposes submission to him, worship, in its highest sense, is "the occupation of the soul with God himself."[5] However practiced, the end of it all is the pure joy of magnifying the One who alone is worthy.[6]

We are made for this purpose—to glorify God, to adore him, and to rejoice in him forever. The creature is never so invigorated as when engaged in this exercise. Haven't you found this to be true in your life? When we magnify his name and celebrate his glory, our own souls partake of greatness.

Such genuine, unabashed happiness in the church attracts lonely, disconsolate people on the outside. Captivated by Christian joy, reinforced by love, "many will see and fear, and put their trust in the LORD" (Ps. 40:3).

The Bible admonishes us to "make a joyful noise to the LORD. . . . Come into his presence with singing" (Ps. 100:1–2). There was a time when the homes of the early Christians could be identified by the sound of singing that came from their houses. Would that this could be said today!

I am reminded of General Stonewall Jackson who one day during the Civil War was told that some soldiers in the camp were singing loudly. He asked what they were singing and was told they were singing hymns. "What's wrong with that?" he asked. "Sir," the officer replied, "the articles of war say that those who make unusual noise should be punished." Whereupon the general replied, "God forbid that praise to God will ever be an unusual noise in this camp."

Of course, worship does not have to be earsplitting or even voiced, but a church alive will cultivate the spirit of praise among her members. Whether in stated meetings or in private meditation, the people of God "worship and bow down" before the Lord (Ps. 95:6; cf. 100:4; Heb. 12:22). This is the DNA of the saints.

From this comes the most powerful motivation for service, especially in bringing the kingdom to people hurting in body and soul. Recognizing need may arouse concern, and the call of duty may provoke effort, but finally it is love for Jesus that constrains one to go (2 Cor. 5:14). In its highest sense, ministry is an offering of praise to God.

### Fellowship of Prayer

Adoration overflows in prayer—the language of the soul in communion with the Spirit. While contemplating the divine glory, we become acutely conscious of our own shortcomings, which brings forth sincere confession of sin and renewal of faith (Ps. 66:18; James 4:3). Then with a clean heart, we can lay personal burdens before the Lord and intercede for others (Matt. 7:7–8; Luke 11:9), not forgetting to praise God from whom all blessings flow.

Prayer involves the whole council of the Holy Trinity. We pray to the Father (Eph. 3:14), coming to him in dependence as a child (Rom. 8:15), and he hears and answers (Matt. 7:11). We pray through the Son, our Mediator (Heb. 12:24), in whom we have identity (John 15:7), and Christ is glorified in the answer (John 13:32). We pray in the Spirit (Eph. 6:18), the activator of worship and truth (John 4:23), who helps us in our weakness and intercedes for us (Rom. 8:26–27).

Nothing in the will of God is beyond the reach of this ministry. Jesus has promised that "whatever you ask in my name, this I will do. . . . If you ask me anything in my name, I will do it" (John 14:13–14; cf. 15:7, 16; 16:23–26). The "name" of Jesus, of course, is another way of saying his person and work. To pray in his name is to pray in his character, to pray as Jesus himself is praying for us, before the Father. Viewed this way, prayer implies the alignment of our will with the purposes of God.

A church alive in the Spirit knows this secret, and by every possible means seeks to involve her people in this ministry. It has been said that one can generally discover how popular God is in a congregation by the way people turn out to pray.

What is seen in the corporate activities of the church, of course, has its most meaningful expression in the personal prayer life of her members. We can get along without some things but we cannot live without prayer. The quality time we have alone with God every day is the best index of our own spiritual vitality.

### Ministering Servants

Undergirded by worship and prayer, the church moves out into the world in ministry. Just as Jesus "came not to be served but to serve, and to give his life as a ransom for many" (Matt. 20:28; Mark 10:45), so the body of Christ on earth becomes a ministering servant.

Every member of the church becomes part of "a holy priesthood, to offer spiritual sacrifices acceptable to God through Jesus Christ" (1 Pet. 2:5; cf. v. 9), fulfilling the prophecy of Moses that we "shall be . . . a kingdom of priests and a holy nation" (Exod. 19:6). No one is excluded. This is rightly called "the priesthood of all believers."

The Protestant Reformation brought this submerged doctrine back into focus. Unfortunately, by and large, only half of the church's priesthood got attention—the perpendicular aspect that in Christ every believer can go directly to God for spiritual ministry. No human intermediary is needed to facilitate access to the throne of God. But in the other dimension of our priesthood—the horizontal outreach to our fellow men—the church has a long way to go. In most parishes, ministry is still largely consigned to duly ordained clergymen or especially favored local leaders.[7]

Offices of individuals within the church, of course, will differ according to their gifts and callings. In the economy of God's design, some gifted persons are prepared for particular roles of leadership in the church, as Paul explains in Ephesians 4:11–12. Apostles serve as foundation builders, sent in a missionary capacity. Prophets proclaim the message of God, an office almost comparable to preaching. Evangelists are particularly gifted in speaking to the lost. Pastors are overseers and shepherds of the flock, an office closely associated with, if not identical to, that of teacher.

These persons are in a unique position to prepare the church for the work of ministry that they share together. It is not their place to do all this work themselves, but rather to "equip the saints" for the work committed by Christ to his whole body. By so doing, the members of the church are built up to a place of strength and maturity, until all become full grown in the Lord (Eph. 4:13).

Many find this concept hard to grasp. For example, as Richard Halverson observed:

> When we ask, "How many ministers does your church have?" the traditional answer is "one" or "two" or "five," depending upon how large the paid staff is. But the true answer is "two hundred" or "two thousand," depending on how large the membership is! Every believer is a minister! Or when we ask, "Where is your church?" the traditional reply is "on the corner of Broad and Main."

But the correct reply is "What time is it?" If it is 11:00 a.m., Sunday, the church is "on the corner of Broad and Main" (that is where the headquarter building is). But if it is 11:00 a.m., Tuesday, then my church is in Room 511 in the Professional Building, where Bill White, Christian attorney, is practicing law. It is at 3009 Melody Lane where Jane White, Christian housewife, is making a home. It is at Central High, where Jimmy White, Christian student, is studying to the glory of God. There is the church in action.[8]

This lifts the concept of ministry into the daily life of mothers, factory workers, clerks, soldiers, farmers, students—every Christ-honoring vocation becomes a means of service and every location a place of witness.

### Celebrating the Sacraments

Sacraments of the church, sometimes called "ordinances," are outward signs of an inward spiritual reality. They signify and seal to those within the covenant of grace the benefits of redemption, increase their faith, and testify of their communion with one another. Also, in receiving them, Christians pledge their fidelity to God.[9]

Roman Catholic and Eastern Orthodox churches have seven sacraments: the Eucharist (Lord's Supper), baptism, confirmation, penance, matrimony, ordination, and extreme unction (the anointing of persons in danger of death). They hold that these sacraments impart grace to the persons who, without moral sin, receive them.

Most Protestants observe only baptism and the Lord's Supper.[10] Baptism, whether performed by sprinkling, pouring, or immersion, represents the believer's faith in Jesus Christ and initiation into the church (Matt. 28:19; cf. John 4:1–2; Acts 2:8–11). Water baptism had long been practiced by Jews when proselytes were inducted into their religion, so the observance was not new. Some link the Christian rite with the Old Testament custom of circumcision, symbolizing the cutting away of sin and entering the covenant of grace. When immersion is the custom, going beneath the water represents burial with Christ in his death, and coming up from the water his resurrection.

The Lord's Supper is a thank offering in remembrance of Christ (Matt. 26:26–29; Mark 14:22–25), and "as often as you eat this bread and drink the cup, you proclaim the Lord's death until he comes" (1 Cor. 11:26). It emphasizes the communion members of the church have with one another (1 Cor. 10:16–17) and foreshadows the "marriage supper of the Lamb" (Rev. 19:9). As a Christian Passover, it also recalls the Old Testament miracle of God delivering his people from bondage (Matt. 26:18–19; cf. Exod. 12:43–49).

In Catholicism, the Eucharist, or "Mass" as it came to be called, is understood as a sacrifice, with the bread and wine, duly consecrated, becoming the actual body and blood of Jesus. Lutherans believe that Christ is literally present in, with, and under the elements, but not in bodily form. Followers of

Ulrich Zwingli have reduced it all essentially to symbolism. Most Calvinists and Arminians think of Christ as being spiritually present in the sacrament and that worthy receivers partake of the blessings of grace for their nourishment and growth.

While the sacraments are intended for believers, the performance of them offers real opportunities for evangelism. Preparing people for baptism presents a natural occasion to explain the Gospel to make sure they can take their vows sincerely. At the time of the baptism, after the candidates give their testimony, the officiating minister can also invite any other person present to come to Jesus.

Probably the greatest opening for presenting the claims of Christ comes at the Lord's Supper. When its meaning is clarified by the celebrant, the invitation is extended. Every church will have their own way of phrasing it, but the one which I have given through the years is typical:

> You that do truly and earnestly repent of your sins, and are in love and charity with your neighbor, and called to lead a new life, following the Commandments of God, and walking from henceforth in his holy ways; draw near with faith, and take this sacrament to your comfort; and make your humble confession to Almighty God.[11]

If these words are sincerely received, no one should leave the Lord's Supper without the assurance of salvation.

### The Great Commission

Christ's last command to the church is recorded variously in all the Gospels: "Go into all the world and proclaim the gospel to the whole creation" (Mark 16:15); "As the Father has sent me, even so I am sending you" (John 20:21; cf. 17:18); "You will receive power when the Holy Spirit has come upon you, and you will be my witnesses in Jerusalem and in all Judea and Samaria, and to the end of the earth" (Acts 1:8; cf. Luke 24:38–49); "Go therefore and make disciples of all nations, baptizing them in the name of the Father and of the Son and of the Holy Spirit, teaching them to observe all that I have commanded you. And behold, I am with you always, to the end of the age" (Matt. 28:19–20).

Clearly Christ intends for his church to reach the world, fulfilling the commission given to our forebearers in the garden to "be fruitful and multiply and fill the earth" (Gen. 1:28).[12] In God's eyes there is no distinction between home and foreign missions. It is just one big world that God loves and for which Jesus died. The objective of going, sending, witnessing, preaching, teaching, baptizing, and receiving the Spirit's power is to "make disciples of all nations."

Christ does not ask us to make converts. Certainly, he made clear that one must be converted to enter the kingdom (Matt. 18:3), but the commission is to "make disciples." A disciple is a learner—one resolved to follow the teacher.

Responding to the Gospel call, thus, commits us to an ongoing process of learning, whereby we are progressively conformed to the image of our Lord.

Implicit in this mandate is the summons to a life of disciplined obedience to the Word of God in the fellowship of the church. Evangelism and training are complementary. To stress conversion and neglect growth eventually demeans the church by bringing in babes who do not grow. On the other hand, to emphasize education to the exclusion of outreach eventually stagnates the church by cutting off the flow of new life.

Jesus went about continually serving people—healing the sick, feeding the hungry, preaching the Gospel to the poor—but he did not let this ministry distract him from the training of a few men. So in his role as a servant, he drew some disciples close to himself. It was like a family relationship. They saw how he lived, even as they gradually got involved in his ministry. When finally he told them to go and make disciples, they understood what he meant, for that was what he had done with them.[13]

His example brings ministry into the diverse vocations of all believers. We should not minimize preaching or healing or any special calling. But discipling is more basic to the pattern of daily living. This ministry is not a gift; it is a command to every Christian. In the routine associations with family and friends—being alert to their desire to learn of Christ, showing them how to relate faith to life, helping them discern the joy of service through their gifts— we can live every day in the excitement of the Great Commission. Moreover, since close relationships are possible only with a few persons at any one time in our lives, we all have about the same opportunity to make disciples.

By placing the emphasis on discipling, the perpetuation of evangelism is assured. One cannot follow Christ without sooner or later learning to become a fisher of men. Not only do true disciples learn to make disciples, but they also teach them to do the same, and through the process of multiplication, someday the world will hear the Gospel.

## Problem Issues

### Confusing the Material Form with the Spiritual Reality

What the world sees as the church may not be the church at all. Buildings, schools, programs, sacraments, rituals, crusades, and the like may be identified with the church of God but in their visible form are fashioned by man. The body of Christ is the creation of the Spirit, supernatural in her origin, incorruptible in her life, and in her spiritual essence, invisible to the world.

But to operate in society, the church is clothed with a material form. The divine and the human are cojoined in one body. The man-made vessel of communication is not necessarily a valid manifestation of the Spirit, just as church ministry is not the same as the Spirit's ministry. Only as the church is controlled by the Holy Spirit can the church properly function as the body of Christ.

Here is our challenge—to close the gap between the human and the divine in the church. To the degree that the Spirit fills the human vessel, the church fulfills her purpose and destiny.

### The Clergy and Laity Divide

Distinctions in the church between ordained clergy and unordained laymen are unnecessary. Biblically speaking, "clergy" and "laity" cannot be defined as mutually exclusive terms. In the bonds of Christ, all are laity (or the people of God) and equally share the responsibility to make disciples. By the same criteria, the whole body of believers receives the inheritance of Christ, which is the root idea of the term in the New Testament from which "clergy" is derived.[14] Radical distinctions between the pulpit and the pew did not develop until well into the second century.

The establishment of a professional clergy has confused the priesthood of all Christians. Regrettably, many feel quite satisfied with the situation, content to allow paid clergy and staff to do all the work of the church. Even those who are more sensitive to their calling and want to be involved may experience a sense of frustration as they try to find their place of service. "After all," they may ask, "if I'm not a preacher or missionary or something of the kind, how can I be properly engaged in ministry?"

The answer lies, of course, in their seeing the Great Commission as a lifestyle encompassing the total resources of every child of God. Here the ministry of Christ comes alive in the day-to-day activity of discipling, whether in a "secular" job or ecclesiastical office.

### Questioning the Unity of the Church

Disagreements among believers have been commonplace through the history of the church, and sometimes these arguments result in a split. Just this week I learned that in one of the oldest churches in the country, a large part of the membership had left to form a rival congregation. And these partings are seldom amicable. Little wonder that observers on the outside become cynical about the church. I understand, too, why my friends in the historic Roman Catholic and Orthodox communions look with dismay at the multiplication of different Protestant denominations around the world, numbering into the thousands.

Let us admit the regrettable fracture of fellowship and bear the sorrow with grace. But discontent in denominations need not disrupt the solidarity of evangelical Christians. Our unity is not dependent on ecclesiastical structures or world councils: unity is not organized; it is affirmed as a present reality. The only thing that can destroy our oneness in Christ is unbelief in the basic truth of the Gospel. Notwithstanding the critiques of a generally disoriented society, sometimes even the pronouncements of compromised ecumenical officials, the real church, inclusive of all born-again believers, is not divided in the Word of God. "There is one body and one Spirit . . . one Lord, one faith, one baptism, one God and Father of all" (Eph. 4:4–6).

We should cherish our common faith and mission, celebrate it with gladness, seek to cooperate in evangelistic endeavors of all kinds, and move out together to storm the gates of hell.


## Summary Applications

*1. The priority of the church is evangelism.*

Introducing people to Christ brings the church into existence. In fact, apart from evangelism, the church would soon become extinct. That is why witnessing to the Gospel is the first duty of every Christian.

Though evangelism will always be assailed by the powers of darkness in this world, the ultimate triumph of the church is never in doubt. After Peter's declarations that Christ was "the Son of the living God" (Matt. 16:16; cf. Mark 8:29; Luke 9:26), Jesus said: "On this rock I will build my church, and the gates of hell shall not prevail against it" (Matt. 16:18).

However the affirmation of Peter is interpreted, the relationship between bearing witness of Christ and this ultimate victory over the world is clear. One cannot come without the other. Bringing the two dynamic facts together comes in evangelism. When Christ is faithfully proclaimed, nothing can defeat the mission of the church.[15]

We must take this to heart. An old lady focused the issue exactly when she turned to the guide showing a group through Westminster Abbey and said, "Young man! Young man! Will you stop your chatter for a moment and tell me—has anyone been saved here lately?"[16] A startled silence came over the tour party. Saved in Westminster Abbey? Why not? Isn't that the business of the church?

It is not easy to keep first things first in the church, but it is even harder to face the consequences of not doing so. The harsh truth is that whenever evangelism is relegated to an incidental place in the church's program, the church begins to die. The church can continue only as the people of God reproduce their life in each succeeding generation.

It breaks down to a personal responsibility. The ministry of the congregation is only a reflection of the lives of individuals in the church, and this is nowhere more important than in personal evangelism.[17]

What is stimulated on the personal level, of course, needs to be implemented in the official programs of the church. Winning people to Christ should be so fused into the congregational life that if the organization functions at all, evangelism is inevitable.[18]

## 2. Evangelism flows out of social compassion.

Giving priority to reaching the lost does not mean the church has no other ministry. Jesus saw himself as an evangelist, announcing the coming of the kingdom of God. However, his message was to be proclaimed in the context of demonstrated compassion for the bruised and forgotten people of the world, "recovering of sight to the blind, [and setting] at liberty those who are oppressed" (Luke 4:18–19; cf. Isa. 61:1–2).

At this point, there is often confusion among churchmen. Some contend that evangelism involves only the Gospel declaration, while others identify it essentially with establishing a caring presence in society or seeking to rectify injustice.

It should be clear that both are necessary. One without the other leaves a distorted impression of the Good News. If Jesus had not borne the sorrows of people and performed deeds of mercy among them, we might question his concern. On the other hand, if he had not made clear the Gospel, we would not have known why he came or how we could be saved. The Name above every name must be named. To bind up the wounds of a dying man while withholding the message that could bring deliverance to his soul would still leave him in bondage.

Balancing spiritual transformation with the ever-enlarging needs of the world is not easy, and over time, the church tends to submerge evangelism in a multitude of humanitarian activities.[19] Awareness of this condition, however, is no excuse for believers to neglect engagement with society.[20] As a matter of historical record, it can be said that when the church is at her best, evangelical Christians have been in the forefront of social action.[21]

## 3. The whole church must be mobilized for ministry.

The extent to which church members are involved in her mission to the world will largely determine success. Total mobilization of the total church for total ministry is the goal. Actually this is not something peculiar to Christianity. It is the criteria of accomplishment in any enterprise, be it business, government, military strategy, or evangelism. The children of light must be as wise in the use of resources as the institutions of this world (see Luke 16:8).

What a difference it would make if we would start looking at church ministry this way! Whatever our occupation, it would be rendered as unto the Lord. Wherever we are, it would be as a sanctuary of worship. Every day would be filled with the glory of God. This does not mean that the secular world becomes holy because we are there, but it does mean that we have the opportunity within our sphere of influence to witness for Christ. It is in this sense, like the apostles of old, that we are called and sent into the world.[22]

The church building, if there is one, is simply the "drill hall for the Christian task force."[23] It is the place where the soldiers come together to be strengthened, trained, and briefed in the art of warfare. The battle is not fought in the church. The battle is in the world, and church meetings are intended to prepare the church for the attack.

In this capacity, those in leadership positions may have a strategic influence in setting policy, but no more authority than others in the church for making disciples. The Great Commission is a personal matter. How the authorities of the church prepare members for this ministry is the measure of their relevance—meetings, committees, crusades, retreats, revivals, seminars, parties, schools, projects—everything must contribute to the mission for which we are sent into the world, or it is an exercise in futility.

If this criterion were applied to our present religious activity, I wonder how much of it would be worth the effort. Somewhere in our rush of services we have substituted institutional programs for our own priesthood. Pomp and ceremony all too often have stifled creativity and individual expression. Tradition has taken precedence over the guidelines of Scripture. We must get back to the apostolic norm of ministry and mobilize the whole body of Christ for action.

### 4. A Great Commission lifestyle assures growth in holiness.

Making disciples is more than God's plan to reach the nations with the Gospel; it is also his way to encourage the sanctification of the church. In seeking to lead another person in the way of holiness, we are made aware of our own inadequacies and constrained by the Spirit to draw more deeply from the wellspring of grace.

One does not have to be perfect to make disciples but one has to be transparent. Let us open our lives to each other, confessing our own failures and welcoming correction. The beautiful thing about discipling others is that we, too, are being discipled. And God is not finished with any of us yet.

### 5. The church is charismatic in ministry.

There are many different forms of service, depending on the abilities and qualifications God has given (Rom. 12:6–8; 1 Cor. 12:4–11, 28–30; Eph. 4:7–12; 1 Pet. 4:10). Whether these traits are natural talents under divine control or special endowments resulting from the operation of the Spirit within the believer's life, they evidence a sovereign grace.

Some of these gifts prepare Christians with basic inner motivations for declaring God's truth, serving practical needs, teaching and clarifying facts, exhorting believers concerning the applications of truth, entrusting money and possessions to others, administering activities, and empathizing with the distress of people. Some gifts relate to a special ministry needed in the church, which might be that of a missionary, preacher, explainer of the Scriptures, worker of miracles, healer, helper, administrator, speaker in various kinds of tongues, evangelist, or pastor-teacher. Still other gifts enable one to restore hope by receiving a word of wisdom, distinguishing between spirits, interpreting tongues, or something else necessary to redeem a life situation. The listings given by Paul were probably not intended to be exhaustive but only suggestive of the various ways God enables the church to fulfill his ministry.[24]

Obviously some Christians, like Paul, are more gifted than others. The number and strength of gifts, however, establishes no merit or superiority. It would seem that believers are not responsible for the possession of gifts, but for their use. For example, wrongly employed, spiritual knowledge may puff up (1 Cor. 8:1), just as the gifts of tongues may lead to self-glory (1 Cor. 14:2). Like any true blessing, the gifts can be misused and falsified. Such abuse met with strong reproof in the early church (e.g., Acts 8:18–24; 19:13–16).

The purpose of God's gifts must always be kept in view. They are given not to foster pride in recipients but to perfect the body of Christ and thereby bring glory to God. When exercised within this intention, there is beautiful fulfillment, and the whole body benefits. Love is the supreme fruit. It shines through the harmonious operation of the gifts as the result of their effective function (1 Cor. 13:1–3; Eph. 4:16).

### 6. Ministry will be no greater than our personal prayer life.

On my desk is a little plaque given to me by my Sunday school teacher when I went off to college. Inscribed on it are the words: "Prayer Changes Things," and underneath is the promise of Jesus, "And all things, whatsoever ye shall ask in prayer, believing, ye shall receive" (Matt. 21:22 KJV). Across the years it has been there to remind me that our greatest ministry, flowing out of worship, is prayer.

In this communion with the Spirit, we are being prepared for ministry to others. Without realizing it, too, we are getting ready for that perfect communion with God to come. We are never so close to heaven on earth as when engaged in prayer.

### 7. The believer's priesthood has its highest expression in intercession.

Such praying is the most rewarding, yet most demanding ministry of the church. It will make us face the cross. It means deep searching of soul and sacrifice. When Jesus prayed in Gethsemane for us, the burden of his mission was so intense that "his sweat became like great drops of blood falling down to the ground" (Luke 22:44). Prayer was indeed the sweat, tears, and blood of his ministry (Heb. 5:7).

So it is with every victory of grace, of which evangelism preeminently bears witness. The weapons of this warfare are not fleshly, but are "mighty through God to the pulling down of strong holds" (2 Cor. 10:4 KJV). To paraphrase the words of Dr. Lewis Sperry Chafer: winning men is more a work of pleading *for* souls than a service of pleading *with* them.[25] It reminds me of what Billy Graham said when asked what was the secret of his ministry. Without hesitation he replied, "There are three reasons. The first is prayer. The second is prayer. The third is prayer."

God's response to our supplications may not come quickly or in the way envisioned. Sometimes we may not see the full effect until the next generation. But we can be sure that the prayer of faith will be answered on God's schedule and according to his will. When the completed church is finally gathered in heaven, perhaps then we will see how the course of human events has been determined by prayer, either its use or neglect.

### 8. The church needs revival.

Revival means to wake up and live, to restore life's true nature and purpose.[26] When this concept is applied to redemptive history, revival can be seen as that "strange and sovereign work of God in which he visits his own people, restoring, reanimating and releasing them into the fullness of his blessing."[27]

Evidence of revival is the change wrought in the heart by the Holy Spirit. When one responds fully to divine grace, there is a wonderful assurance of sin forgiven—the heart is clean, the soul is free, and love fills life with spontaneous praise. There is still suffering and temptation, but amid it all is the light of God's face shining on the inner man.

From the standpoint of New Testament Christianity, there is nothing unusual about the revival experience. In this personal sense, it should be a constant reality. Unfortunately, most of us do not live up to our privilege. But if we were living in the continual fullness of the Spirit of Christ, as God desires, revival would be an abiding state.

Yet revival involves more than personal blessing. As individuals come alive to Christ and this experience is multiplied in the lives of others, the church feels a new unity of faith and purpose. The dynamic for a compelling evangelism is born. The commission to make disciples of all nations cannot be ignored. In the same spirit, social concern is quickened for oppressed and lonely people. Duty becomes a joy. Love naturally overflows when hearts are full.

Society feels the impact. As the Gospel goes forth in word and deed, the world takes note that men and women have been with Jesus. Restitutions are made. Broken homes are reunited. Public moral standards improve. Integrity makes its way into government. To the extent that the spirit of revival prevails, mercy, justice, and righteousness sweep over the land.

Let it be clear, however, that authentic revivals are not engineered by men. They are God's work. What he does is by his own sovereign power as his conditions are met (2 Chron. 7:14), and, as is true of all grace, no one can take any credit for it.

Still, whether in individual experience or the corporate life of the church, it is during these seasons of refreshing that the work of the Spirit of holiness is brought into bold relief. There have been times in redemptive history when revival has gathered such strength that the course of nations has been changed. Were it not for the force of revival at several crucial periods in American his-

225

tory, when the republic was in jeopardy, it is doubtful if our country could have survived.[28]

As you think about times of revival in other days and then consider the state of the church today, do you not find yourself praying that God will revive us again, and that a new and mighty demonstration of holy love in Pentecostal power will come on the church (Ps. 85:6)?[29] Lord, send a revival, and let it begin with me.

# 16

# The Return of the King

During the closing days of the Second World War, a hospital in Nuremberg, Germany, was damaged by the extensive bombing. After cleaning up the rubble, someone painted on the wall of one of the wards, as translated: "We don't know what is coming, but we know who is coming."[1]

## The Blessed Hope

### Christ's Return

Christians have always lived with the joyous certainty that Jesus is coming again (Titus 2:13). His return is the concluding act in the drama of redemption. Salvation of believers has already been achieved through the cross and resurrection, but the total victory awaits the day of his return.[2] Christ must remain in heaven "until the time for restoring all the things about which God spoke by the mouth of his holy prophets long ago" (Acts 3:20–21). His coming "a second time" is "not to deal with sin, but to save those who are eagerly waiting for him" (Heb. 9:28; cf. 1 John 3:2).

No teaching of the New Testament could be clearer. Jesus told his disciples on the eve of his death, "I will come again and will take you to myself" (John 14:3). At his ascension, the angel said to the watching believers, "Why do you stand looking into heaven? This Jesus, who was taken up from you into heaven, will come in the same way as you saw him go into heaven" (Acts 1:10–11). Echoing the testimony of the apostolic church, Paul declared: "The

Lord himself will descend from heaven with a cry of command, with the voice of an archangel, and with the sound of the trumpet of God" (1 Thess. 4:16).

With such thunderous sounds rending the heavens, the powers of the physical cosmos will be shaken, "the sun will be darkened, and the moon will not give its light, and the stars will fall from" the sky (Matt. 24:29). As the last trumpet sounds, Jesus appears suddenly, "in a moment, in the twinkling of an eye" (1 Cor. 15:52).

He is "coming on the clouds of heaven" (Matt. 26:64) "with great power and glory" (Mark 13:26), "and every eye will see him," not merely with the eye of faith but in sight of heaven and earth, "even those who pierced him, and all tribes of the earth will wail on account of him" (Rev. 1:7; cf. Matt. 24:30). "As the lightning comes from the east and shines as far as the west, so will be the coming of the Son of Man" (v. 27; cf. vv. 29–31; Luke 17:24).

Awesome beyond description. The heavens open, and he descends in "the glory of his Father" (Matt. 16:27; cf. Mark 8:38), accompanied by an army of "his mighty angels in flaming fire" (2 Thess. 1:7–8; cf. Rev. 19:14). With graphic apocalyptic language, the book of Revelation depicts him "clothed in a robe dipped in blood, and the name by which he is called is The Word of God" (Rev. 19:13).[3] "From his mouth comes a sharp sword," suggestive of the fearsome judgments that he commands, by which he strikes nations and triumphs over all the powers of evil gathered to make war against him (Rev. 19:15–21). And on his resplendent vesture is written, "King of kings and Lord of lords" (Rev. 19:16).

### Signs of His Return

"When will these things be," asked the disciples, "and what will be the sign of your coming and of the close of the age?" (Matt. 24:3; cf. Mark 13:4). In reply, Jesus stressed that concerning the day or hour, "no one knows, not even the angels in heaven, nor the Son, but only the Father" (Matt. 24:32). "The Son of Man is coming at an hour you do not expect" (Matt. 24:44; Luke 12:40). Clearly people will be caught by complete surprise (1 Thess. 5:2; cf. Rev. 16:15).

Nevertheless, Jesus does give some indications of the closing days of history. For one thing, prior to his return, the world will be going through unprecedented upheaval. "Nation will rise against nation, and kingdom against kingdom, and there will be famines and earthquakes in various places," and this is only "the beginning" of sorrows (Matt. 24:7–8). As conditions deteriorate, "there will be great tribulation, such as has not been from the beginning of the world" (v. 21).

Amid this dissolution in society, Christians will be hard-pressed, "hated by all nations" (v. 9). "Many will fall away and betray one another" (v. 10). Contributing to the tragedy, "false prophets will arise and lead many astray" (v. 11; cf. v. 24). And "because lawlessness will be increased, the love of many will grow cold" (v. 12). Encouraging this spirit of rebellion, "the son of destruction" appears "proclaiming himself to be God," casting a pall of delusion across the earth (2 Thess. 2:3–12).[4]

Yet it appears that the trials of the last days will serve to refine the character of the true saints. A purified church will then be able to receive unhindered the power of the outpoured Spirit, and thereby more boldly enter into the mission of Christ in preparation for the Lord's return (James 5:7).[5]

Out of this spiritual rejuvenation, something akin to the first Pentecost, though on a worldwide scale, will emerge as a tremendous surge of evangelism. Recall that Jesus said in these last days, "this gospel of the kingdom will be proclaimed throughout the whole world . . . and then the end will come" (Matt. 24:14). Despite the mounting opposition of the world, doubtless the passion to get out the message will increase, even as the witnesses multiply. Woven into this consummation will likely be the conversion and ingathering of many Jews.[6] That the Gospel will eventually reach every nation, tribe, people, and language is clear from the description of the innumerable multitude of the white-robed saints gathered around the throne of God in heaven (Rev. 7:9; cf. 5:9).

In thinking of these events associated with Christ's return, it is well to keep in mind that prophecy often has both a present and future reference. So it can be said that many of these signs may be present in some degree throughout history, but they will be greatly intensified in the end times.[7]

### Events at His Coming

The second advent of Christ, called the "parousia," unveils the glory of the Son of God.[8] What he has forever accomplished on the cross is now majestically disclosed to his people, while also accenting his lordship over the created elements of the universe and his dominion over the nations of the earth.

With the descent of the Lord from heaven, the dead shall be resurrected and brought to final judgment, both those who have done good and those who have done evil (John 5:28–29). It is a day when "God judges the secrets of men by Christ Jesus" (Rom. 2:16). "People will give account for every careless word they speak" (Matt. 12:36). As noted earlier when discussing sin (chapter 5), everyone in this present time when convicted by the Spirit of Christ makes a decision, which when lived out determines the judgment at his appearing.

Christians will be judged for their deeds done in the flesh. It has nothing to do with salvation—that has already been settled in this life. Rather at this judgment of believers, rewards are given for faithful stewardship and service. The determination is likened to placing our works into a fire. Any work not worthy of Christ is consumed in the flames, like "wood, hay, [or] straw"; works truly done for the glory of God, like "gold, silver, [or] precious stones" will remain. "Each one's work will become manifest, for the Day will disclose it . . .

and the fire will test what sort of work each one has done" (1 Cor. 3:12–13). The saints "will receive a reward" for any work built on the foundation of Christ (v. 14). "If anyone's work is burned up, he will suffer loss, though he himself will be saved, but only as through fire" (v. 15; cf. 2 Cor. 5:10; 1 Thess. 4:13–18; Rev. 11:18; 22:12).

The rewards Christians receive are sometimes called crowns or prizes, which are given in recognition of their faithfulness (Phil. 3:14; 1 Cor. 9:24–27; 2 Tim. 2:5; 4:7–8; Rev. 4:10–11). Let it be clear, however, that anything un-Christlike will be destroyed. Nothing can endure in the refining fire of judgment except that which displays the character of God.

Details are very sketchy and subject to different interpretations, but the judgment of the saints may precede that of the unrighteous.[9] Adding to the mystery, it appears that in some way Christians will assist in the judgment of the world (1 Cor. 6:2–3; cf. Rev. 20:4). Whatever the distinctions in time sequence, the judgments of mankind will climax in one final day of reckoning at the "great white throne" of God (Rev. 20:11; cf. Acts 17:31; Rom. 2:5, 16; 2 Pet. 2:9; 3:7). The "books were opened . . . and the dead were judged by what was written in the books, according to what they had done." And anyone's name "not found written in the book of life" was "thrown into the lake of fire" (Rev. 20:12–15).

Satan and his demon cohorts, along with the "kings of the earth and their armies gathered to make war" against Christ, following their defeat at Armageddon "on the great day of God the Almighty," also are judged and cast into the "lake of fire that burns with sulfur" (Rev. 16:12–16; 19:11–21; cf. Matt. 8:29; 2 Pet. 2:4).

## The Millennium

### Christ's Reign on Earth

Associated with these judgments is the binding of Satan, when all the enemies of Christ are put under his feet and he reigns with his saints on the earth (1 Cor. 15:24–25; Rev. 20:1–6). This period is called the millennium, which literally means a thousand years, though it may be an indefinite period of time. The term is used in Scripture only six times, in Revelation 20:1–7.

Because the biblical reference can be variously understood and is complicated, I think it prudent not to make any interpretation crucial to evangelism. What matters is the Gospel, not one's view of the millennium. Probably no teaching has caused more confusion, if not division, in the evangelical church. We can be thankful that the fact of Christ's return is not in question. The differences concern whether the scriptural texts refer to a literal or symbolic earthly reign of Christ and whether the millennium precedes or follows his return.[10]

## Premillennialism

Basically interpretations of the millennium fall into three categories, with many variations. Premillennialists see the second coming inaugurating the age of blessedness on earth when Christ reigns as King over his saints for a thousand years or its equivalent. Prior to his return, conditions in the world get progressively worse (Matt. 24:21; cf. Rev. 6:1–8:13). As to how this ordeal impacts the church, some hold that Christians will be raptured to heaven before the great tribulation.[11] Others see Christ coming to save a remnant midway during the tribulation, while still others believe that the church must endure the tribulation before the millennial age.[12] However viewed, the resurrection of the saints occurs at the beginning of the millennium and the resurrection of the unsaved at the end, followed by the final judgment.[13]

## Amillennialism

Rejecting a literal interpretation of the thousand-year rule of Christ, amillennialism (sometimes called realized or symbolic millennialism) holds that the promised reign of blessedness is already present in society or it is an emerging reality in the hearts of the born-again. In this view, the millennial promises refer to the church on earth now made alive with Christ (Eph. 2:1–6). The kingdom of God and the kingdom of the world coexist, like the wheat and tares growing together (Matt. 13:30). Though the saints endure increasing tribulation as history draws to a close, they look forward to a glorious future when the King returns.[14]

## Postmillennialism

Still another perspective, called postmillennialism, envisions a period of blessedness on earth prior to the second advent of Christ. In this view it is believed there will be a growing improvement in society through the triumph of the Gospel witness. Contrasted to the other two positions, which tend to see the church in the present age valiantly holding the faith of Christ as conditions on earth become darker, postmillennialists are optimistic about the future. Christians still have to struggle against the contagion of sin in the world, but ultimately evangelism will bring in the kingdom in preparation for the Lord's return.[15]

It's regrettable that many modern churchmen, infatuated with the prospects of a new world order, have abandoned the original evangelical basis for such a transformation and in its place have substituted a social gospel promoting justice, peace, and brotherhood through human effort. This more secularized form of postmillennialism, in as far as it discounts the supernatural power of the Gospel, has no genuine evangelistic message.

All the interpretations of the millennium are ably represented by respected scholars in the church, all of whom appeal to the Bible for support. Many form different positions using the same Scriptures. I think it fair to say, too, that all the viewpoints offer some valuable insights. These ideas can be discussed among Christians with profit, even as we agree to disagree on the specifics.

## Problem Areas

### Spiritualizing the Second Advent

As foretold by the apostles, "scoffers will come in the last days," dismissing the promise of the Lord's return (2 Pet. 3:2–4; Jude 18). So it is not surprising that this doctrine is often obscured, if not outright denied, by many today. Within the church this derision is consistent with theological humanism. Obviously those who reject the bodily resurrection of Christ cannot be expected to affirm his visible, literal, personal return.

It is not uncommon, however, for some to use the language of the parousia, while not meaning an objective event in history. The return of Christ is spiritualized to indicate his moral teaching that penetrates society or deeds of kindness done in his name. The comparison becomes even more confusing when the second coming is identified with Pentecost, or on a personal level, when one receives Christ as Savior.

These associations have substance in reference to the work of the Holy Spirit, of course, but contradict the distinctive ministry of the Second Person of the Holy Trinity. Yes, the Spirit does carry on the ministry of Christ, but to relegate the return of Christ merely to his spiritual presence in the world violates the testimony of Scripture and confounds any explanation of the end of history.

### Last Day Speculation

The certainty of Christ's return does not imply that we can predict the time of his coming. Though God has revealed some general things to look for, the details remain obscure. It is clear, for example, that God wants no one to perish and that the Gospel will be preached to all nations before the world ends, but when can we say that the last person has been reached? There may be people out there we know nothing about, even when we think the task is completed.

Biblically speaking, we live now in the last days, a period extending from Christ's resurrection to his return and the final judgment (1 Cor. 15:24). It is healthy to believe that his coming is near (Rev. 22:20), but we also know that God does not reckon time as we do, "that with the Lord one day is as a thousand years, and a thousand years as one day" (2 Pet. 3:8).

Unfortunately, throughout the history of the church, there have been persons who have presumed to know the exact day of Christ's return. Of course when their predictions failed, many people were disillusioned, and worldlings looking on were given cause to ridicule the church. For this reason, we should be cautious when it comes to the chronology of events, like Armageddon (Rev. 16:16), associated with the last days. With the same modesty, we do not have to identify by name the characters that have a role in the last days, like "the man of lawlessness" (2 Thess. 2:2–3) or the Antichrist (1 John 2:18; 4:3). Sometimes the better part of discretion is to confess that we do not know.

## Summary Applications

*1. Jesus always lived in the triumph of his return.*

This assurance shines through his constant reference to himself as the Son of Man.[16] The title relates to the one in human form foreseen by Daniel who was coming in the clouds of heaven, "and to him was given dominion and glory and a kingdom, that all peoples, nations, and languages should serve him." The prophet adds that "his dominion is an everlasting dominion, which shall not pass away, and his kingdom one that shall not be destroyed" (Dan. 7:13–14; cf. vv. 15–28). While much about the passage remains unclear, one cannot mistake its dominant note, which is the ultimate victory of the Son of Man and of those associated with him.

This messianic figure also has the qualities of the universal divine Savior and the servant of God. Within this context, yet bringing it new meaning, Jesus alluded to his earthly ministry. He pictured himself coming from heaven as the Son of Man (John 3:13) and in this exalted state going about his mission of sowing the good seed and seeking the lost (Matt. 13:37–38; Luke 19:10). What difference did it make that he lived in lowly circumstances? He was still the Son of Man (Matt. 11:19; Luke 7:34). When the disciples were rebuked for plucking corn unlawfully, he responded with the same refrain, "For the Son of Man is lord of the Sabbath" (Matt. 12:8; Mark 2:28; Luke 6:5). In his own right, "the Son of Man" had authority to forgive sins (Matt. 9:6; Mark 2:10; Luke 5:24), execute judgment (John 5:27), and give everlasting life (John 6:27). When he spoke of his rejection, betrayal, and crucifixion, he was aware that "the Son of Man" would suffer these things (Matt. 17:12, 22; 20:28; 26:24–25; Mark 8:31; 9:12, 31; 10:45; 14:21; Luke 9:22, 44; 22:22; John 3:14; 6:53; 8:28; 12:23). Of course he would die, but the grave could not hold "the Son of Man" (Matt. 17:9; 20:19; Mark 9:9; 10:34; Luke 18:31).

Every time he used this name, it was more than a prophecy of his coming rule; it indicated that in his mind that reign was already a reality. He never thought of himself any other way. Even when no one else seemed to understand, he was no less the Son of Man—the mighty conqueror of evil, destined to rule the universe with invisible, holy love.

*2. The second coming of Christ completes the purpose of his first coming.*

So it can be said that Christ's return in exaltation gives meaning to his life of suffering on earth.

Contrasted to the birth of royalty in the world, when Jesus was born, only some shepherds of the field and a few wise men from the East came to worship him. But when he descends on clouds of glory, all creation will celebrate and people from every tongue and tribe and nation will bow before him.

In his first coming he came as a servant, to offer himself an atoning sacrifice for the world, so that mankind can be saved from the guilt and power of iniquity. Coming the second time, he will take his people away from the very presence of sin.

The first advent was marked by humiliation and rejection: "His own people did not receive him" (John 1:11). But he will return in triumph as the King who will sit on the throne of his majesty and reign over his kingdom.

Though foretold, his first appearing in Bethlehem was obscure, but "the second is to be brilliant, and so manifest that even his enemies will recognize it."[17]

*3. Righteousness will shine forth at his return.*

For the present, society, captivated by Satan and principalities of darkness, flaunts the law of God. Sin arrogantly breeds contempt for truth, mocking justice and human rights. The oppression of wickedness lies like a heavy fog over the land.

But the day of reckoning is coming when Jesus returns to execute judgment. We need not worry about the timing or circumstances of the day. What matters is his coming and the exacting way everyone will give account. We can be sure that the judge of all the earth will do right (Gen. 18:22–33; Jer. 11:20; Rev. 16:7).

*4. The coming judgment calls for faithful stewardship in our work.*

Driving home this point, Jesus told of a nobleman who, before going away to receive a kingdom, gave his servants ten minas (each equal to about one hundred days' wages) and entrusted them to "engage in business until I come" (Luke 19:13). On the nobleman's return each servant was asked what he had gained. Two reported a good increase and were appropriately rewarded, but the third did nothing with his gift and was severely reproved (Luke 19:11–27).

Similarly, in his parable of the talents, the master gave to his servants different proportions of talents to invest "each according to [their] ability" (Matt. 25:15). When the master returned to settle accounts, two were "good and faithful" servants, having doubled their investment, but the third did not utilize his opportunity at all, hiding his talent in the ground. This "worthless servant" was cast into outer darkness (vv. 14–30).

Many lessons can be drawn from the parables, but surely among them is the principle that Christ's gifts cannot be wasted and that it is required of servants to be faithful.

### 5. *Christians must be ready to meet the Lord.*

That Christ's sudden appearing will be unexpected is all the more reason to live always in a state of readiness (Matt. 24:44; 25:13; Luke 12:40). "Blessed are those servants whom the master finds awake when he comes" (Luke 12:37).

Recall the parable of the ten virgins invited to a wedding feast. Five were wise and had their lamps filled with oil as they awaited the bridegroom. The others, however, neglecting to fill their lamps in advance, were unprepared to enter when the bridegroom came, thereby missing the wedding. "And the door was shut" (Matt. 25:1–13).

Emphasizing the lesson, though in a different context, Jesus told his disciples: "Stay dressed for action and keep your lamps burning, and be like men who are waiting for their master" (Luke 12:35).

The story is told of a traveler who visited an exquisite garden situated on the shore of a lake in Switzerland. Knocking at the gate, he was met by an elderly caretaker who invited him in. The old man seemed glad to have someone to talk to.

"How long have you been here?" asked the tourist. Learning that the man had worked there twenty-four years, he inquired how often the owner came to see the garden. Told that he seldom visited and that the last time was twelve years ago, the traveler was surprised. "Yet," he said, "you have the garden in such perfect condition that one would think that you were expecting the owner tomorrow." "No, sir," exclaimed the caretaker, "I have it tended as if he were coming today."[18]

Actually the expectation of the imminent return of Christ has characterized believers from the beginning. The early church lived in the realization that "the Lord is at hand" (Phil. 4:5), remembering how Jesus said, "I am coming soon" (Rev. 3:11; 22:7, 12, 20; cf. Heb. 10:37). It is the reasonable way to live. The signs of his coming are never so clear as to exclude his return anytime.

As a good rule for us all, to paraphrase the advice of Luther, we should live as though Christ had been crucified yesterday, had risen today, and is coming again tomorrow.

### 6. *His imminent coming summons us to personal holiness.*

Reflecting on the end times, Peter said to the church to have "lives of holiness and godliness, waiting for and hastening the coming of the day of God" (2 Pet. 3:11–12). Likewise, John said that everyone who hopes in him purifies himself even as he is pure (1 John 3:3). Appealing to the same incentive, Paul exhorted Timothy to "pursue righteousness (right standing with God and true goodness), godliness (which is the loving fear of God and being Christlike), faith, love, steadfastness (patience), and gentleness of heart." And with the determination of a fighter, "keep all His precepts unsullied and flawless, irreproachable, until the appearing of our Lord Jesus Christ (the Anointed One)" (1 Tim. 6:11–14 AMP; cf. 1 Thess. 5:23).

*7. World evangelization prepares the coming of the Lord.*

As his last command to the church (Matt. 28:19–20; Mark 16:15; Acts 1:8), the fulfillment of this commission becomes the most obvious prelude to his return. Jesus has said that the "gospel of the kingdom will be proclaimed throughout the whole world as a testimony to all nations, and then the end will come" (Matt. 24:14).

That this assignment has not been completed may explain why Jesus has delayed his return. One can only conjecture that had the church been more faithful in discipling the nations, the Lord might have already returned. Certainly this remains our greatest task, and with renewed dedication, we must set ourselves to finish the work.

## 8. The glorious coming of Christ is the blessed hope of the church.

It is this hope that the attacks of demons cannot take away; this hope gives courage to the fainthearted and persecuted; this hope rises above the dissonant noise of the world to bring peace to the soul—Jesus is coming again!

Yet it is more than a hope. It is the unshakable affirmation that the King of heaven has taken to himself his own great power, and his kingdom will never perish. In this anticipation, our longing eyes turn toward the eastern skies, looking to that time when our majestic Savior, crowned with glory and honor, returns to rule over all.

I cannot forget an experience a few years ago in a Billy Graham–sponsored pastors' school in a remote region in Peru near the headwaters of the Amazon River. It was an impoverished area, rife with diseases, where most people had little access to medical care or formal education. Adding to their suffering, corrupt political officials as well as the hierarchy of the government-favored religion oppressed evangelical believers.

In one of the sessions I spoke on the completion of the Great Commission. When I mentioned that Jesus would come back in trailing clouds of splendor, the pastors began to cheer and shout. They became so vociferous in their joy that I could not be heard, so I stepped back from the pulpit until they settled down.

After the service one of the pastors graciously came up to thank me for the message. He told me about his growing congregation and some of the harassment they were enduring—in fact, one night just two weeks before, their church building mysteriously burned to the ground. Though arson seemed apparent, the police made no effort to investigate. Two other churches whose buildings burned earlier had experienced the same indifference of the government. But there was no bitterness in his voice; rather a big smile spread across his face as he told me that his congregation had already started to build another church, and the new one would be twice as big. While still grinning, he said he had noticed my surprise at the way the people had celebrated when I mentioned the second coming of Christ. Then he explained, "You see, sir, down here, that's our only hope."

Those words have resounded in my mind many times since then. The dear pastor was right. In our easygoing, affluent, secure way of life, it is difficult to realize that all these things are passing away, that nothing down here will last, and that there will be no real, no permanent peace until Jesus comes to reign.

Yes, whether realized or not, his return is our only hope—and what a blessed hope it is! It is reason to celebrate. I feel like singing with Wesley.

> Lo! He comes with clouds descending,
> Once for favored sinners slain;
> Thousand, thousand saints attending
> Swell the triumph of his train.
> > Alleluia! Alleluia! Alleluia!
> > God appears on earth to reign!
>
> Ev'ry eye shall now behold him,
> Robed in dreadful majesty;
> Those who set at naught and sold him,
> Pierced and nailed him to the tree,
> > Deeply wailing, deeply wailing,
> > Shall the true Messiah see.
>
> Yea, amen! Let all adore thee,
> High on thy eternal throne;
> Savior, take the pow'r and glory,
> Claim the kingdom for thine own.
> > Alleluia! Alleluia! Alleluia!
> > Everlasting God, come down![19]

# 17

## The Providence of God

When Robert Morrison, the pioneer missionary, was about to sail to China in 1867, a merchant, looking at him with an amused smile, asked, "And so, Mr. Morrison, you really expect that you will make an impression on the idolatry of the great Chinese Empire?" Morrison replied with dignified sternness, "No, sir, I expect God will."[1]

The young missionary's assurance was right. God accomplishes what he pleases according to his purpose to display his glory.

### God's Ordering of All Things

#### The Care of Creation

Christ's glorious descent from heaven brings into focus the outworking of divine providence from the beginning of time. God, being infinite in wisdom and power, perfect in holiness and love, looked ahead in creation and planned in advance the whole course of history. It would be inconsistent with the character of God that he would make something that would not disclose his glory. The "divine attributes" that are intrinsic to his nature "logically require and imply" his "gracious preservation and governance of the world."[2]

Having planned creation, he sustains and directs all that is made to their ultimate destiny. The whole compact of the universe is upheld "by the greatness of his might" (Isa. 40:26; Heb. 1:3). Whether physical matter, like the stars; living vegetation, like plants or trees; animal creations or human beings—each according to their nature have their continuance from the will of

God (Ps. 104:1–35). Everything in the cosmos is totally dependent on him, and apart from his care all would dissolve into nothing. Even the so-called laws of nature, which he established, can be set aside as he pleases, so that what we may call miraculous is perfectly natural to the creation.

His providence, in its highest expression, embraces all rational, self-determining moral beings, especially creatures made in his own image, "since he himself gives to all mankind life and breath and everything" (Acts 17:25; cf. v. 28; Ps. 104:27–28; 145:15–16; Prov. 30:25). Never removed from what happens in the world, the Lord "fashions the hearts" of the inhabitants of the earth "and observes all their deeds" (Ps. 33:14–15; cf. Job 12:23; Isa. 10:12–15).

Thus whatever is done is done only by the will of God, either his permissive or directed will.[3] "He changes times and seasons; he removes kings and sets up kings; he gives wisdom to the wise and knowledge to those who have understanding" (Dan. 2:20–21). Throughout history, "it is God who executes judgment, putting down one and lifting up another" (Ps. 75:7; cf. 1 Sam. 2:6; Matt. 5:45; Luke 11:52–53; Rom. 13:1; James 4:14–15). Even little things that seem to happen by chance, like the casting of lots, fall within his providence. "The lot is cast into the lap, but its every decision is from the Lord" (Prov. 16:33). Nothing is beyond his care.

### Redemptive Providence

Within God's general oversight of the world, there is a special care for individuals and peoples according to his plan of redemption. It emerges clearly in the call of Abraham to leave his own country and go to a new land of promise, where God will raise up from his seed a great nation through which all the families of the earth will be blessed (Gen. 12:1–3). The rest of the Old Testament tells the story of God sovereignly working through his chosen people to teach his law and character. Israel becomes an object lesson in God's care for the world to see.

Finally, the journey leads to Calvary, when God supremely unveils the glory of his love in the atoning sacrifice of his Son. "For this purpose," Jesus came into the world (John 12:27; 18:37). As had been decreed in the councils of the Holy Trinity from the beginning of time, he was "delivered up according to the definite plan and foreknowledge of God" (Acts 2:23). After which "God raised him up, loosing the pangs of death, because it was not possible for him to be held by it" (v. 24). It was all "predestined to take place" (Acts 4:28).

The Bible shows one long history of divine government, as justice is administered and mercy disclosed. Underlying it is the certainty that all things are moving to the end purposed by God. The end has been determined from the beginning, including both the curse and the cure of sin. Inevitably history will disclose fully God's purpose and glory.

## What about Freedom?

At this point, the issue of human willfulness again comes to the fore. Many things happen that, from our limited point of view, seem fortuitous, yet from God's infinitely larger perspective, are not accidental. Thomas Aquinas illustrates by an employer sending two workers to the same place; the two men meet by chance, but from the employer's view, their meeting, though not initially intended, was caused by him and "understandable as orderly in relation to him." In the same way, God foresees everything and knows their causal connection, "but not in such a way as to preempt secondary causes."[4]

The question of freedom gets more complicated when evil is brought into the equation. If a holy God orders all things according to his will, how can we account for sin?

As seen before, the answer resides in the recognition that freedom is a constituent part of human nature. The will of man is corrupted by sin and inclined toward evil, but his willful choice is free. By God's all-sufficient grace everyone can freely choose the way of life or death (Deut. 30:15). Rightfully used, freedom to choose enables man to respond to God's will and receive all his blessings. There could be no character development without it.

Sin results from the misuse of freedom. "Evil is not an effect caused by God, but a *defect* of secondary causes that are permitted by God."[5] Yet because God knows every defect of our lives, even wrong choices, sin and its consequences are absorbed into the all-inclusive divine providence. Human freedom operates in history but it can never overrule God's purposes. "Many are the plans in the mind of a man, but it is the purpose of the LORD that will stand" (Prov. 19:21).

## Fatherly Guidance in Providence

How God directs persons has been variously understood in classical exegeses, all of which resemble human parenting.[6] One way is by permitting persons to use their freedom to discover their competencies and the blessing of obedience, even though it may lead to suffering and sin. Freedom always runs the risk that wrong choices will be made, but by enduring the consequences, we can learn from our mistakes. All through the Bible we can see this divine permission in operation (e.g., Ps. 18:11–13; Jer. 18:12; Acts 14:16–17).

Another way God guides us is by hindering our wrong actions. He does not coerce, but puts obstacles in the way of the ill-conceived course of action. "It was I who kept you from sinning," God said to Abimelech. "Therefore I did not let you touch her" (Gen. 20:6). Israel's complaint in captivity was that God had so "walled" them from escape that repentance was their only hope for deliverance (Lam. 3:7). A beautiful example of such hindering is the way the Spirit closed the doors of Paul's ministry in Asia Minor, which made his Macedonian call to Europe more obvious (Acts 16:6–10).

Also God may overrule a wayward course when it is completely out of line with his purpose. By such direct intervention we are saved from harm and missing the divine will. "Blessed is the one whom God reproves" (Job 5:17; cf. Mic. 4:7). Consider the decision of the sons of Jacob when they sold Joseph into slavery. The ill-motivated act was meant for evil, but God intended it for good (Gen. 50:20).

A final way providence guides us is by preventing undue challenges to our faith. God knows our weakness in temptation, and does not permit us to be tested more than we can endure (Job 1:12; 2:6; 1 Cor. 10:13). In multiple unseen ways far beyond our understanding God is looking after the well-being of his children.

### Predestined to Glory

God wants the best for his people, so before the worlds were made he decreed the redemption of a people for his glory. This decision comes out in the word *predestination*. It is a very positive term that emphasizes God's determination to restore men and women to their created purpose.[7] Related to divine foreknowledge, as St. Justin Martyr aptly put it, "He did not predestinate them before he knew them, but he did predestinate the reward of those whose merits he foreknew."[8]

Wrapped up in the word is the concept of election. "In love he predestined us for adoption as sons through Jesus Christ," in accordance with his pleasure and will (Eph. 1:4–5).[9] We are loved in Christ, the beloved Son of God, in whom the love of the Father eternally rests. "In him we have obtained an inheritance, having been predestined according to the purpose of him who works all things according to the counsel of his will . . . to the praise of his glory" (vv. 11–12).

The election in Christ is all by grace, the free gift of God, "with which he has blessed us in the Beloved" (v. 6; cf. Rom. 9:11–13; Titus 2:11), "of his own purpose and grace," which was given us "in Christ Jesus before the ages began" (2 Tim. 1:9). That is, persons who come to Christ were already God's elect in his heart while they were one time in themselves enemies. "For those whom he foreknew he also predestined to be conformed to the image of his Son. . . . And those whom he predestined he also called, and those whom he called he also justified, and those whom he justified he also glorified" (Rom. 8:29–30).

### Whosoever Will May Come

In God's providence everyone is free to come to Christ. God would have "all people to be saved and to come to the knowledge of the truth" (1 Tim. 2:4). The Lord does not want anyone to perish, "but that all should reach repentance" (2 Pet. 3:9).

No one can say they are excluded from God's plan of salvation. The invitation is to "all who labor and are heavy laden" (Matt. 11:28), to "anyone" who thirsts (John 7:37), to "whoever believes" (John 3:16, 36). Again and again we hear it: "Everyone who calls on the name of the Lord will be saved" (Rom. 10:13; cf. 10:11; 1 John 5:1). So appropriately the Bible closes with the call: "The Spirit and the Bride say, 'Come.' And let the one who hears say, 'Come.' And let the one who is thirsty come; and let the one who desires take the water of life without price" (Rev. 22:17).

Clearly God invites everyone to come and partake at the table of grace. But let us dispel the notion that our choices are completely undetermined. Freedom in human experience is always conditioned by other factors, including the prayers of others, and all of these things impact our liberty to choose. Only God, who is unlimited and able to control all things, can be unconditionally free in making decisions.

Still though limited in what we can do, we are free to respond to the invitation of God. We can accept or reject his will, but we cannot change it. God will not stop loving us, even if we turn from him. But whatever our willing choice, his omniscience and foreknowledge covers every decision throughout life. That is why God is never taken by surprise. He already knows the outcome of our decisions.

Persons are lost by their own refusal to align their will with God's desire. No one can blame God that he or she is lost. All who go to hell are there by their own willful choice in rejecting the Gospel of grace.

## Divine Sovereignty and Human Freedom

### The Problem

Throughout the history of the church, theologians have tried to relate two facts that appear irreconcilable—divine sovereignty and human freedom. Both are taught in Scripture. Take the statement of Jesus: "All that the Father gives me will come to me"—God's determination; "and whoever comes to me I will never cast out"—human free choice (John 6:37). Or put it in the words of Paul: "Work out your own salvation with fear and trembling"—human will; "for it is God who works in you, both to will and to work for his good pleasure"—determination (Phil. 2:12–13).

This is a mystery, but clearly it is God who calls and man who responds. Theologically, the problem is resolved among evangelicals primarily in two ways: the Reformed view and the Evangelical Arminian view.

#### THE REFORMED VIEW

Calvinism looks at providence from the standpoint of God's eternal decrees. He knows what will happen because he has said that it will happen, and it does. In effect, this view identifies foreknowledge and predestination, maintaining that the divine decrees are the basis for the happening. This includes the voluntary actions of people. God foresees future events in consequence of his decision that they should happen.

In respect to redemption of persons, God has foreordained by his own "effectual calling" some to be saved by grace. These are "the elect"—persons whom God has chosen in Christ to be holy before him.

These elected ones are disposed to believe unto salvation.[10] That is, their wills are made responsive to God's call. Ultimately they can do nothing else, for God is sovereign over all. Hence, his saving grace is irresistible, for persons called by God to be saved must respond; otherwise God would not be sovereign in his decree.

Persons who do not believe in Christ are still responsible for their will to sin. Sin is our doing. Jonathan Edwards in his *Freedom of the Will*[11] has the best rationale for this position. He approaches the issue by dividing the moral nature of man from his will. All men are able voluntarily to turn to God and be saved, he believes, but because of our depravity, no one wants to do it. Our natural course is to sin, and by our nature, we are unable to do otherwise. This view makes sin a matter of human volition. That some people do not believe in Christ is no reflection on God's love. It is only an evidence of human depravity. But, by contrast, those who do believe in Christ disclose God's eternal decree.

If taken out of the context of grace, this position can tend toward human irresponsibility. Taken to an extreme, it may encourage antinomianism or legalism. In reaction to this teaching, some people have gone to the other extreme and rejected the whole concept of divine providence. It is interesting that the heaviest casualties to deistic Unitarianism in the eighteenth century came out of Calvinistic churches.

### THE EVANGELICAL ARMINIAN VIEW

Arminianism looks at providence from the standpoint of God's foreknowledge. It is his perfect knowledge of all things that determines his decree. What human freedom does, God knows. The power of contrary choice is essential to human freedom, and therefore the foreknowledge of God refers to free acts of man.[12] Man and woman make a choice, right or wrong, and knowing its consequences, God has planned accordingly.[13]

In respect to redemption of persons, God has enabled everyone to be saved by grace. There is a valid opportunity for all to respond to the call of God. Arminians insist that by "prevenient grace" everyone has the ability to believe in Christ.

Those who believe in Christ are "the elect." The choice is made by us in the present, even though it was foreknown by God from the beginning of time, and by virtue of that knowledge, the believer has been predestined to salvation.

Persons who do not believe are accountable for their will to sin. They have determined their choice to live as they please, and hence cannot claim there was no opportunity of salvation.

If taken out of the context of grace, this position can lead to human determinism. The effort of Arminianism to give place to human freedom presents the temptation to think that, after all, man determines what he will do. This notion, however innocent, can be disastrous and too often has been. The wreckage of humanistic theology seen in so many churches today bears testimony to what can happen.

### Coming Together around Evangelism

Since the streams of both Reformed and Arminian theology flow through the church and have nurtured Christians throughout the centuries, is there a synthesis of the different positions? Perhaps the disparities between them in God's providence can teach us that none of us is as smart as we think we are. At least they should help us realize that we do not have all the answers and also help us to become more reverent in the presence of mystery.

Certainly, the truth that binds Reformed and Arminian together in the Gospel is far stronger than our differences. Both agree that there is a divine purpose and providence in God's creation. Both agree that God has a perfect knowledge of himself and all that he has made. Both agree that God's sovereign will is exercised in consistency with his personal moral nature. Both recognize that the permissive will of God is resolved in his perfect will. Both understand that God respects the integrity built into his creation of man and woman, including their freedom of choice. Both affirm that sin is the result of human refusal to accept God's will. Both agree that God's foreordination does not take away human liability resulting from the fall. Both realize that God must himself take the initiative in our redemption from sin. Both believe that only by response to the Gospel can a person be saved by grace. And as faith is defined, both agree that Christians are eternally secure.

In reality, then, from the standpoint of evangelism, the distinction between the two is more theoretical than practical. Here we come together around what really matters.

## Problem Areas

### Depersonalizing Providence

Divine providence stands in antithesis to any idea that diminishes personal involvement in the movement of history, both by God in his decrees and by man in our response to his will. For this reason, it gives no comfort to deists, who hold that after God created the world, he removed himself from it, leaving mankind on its own. Such thinking allows no place for divine direction in our lives and borders on the notion of indeterminism—that there is no intelligible control operative in the world at all.

Likewise, providence opposes the concept of pantheism, which believes the natural universe, taken or conceived as a whole, is God. Failing to distinguish God from what he created, this view not only belittles the majesty of God but confounds his communion with persons made in his image.

Dualism, which holds that powers of good and evil compete for control in the world, also contradicts the almighty and benevolent providence of God. There is never any question in Scripture about God's universality and sovereignty over all.

Nor can one imagine that God is available only when something goes wrong in the universe, as if he is not always present to preserve and govern what he has made. The God of providence "will neither slumber nor sleep" (Ps. 121:4).

### Human Irresponsibility

Probably the most persistent error in removing control of history from the personal care of God comes in fatalism, the idea that all events are so determined by necessity that humans have no choice in what happens. The divine will is believed to be inexorable and man has no way to effect change. Such a "fate," of course, destroys any basis for human freedom and accountability.

What this view fails to realize is that divine determination does not negate human freedom in the outworking of providence. God's sovereignty and human freedom move along two different but parallel lines, so that every event in history is determined from the beginning in light of what God knows man willfully chooses.

We recognize, however, that as a result of the fall of man, our freedom to choose is now bent toward sin. Free will is sufficient for evil, but it cannot bring forth good unless aided by divine grace. Yet grace, though sufficient to enable a person freely to choose good, does not make the choice. That is why we are all accountable for our decisions. God is not responsible for the mess the world is in.

The Gospel has no common ground with any view that undermines human freedom and responsibility. Providence makes painfully evident that our choices have consequences.

### Aimlessness in History

The movement of providence toward its divinely appointed end is a foreign concept to a humanistic-oriented society. Naturalists, especially, who allow no place for God, have no sense of the purposeful end of history because they have no understanding of its beginning. Having fallen for the notion that people are mere superior organisms of some primeval osmosis, they have no idea where life will end, except the grave.

Persons, however, with a spiritual sensitivity may fall into the same delusion. Taking the physical world as a pattern, to them the drama of humanity unfolds around a cycle of life: birth, growth, maturity, death. Everything comes and goes and comes around again, like the changing seasons of nature. Reincarnation, seen in Hinduism and Buddhism, popularized now in modern forms of Eastern religion, are an outworking of this recycling motif.

Such thinking views history as always repeating itself in an endless rotation of events, evolving without purpose or meaning. To be sure, things do tend to be repeated in life, but Christians, taking their cue from Scripture, affirm that redemption governs the movement of history and that all things will end as planned by God in the beginning to show his glory.

## Summary Applications

### 1. God is always for us.

He cannot be otherwise, for this is his nature. His holiness, his love, his goodness find expression in everything he does. The acclamation sometimes heard in church gatherings sums up this basic premise in divine providence: "God is good all the time; all the time God is good."

Because he is always seeking the salvation of a rebellious world, even his judgments work for good. He will not shield his church from hardship and suffering when he knows they are needed to further our sanctification. God loves us too much to compromise his plan for our lives. So whatever we may be going through, "if God is for us, who can be against us?" (Rom. 8:31). That being true, we can rest in his assurance:

> Fear not, for I have redeemed you;
> I have summoned you by name; you are mine.
> When you pass through the waters,
> I will be with you;
> and when you pass through the rivers,
> they will not sweep over you.
> When you walk through the fire,
> you will not be burned;
> the flames will not set you ablaze.
> For I am the Lord, your God,
> the Holy One of Israel, your Savior.
>
> Isaiah 43:1–3 (cf. Ps. 118:6–7, 14; Isa. 41:10)

### 2. Wonderful, too, is the realization that God does not make mistakes.

"His way is perfect" (Ps. 18:30). "All his works are right and his ways are just" (Dan. 4:37; cf. Matt. 5:45). With this certainty, we can rest assured that nothing is haphazard in God's plan. There are no accidents. John Oxenham has said it well:

246

He writes in characters too grand
For our short sight to understand;
We catch but broken strokes, and try
To fathom all the mystery
Of withered hopes, of death, of life,
The endless war, the useless strife—
But there with larger, clearer sight,
We shall see this—His way was right.[14]

### 3. We should try to see God's larger purpose in providence.

Since everything that happens, whether good or evil, must first pass through his will, what is God teaching us about his character in the events of history? With this perspective, we can learn more than meets the eye when reading the newspaper.

The story is told of a common laborer who worked on the construction of Westminster Abbey. His task was to carry brick and mortar for the stone masons. Day after day he did the same thing. The monotony of the work finally got to him, and he decided to quit.

On the way to the timekeeper's office to get his wages, he passed the architect's hut and saw some large drawings spread out on the table. "What is that?" he asked. Told that they were the completed plans for the cathedral, the worker paused to look at them, and wonder filled his eyes. For the first time he realized what was being built and now knew it was more than brick and mortar. He had seen the end product of all his labor and returned to his task with excitement and determination, saying, "I want to have a part in this building."

Knowing that God is in the process of making something beautiful for his glory gives meaning to all the tedious, painstaking, menial tasks in our lives. Nothing is insignificant. It is all part of the plan.

### 4. The outworking of God's will in history is fully revealed in Christ.

What we know as past, present, and future focus on him who is "the Alpha and the Omega, the first and the last, the beginning and the end" (Rev. 22:13; cf. 1:8; 21:6). "In him all things hold together" (Col. 1:17).

To approach any of the unsolvable problems of a world in disarray, we must first try to comprehend how God addressed the issue when he lived among us. The struggles of a disoriented society and the martyrdom of saints make no sense until we see Jesus on the cross bearing the iniquity of us all. There we begin to understand that God is never defeated in his purpose, even when mankind rejects his will.

Jesus is the key to unlock the mystery of divine providence. In him we are given a historical perspective on the future. What he did at Calvary and verified in his resurrection reaches into eternity.

*5. Following Jesus requires submission to his will.*

There is a cross in it (Matt. 10:38; Luke 9:23). The apostolic believers already considered themselves crucified with Christ—dead to sin, dead to the world, but alive to God (Rom. 6:11; Gal. 2:20).

That commitment reminds me of the five missionaries who were killed some years ago while they were seeking to bring the Gospel to the Auca Indians in Ecuador. What most gripped me about the incident was an interview a reporter had with the widowed wives. "Why would God permit this to happen?" he asked. "After all, were not the men on an errand of mercy?" One of the wives turned to the incredulous man and quietly replied, "Sir, God delivered my husband from the possibility of disobedience."[15]

That is what the Christian fears. It is not death. Our Lord has delivered us from that enemy. The grave has lost its sting. But there is a holy fear of disobeying the will of God, for that alone can mar the relationship that binds us to his love.

*6. Resting in the will of God gives perfect peace.*

Often things do not turn out as we would like, and we cannot understand why. But God is still keeping watch over his own.

This was vividly impressed on me one summer in 1957. I had been invited to go with the Billy Graham team for a one-night rally in Tulsa, Oklahoma. On arriving at the hotel where the team was staying, I was assigned to a room with Lorne Sanny, who that night was in charge of the crusade follow-up. Actually Dawson Trotman, founder of the Navigators, was the head man, but he had gone for the weekend to speak at a youth camp in New York.

While we waited in the room, the phone rang. Lorne picked it up and after listening, turned to me and said, as if in disbelief, "Daws is dead."

He related the message, how just a few minutes before, Trotman was out on Schroon Lake with Jack Wyrtzen and some young people in a motorboat. The girl sitting next to Daws had told him that she could not swim. Suddenly the boat hit a wave and Daws and the nonswimmer were catapulted into the lake. When the boat turned back, someone pulled in the girl, but Daws, who had been holding her up, disappeared beneath the water. It was two days before his body was recovered.

At the time the call came, Dawson's wife, Lila, was still at the lake. She had sent word by a messenger to get in touch with Lorne Sanny and relay the news to Billy Graham. Then, as an afterthought, she added, "Tell Lorne, Psalm 115, verse 3." It is a custom among Navigators to close a greeting with a verse of Scripture.

As Lorne went to tell Mr. Graham, I called his secretary to pass word to the others. While the team members began to gather in the hotel lobby, still stunned by the news, I had opportunity to look up that verse in the little Bible I had with me. My eyes filled with tears as I read the words:

"But our God is in the heavens: he hath done whatsoever he hath pleased" (Ps. 115:3 KJV).

I thought of that dear wife and mother standing at the lake there watching men grabble for her husband's body. I could imagine what was going through her mind—the agonizing unanswered question, *Why?* Yet, amid the heartbreak, there was a quiet confidence that God was still in control, that even in this tragedy, he would somehow bring forth good to those who love him, "who are called according to his purpose" (Rom. 8:28).[16]

Far from stoic resignation to meaningless fate, this is the confidence a believer has resting in the will of God. Whatever happens he keeps "in perfect peace [those] whose mind is stayed" on him (Isa. 26:3).

*7. Making Christ known gives direction to the divinely orchestrated providence of history.*

This is why it can be said that evangelism keeps the church on the course to which all things are moving, when finally the Gospel will be heard to the ends of the earth and disciples made of all nations (Matt. 28:19–20).

That goal, in turn, establishes the priorities around which our lives should be ordered. Everyone has some part in the mission. We may be sure, too, that however slow and difficult that task, what God decreed in the beginning shall be accomplished.

Envision that awesome day to come. The redeemed of the Lord are assembled around the throne of grace. As far as the eye can see, they are gathered in every direction. So great is the multitude that the number cannot be counted. They come from the east and from the west, from the north and from the south (Matt. 8:11; Luke 13:29); "from every nation, from all tribes and peoples and languages" (Rev. 7:9). The Great Commission is fulfilled.

In your eyes of faith, see them standing there before the reigning King of kings and Lord of lords, "clothed in white robes," symbolic of their purity and victory, waving "palm branches in their hands," descriptive of their irrepressible joy (v. 9).

Listen! They are "crying out with a loud voice, 'Salvation belongs to our God who sits on the throne, and to the Lamb'" (v. 10). And as the blood-washed saints shout their praises, all the celestial hosts fall on their faces before the throne, saying, "Amen! Blessing and glory and wisdom and thanksgiving and honor and power and might be to our God forever and ever!" (vv. 11–12).

This is reality! This is eternity! And, by faith, we can live in that certainty now.

# 18

# The Coming Glory

Dr. H. C. Morrison, founder of Asbury Theological Seminary, liked to tell about his return from a long missionary trip overseas. It happened that Teddy Roosevelt, who had been hunting in Africa, was on the same boat. As the ship docked in New York harbor, throngs of people had turned out to welcome back Roosevelt. Tugboats were blowing their horns, a band was playing at the pier, and the mayor was there with the key to the city. But when Morrison left the ship, no one was there to meet him.

At first, the minister, worn out after months of labor, was saddened, feeling forgotten. Morrison said he felt like the loneliest man in the world. Then the Spirit of God spoke to him, and the scene around him began to fade as he heard a still, small voice within saying, *Morrison, why are you so disappointed? Get hold of yourself. There will be a celebration for you—far greater than anything here. But you are not home yet.*

All of us need that reminder. Though the glory of this eternal home can scarcely be imagined, no subject brings more joy in evangelism.

## The Transition of Death

### Where the Spirit Belongs

A hospital attendant, trying to comfort a man coming out of anesthesia after an operation, assured the patient that he was still in the land of the living. "No," said the Christian, "I'm still in the land of the dying but someday I will go to the land of the living."

Yes, in this interval of time, before the return of Christ, all of us, as a consequence of the fall, live in the land of the dying. It is also certain that after death comes the judgment, which will determine the place of our eternal habitation.

Whenever the final day of reckoning comes, "multitudes who sleep in the dust of the earth will awake, some to everlasting life, others to shame and everlasting contempt" (Dan. 12:2 NIV; cf. Isa. 26:19 NIV). A "time is coming," Jesus said, "when all who are in their graves will hear his voice and come out—those who have done good will rise to live, and those who have done evil will rise to be condemned" (John 5:28 NIV; cf. 11:25–26 NIV).

Death, thus, releases the human soul or spirit to go where it belongs. For those who have rejected the Gospel of saving grace, there awaits the sentence of endless separation from God, called in the Bible "the second death" or hell (Rev. 20:6, 14). But for those who die in the Lord, death brings release from suffering, and the liberated spirit goes into the presence of God.

### Before the Resurrection

To be absent from the body and present with the Lord leaves unclear what this relationship is before the final resurrection. Allusions to death as "sleep" suggest some kind of a waiting period prior to Christ's return (e.g., Acts 7:60; 1 Cor. 15:18, 20, 51). If there is such a state, however, the Scriptures indicate that the redeemed are conscious of what is happening on earth. "The souls of those who had been slain" because of their testimony, John observed, were fully aware of the struggles of their "fellow servants" in the world (Rev. 6:9–11).

It also appears that this intermediate state is characterized by activity. Those washed "in the blood of the Lamb" are said to serve God "day and night in his temple" (Rev. 7:14–15). In the vision of John, seeing one of the redeemed in God's presence, he "fell down at his feet to worship him," so beautiful was the sight. Whereupon the apostle was told: "I am a fellow servant with you and your brothers" (Rev. 19:10).

Whatever the state of the righteous during this time while the body returns to dust, their spirit is with the Lord. As the psalmist wrote, "God will redeem my life from the grave; he will surely take me to himself" (Ps. 49:15 NIV). Jesus told the repentant thief on the cross, "Today you will be with me in Paradise" (Luke 23:43). So real is this truth that the battle-weary apostle Paul, writing to the church in Philippi, said, "My desire is to depart and be with Christ, for that is far better" (Phil. 1:23).

What is clear is that when Christ returns in the clouds of heaven, the spirits of the departed saints shall be with him. And "with the voice of an archangel, and with the sound of the trumpet of God," the bodies of the dead in Christ shall come from their graves and be joined with their spirits. The redeemed still living on earth will be "caught up together with them in the clouds to meet the Lord in the air" (1 Thess. 4:16–17).

### Escorted by the Angels

With the return of the Son of Man, one of the ministries of the angels is to conduct "his elect" into the presence of God, when the spirit is separated from the body (Matt. 24:30–31; cf. 13:39). This heavenly escort seems a provision God has already provided for the righteous, as may be inferred from the story Jesus told about the beggar who dies "and was carried by the angels to Abraham's side" (Luke 16:22).

What a comfort this brings to one going through the valley of death when the shadows close in at the ending of day. The old Negro spiritual expresses it well: "I won't have to cross Jordan alone."[1]

I recall the late Harold Paul Sloan, a beloved Methodist pastor in Philadelphia, talking about the death of his mother. Because of the nature of her condition during the last months of her illness, she could not lie down on the bed but was confined to a wheelchair. Dr. Sloan was with her during the last hours. As she died, he said, it seemed that someone entered the room. He started to turn around to see who it was, when suddenly his mother rose completely out of the chair, lifted her hands in the air, and shouted the praises of God. Then her limp body fell back in the wheelchair, but her spirit was taken by the unseen angel into the presence of God.

### Home at Last

Probably no description of heaven is more familiar than the homily of Jesus to his distraught disciples on the eve of his crucifixion: "Do not let your hearts be troubled. . . . In my Father's house are many rooms; if it were not so, I would have told you. I am going there to prepare a place for you. And if I go and prepare a place for you, I will come back and take you to be with me that you also may be where I am" (John 14:1–3 NIV).

Oh, to be with Jesus, to move in with him, to live eternally where the love within the Holy Trinity engulfs the whole family of God. What a glorious habitation, this mansion of many rooms that is being prepared with meticulous care for the heirs of Christ!

The Bible projects this idea of a divine household when speaking of God as the Father in heaven and the redeemed as his children, sons and daughters, and members of his family are brothers and sisters in the kingdom. What a reunion that will be! Though its ultimate meaning is veiled, the analogy awakens warm thoughts of a home where love abounds, a house filled with singing and frolicking fun, a place of perfect rest where everyone feels secure in the Father's embrace.

Peter Marshall in one of his sermons told of a child with a crippling terminal disease that progressively depleted his strength. As his body weakened, he began to realize that he was not like the other boys he could see playing outside his window. One morning, quite unexpectedly, he asked his mother what it is like to die.

She had not faced that question before and did not know what to say. Quickly excusing herself to go to the kitchen, she prayed that God would help her know how to answer her son.

Returning to the room, she cuddled up beside him, stroked his hair, and said, "Kenneth, you remember how it is in the evening, when all of us are home and sitting together in the living room. After a while, you begin to get tired and come over to lie down in Daddy's lap, then soon go to sleep. But the next morning, when you wake up, you are in your own little bed in your own room. For after you went to sleep, your daddy picked you up in his big arms and carried you to where you belong. That is the way it is when you die. After a while, the old body gets tired; finally, you go to sleep and wake up in your own room where you belong."[2]

## The City of God

### Wonderful beyond Comprehension

John Bunyan in *The Pilgrim's Progress* describes the feeling of Christian and his companion when they finally behold the celestial city. Such was its beauty that the pilgrims fell sick with happiness, crying out because of their pangs. "If you see my Beloved, tell him I am sick with love." So glorious was the city, reflected in the brilliant sunlight of the cloudless day, that they could not as yet with open face look on it but had to use an instrument made for the purpose.[3]

This reflects my feeling as I try to speak of this home of the redeemed. The glory surpasses my ability to comprehend it, much less explain it. If no eye has seen nor ear heard nor mind conceived "what God has prepared for those who love him" in this present life (1 Cor. 2:9), how much more are the human faculties of reason exhausted when thinking of the glory yet to come?

To help us project our thoughts into this future experience, God has clothed the revelation with pictorial images and parables that appeal to our imagination. Such apocalyptic language, though often mystifying, makes the spiritual truth more vivid to the human senses. The idea conveyed is more than allegory, more than symbol; it expresses the reality itself.

### A New Heaven and a New Earth

What has long been promised and anticipated, God will do. He will make "new heavens and a new earth" (Isa. 65:17; 66:22; 2 Pet. 3:13; Rev. 21:1). The former creation will be dissolved, as the old earth and heaven are laid aside like a garment that has outgrown its usefulness (Ps. 102:25–26; Isa. 34:4; 51:6; Heb. 1:10–12).

Some understand this to mean a demolition of the present world, the physical elements being "destroyed by fire, and the earth and everything in it will be laid bare" (2 Pet. 3:10–11 NIV). Passages in Scripture that speak of the heavens and earth being removed or passing away may support this view (e.g., Heb. 12:26; Rev. 21:1).

Others, however, interpret this new creation as the renewal of the old earth, "new in the qualitative sense of something previously unknown, unprecedented, marvelous."[4] The idea is that God will consume the earth with fire, "reduce matter to its basic elements, split its atoms, free it from all restrictions, transform all things," and then make the new out of the old. It would be like placing a solid lump of coal in a retort, and by "great heat made fluid as gas, and then afterwards crystallized again into a glorious diamond."[5] Thus God does not abolish the temporal creation but reconstructs it according to the Spirit's eternal order.

### Creation Redeemed

The physical universe longs for this redemption. Because the sentence of mankind's sin carried consequences that extended to the whole realm of his habitat, the earth has been waiting "in eager expectation for the sons of God to be revealed" (Rom. 8:19 NIV). The glorification of the saints has its counterpart in nature. For when the curse of sin is removed, then "creation itself will be liberated from its bondage to decay and brought into the glorious freedom of the children of God" (v. 21 NIV).

Not only is the earth redeemed from the pollution of sin, but also "the heavenly things" are "purified" (Heb. 9:23). Since Satan and "spiritual forces of evil" had been active in the realms above (Eph. 6:12), conspiring rebellion against God and accusing his saints (Job 1:6; 2:1; Eph. 2:2; Rev. 12:7–10), it was necessary to cleanse the heavenly domain that had been corrupted by these pernicious schemes (see Job 15:15).

Everything in the universe has been affected by the completed work of Christ. In releasing mankind from bondage, so too the cosmos is set free. What this involves is not explained, but of this we can be sure: salvation embraces the farthest reaches of creation, so that all God has made will never cease to praise him (Psalm 148).

### Glory Personified

Into this glorified atmosphere appears "the holy city, the new Jerusalem, coming down out of heaven from God" (Rev. 21:2, 10). That the city descends from heaven to earth, underscores the relationship between God's residence and the place where redemption was secured for his people. It may suggest, too, keeping in mind the cataclysmic transformation of all things, that the new heaven actually becomes the transfigured earth.

What makes the city distinctively the habitation of God is holiness. Everything about the city reflects the character of him who reigns on the throne.

He is holy—utterly separate from any iniquity or defilement, of purer eyes than to look on evil (Hab. 1:13). Nothing that is unclean can enter into his presence (Rev. 21:8; 22:15).

The city radiates "the glory of God" (Rev. 21:11), magnifying the all-encompassing divine presence. It brings to mind Isaiah's promise: "Arise, shine, for your light has come, and the glory of the LORD has risen upon you" (Isa. 60:1–2, 19; cf. Ezek. 43:5). Prefigured by the city of David, where "great is the LORD and greatly to be praised" (Ps. 48:1), this is "the heavenly Jerusalem, the city of the living God" (Heb. 12:22 NIV).

Seeking to describe the grandeur of the Holy City, John likens it to a "bride adorned for her husband" (Rev. 21:2). Her radiance is "like that of a very precious jewel, like a jasper, clear as crystal," a beautiful hue associated with the nature of God (v. 11 NIV).

That it is called a city, a community of shared dependence and responsibility, emphasizes the corporate life of all those who reside within its boundaries. Everyone in the new Jerusalem partakes of its glory. Indeed, "blessed are those who wash their robes," that they "may go through the gates into the city" (Rev. 22:14 NIV).

### Consequences of Sin Removed

The first act of God for his saints in this new state of felicity is to "wipe every tear from their eyes" (Rev. 21:4 NIV; cf. 7:17). Recall that just prior to the new creation, the church has witnessed the last judgment and final separation of everyone "not found written in the book of life" (Rev. 20:15). The trauma of the experience can only be imagined—seeing persons who were loved on earth assigned to the lake of fire. It is comforting to know that God will erase the sorrow of that parting. This healing of unpleasant memories to me is one of the greatest miracles of heaven.

So far above present earthly experiences is the glorified state that, like the character of God, it can best be conceived in negatives. "Death shall be no more" (Rev. 21:4). There are no funerals in the city of God. "Death is swallowed up in victory" (Isa. 25:8; 1 Cor. 15:54). Neither shall there be any more "mourning, nor crying, nor pain any more, for the former things have passed away" (Rev. 21:4). All the agonizing effects of sin are gone forever. There is not even a semblance of the raging sea; that barrier to the Promised Land and emblem of the world's evil has passed away (v. 1). Nothing in heaven can ever cause a tremor in the everlasting song. If happiness is the opposite of sadness, then conversations of heaven shall be punctuated with the sound of laughter.

### Magnificent Immensity

A wall surrounds the city, conveying a sense of security to those within (Rev. 21:12, 17–18). Though the wall is not large, compared to the height of the city that it surrounds, still it is too high to scale, making access possible only through the proper entrances.

The foundations of the wall are inlaid with jewels that parallel roughly the twelve gems in the breastplate of the High Priest (vv. 19–20; cf. Exod. 28:17–20), suggestive of the heavenly communion of God's people.

Continuing this symbolism in the wall are twelve gates, each composed of a single pearl, expressive of the entrance into the kingdom (Rev. 21:12, 21). Recall that a pearl is made from the secretion in an oyster, to protect an injury. Without a wound, there would be no pearl. The pearl gates, thus, furnish a fitting emblem of the Savior by whose wounds we obtain salvation (Matt. 13:46).

The gates are arranged in three groups, separately open to the east, the north, the south, and the west, for the Gospel reaches to all people and nations; and the gates will never be closed (Rev. 21:12–13, 25). Stationed at the gates are twelve sentinel angels, the ministering servants of God, and written on the gates are the names of the twelve tribes of the sons of Israel, the heirs of the covenant (v. 12; cf. Ezek. 48:30–34). Inscribed on the foundation stones of the walls are the names of the twelve apostles of the Lamb, underscoring the faith and mission of the church (Rev. 21:14). By engraving both the names of the tribes and the apostles on the city structure, God again brings into focus the unity of his work throughout history.

Intensifying the immaculate splendor is the "pure gold" of which the city is made (v. 18). Even the streets are "pure gold, transparent as glass" (v. 21). Nothing about it can hinder the transfusion of the glory of God. These construction materials of gold, pearls, and precious jewels, among the most valuable substances known, convey a feeling of indescribable affluence and costliness. The treasures of this world heaped together pale into nothing by comparison.

Still employing poetic imagery, attention is given to the dimensions of the city. Foursquare in design, its length and width and height are equal, one harmonious structure, symmetrical in all its parts (v. 16). Doubtless it is an allusion to the Holy of Holies in ancient Israel (1 Kings 6:20). That hallowed place where the Shekinah glory of God would come on the Day of Atonement now characterizes the whole habitation of the saints.

Yet in contrast to the small cubicle of the earth's sanctuary, the new Jerusalem measures 12,000 furlongs on each side, the equivalent of about 1,500 miles, or 2,250,000 square miles, an immensity of fantastic proportions. There is surely room for everyone. When the dimensions of the city are seen, too, as in infinite multiples of the number 12, one can see how everything symbolically magnifies the perfection of God's provision for his bride.

### Emmanuel's Land

A voice from the throne proclaims, "Now the dwelling of God is with men, and he will live with them. They will be his people, and God himself will be with them and be their God" (Rev. 21:3 NIV). The announcement recalls the promise made through Moses: "I will make my dwelling among you. . . . I will walk among you and will be your God, and you shall be my people" (Lev. 26:11–12).

John picks up this familiar association in his Gospel, when he says: "The Word became flesh and dwelt among us, and we have seen his glory, glory as of the only Son from the Father, full of grace and truth" (John 1:14). When he uses this analogy in describing heaven, he is affirming that Emmanuel has come to abide with his people forever.

This life in the glorious presence of God, constantly sustained by the ever-present Spirit, is depicted by a sparkling pure river of water proceeding out of the throne. God is sometimes described in Scripture as "the fountain of living water" (Jer. 2:13; cf. Ps. 36:9), "welling up to eternal life" (John 4:14).

The waters in heaven are pictured as nourishing twelve trees of life along the banks of the stream, which bear perpetual fruit to bring healing to the nations (Rev. 22:1–2; cf. Gen. 2:9; 3:22; Ezek. 47:12). That the saints will continually partake of this life-giving fruit indicates again that they are always dependent on divine grace. We never get a hint that life comes as a result of human accomplishment—it ever flows out of God.

Living in the presence of the Lord and gazing on his beauty will satisfy every longing of the soul (Ps. 27:4). What greater blessing can be imagined? For in his presence is fullness of joy (Ps. 16:11). Enraptured in the delight, the psalmist honestly could say, "Whom have I in heaven but you? And there is nothing on earth that I desire besides you" (Ps. 73:25).

### Faith Turns to Sight

Amplifying this sense of divine fellowship is the absence of a temple in the city. This physical symbol of God's dwelling has been replaced by the spiritual reality itself "for its temple is the Lord God the Almighty and the Lamb" (Rev. 21:22). As Jesus had said, the time has come when all who worship God do so "in Spirit and in truth" (John 4:24 NIV).

Moreover, the city does not need the sun or the moon to shine on it. Secondary means of illumination are superfluous, "for the glory of God gives it light, and its lamp is the Lamb" (Rev. 21:23). And, "the nations will walk in its light, and the kings of the earth will bring their splendor into it" (v. 24 NIV).

In this rarified atmosphere our eyes will be opened to see Christ in his resplendent glory. He is the light that banishes every vestige of darkness. What we now see only through a glass in shadows, will then be seen in the full light of endless day. Faith shall turn to sight, and we shall see Jesus in all his glory, face-to-face (Rev. 22:4).

Anne R. Cousin captures the feeling of the saints in her hymn:

The bride eyes not her garment, but her dear bridegroom's face;
I will not gaze at glory, but on my king of grace;
Not on the crown he giveth, but on his pierced hand;
The Lamb is all the glory of Emmanuel's land.[6]

## Glorification of the Saints

### The Resurrection Body

Jesus assures his followers: "Whoever hears my word and believes him who sent me has eternal life and will not be condemned; he has crossed over from death to life" (John 5:24 NIV). This new undying life of the believer through eternity can be understood best through the lens of Christ's own resurrection.

Much about this glorified life of the Christian "has not yet appeared," of course. However, John says, "we know that when he appears, we shall be like him" (1 John 3:2). Also, Paul, looking to the second coming of Christ, affirms "the power that enables him to bring everything under his control, will transform our lowly bodies so that they will be like his glorious body" (Phil. 3:21 NIV; cf. Rom. 8:11 NIV).

Thus the resurrection body of Jesus indicates the nature of the heavenly body of the saints. Using the analogy of a seed, it is perishable when planted in the soil, but "it is raised imperishable; it is sown in dishonor, it is raised in glory; it is sown in weakness, it is raised in power; it is sown a natural body; it is raised a spiritual body" (1 Cor. 15:42–44 NIV). It is the same body as was fashioned from the dust in the first Adam, but now through the resurrection, it has the "life-giving spirit" of "the last Adam," the "man from heaven" (vv. 45–49).

Difficult as it is now to conceive of a human body utterly free from the limitations of the flesh, this is the kind of body we recognize in appearances of Jesus after his resurrection. He could walk out of a sealed tomb; he could travel from one place to another without any regard to time or distance; he could appear and disappear at will; and, in contradiction to the laws of gravity, he ascended back into the heavens (Matt. 28:1–20; Mark 16:9–20; Luke 24:1–53; John 20–21; Acts 1:6–11).

It is also obvious that Jesus could manifest himself to others in the way most appropriate to accomplish his purpose. He talked to his disciples and expounded the Scriptures to them. On occasion he ate with them. And to allay their doubts, he showed them the wound in his side and the nail prints in his hands. Clearly, he wanted them to identify his glorified body with his previous life and death in the world.

### Authentic Spiritual Identity

Here we can begin to understand how the spiritual body of the saints will be recognized in heaven. As with Jesus, the identity and personality of each child of God is preserved. People are known for who they were on earth (e.g., 1 Thess. 2:19; Heb. 12:23).

In our present experience, we really do not get to know each other very well, so limited is our knowledge. Paul likened it to seeing a poor reflection of someone in a mirror. But when the restrictions of our natural situation are removed, then we "shall know fully," even as we are known (1 Cor. 13:11–12). Think of it! All the twisted, inaccurate, often blatantly false assumptions by which we have evaluated earthly acquaintances will no longer hinder genuine friendship. We will actually see the true values and motivations of the redeemed, and know them for who they are in Christ.

Probably nowhere does this realization bring more comfort than in the preservation of family relationships. True, the propagation of the race through marriage will cease in heaven; people "neither marry nor are given in marriage," like the angels (Matt. 22:30). But the end of procreation does not erase the happy memories of earthly associations, especially in the home. Indeed, the deep endearments the saints have known will be enhanced in the ever-expanding realization of the glory of God.

### Unimpaired Life

Wonderful, too, is the realization that, unencumbered with physical infirmities, the saints will be able to develop the full potential of their created life. Latent gifts and abilities, which had long been dormant or suppressed on earth, will come forth invigorated. Even those innocent ones whose life was aborted in the womb, I expect, will rise to fulfill their God-intended destiny.

Intriguing, too, the resurrection body, made spirit and incorruptible, never gets sick or tired. Also, being immortal, it is unaffected by time. There is sequence in heaven but no age.

I think of my dear mother before she died. Her depleted body was so emaciated that the children closed the casket at her funeral and placed on the floral wreath resting on the coffin a picture of her earlier in her splendorous beauty. That is the way I like to remember Mom and that is the way I expect to recognize her in heaven.

Imagine a body fully adapted to the new environment of eternal life, a body that can serve all the desires of the soul in harmony with the law of the Spirit that governs heaven. In this devotion, the saints, without any hindrances, will be able always to respond to the will of him who sits on the throne.

### Perfected in Holiness

Translated into "the heavenly realms," the human spirit will enjoy "every spiritual blessing" (Eph. 1:3 NIV). It is spoken of as a "glorious inheritance" belonging to the Son of God to which the saints are made "co-heirs with Christ" (Matt. 25:34; Rom. 8:17 NIV; Eph. 1:14, 18), "an inheritance that can never perish, spoil or fade—kept in heaven . . . ready to be revealed in the last time" (1 Pet. 1:4–5 NIV).

That revelation has come, and the bride of Christ, clothed in garments of holiness, washed spotlessly clean through the blood, is presented before the "glorious presence" of God "without fault and with great joy" (Jude 24 NIV; cf. Rev. 19:8 NIV). The goal to "present everyone perfect in Christ," which has always directed the saints, has been attained (Col. 1:28 NIV).

In token of the character of the Lord whom they serve, and whose Spirit continually nourishes their life, "his name will be on their foreheads" (Rev. 22:4). It is a way of indicating their oneness with Christ. The saints now are totally under his ownership and care, sealed in perfect love forever.

Magnifying this perfection is their love displayed in the church. What may have been confessed on earth now is fact—the saints live as "members together of one body" (Eph. 3:6 NIV; Col. 1:12 NIV). Behold, "how good and pleasant it is when brothers live together in unity" (Ps. 133:1 NIV). Everyone cherishes the best for others in the family of God.

In this mutual giving and receiving of holy blessings, the uniqueness of each individual personality is enhanced, adding to the beauty of the whole. Since this life together finds expression in holy love for God and each other, the new Jerusalem will never be marred by deceit or disrupted by disunity.

The splendor of holiness mirrored in the multiplicity of the heavenly host fills the saints with unspeakable joy, as all are being perfected in the love of God and the unity of the Spirit. Jesus prayed that his church might have this oneness of heart with him, and that prayer is being answered (John 17:22–26).

### Unceasing Growth and Activity

Giving further meaning to this reality is the expanding capacity of the church to experience more of the unsearchable riches of Christ. Though the joy of the saints is full in glorification, it continues to intensify as comprehension of God grows "with ever-increasing glory" (2 Cor. 3:18 NIV; cf. Eph. 3:18–19). Learning never ceases through eternity. God alone is infinite, so there will always be more for finite children of grace to explore in the limitless reaches of him who is above all and through all, and by whom all things have their proper place (Eph. 1:20–21; 3:16; Phil. 2:9–10; Col. 1:17).

I can only imagine the delight that will come in exploring the universe of truth, free to think with purified reason, and unencumbered with the pressure of time limits. Oh, what a treat that will be!

With the learning, too, there will be endless ways to develop in ministry. We are called "servants" of the throne (Rev. 7:15; 22:3), which indicates that in heaven there is no idleness. Every person will be involved some way in ministry to the Lord, which, as on earth, finds expression in deeds. Recall that in the parable of the ten men the faithful servants received new tasks for rendering glory to God (Luke 19:11–27).

However the activity takes form, it will have a royal and priestly function. For the saints are made "to be a kingdom and priests to serve" God (1 Pet. 2:5 NIV; Rev. 1:6 NIV). For this ministry, they are said to "reign" with Christ in the discharge of his kingly rule (Rev. 5:10; 22:5). All that this involves is not explained, though it implies a regal occupation, a work that carries the trust and dignity of the King.

## Summary Applications

### 1. Heaven is where the heart is.

One does not have to understand all the strange and fascinating imagery of heaven to know its reality. It is enough to know Christ, for in him are found all the treasures of the kingdom.

A man was asked if he expected to go to heaven when he died. "Why," he replied, "I live there." Indeed, in the deepest sense of our spiritual being, persons indwelt with the Spirit of Christ already sit with him in the "heavenly places" (Eph. 2:6; cf. 1:3; 3:10; Col. 3:1–2). There we have "citizenship" (Phil. 3:20); his inheritance is already possessed by faith (Eph. 1:11, 14; Col. 1:12; Titus 2:14), for the future is present in him who is ever "the same yesterday and today and forever" (Heb. 13:8).

So it can be said that heaven begins when one falls in love with Jesus. That is where the heart is at home. Neither time nor distance should impede this assurance of the soul.

### 2. The Gospel begins and ends in heaven.

In the councils of eternity, our Triune God decided to create a man and a woman in his image, with the capability to know him and to love him. They were to multiply and "fill the earth" (Gen. 1:28). Though our forebearers chose to forfeit their inheritance, God loved them and had already determined from the beginning to save out of humanity a people for his glory. This he would accomplish by taking on himself the judgment of our sin (Rev. 13:8).

His sovereign purpose, revealed through the history of Israel, finally became visibly incarnate on that Judean night two thousand years ago when the angels announced: "Unto you is born a Savior . . . who is Christ the Lord" (Luke 2:11). His journey would lead to Calvary when Jesus took our place on the cross. Behold, the love of God, that "while we were still sinners, Christ died for us" (Rom. 5:8).

Just as evangelism began in heaven, so it will consummate there when the Gospel has been preached to the ends of the earth and all the redeemed are gathered from the nations (Matt. 24:14; Rev. 7:9).

Fulfilling this mission is the primary occupation of the church today—to call out from the world the people of God, and thereby to populate heaven. Jesus likens it to gathering a harvest "for eternal life" (John 4:36).

That everyone hears the Gospel of salvation, thus, becomes the imperative of the saints. For not to believe in Jesus is to miss heaven. "But how, then, can they call on the one they have not believed in? And how can they believe in the one of whom they have not heard? And how can they hear without someone preaching to them?" (Rom. 10:14 NIV).

Aware of the judgment following the resurrection of the dead who will awake, some to everlasting life, others to eternal contempt, we should heed the admonition of the prophet: "Those who are wise will shine like the brightness of the heavens, and those who lead many to righteousness, like the stars for ever and ever" (Dan. 12:3 NIV).

### 3. We should measure life now by the values of eternity.

Heaven gives a different perspective on what is important. Jesus taught his disciples to keep eternity in mind when deciding on where we want to invest the labor of our so brief lives. "Store up for yourselves treasures in heaven," he advises, "where moth and rust do not destroy, and where thieves do not break in and steal" (Matt. 6:20 NIV; cf. 19:21; Luke 12:33).

I suspect that if we would earnestly seek to measure what we value now by these criteria, there would be a lot of changes in our investments. Most of the things cherished today would be seen as very temporary and perishable. In fact everything in the world passes away. Nothing will remain except the Word of God and the souls of men and women. That is why bearing witness to the Gospel and making disciples of Christ has such high priority in preparing for eternity.

Randy Alcorn, in his historical novel *Safely Home*, gives a moving insight into the persecuted church today in China.[7] The story depicts the suffering Christians, who, because of their unwillingness to collaborate with the Communist government, endure constant harassment. Many are imprisoned and subjected to unspeakable tortures. Yet through it all the joy of the Lord overflows in their lives and the imminence of martyrdom only heightens the anticipation of seeing Jesus, as they continually ask themselves: "Is this the day?"

Can you imagine the change that would come in our lives if we greeted each morning with that same question?

### 4. Earth holds no sorrow that heaven cannot heal.

Pain is the common experience of everyone on earth (Gen. 3:17–19). Not a second goes by without multiplied millions of people bearing physical, emotional, mental, or spiritual suffering.

But "our light affliction, which is but for a moment, worketh for us a far more exceeding and eternal weight of glory" (2 Cor. 4:17 KJV). The day is coming when it will vanish like the morning dew in the light of the sun. The injustice, inequality, and poverty rampant in this world will be gone. Disease will no longer torment feverish bodies. Never again will one know that terrible feeling of being left alone at an open grave. In Emmanuel's land there will be only the joy of eternal life, to which our present suffering cannot be compared (Rom. 8:18).

A beautiful example of this assurance comes out in the martyrdom of Pastor Yona in eastern Rwanda during an uprising in 1964.[8] In the evening of Thursday, January 23, a jeep laden with soldiers pulled up in front of the pastor's house, and he was ordered to go with them. The soldiers also arrested the schoolmaster.

They drove away in the direction of Kigali. When they crossed the river some miles away, they were met by more soldiers. The prisoners were ordered out of the jeep and told to surrender everything they had. One of the soldiers sneered, "You had better pray to your God." So the men stood up and the pastor prayed, after which they joined in singing:

> There is a happy land,
>     Far, far away.
> Where saints in glory stand,
>     Bright, bright as day.
> Oh, how they sweetly sing,
>     Worthy is our Savior King.
> Lord, let his praises sing—
>     Praise, praise for aye!

They had scarcely finished singing when the pastor was told to walk back to the bridge over the river. He complied but, as he went, he lifted his voice and began to sing:

> There's a land that is fairer than day,
>     And by faith we can see it afar;
> For the Father waits over the way
>     To prepare us a dwelling place there.
> For in the sweet by and by
>     We shall meet on that beautiful shore,
> In the sweet by and by
>     We shall meet on that beautiful shore.

The last words of the song, however, were not heard on earth, for when the pastor reached the bridge, he was shot, and a soldier threw his body into the river.

The schoolmaster fully expected to be next. But to his surprise, he was released. Later, after making his way to another country, where he found refuge, he told what had happened. "The soldiers were all amazed," he said. "They had never before seen someone go singing to his death."

That is what the assurance of heaven does for the soul.

### 5. The heavenly vision energizes obedience.

Once the glory of the coming kingdom is in focus, the allurements of this world begin to lose appeal while the resolve to follow Christ intensifies. Disciplines that nourish faith—communion with God in prayer, study of his Word, participation in the ministries of the church, the practice of worship—become all-important. Other things cannot satisfy the yearnings of the soul.

I will never forget my dad one day before his death, turning to me and asking, "Son, where does a man go when he goes out with God?"

The question came as such a surprise that I was a bit confused. Seeing my perplexity, Dad smiled, then in a quiet voice said, "Does it matter? You just go wherever he wants to take you. There is nothing to worry about. He knows the way. All you have to do is follow."

He was thinking of that passage in the old King James version that says of Abraham:

> When he was called to go out into a place which he should after receive for an inheritance, obeyed: and he went out, not knowing whither he went. By faith he sojourned in the land of promise, as in a strange country, dwelling in tabernacles with Isaac and Jacob, the heirs with him of the same promise: for he looked for a city which hath foundations, whose builder and maker is God.
>
> Hebrews 11:8–10 KJV

That is the way it is with everyone who obeys the voice from above. Once we have been called to go "out," we know that we can never be satisfied to stay in the old country. God has something better for us. It really does not make any difference where we go, as long as we are together, for where he is, there is heaven. Following him, we have perfect peace. Our part is simply to trust and obey. In this pilgrimage of faith, we are content to live as aliens in this world, as in a foreign land, for we have been spoiled by the vision of another world, "a city which hath foundations, whose builder and maker is God."

### 6. The saints are presented to Christ in holy wedlock.

With the completion of events related to the second advent of Christ, as shouts of hallelujah resound through heaven, at last comes the "marriage of the Lamb" with his church (Rev. 19:7). The bond of marriage, as a symbol of the relationship between God and his beloved, occurs all through Scripture (e.g., Isa. 54:5–6; Hosea 2:20; Matt. 22:1–10; 25:1; Eph. 5:25–32). So it is not strange that the Bible ends, as it began, in a wedding.

264

What is most significant for us is that the bride is properly attired to meet her Lord. "Fine linen, bright and clean, was given her to wear. (Fine linen stands for the righteous acts of the saints.)" (Rev. 19:8 NIV). Again we are reminded that holiness becomes the people of God, a positive way of life that finds expression in deeds of mercy and truth. Lest we imagine that such works flow from human initiative, the Revelator takes care to point out that this righteous covering for the wedding feast is "given" by the Lamb. The adornment of holiness is a witness to the grace of God.

Thinking of this presentation of the bride reminds me of my own wedding day. It was June 3, 1951. As the time drew near, my bride, with one of her seamstress friends, began to make her wedding gown. Though we were observing the custom of the fiancé not seeing the bride in her dress until the wedding, I was told something of its design and material, and was sure that it was going to be the most beautiful dress that had ever been made.

At last the day came. I was standing at the altar of the church when the door opened and I saw for the first time my bride, coming down the aisle wearing the wedding garment. Indeed, it was the most beautiful dress I had ever seen—a long, flowing, glistening, white satin gown, without any spot or wrinkle or any such thing. And as I looked into my beloved's face, I saw love that corresponded to her wedding garment—a love that was pure, a love that reached out and embraced me with all that she was and hoped to be. The vows we took at the altar, pledging ourselves each to the other, were but a public affirmation of a love between us that was perfect.

I have to say that in these intervening years, I have learned a great deal more about the meaning of those vows. There have been some strains, times of sorrow and suffering, but we have gone through them together, and the experiences through which we have passed have only made us more conscious of our love. Yet because our capacity to understand and appreciate each other has grown, it might be said that we love now more than we did then, even though in the beginning as we knew our hearts, we loved with all our souls, with all our minds, and with all our strength.

I have often thought that this is an illustration of the way Jesus wants us to love him. However limited our comprehension of his will, he wants us to give ourselves unreservedly to him—to love him and trust him with all that we are, all that we hope to be. This is the fulfillment of the law and the prophets (Matt. 22:37–40). It is the bond of perfection (Col. 3:14). In this devotion we are to live every day in exciting readiness to meet him when the shout is heard, "Behold, the Bridegroom comes!"

*7. The longing for heaven grows with the years.*

This anticipation comes out beautifully in the closing stanza of Augustus Toplady's hymn "Rock of Ages":

> While I draw this fleeting breath,
> When my eyes shall close in death,
> When I rise to worlds unknown,
> See Thee on Thy Judgment Throne,
> Rock of Ages, cleft for me,
> Let me hide myself in Thee.

A short time before his death, Toplady asked his physician about his condition. The reply was that his pulse indicated that his heart was beating weaker every day. The patient replied with a smile, "Why, that is a good sign that my death is fast approaching, and blessed be God, I can add that my heart beats stronger and stronger every day for glory."

To another friend he said, "O, my dear sir, I cannot tell you the comfort I feel in my soul; they are past expression . . . my prayers are all converted into praise."[9]

### 8. Heaven resounds with the praise of God forever.

In Emmanuel's land everything that has breath will praise the Lord.

Then let us get acclimated to the occupation of heaven. As best we can, we should develop this lifestyle now. Life at its best becomes doxology. To the degree this is accomplished, our spirits pulsate with the heartbeat of God, and life takes on deathless, joyous meaning.

John Wesley's last hours on earth vividly portray this truth. One who was present when he died has written that as his strength failed, to the astonishment of those gathered in the room, Wesley broke out singing:

> I'll praise my maker while I've breath,
> And when my voice is lost in death,
>    Praise shall employ my nobler powers;
> My days of praise shall ne'er be past,
> While life, and thought, and being last,
>    Or immortality endures.

Struggling for breath, he lay down on his bed and asked the people about him to "pray and praise." Then, as if to comfort his weeping friends kneeling by the bedside, "lifting up his dying arm in token of victory, and raising his feeble voice with a holy triumph not to be expressed he repeated the heart-reviving words, 'the best of all is, God is with us!'"

Thereafter in the few remaining hours that his soul lingered between two worlds, he was heard to whisper again and again, "I'll praise . . . I'll praise . . . I'll praise."[10]

It's a beautiful way to conclude a theology of evangelism. The praise of God was in our Creator's mind when he spoke the Gospel into existence, determined to make a people to know him, to love him, and to rejoice in him.

This is the heart of the Gospel. May the day be hastened when God's Good News will be heard to the ends of the earth, and all the nations, redeemed by grace, cleansed by the blood, will be gathered at the throne of the Lamb to celebrate his glory forever.

Every sinner saved by grace lives with this destiny. Yes, we are going home. Though our body is still held by the earth, our spirits can soar with the angels in the city of God. In the inner sanctuary of our being, we are already beginning to learn something of that worship in which the King of heaven dwells.[11]

> All creatures of our God and King
> Lift up your voice and with us sing,
>     Alleluia! Alleluia!
> Thou burning sun with golden beam,
> Thou silver moon with softer gleam!
>         O praise Him! O praise Him!
>         Alleluia! Alleluia! Alleluia!
>
> And thou most kind and gentle death,
> Waiting to hush our latest breath,
>     O praise Him! Alleluia!
> Thou leadest home the child of God,
> And Christ our Lord the way hath trod.
>         O praise Him! O praise Him!
>         Alleluia! Alleluia! Alleluia!
>
> Let all things their Creator bless,
> And worship Him in humbleness,
>     O praise Him! Alleluia!
> Praise, praise the Father, praise the Son,
> And praise the Spirit, Three in One!
>         O praise Him! O praise Him!
>         Alleluia! Alleluia! Alleluia![12]

# Notes

## Introduction

1. C. E. Autrey, *Basic Evangelism* (Grand Rapids: Zondervan, 1954), 16.

2. J. I. Packer, cited in an article by Krish Kandiah, "Lesslie Newbigin's Contribution to a Theology of Evangelism," *Transformation* 24, no. 1 (January 2007): 51.

3. James Denny, *The Death of Christ* (London: Hodder & Stoughton, 1902), 7.

4. J. I. Packer, from *The Evangelical Anglican Identity Problem: An Analysis* (Oxford: Latimer House, 1978), 15–23; cited in John Stott, *Evangelical Truth: A Personal Plea for Unity, Integrity and Faithfulness* (Downers Grove, IL: InterVarsity, 1999), 23–25.

5. Stott, *Evangelical Truth*, 25.

6. C. H. Dodd, *The Apostolic Preaching and Its Development* (London: Hodder & Stoughton, 1936).

7. Michael Green, *Evangelism in the Early Church* (London: Hodder & Stoughton, 1970); a full-scale treatment of this issue is in R. C. Worley, *Preaching and Teaching in the Earliest Church* (Philadelphia: Westminster, 1967).

8. Stott, *Evangelical Truth*, 25.

9. Two church statesmen I have studied with special interest are John Wesley and Jonathan Edwards. Though different in temperament and theological perspective, both labored with a passion for spiritual revival and understood the priority of evangelism and personal holiness. Other astute theologians to which I have often turned, in addition to the fathers and reformers, include Wayne Grudem, H. Orton Wiley, Carl F. H. Henry, Dennis Kinlaw, F. J. Sheed, J. I. Packer, Allan Coppedge, Donald G. Bloesch, Millard Erickson, Charles G. Finney, John Stott, Ajith Fernando, C. S. Lewis, Walter Kaiser, and Thomas Oden.

10. Two small books deserving of note are T. A. Kantonen, *The Theology of Evangelism* (Philadelphia: Muhlenberg Press, 1954); and A. Skevington Wood, *Evangelism: Its Theology and Practice* (Grand Rapids: Zondervan, 1966).

11. Lewis A. Drummond, *The Word of the Cross: A Contemporary Theology of Evangelism* (Nashville: Broadman Press, 1992). A later book extends his research: *Reaching Generation Next: Effective Evangelism in Today's Culture* (Grand Rapids: Baker, 2002).

12. Paulus Scharpff, *History of Evangelism* (Grand Rapids: Eerdmans, 1966), 118.

## Chapter 1  The Character of God

1. The meaning of this personal name for God was considered by the Israelites too sacred even to be pronounced, so it was first written by four consonants, YHWH, and read as Adonai, "Lord." Putting together the consonants with the vowels in Adonai gives the name Jehovah.

2. For a discussion of the creeds developed through the church across the years, see Philip Schaff, *The Creeds of Christendom* III (1931; repr., Grand Rapids: Baker, 1983). A citation of the historic Conferences of Faith is quoted in Wayne Grudem, *Systematic Theology* (Grand Rapids: Zondervan, 1994), 1168–221.

3. Article I, "Of Faith in the Holy Trinity," quoted in Grudem, *Systematic Theology*, 1171.

4. A story told by James Henry White, "God's Most Defining Trait," *Decisions* (July–August 2007), 15.

5. Walter Kasper, *The God of Jesus Christ* (New York: Crossroad, 1996), 30. A masterful treatment of this concept is in Dennis F. Kinlaw, *Let's Start with Jesus: In Search of a New Paradigm* (Grand Rapids: Zondervan, 2005), especially pp. 34–106.

6. Dennis F. Kinlaw, from his devotion for November in *This Day with the Master* (Nappanee, IN: Francis Asbury Press, Evangel Publishing House, 2002).

7. Kantonen, *Theology of Evangelism*, 25.

8. Timothy C. Tennent, *Invitation to World Missions: A Trinitarian Missiology for the Twenty-First Century* (Grand Rapids: Kregel, 2010), 74–101, 147, 187.

9. Adapted from a story told by Dennis Kinlaw, *Let's Start with Jesus*, 15.

10. The idea that God can be known not by what he is, but by what he is not, was first advocated by Moses Maimonides, a physician of the Sultan and leader of the Jewish community in Cairo in the twelfth century.

11. H. Orton Wiley, *Christian Theology*, vol. 1 (Kansas City, MO: Beacon Hill Press, 1949), 389.

12. Openness theologians believe that God does not know human decisions in advance, for they do not yet exist to know, they contend. While God is seen as immutable in character, he is thought to be limited in his foreknowledge of events caused by human agency. Presentation of this position is by Clark H. Pinnock, *Most Moved Mover* (Grand Rapids: Baker, 2001). For a good rebuttal, see Bruce A. Ware, *God's Lesser Glory: The Diminished God of Open Theism* (Wheaton: Crossway, 2000).

13. In reference to the doctrine of God, this theme is no better treated than by Allan Coppedge, *Portraits of God* (Downers Grove, IL: InterVarsity, 2001). The author traces the centrality of holiness in various roles of God—Transcendent Creator, Sovereign King, Personal Revealer, Priest, Righteous Judge, Loving Father, Powerful Redeemer, and Good Shepherd.

14. The three ecumenical creeds all address attacks on the Trinity. The Apostles' Creed (AD 100–150) expands on the baptismal formula—the Father, the Son, and the Holy Spirit. The Nicene Creed (AD 325) spoke to the Arian controversy, which relegated Christ and the Spirit to a position less than God. The most explicit statement on this issue was the Athanasian Creed (fifth century), which said: "We worship our God in Trinity, and Trinity in Unity. Neither confounding the Person; not dividing the substance for there is one Person of the Father; another of the Son; and another of the Holy Spirit. But the Godhead of the Father, of the Son, and of the Holy Spirit is all one: The Glory equal, the Majesty eternal."

15. The effect of this heresy was to deny the equality of Christ and the Spirit with the Father. When it is followed out in history, the divine significance of the atonement in redemption is lost.

16. This view arose during the Enlightenment and the growing infatuation with science in the seventeenth century. It neglected any need of divine revelation. Voltaire and Thomas Payne were typical exponents. The ancient philosophy of Stoicism, with its emphasis on natural law and high ethics, has much in common with this view. Also it has similarities with Epicureanism. Paul encountered these philosophers in Athens (Acts 17:12–34).

17. Reasons for the existence of God can take different courses—the ontological approach, showing the necessity for absolute perfection; the cosmological, arguing from the presence of cause and effect in the universe; the teleological, reasoning from the obvious design in the universe to a Master Designer; the anthropological, showing the need for some infinite personality; the moral purpose position, contending for some moral end in the universe; added to these classical arguments could be the testimony of human reason, experience, and devotion in their various forms. These arguments can be found in any standard systematic theology text.

18. Apologetics refers to the science of defending or explaining the Christian faith to nonbelievers, and therefore, complements a theology of evangelism. Resources on this discipline are abundant and are especially helpful in answering skeptics. For an introduction to this discipline, see William Lane Craig, *Reasonable Faith: Christian Truth and Apologetics* (Wheaton: Crossway, 1984); Norman Geisler and Peter Bocchino, *Unshakable Foundations* (Minneapolis: Bethany, 2001); Peter Kreeft and Ronald K. Tacelli, *Handbook of Christian Apologetics: Hundreds of Answers to Crucial Questions* (Downers Grove, IL: InterVarsity, 1994).

A powerful application to our contemporary culture is by Ravi Zacharias, *A Shattered Visage: The Real Face of Atheism* (Brentwood, TN: Wolgemuth and Hyatt, 1990).

19. Augustine is reported to have said, perhaps tongue in cheek, "Anyone who denies the Trinity is in danger of losing their salvation, but anyone who tries to understand the Trinity is in danger of losing their mind." Quoted in Roger E. Olsen and Christopher A. Hall, *The Trinity* (Grand Rapids: Eerdmans, 2002), 1.

20. John Wesley, "On the Trinity," *The Works of John Wesley*, vol. 2, ed. Albert C. Outler (Nashville: Abingdon, 1985), 384.

21. Jonathan Edwards, "Sinners in the Hands of an Angry God," in *Puritan Sage: Collected Writings of Jonathan Edwards*, vol. 1, ed. Vergilius Ferm (New York: Library Publishers, 1953), 366.

22. Jonathan Edwards, "Personal Narrative," quoted in *Resolutions of a Saintly Scholar* (Minneapolis: World Wide Publications, 1992), 15.

## Chapter 2  Revelation and the Bible

1. Often the Bible refers to God speaking, which is a way of indicating communication appropriate for the occasion (e.g., Jer. 18:1; Hosea 1:1; Amos 3:1; Heb. 1:1–2). The language may be audible, may be a silent hearing of God's voice, or may come through a dream or vision. Then, too, God may be described as speaking to us in mighty acts, as in creation (Genesis 1) or in Christ (John 1:1).

2. This natural order in creation is called general revelation, indicating what can be learned about God through nature, history, and the nature of man. Human ability, however, corrupted by sin, can no longer perceive clearly God's revelation in nature (Rom. 8:19–23; 2 Cor. 4:4). An excellent treatment of this subject, with its many ramifications, is in Millard J. Erickson, *Christian Theology*, vol. 1 (Grand Rapids: Baker, 1983), 153–298.

3. Some scholars hold that one can come to a genuine knowledge of God on the basis of reason, without any special divine revelation. The most prominent work in this regard was by Thomas Aquinas in his *Summa Theologica* (Part I). He argued that certain beliefs can be proved in the realm of nature, like the existence of God and the immortality of the soul. There are certain truths in the realm of grace, however, that can only be known by special revelation received by faith. Unlike Aquinas, who had a high view of Scripture, persons who have questions about the authority of the Bible build a natural theology on general revelation, relying heavily on reason. Seeing the bankruptcy of his humanistic thinking, Karl Barth, for example, rejected both natural theology and general revelation.

4. For an excellent treatment of this subject, though a bit heavy, see Carl F. H. Henry, *God, Revelation and Authority: God Who Speaks and Shows*, vols. 3 and 4 (Waco: Word, 1979). There is no want of other evangelical scholars who explain biblical inspiration, among them Erickson, *Christian Theology*, vol. 1; and Norman Geisler, *Systematic Theology*, vol. 1 (Minneapolis: Bethany, 2003).

5. The so-called mechanical dictation theory of inspiration, whereby those who wrote the Scriptures were totally passive in the transmission, is subject to misunderstanding. Most evangelicals contend for a verbal inspiration of Scripture, which recognizes the humanness of the biblical authors.

6. John Wesley, "Sermons of Social Occasions," in *The Words of John Wesley*, vol. 1, ed. Albert C. Outler (Nashville: Abingdon, 1984), 105–6.

7. Modern liberalism has many spokesmen. Its anti-supernaturalism in regard to Scripture goes as far back as the seventeenth century and Thomas Hobbes and Benedict Spinoza, gathering fellow travelers through the years such as Immanuel Kant, Georg Wilhelm Friedrich Hegel, Herbert Spencer, and Charles Darwin. Its destructive biblical criticism found expression in such scholars as Friedrich Schleiermacher, David Friedrich Strauss, and Rudolf Bultmann. More recent theologians with this outlook are represented by Harold DeWolf, Schubert Ogden, and John Cobb. The many developments of liberalism, and their distinctive forms, may be seen in any standard systematic theology.

8. This movement had its roots in the work of Søren Kierkegaard, who, though orthodox in basic theology, had shifted the emphasis in salvation from doctrine to an existential encounter with Christ through a "leap of faith." Influenced by this thinking, Karl Barth, a German Swiss pastor, seeing the utter bankruptcy of liberalism during the evil of World War I, turned to

the Bible for direction, especially the book of Romans (*Commentary on Romans*, 1919). Though he had a flawed view of Scripture, his vigorous teaching and writing (e.g., *Church Dogmatics*, 1961) has had tremendous impact on the church. Others who have followed his thinking, with their own variations, include notables like John Baillie, Emil Brunner, Reinhold Niebuhr, and Paul Tillich. Remnants of this thinking can be seen in some of the writings of accommodating evangelicals today, like G. C. Berkouwer and Jack Rogers.

9. J. I. Packer, "Contemporary Views of Revelation, Part 2," *Christianity Today*, December 8, 1958, 17.

10. Frequently this criticism comes out in the debate between science and religion. An example is reported in the November 13, 2006, issue of *Time*, pp. 48–50. Here the atheist biologist and Oxford professor Richard Dawkins characterizes believers in the Genesis account of creation as "clowns." Respectfully answering him is Francis Collins, director of the National Human Genome Research Institute and foremost geneticist (*The Language of God: A Scientist Presents Evidence for Belief* [New York: Free Press, 2006]). He points out that God cannot be contained within nature, and when the evidence for God is put into the equation, there need be no conflict between science and faith in Christian revelation.

11. John Clifford, *The Inspiration and Authority of the Bible* (London: James Clarke & Co., 1895), 106.

12. This illustration I expect has been told many times, but I came across it in the book by Herb Hodges, *Tally Ho the Fox!* (Memphis: Spiritual Life Ministries, 2001), 183–84.

13. John Bunyan's *Pilgrim's Progress* was written in 1678 and is still in print in several editions. Because of its simplicity and profound application to any Christian, I believe it is the best introduction to the theology of evangelism. It has been a basic text in my classes for many years. The version I like best is *The New Pilgrim's Progress*, revised for today by Warren W. Wiersbe (Grand Rapids: Discovery House, 1989).

14. St. Jerome, quoted in Mike MacIntosh, *Falling in Love with the Bible* (Wheaton: Victor, 2005), 173.

15. Officially Roman Catholics, like evangelical Protestants, affirm the inerrancy of Scripture. The doctrine of revelation of Vatican II, following Pope Pius XII's *Encyclical Divino Afflante Spiritu*, states: "The book of Scripture must be acknowledged as teaching firmly, faithfully and without error, that truth which God wanted was put into the sacred writings for the sake of our salvation." Richard P. McBrien, gen. ed., *HarperCollins Encyclopedia of Catholicism* (San Francisco: Harper, 1995), 165. *A Catholic Dictionary* sums it up this way: "Inspiration comes with it absolute absence of error, God's infinite veracity being incompatible with error in any form" (New York: Macmillan, 1962), 256.

16. Sir Walter Scott, *Masterpieces of Religious Verse*, ed. James D. Morrison (New York: Harper and Brothers, 1948), 384.

17. For a full treatment of this word *preach*, see Gerhard Kittel, *Theological Dictionary of the New Testament*, vol. 3, trans. Gerhard Friedrich (Grand Rapids: Eerdmans, 1966), 697–714. Consult A. T. Robertson, *Word Pictures in the New Testament*, vol. 4 (New York: Harper and Brothers, 1931), 629, for an exegesis of the word in this passage.

18. Taken from Billy Graham's personal explanation of his preaching ministry, "Biblical Authority in Evangelism" in the first edition of *Christianity Today*, October 15, 1956, 6.

19. Ibid.

20. Ibid. For a more complete account of this experience, see Billy Graham, *Just As I Am: The Autobiography of Billy Graham* (San Francisco: Harper, 1997), 137–40.

## Chapter 3 Creation and the Celestial Hosts

1. The creative sequences in Genesis are viewed in various ways by evangelicals. Some see a gap of an indeterminate amount of time between Genesis 1:1 and 1:2. This period is ruined by the fall of Satan and the judgment of God on the earth so that it becomes "without form and void." Taking this perspective, Genesis 1:3–2:3 really refers to a second creation by God in a series of six twenty-four-hour days. Others understand the days of Genesis 1 as ages of geological periods, though there are differences in the order of details, especially with the creation of the earth and its vegetation. Still another group, dating back to Augustine, believes that the Genesis account is not intended to supply a chronology of origins, but rather brings out certain themes to provide a theology of the Sabbath. They distinguish the

works of separation (days 1–3) from the works of adornment (days 4–6), seeing the creation story as a hymn-narrative. I will leave the reasoning for these and other interpretations to their defenders. My point is that whatever position one takes, creation was God's work, and that is what matters in the Gospel. For a full treatment of the subject, consult a good systematic theology.

2. These heavenly beings, in various orders of created personalities, are mentioned in the Scriptures more than 325 times, including those fallen with Satan.

3. Some speculate that the angels were created on the first day of creation, when "heaven and the earth" were made (Gen. 1:1 KJV), followed by the statement that "the earth was without form" without any reference to heaven (Gen. 2:1 KJV). The assumption is that the uninhabitable state of the earth is contrasted with the heavens where the angels had already been created. This view finds some support, too, when it is said that angels rejoiced when God made the earth habitable (Job 38:6–7). See Grudem, *Systematic Theology*, 401–2.

4. Among the angels, only two are identified by name: Michael (Dan. 10:13, 21; Jude 9; Rev. 12:7–8) and Gabriel (Dan. 8:16; 9:21; Luke 1:19, 26–27).

5. Fallen angels cannot be evangelized, for there is no provision for their salvation. It would appear that all the angels after their creation were in some kind of probationary state in which they had to prove their devotion to God, and that decision having been made is now fixed eternally.

6. The descriptions used here seem much stronger than we would normally associate with an earthly ruler and are consistent with what we know elsewhere about the devil—for example, Jesus's reference to seeing "Satan fall like lightning from heaven" (Luke 10:18; cf. Rev. 12:9). Also it was common for prophets to parallel events in the world with heavenly events (e.g., Psalm 45).

7. This does not explain all illness, of course. Most sickness results from organic dysfunctions in the body, or simply, carelessness in proper hygiene. In time these people get well or respond to medical treatment. The Gospel writers carefully distinguish between demon-caused disease and those that are not (e.g., Matt. 4:23–24; 8:16–17; Mark 1:34; Luke 4:40–41).

8. This description probably suits the condition better than the term "demon possession"

(Matt. 4:24; 8:16, 28, 33; John 10:21). How a person can become so demonized is not explained, but it would seem the result of weakness in the face of demonic attack. For helpful insights to this problem, see Timothy Warner, *Spiritual Warfare* (Wheaton: Crossway, 1991); or a more exhaustive treatment of the subject by C. Fred Dickason, *Demon Possession and the Christian* (Chicago: Moody, 1987). Addressing the question, Can a Christian be demon possessed? a good answer is in Clinton Arnold, *Three Crucial Questions about Spiritual Warfare* (Grand Rapids: Baker, 1997).

9. These heavenly creatures all appear to belong to the angelic class, though the distinctions between them are not clear. Specific Scripture explanation of the particular roles is limited, but we do know that they have a special ministry at the throne of God. For more information, see C. Fred Dickason, *Angels: Elect and Evil* (1975; repr., Chicago: Moody, 1996), 64–69.

10. In this instance, the reference to "the angel of the Lord" seems to relate to a created being, not Christ. However, in most instances where the definite article "the" is used, as is the case here, the description probably represents God revealing himself in angelic form as Christ or speaking through the Holy Spirit (e.g., Gen. 16:7–12; 22:11–18; 31:11–13; Exod. 3:2–6; Num. 22:22).

11. The full sermon of Paul Tillich is published in "The Princeton Seminary Bulletin" 57, no. 1 (October 1963): 4–9.

12. How demonic presence in social structures works to bring the church to dig her own grave is aptly portrayed by Os Guinness, *The Gravedigger File: Papers on the Subversion of the Modern Church* (Downers Grove, IL: InterVarsity, 1983). The ingenious way that the devil subverts people is no better described than in C. S. Lewis's classic *The Screwtape Letters* (New York: Macmillan, 1982).

13. Laura Whitlock, NASA, Goddard Space Flight Center, www.imagine.gsfc.nasa.gov.

14. Article on "quark," *Encyclopedia Britannica* (2009), www.britannica.com.

15. Those who would like to pursue this subject further will find helpful Michael Green, *I Believe in Satan's Downfall* (Grand Rapids: Eerdmans, 1981); Heinrich Schlier, *Principalities and Powers in the New Testament* (New York: Herder and Herder, 1961).

16. Isaac Watts, "Jesus My Great High Priest."

17. A story recounted by Billy Graham, *Angels: God's Secret Agents* (New York: Doubleday, 1975), 3.

## Chapter 4  Creation of Man and Woman

1. The word translated "man" in Hebrew is the same term used for the naming of Adam and generally refers to all mankind.

2. Marcus Dods, "Book of Genesis," ed. W. Robertson Nicoll and Marcus Dods, *The Expositor's Bible* (New York: George H. Doran, 1907), 7.

3. Some contend that animal creatures with physical characteristics like those of man preceded the actual creation of a human being. This view of theistic evolution, as distinct from Darwinian natural evolution, presents more problems than it solves and is not generally held by evangelicals.

4. Not only in the Genesis account, Adam is also mentioned as a real person in the genealogies in Jude 14 and Luke 3:38. He is also compared to and contrasted with Jesus as a historical person (Rom. 5:12–21; 1 Cor. 15:22).

5. The English Standard Version says "the LORD God caused a deep sleep to fall upon the man, and while he slept took one of his ribs . . . and the rib that the LORD God had taken from the man he made into a woman" (Gen. 2:21–22). However, the word *rib* is better translated "side," which is the way the term usually is rendered elsewhere in Scripture.

6. This same command is given to Noah and his sons after the flood when God starts over again to "fill the earth" (Gen. 9:1).

7. Joseph Parker, "The Making of Man," in *The People's Bible: Discourses upon the Holy Scripture*, vol. 1 (New York: Funk and Wagnalls, 1886), 111–12.

8. These terms are used by Dennis Kinlaw in his book *Let's Start with Jesus*. Dr. Kinlaw draws on the work of Jaroslaw Kupczak, *Destined for Liberty* (Washington, DC: The Catholic University of America Press, 2000), 114.

9. Though it makes no difference to the Gospel, an interesting subject among theologians concerns when a person receives this spiritual nature in creation. Some believe that the soul or spirit comes into existence when the person's body is formed by parent conception. This position, called "traducianism," emphasizes the unity of body and spirit and brings the parents more directly into inherited emphasis of the human race. Another view, called "creationism," holds that God creates a soul for each individual at conception or birth, although not limited by these options. In this view, God is the sole originator of the personal soul, and inbred sin is entirely physical. A third view, called "pre-existentianism," contends that souls existed in an ideal world before being infused into the embryo or fetus before conception; this is pure speculation with no scriptural support.

10. Termed the "dichotomy" theory, it contends that man is composed of only two kinds of essence—a material portion called the body, and an immaterial portion called the soul or spirit (the part that never dies). Defenders of this view point out that the words *soul* and *spirit* are generally used interchangeably in Scripture (e.g., Luke 1:46–47; John 12:27; cf. John 13:21; 1 Pet. 3:19; Rev. 6:9). Also, man is said to be "body and soul" or "body and spirit" (Matt. 10:28; 1 Cor. 5:5; 7:34; James 2:26). A related view, called "monism," though not widely held, regards man as having only one element, the person or life, and that the body is the person, as well as the soul or spirit.

11. Termed the "trichotomy" theory, it means that man is composed of three consistent elements: the body, the animal soul, and the rational spirit. In this view, whereas everyone has a material body and soul, the spirit is that part of man that can communicate with God and comes alive in the new birth of a Christian. Much is made of 1 Thessalonians 5:23; Hebrews 4:12; 1 Corinthians 2:14–3:23. For a good analysis of both these views, see Grudem, *Systematic Theology*, 472–83.

12. Elaboration of this subject will be treated in later chapters, including the position of the annihilation of the soul.

13. Many theologians speak of this aspect of man's image in God as "original righteousness." Luther, however, according to Louis Berkhof, "did not seek the image of God in any of the natural endowments of man, such as his rational and moral powers, but exclusively in original righteousness, and therefore regarded it as entirely lost by sin." Louis Berkhof, *Systematic Theology* (Grand Rapids: Eerdmans, 1941), 202–3.

14. Since we are concerned here with evangelism, it is well to note that the flagrant display of pornography in the media and Hollywood films is probably the most formidable barrier to reaching the non-Western world with the Gospel, particularly Muslims. Whether justified or not, they generally associate Western nations with

the Christian faith and thereby say they want no part of that perverted lifestyle. Evangelization must confront this. For a brief statement of this problem, read Dinesh D'Souza, "The Clash of Stereotypes," *Christianity Today* 53, no. 7 (July 2009): 54.

15. H. C. Morrison, "The Value of Souls," *The Herald* (March 5, 1958): 3.

16. "The Confession of Faith," *The Westminster Shorter Catechism* (Richmond: John Knox Press, 1964), 391.

17. Jonathan Edwards, "Dissertation Concerning the End for Which God Created the World," *Works of President Edwards* II (New York: Leavitt and Allen, 1858), 255. The ambitious student who does not mind laborious reading will be abundantly rewarded in working through this whole dissertation.

18. Charles Wesley, "O All-Creating God."

## Chapter 5 Rebellion against God

1. Aleksandr Solzhenitsyn in an address when he received the Templeton Prize for Progress in Religion in London, England, in 1980, quoted in *Pastoral Renewal* 8, no. 10 (April 1984): 116.

2. Many scholars do not identify this crafty creature with a reptile, but rather see the term as the description of a person with the characteristics of a serpent. It does seem that this serpent is a person in Revelation 12:9 and 20:2.

3. The word *chatteh* in the Hebrew and *hamartia* in the Greek. Other important terms used to describe sin in the Old Testament are the nouns *rasha*, wickedness, confusion; *avon*, iniquity, perversion, guilt; *pasha*, wrongness, vanity; *sheger*, deceit or lying; *nra*, evil; *maal*, trespass; *auvel*, injustice; *asham*, error. Hebrew verbs for sin include *sarar*, to disobey; and *abar*, to transgress. New Testament words include *adikia*, unrighteous, injustice, stressing conduct incongruous with God's nature; *anomia*, iniquity, lawlessness; *asebeia*, impiety; *parabasis*, transgression; *paraptoma*, having a wrong relationship with God; *peoneria*, depravity; *epithumia*, lust; and *apeitheia*, disobedience; among others. Descriptions of these and other terms may be found in any good lexicon.

4. No one has made the point more emphatically than John Wesley. "Is man by nature filled with all manner of evil?" he asked. "Is he void of all good? Is he wholly fallen? Is his soul totally corrupted? . . . Allow this, and you are so far a

Christian. Deny it, and you are a Heathen still." John Wesley, "Original Sin," *Wesley Standard Sermons*, ed. Edward H. Sugden, vol. 2 (1921; repr., London: The Epworth Press, 1968), 223.

5. *The Confession of Faith of the Presbyterian Church in the United States Together with the Larger Catechism and the Shorter Catechism* (Richmond: John Knox, 1964), 330, 428. It's interesting that John Wesley made this confession when taking Holy Communion, and it is still followed by Methodists at the Lord's Table today. See "An Order for the Administration of the Sacrament of the Lord's Supper or Holy Communion," Letter Order, I or II, in any standard Methodist hymnal or *Book of Discipline*.

6. Such a distinction was made in the Law of Moses when dealing with degrees of the seriousness of a sin (e.g., Lev. 4:2, 13, 23, 27; 5:14). "Unintentional" sins pertained to lesser offenses against the commands of God, like touching anything ceremonially unclean or thoughtlessly taking an oath (Lev. 5:1–4). Though the person still bore guilt for his offense (e.g., v. 17), provision was made for forgiveness through the sacrificial offerings. However, for intentional sins, usually of a greater offense, like idolatry, murder, or adultery (Num. 15:30), recourse had to be made directly to God (e.g., the prayer of David after his adultery with Bathsheba in Psalm 51). The differentiation can be seen again in the way one who had killed a person could flee to a city of refuge for safety from an avenger of blood, but this provision only applied if the manslayer had committed the act "unintentionally" without malice aforethought (Deut. 4:42; cf. 19:1–14; Joshua 20).

7. It is well to note, too, that within the category of carnality many Arminians make a distinction between willful selfishness, which exists by our permission, and the human infirmities, which still remain in the physical body. Implications of this will be discussed later when considering sanctification.

8. The word for hell, *Gehenna*, used by Jesus eleven times, as distinct from the word *Hades*, is equated with a corresponding Hebrew word denoting a place of perpetual separation from God.

9. Roman Catholic thought distinguishes between the turning away of the soul from God, called "mortal" sin, and an action that only impedes the course of the soul to God, called "venial" sin. Mortal sins like adultery, murder, and especially idolatry cause the loss of grace

by defying the majesty of God and thus deserve eternal punishment; while a venial sin entails no loss of grace, but requires submission to disciplines of penance. This may serve some liturgical purpose, but I wonder how the church has the knowledge to make such a distinction. Ultimately, all sin is mortal.

10. The question might be raised about infants who are not old enough to understand their sinful condition and may die without hearing about Christ. They bear the marks of original sin, but can they be saved without calling on the Name of the Lord? The Scripture at this point seems silent. However, we know that God is just and merciful and he can do anything he pleases. There are instances when children of believers are saved (e.g., Gen. 7:1; Josh. 2:18; Heb. 11:7). Recall, too, the promise to the Philippian jailer (Acts 16:31). In truth, no one is saved by his own merit; it is all by the grace of God. So, based on the principle of privilege noted here, I find it easy to believe that the redeeming love of Christ embraces helpless persons, like infants or the mentally deranged, who have had no means of knowing the Gospel.

11. Representative of this group would be Karl Barth. Though he may obscure the judgment of sin in terms of damnation, leading to the idea that ultimately no one will be lost, he has no illusion about the sinfulness of men or the necessity of God's supernatural intervention of grace to bring salvation.

12. Pelagianism is a rationalistic system of thought that originated with Pelagius, who taught that Adam was born spiritually neutral and that his sin affected only himself, not his descendants. Denying original sin, he believed that people can do all that God expects. The teaching was condemned by the Church Council of Ephesus in AD 431.

13. These broad generalizations find expression in different ways. In theology and philosophy it comes out in humanism, rationalism, and to some degree, in deism. In education a modern reflection of it flows through Dewey's progressive ideas, a theory that has invaded much of the religious education movement. In psychology the heresy is represented by such schools as behaviorism and Freudianism. In science, materialism and evolution bring out the same theme, while in political science its extreme form is communism.

14. First advocated by Origen in the third century, and intermittently reappearing through the centuries, this view has received new impetus in recent years through the rise of postmodernism and existential theology. Such thinking confuses the eternity and unity of God's nature by not keeping his love consistent with his holiness and justice. For an excellent treatment of this issue, see Timothy K. Beougher, "Are All 'Doomed to Be Saved'? The Rise of Modern Universalism," *The Southern Baptist Journal of Theology* 2, no. 2 (Summer 1998): 6–24.

15. An excellent overview of this subject is by J. I. Packer, "Evangelical Annihilationism," *Reformation & Revival* 6, no. 2 (Spring 1997): 37–51.

16. Susanna Wesley, in a letter to her son John, June 8, 1725. *The Oxford Edition of the Words of John Wesley*, vol. 1, ed. Frank Baker (Oxford: Clarendon Press, 1980), 166.

17. William Ernest Henley, from his poem "Invictus."

18. Bunyan, *New Pilgrim's Progress*, 91.

19. Quoted by Luis Palau, *Everything You've Longed For* (New York: Doubleday, 2002), 77.

20. *Chicago Sun Times*, August 6, 1962, 112.

21. Quoted by Paul Rees, "Pleasure in a Package," *The Herald* 73, no. 20, 2.

22. Quoted in Norman Grubb, *C. T. Studd* (Atlantic City, NJ: World Wide Prayer Movement, 1935), 40.

23. Francis Asbury, *Journal and Letters of Francis Asbury*, vol. 2, ed. Elmer T. Clark (Nashville: Abingdon, 1958), 784–85.

24. John Wesley, *The Letters of the Reverend John Wesley*, vol. 8, ed. John Telford (1931; repr., London: The Epiworth Press, 1960), 271–72.

## Chapter 6 The Son of God

1. Seeking to bear witness to this fact, while also protecting it from unscriptural interpretations, theologians of the church have tried to work out clarifications in the early creeds of Christendom. It would be well to read some of these early creeds. See Schaff, *Creeds of Christendom*.

2. Saint Chrysostom quoted in *Greatest Thoughts about Jesus Christ*, comp. J. Gilchrist Lawson (New York: Richard R. Smith, 1930), 115.

3. Joseph is not mentioned in the accounts of Jesus's later life, which leads to the assumption that he had died earlier.

4. For a more complete description of Christ's devotional life of prayer and dependence on the Word of God, see my book, *The Mind of the*

*Master* (Wilmore, KY: Christian Outreach, 2003), 37–68.

5. A succinct treatment of this question is by Ronald H. Nash, *Is Jesus the Only Savior?* (Grand Rapids: Zondervan, 1999).

6. For more discussion of this position by some of its proponents, see John B. Cobb Jr., "The Meaning of Pluralism for Christian Self-Understanding," in *Religious Pluralism*, ed. Leroy S. Rouner (South Bend, IN: University of Notre Dame Press, 1984); and John Hick, *God Has Many Names* (London: Macmillan, 1980), and *Problems of Religious Pluralism* (New York: St. Martin's Press, 1985).

7. An inclusivist number of Christians, generally of evangelical persuasion, expound this view. Much is made of the condition of millions of people, past and present, who have never had the opportunity to understand the Gospel. Would God have condemned them to perdition in their ignorance? Does God's love reach all people? While affirming that Christ is the only authoritative revelation of God, it is contended that some specific presence of God can be recognized in non-Christian religions. Though the Gospel has not been heard, it is believed that persons can still benefit from the saving work of Christ. The idea is that saving faith does not require Christian content in the object of that faith. It is the spirit of faith that matters. Examples of such believers may be noted in the Old Testament, like Job, Jethro, or Naaman. Persons who receive God's offer of grace and truth through non-Christian religions may be regarded as "anonymous Christians" to use Karl Rahner's description. However, there is a time limit on this period of innocence. When the message of Christ penetrates their culture, it is said, these saved "pagans" will then make explicit what was before implicit in their faith and devotion by divine grace. Inclusivists generally disagree with the universalists who hold that eventually everyone will be saved. Representative spokesmen for this point of view, with variations, include Karl Rahner, *Theological Investigations*, vols. 5 and 6 (New York: Herder and Herder, 1966); John Sanders, *No Other Name* (Grand Rapids: Eerdmans, 1992); and Clark Pinnock, *A Wideness in God's Mercy* (Grand Rapids: Zondervan, 1992).

8. Messianic prophecies flow all through the Old Testament. No two authorities agree on their number or on how to interpret them, but it would appear that more than one hundred personal predictions can be found, involving more than three thousand verses. For helpful summaries, including charts and lists, see Alfred Edersheim, *The Life and Times of Jesus the Messiah*, vol. 2 (London: Longmans, 1915), appendix IX; J. Benton Payne, *Encyclopedia in the Old Testament* (Grand Rapids: Zondervan, 1995), 237–42; and James E. Smith, *What the Bible Teaches about the Promised Messiah* (Nashville: Thomas Nelson, 1993), appendix 3, 475–501. One interested in a more exhaustive study may turn to the four-volume work of E. W. Hengstenberg, *Christology of the Old Testament and a Commentary on the Messianic Predictions* (1872–78; repr., Grand Rapids: Kregel, 1956). An excellent review of the whole subject is Walter C. Kaiser, *The Messiah in the Old Testament* (Grand Rapids: Zondervan, 1995).

9. For a fascinating treatment of the fulfillment of prophecy proving the deity of Christ, see Pascal's *Pensées* (New York: E. P. Dutton, 1958), Articles 692–801, 198–237. In his discussion, he raises the question, "Why did not the Jews believe, since the prophesies were so clearly fulfilled in Christ?" His intriguing answer is that their rejecting was itself part of the prediction, which then to him proves their validity.

10. As an illustration of the amazing accuracy with which God's Word is fulfilled, contrast the right of Jesus to the throne of David to that of his brothers (Ps. 89:3–4; 110:1; 132:11; Isa. 9:7; 11:1–5; Matt. 1:16; Acts 2:30). The fact that the other children of Mary were generic descendants of David through their father Joseph excluded them from the promise, since Joseph came through the line of Jechoniah (Matt. 1:10–11), also called Coniah, and the descendants of this king were declared ineligible to sit on David's throne (Jer. 22:28–30). Yet this prohibition did not rest on the lineal descendants of Mary, of whom Jesus had generic birth. Hence, the peculiar relationship that Jesus sustained with his parents, making him a legal heir to David's throne, while not being affected by any sin, made him the only person on earth eligible for the promise.

11. C. S. Lewis, *The Case for Christianity* (New York: Macmillan, 1944), 45.

12. Quoted in Samuel M. Moffet, "What Is Evangelism?" *Christianity Today*, August 22, 1969, 5.

13. I have heard the story in various ways. The version adapted here comes from two sources. One is credited to Paul Harvey in one of his radio

broadcasts, reported by Charles Swindoll at First Evangelical Church of Fullerton, "Newsbreak," vol. 13, no. 46 (December 19–25, 1993), 1, 4. The other account is credited to Louis Carpels, by Brimwell H. Tillsley, "The Salvation Army Supplier" (Atlanta, n.d.), 41–43.

14. The story is pieced together from two slightly different accounts—two biographies of the missionary. John Farrow, *Damien, the Leper* (New York: Sheed and Ward, 1937), 156–59; and Irene Caudwell, *Damien of Malakai, 1840–1889* (New York: Macmillan, 1932), 125; along with a sermon by William Richard Ezell in *Preaching* (November–December, 2002), 18. While some details in the sources vary, all agree in the substance of the story.

15. Pascal, *Pensées*, Article 54, 147.

16. Bernard of Clairvaux, Latin, twelfth-century hymn, trans. Edward Caswall.

17. This description has been adapted from a collection of tracts from unknown authors. The one to which I am most indebted is an anonymous author in Terry D. Bilhartz, *Sacred Words: A Source Book of the Great Religions of the World* (New York: McGraw-Hill, 2006), 55.

18. Wesley, in a letter to Arthur Keene, Dublin, July 1, 1789, in *Letters of the Reverend John Wesley*, 150.

## Chapter 7 The Death of Christ

1. Much of this chapter, including this story, is taken from my study on the blood, *The New Covenant* (Colorado Springs: NavPress, 1984), now published by Christian Outreach, 9685 Harrodsburg Road, Wilmore, KY 40390. This book notes many other works treating various aspects of the subject.

2. Information respecting ceremonial rites involving blood in primitive societies may be found in almost any standard work on cultural anthropology. Unfortunately the intended use of the blood became perverted in pagan cultures. Were it not for the Bible, we would not know its original meaning. Some of the most extensive research in this area has been done by H. Clay Trumball, published in *The Blood Covenant* (London: George Redway, 1887); and *Studies in Oriental Social Life* (Philadelphia: Sunday School Times, 1907).

3. The result of the atoning death of Christ is set forth in Scripture many ways, but the scope of this study permits only a few. For a more complete survey, see Leon Morris, *The Atonement: Its Meaning and Significance* (Downers Grove, IL: InterVarsity, 1983).

4. In Scripture the term applies to various transactions between God and man, as well as man and his fellow man. For coverage of all the aspects of a covenant, see G. E. Mendenhall, *Law and Covenant in Israel and the Ancient Near East* (Pittsburgh: The Biblical Colloquium, 1955); and Roderick Campbell, *Israel and the New Covenant* (Rome: Pontifical Biblical Institute, 1963). A good short treatment of the subject is Leon Morris, *The Apostolic Preaching of the Cross* (London: Tyndale Press, 1965), 65–111.

5. Evidence supporting this idea is recorded by Trumbull, *Blood Covenant*, 234–36.

6. The term can also be translated "expiation," which agrees in meaning—to make satisfaction for an offense or to undo a wrong one has done by suffering the penalty. The word is sometimes rendered "atonement," which has the same idea of reconciling persons at odds with each other. From a theological perspective, it could be said that through Christ's blood God's wrath is propitiated and human guilt is expiated. The important thing is that in the atonement God was both reconciled to man and man was reconciled to God (2 Cor. 5:18–20).

7. The essence of this story is authenticated from several sources, as told by Billy Sunday in *Wonderful, and Other Sermons* (Grand Rapids: Zondervan, 1958), 37–39.

8. An excellent general statement of different theories of the atonement, going back to the New Testament, is the work of Sydney Cave, *The Doctrine of the Work of Christ* (Nashville: Cokesbury, 1937). The book includes a bibliography of other significant English works. Among more recent summaries of atonement views, with their history, are Bruce Demarest, *The Cross and Salvation* (Wheaton: Crossway, 1997), 147–99; and Alan F. Johnson and Robert E. Webber, *What Christians Believe* (Grand Rapids: Zondervan, 1993), 257–76. Of course any good systematic theology will cover the subject, giving particular attention to the author's own position. An example of solid Calvinistic perspective is Benjamin Breckinridge Warfield, *The Person and Work of Christ*, ed. Samuel G. Craig (Phillipsburg, NJ: Presbyterian and Reformed, 1950), 325–426; and from a good Wesleyan scholar, H. Orton Wiley,

*Christian Theology*, vol. 2 (Kansas City, MO: Beacon Hill Press, 1952), 217–300. Also there is no end to specialized studies—for example, the critique of Karl Barth's understanding of the atonement, Donald G. Bloesch, *Jesus Is Victor!* (Nashville: Abingdon, 1976).

9. Probably the best contemporary discussion of this view is by Gustaf Aulen, in his book *Christus Victor* (New York: Macmillan, 1969). Also helpful is Malcolm Furness, *Vital Doctrines of the Faith* (Grand Rapids: Eerdmans, 1973), 55–60. Since this theory dominated the first millennium of Christian thought, Sydney Cave calls it the "patristic" view. Most of the early fathers take this position. As an evangelist, Augustine held that God's justice delivered the human race into the power of the devil, and that this could only be reversed by the righteousness of Christ. When the devil could "find nothing in Christ worthy of death, he killed him. In this way it is said that we are justified by the innocent blood of Christ" (Cave, *The Doctrine of the Work of Christ*, 141).

10. This interpretation may explain why the devil tempted Jesus in the wilderness to take a course of action that would avoid the cross (Matt. 4:1–11; Mark 1:12–13; Luke 4:1–13). For the same reason the dragon or "Satan, who leads the whole world astray" tried to kill Jesus, the "male child," when he was born, possibly alluding to the massacre of the baby boys in Jerusalem after Christ's birth (Rev. 12:1–9). This view does not explain, however, why the devil would bring Judas to turn Christ over to those who would kill him (Matt. 26:14–16).

11. My book *The Mind of the Master* attempts to see in the life of Christ some of the motivations for holy living. Many other books that speak to this same theme are mentioned in the notes.

12. This "subjective" or "moral" theory is associated with Abelard in the twelfth century, though there were earlier antecedents. Taken by itself, the theory reflects the Pelagian idea of humanity's essential goodness, and that God's justice did not need satisfaction. It also takes on an adoptionist concept of Jesus, thereby rejecting his incarnate deity. In various forms, the view has become common among liberal theologians of the last two centuries, like Schleiermacher, Horace Bushnell, and L. H. DeWolf.

13. This is called "juridical" or "objective" theory, though overtones of the idea will appear in other views. The concept is usually credited to Anselm in the eleventh century, and with some modifications, generally characterizes later Catholic and Protestant orthodoxy. What is called the "governmental" or "rectorial" theory has many similarities yet avoids the concept of penal satisfaction. In this view, while Christ did not bear the actual punishment due to sinners, his suffering did take its place in a rectorial sense, thereby upholding the moral order of the universe.

14. It is believed that since Christ was sinless, divine justice need not punish him. Therefore, Christ suffered rather than being punished. His death "provided a moral basis for clemency." J. Kenneth Grider, "Governmental Theory of the Atonement," *Beacon Dictionary of Theology* (Kansas City, MO: Beacon Hill Press, 1984). For a complete explanation of this view, see John Miley, *Systematic Theology*, vol. 2 (New York: Hunt & Eaton, 1892–94).

15. Charles Wesley, from his hymn "And Can It Be That I Should Gain."

16. The Reformed Calvinist position is often represented by the acronym TULIP, which stands for total depravity, unconditional election, limited atonement, irresistible grace, and perseverance of the saints. The idea is that in the complete lostness of mankind, God by his sovereign decree elects from eternity some persons to be saved, and for these effectually called ones Christ actually died, and they will be constrained by grace to believe the Gospel and continue to follow Christ. From the standpoint of including all believers, it might be said that the atonement was unlimited. But in actuality, the merit of Christ's death was limited to those persons who were decreed by God to be saved. For a good discussion of this question, see Grudem, *Systematic Theology*, 594–603. From the Arminian side, a strong rebuttal is by David L. Larsen, *God, Free Choice and Human Responsibility* (Kearney, NE: Morris, 2003).

17. This is the conclusion of many medical authorities who have evaluated the record of water and blood gushing from Jesus's pierced side. Apparently during the suffering on the cross, his heart swelled until it burst. The blood was effused into the enlarged sac of the pericardium, where it afterward separated into real clots and watery serum. When the distended sac was punctured by the soldier's spear, the water and blood discharged, as described by John. See S. J. Andrews, *Life of Our Lord upon the Earth* (New

York: Charles Scribner, 1863), 553–55; and David Smith, *The Days of His Flesh* (New York: Harper and Brothers), 506.

18. Taken from a sermon of James Kennedy, in *Preaching* (September–October, 1991), 10–12. Used by permission.

19. This account is taken from "The Story of the Alamo," a folder prepared by The Daughters of the Republic of Texas and available to visitors at the Alamo.

20. Isaac Watts, from his hymn "When I Survey the Wondrous Cross."

21. Charlotte Elliott, from her hymn "Just As I Am."

## Chapter 8 The Triumph of Christ

1. No vital purpose is served in trying to explain all the ways these verses have been interpreted, for, I believe, it really makes no difference in terms of evangelism. Here is a good example of the rule that the less revelation we have the more opportunity there is for speculation. In this instance, what matters is not the activity of Christ in the grave but his resurrection.

2. Noted by Philip Schaff, *A History of the Creeds of Christendom*, vol. 1 (New York: Bible House, Harper and Brothers, 1876), 21.

3. Though Calvin acknowledged that "descended into hell" was introduced into the Creed after a considerable lapse of time, he notes that it came into use early by Christian believers and was mentioned by all the fathers, excluding Augustine. Therefore he said that it should not be disregarded, "as containing a matter of great importance." "It was necessary," he believed, "that Christ should engage, as it were, at close quarters with the power of hell and the horrors of eternal death." Hence, the descent "appropriately adds the invisible and incomprehensible judgment which he endured before God, to teach us that not only was the body of Christ given up as the price of redemption, but that there was a greater and more excellent price—that he bore in his soul the tortures of condemned and ruined men." John Calvin, *Institutes of the Christian Religion*, vol. 1 (Grand Rapids: Eerdmans, 1953), 241–43.

4. The response to Question 44, which asks, "Why is it added: he descended into Hades?" The Heidelberg Catechism, AD 1563 in *The Creeds of the Evangelical Protestant Churches*, vol. 3 (New York: Harper and Brothers, 1876), 321. A good

discussion of this subject is in Grudem, *Systematic Theology*, 586–94.

5. The empty tomb in Joseph's garden became a place where people would go to view the site of the resurrection. It became so embarrassing to the Jews that the holy cave was sealed with earth and then covered over with stones. It remained that way until the fourth century when, after the conversion of Constantine, one of his first acts was to order the uncovering of the site. Unfortunately, the exact location of the tomb has been disputed, and there are two places today that claim the distinction. As to which one is the authentic tomb, I am not able to determine. But one thing is clear, both are empty. The bones of Jesus are nowhere to be found on earth.

6. It's interesting that there is no record Jesus ever appeared to nonbelievers during this period after his resurrection. One might wonder why he did not go to his enemies and show them how wrong they were. Trying to approach an answer makes me aware again of the priority of Jesus's ministry in developing leaders for his church, men and women who needed assurance and courage for the ministry that awaited them.

7. Others have been brought back to life again, like some saints who came out of the tombs at Christ's resurrection (Matt. 27:52–53), but they still died.

8. Rudolf Bultmann, *Kerygma and Myth*, vol. 1, ed. H. W. Bartsch (London: S.P.C.K., 1962), 39. Proponents of this view in recent years have become brazen and vehement in their attacks on the credibility of historical accounts of the resurrection, as well as the Gospel. The self-appointed scholars of "the Jesus Seminar" and the promoters of the da Vinci Code, who are given prominence in the popular media, seem more desperate for attention than for biblical truth.

9. A good representative apologetic for the resurrection is compiled by Josh McDowell, *Evidence that Demands a Verdict*, vol. 1 (Nashville: Thomas Nelson, 1970), 179–259. Other easily read studies are by William Lane Craig, *The Son Rises* (Chicago: Moody, 1981); Frank Morison, *Who Moved the Stone?* (London: Faber and Faber, 1944); J. N. D. Anderson, *The Evidence for the Resurrection* (London: Inter-Varsity, 1956); and Ajith Fernando, *The Supremacy of Christ* (Wheaton: Crossway, 1995), 225–59.

10. Other confirmations of the resurrection can be seen in the Christians' changing of their

Sabbath day of worship to the first day of the week, for it was on that day that Jesus rose from the dead (Mark 16:2; Luke 24:1; John 20:1). Likewise, the practice of baptism depicted for them being "buried with [Christ]" unto death and "united with him in his resurrection" (Rom. 6:4–5 NIV; cf. Col. 2:12). Also their observance of the Lord's Supper proclaimed "the Lord's death until he comes" (1 Cor. 11:26; cf. Acts 2:46). Of course the preaching of the Gospel powerfully stressed the resurrection, as is evidenced in the book of Acts.

11. Paul's confrontation with the glorified Christ on the Damascus Road led to the same acknowledgments. He saw the evidence of the glorified Christ and knew that he had seen the Lord (Acts 22:8–10).

12. There is no historical evidence that Buddha, Muhammad, Confucius, or any other religious leader ever had a bodily resurrection, nor has this been claimed by their original followers. Wilbur M. Smith, *Therefore Stand* (Boston: W. W. Wilde, 1945), 385; see also McDowell, *Evidence that Demands a Verdict*, 180.

13. Alfred H. Ackley, from his hymn "He Lives."

14. Told by Louis Albert Banks, *Immortal Hymns and Their Stories* (Cleveland: Burrows Brothers, 1898), 312–13; see also Amos R. Wells, "All Hail the Power of Jesus' Name," *The Christian World*, May 26, 1904.

15. A paraphrase of Isaac Watts's hymn, "Jesus Shall Reign Where'er the Sun."

## Chapter 9  The Holy Spirit

1. A story attributed to Dr. Norman McLeon, *Evangelical Beacon*, July 11, 1988, 5.

2. The Greek word for Spirit, *pneuma*, is neuter, but when the noun occurs with a pronoun, the masculine pronoun is used. Personality is understood.

3. The Nicene Creed originally (AD 325) referred to the Holy Spirit as proceeding from the Father, which seemed to indicate a subordinate of God the Son. To avoid this thought, and in keeping with other passages of Scripture (John 14:26; 15:26; 16:7), the Western Church at the Council of Toledo (AD 589) added the *filioque* "and of the son." The Eastern Church, however, has stayed with the earlier version. Contention over this point, largely arising from the way John 15:26 is interpreted, has not been resolved to this day.

4. In the Hebrew language, the words for "breath," "wind," and "Spirit" come from the same root. So it can be said that God breathed the world into existence. Later this same word appears when God creates a man. Altogether there are about one hundred times when words associated with the Holy Spirit are used in the Old Testament. A fairly complete listing is in James Elder Cumming, *Through the Eternal Spirit* (Chicago: Revell, 1890). More developed is Leon J. Wood, *The Holy Spirit in the Old Testament* (Grand Rapids: Zondervan, 1976). For more background, see *The New Testament Dictionary of the New Testament Theology*, vol. 3 (Grand Rapids: Zondervan, 1976), 689–709.

5. Some of this section is adapted from my book *The Mind of the Master*, 21–35; and from *The Master Plan of Discipleship* (1987; repr., Grand Rapids: Revell, 1998), 101–20.

6. The Holy Spirit was prominent in the preparation of John the Baptist for his prophetic ministry that introduced Christ. Both his father and mother were filled with the Spirit (Luke 1:41, 67), while John was filled with the Spirit when still in his mother's womb (Luke 1:15).

7. One may find an excellent treatment of Jesus's teaching about the Spirit's work in Louis Burton Crane, *The Teaching of Jesus concerning the Holy Spirit* (New York: American Tract Society, 1905); and Henry Barclay Swete, *The Holy Spirit in the New Testament* (Grand Rapids: Baker, 1976).

8. For a discussion of this point, see Joachim Jeremias, *New Testament Theology* (New York: Charles Scribner, 1971), 80–85.

9. It is well to note that in this reference Jesus did not say that the Pharisees were beyond redemption, but by their hostile attitude they displayed a condition that, unless reversed, would bring final separation from God's mercy. To scorn Christ is to reject the only way of salvation, and hence, to be in a state of unforgiveness. If one persists in this rejection, the state of judgment becomes permanent—one is guilty of an eternal sin.

10. The word *Helper* can also be translated "Counselor" or "Comforter." It has the meaning of "one who strengthens or stands beside," whereas the word *another* stresses the sameness of quality between Christ's life and that of the Spirit. An enlargement of this idea will be found in my book *The Master Plan of Evangelism* (1963; repr., Grand Rapids: Revell, 1993), 67–69; and

G. Campbell Morgan, *The Teaching of Christ* (New York: Revell, 1913), 65.

11. Andrew Murray comments: "When the Holy Spirit came down, he brought as a personal life within them what had previously only been a life near them, but yet outside their own. The very Spirit of God's own Son, as he lived and loved, had obeyed and died, was now to become their personal life." *The Spirit of Christ* (London: Nisbet, 1889), 149.

12. When thinking of the Holy Trinity at work in this personal transformation, it can be said that the Father elects, the Son redeems, and the Spirit dispenses the grace of God. Some may speak of these different functions of the Persons within the Godhead as the "economic Trinity," in contrast to the "essential Trinity," which thinks of God without reference to the order of creation and personality. Actually, both ways of looking at it are true and should be kept in balance. The essential relations of God within the Trinity are eternal. But in function the Holy Spirit has a subordinate role to the Father and the Son, just as the Son has a subordinate role to the Father. While there is no subordination of essence (the eternal Trinity), there is subordination of order, office, and operation (economic Trinity). For a careful description of this point, see A. H. Strong, *Systematic Theology* (Valley Forge, PA: Judson, 1907), 342.

13. Charles Spurgeon recounts this in *Metropolitan Tabernacle Pulpit*, cited by Mark Dever and C. J. Mahaney, *The Gospel and Personal Evangelism* (Wheaton: Crossway, 2007), 110.

## Chapter 10 The Grace of God

1. John Newton, from his hymn "Amazing Grace."

2. Some theologians relate Christ's saving grace only to persons who come to faith. However, that leaves unexplained why God would show kindness to unbelievers.

3. Not all Christian theologians recognize the concept of common grace, thinking that it diminishes God's sovereignty and the state of the reprobate. For such reasoning, see Herman Hoeksema, *Reformed Dogmatics* (Grand Rapids: Reformed Free Publishing Association, 1966). Most scholars, however, use the common grace category. An able exponent is Abraham Kuyper, *Particular Grace: A Defense of God's Sovereignty in Salvation* (Grandville, MI: Reformed Free Pub-

lishing Association, 2001). For a good review of the issues, see Richard J. Mouw, *He Shines in All That's Fair* (Grand Rapids: Eerdmans, 2001).

4. Wilfred Thomason Grenfell, *A Labrador Doctor* (Boston: Houghton Mifflin, 1919), 77.

5. John Wesley, "Working Out Your Salvation," *The Work of John Wesley*, vol. 3, ed. Albert C. Outler (Nashville: Abingdon, 1986), 203.

6. Though the word no longer commonly has this use today, it may be found in the King James Version of the Bible, for example in Psalm 79:8: "O remember not against us former iniquities: let thy tender mercies speedily prevent us" (cf. 2 Sam. 22:6; Ps. 18:5; 21:3; 88:13; 119:147–48; 1 Thess. 4:15).

7. Quoted in C. E. Elliott, *The Life of the Reverend Robert B. Roberts* (Cincinnati: J. F. Wright and L. Formsteat, 1844), 121–22.

8. Antinomianism is the idea that the moral law of God is no longer binding on those who believe in Christ.

9. Jerry Bridges, *Transforming Grace* (Colorado Springs: NavPress, 1991), 92. This is a great book and for anyone desiring more solid reading on God's unfailing love, this would be a good place to turn.

10. William Carey, quoted by Ruth A. Tucker, *From Jerusalem to Irian Jaya* (Grand Rapids: Zondervan, 1983). Carey is often called the Father of Modern Missions.

11. I have forgotten when I first heard the story, or where it was, and I have not been able to find an authenticated published account. My suspicion is that the idea originated with an imaginative preacher and has been revised many times. Doubtless with the retelling, it has taken on more color. That being my assumption, I have taken the liberty to add yet another version.

12. Martin Luther, "Lectures on Deuteronomy," in *Works*, vol. 9, ed. Jaroslav Pelikan (St. Louis: Concordia, 1960), 96.

13. Martin Luther commenting on Romans 12:1, as quoted by R. C. H. Lenski, *The Interpretation of St. Paul's Epistle to the Romans* (Minneapolis: Augsburg, 1936), 746; called to my attention by Jerry Bridges, *Transforming Grace*, 78.

14. Philip Yancey, *What's So Amazing about Grace?* (Grand Rapids: Zondervan, 1997), 45.

15. The sacrifice of Christ on the cross was a display to the Jews that salvation comes because another has paid the price of redemption. Salvation from the book of Genesis to the praise of

the Lamb in heaven is by grace received by faith in the blood.

16. An excellent guide to understanding the basic concepts of world religions is Dean C. Halverson, gen. ed., *The Compact Guide to World Religions* (Minneapolis: Bethany, 1996). There is no want of resources in this area, as any search of the internet will reveal. One caution, however. Much of the work in comparative religions has been done from a naturalistic viewpoint, and with liberal theological presuppositions.

17. Bill Hybels and Mark Mittelberg, *Becoming a Contagious Christian* (Grand Rapids: Zondervan, 1996), 155–56.

18. J. W. Fletcher, quoted in *Illustrative Gatherings* (London: Wertheim, MacIntosh, and Hunt, 1860), 175–76.

19. Author unknown; quoted in Walter B. Knight, *Three Thousand Illustrations for Christian Service* (Grand Rapids: Eerdmans, 1954), 324.

20. Charles Simeon, *Expository Outlines on the Whole Bible: Genesis–Leviticus*, vol. 1 (Grand Rapids: Zondervan, 1956), xvii–xviii.

21. John Newton, the last stanza of his hymn "Amazing Grace."

## Chapter 11 Coming to Christ

1. Theologians will differ as to which comes first. Those from a Reformed perspective contend that a spiritual regeneration must awaken saving faith out of which genuine repentance comes. On the other hand, most Arminians reverse the order. Though one can read theological overtures into the sequence, the order has no practical bearing on evangelism, for both flow together.

2. Conversion may be sudden and attended with great emotion. Frequently this turning can be recognized at a precise time. For other people, conversion may be gradual, with no emotion, and the person has no clear sense of when it occurred. What matters is not the manner or timing of the change of direction, but that it has happened. Some theologians look on conversion as the human side to regeneration, though distinctions may be made as to when God gives grace to believe.

3. Doubtless this awakening begins in childhood, and unless suppressed, can lead one very early to the consciousness of need for a Savior. I believe that children given proper direction and encouragement, by God's grace, ideally will re-

spond to the Gospel call. Believers still need spiritual insight to human failures, of course, and this gracious correction will continue, at deeper levels of our humanity, all the way to heaven.

4. Billy Graham, "True Repentance, Real Change," *Decision*, January 2007, 4.

5. Confession of sin is always made to God (1 Kings 8:33–34; Ps. 51:3–4; Rom. 14:10–12). Sins against people, as the Spirit may lead, call for private confession to the offended person. Some persons sinned against may not need to hear all about the sinner's previous sin. We should be sensitive to the feelings of those hurt. For example, I doubt that a newly married man who had lived promiscuously before meeting Christ need tell his wife all the shameful details of his past. A public confession of sin may be appropriate when the church or community is involved (2 Cor. 2:5–7; Gal. 6:1). However, caution should be exercised when going into lurid details that can border on exhibitionism. Confession to others in the bonds of Christ also can bring blessing to the saints as we pray together (James 5:16). An example of the practice can be seen in the hand and class meetings of the early Methodists. An excellent treatment of this practice is D. Michael Henderson, *A Model for Making Disciples: John Wesley's Class Meeting* (Nappanee, IN: Francis Asbury Press, 1997).

6. The story of this revival is told in *One Divine Moment*, ed. Robert E. Coleman (Old Tappan, NJ: Revell, 1970), 85. A moving documentary of this epic is told twenty-five years later in a DVD, *When God Comes* (Wilmore, KY: Francis Asbury Society, 1995).

7. This should not be understood to mean that all adversity comes in consequence of persistent sin, of course. There are many other reasons for suffering. Whatever the cause may be, however, God will work through it for good to those who love him.

8. I have forgotten where I heard the substance of this well-known story. Though imaginary, of course, the principle it illustrates is clear.

9. The word *believe* in its various forms simply means "to trust or to rely on." Consulting some good lexicons and dictionaries in reference to faith and belief in its various forms will bring rich reward.

10. It is because of who Christ is that his Word can be accepted with perfect confidence. Take as an example the centurion who, concerned for his servant's welfare, not feeling worthy of the Mas-

ter entering his house, asked Jesus only to "say the word" and his servant would be healed. As a soldier who lived under orders, he knew that one in authority would be obeyed. Turning to the officer, Jesus said, "Go; let it be done for you as you have believed" (Matt. 8:5–13). Other examples of the same principle can be seen in the nobleman's request for his son (John 4:46–53) and the Syrophoenician mother's faith for her daughter (Matt. 15:21–28; Mark 7:24–30).

11. Joseph Henry Thayer, *A Greek-English Lexicon of the New Testament* (New York: American Book Company, 1886), 511.

12. Martin Luther, "Preface to the Epistle to the Romans," *Works of Martin Luther*, vol. 6 (Philadelphia: Muhlenberg, 1936), 449–52.

13. John Wesley, *The Journal of John Wesley*, vol. 1, ed. Nehemiah Cuonock (London: Epworth, 1909), 476. This experience came in a Moravian Chapel at Aldersgate in London on May 24, 1738.

14. There were evidences of spiritual awakening much earlier, as far back as 1725, but it was not until Wesley came to this realization at Aldersgate that a complete turning point in his life became obvious. Commentary on this position may be found in J. E. Rattenburg, *The Conversion of the Wesleys* (London: Epworth, 1938).

15. The generally recurring present tense of the word *believe* in the New Testament emphasizes the continuing action of faith (e.g., Mark 5:36; John 3:15, 16, 18, 36; 5:24; Acts 13:39). It is ongoing as a present fact. Less frequently, the aorist tense is used for "believe," which describes a completed action in past time, something which has happened. This is significant in both tenses as applied to faith; that is, faith does have a definite beginning point, but in consequence, it is a present fact.

16. The content and intensity of faith in coming to Christ may not be located in a precise understanding of the plan of salvation or a moment when one prayed the "sinner's prayer." Take Peter as an example. When was he converted? Was it at his first introduction to Jesus during the revival of John the Baptist (John 1:42)? Or was it when he and the other fishermen left their nets to follow him (Matt. 16:13–20; Mark 1:16–20; Luke 9:18–21)? Or was it at the transfiguration of Jesus on the mount (Matt. 17:1–8; Mark 9:2–8; Luke 9:28–33)? Or was it sometime during their travels together after beholding some awesome miracle? Or were they not really converted until after the cross and resurrection? Clearly they struggled with their understanding of both until after the fact (Matt. 16:21–23; Mark 8:31–33; 16:11–14; Luke 24:36–43; John 20:19–25).

17. Since Christ is not divided, to receive him as Savior is to surrender to him as Lord. I see no biblical reason to separate the two, as if we could have one part of Jesus without the other. For pros and cons of this issue, briefly stated, see Grudem, *Systematic Theology*, 713–17. For a larger discussion, consult John MacArthur, *The Gospel According to Jesus* (1988; repr., Grand Rapids: Zondervan, 1994); cf. Zane C. Hodgen, *The Gospel under Siege* (Dallas: Redención Viva, 1981).

18. For example, it was hard for them to accept Jesus's teaching of lowly servitude for the sake of others (Luke 22:24–30; John 13:1–20). They bickered among themselves who would be greatest in the kingdom (Matt. 18:1–5; Mark 9:33–37). James and John wanted to have prominent places, and the other ten, displaying an envious spirit, were indignant about it. They were necessarily harsh in their judgment of those who did not agree with them. And in countless other ways one can recognize how much more they had to learn.

19. The Gospels record at least sixteen times prior to his actual arrest by the soldiers that Jesus spoke of his suffering and death, yet the disciples did not grasp what he meant. For a listing of those occasions, see Coleman, *Master Plan of Evangelism*, footnote on p. 114.

20. This principle raises the question about those who respond to the light given by God but with an incomplete knowledge of Christ. Take Cornelius as an example. Was his desire to know the Gospel adequate for salvation? Apparently not, for Peter came to bring a message by which he and his family could be "saved" (Acts 11:14; cf. 10:30–48). It may be helpful to look again at "the measure of judgment" I discussed in chapter 5.

21. When there is no word in another language for a biblical term, translators have to find its meaning in another term, and sometimes the equivalent word makes the text even more profound. Bruce Olson's translation of "faith" in the Motilone tongue is another example. He used the word for "tie into" God, just as they tie their hammocks onto the high rafters of their communal homes in the jungle of Columbia. Bruce Olsen, *For This Cross I'll Kill You* (Carol Stream, IL: Creation House, 1973), 16.

22. R. Kelso Carter, "Standing on the Promise," *Echoes of Praise* (Anderson, IN: Warner Press, n.d.), 29.

23. Taken from a sermon of H. C. Morrison on Abraham, as recounted by Dennis Kinlaw, "A Significant Moment," *The High Calling*, Winter 2008, 9.

24. Recounted by Mark Dever in *The Gospel and Personal Evangelism* (Wheaton: Crossway, 2006).

25. For a more complete account of this scene, see Robert Coleman, *The Master's Way of Personal Evangelism* (Wheaton: Crossway, 1997), 123–32.

## Chapter 12  The New Life

1. Regarding the statement of James "that a person is justified by works and not by faith alone" (James 2:24, cf. 2:14, 17–18, 22), it would appear that justification is by what a person does, in opposition to Romans 3:28, which states that one is "justified by faith apart from works of the law." Though the same word for works is used in both verses, they refer to two different things. Paul is speaking of observances of the Jewish religion, like circumcision or purification rituals, while James is talking about works of mercy. The point is that after receiving the free gift of grace, a Christian serves the Lord with spiritual works consistent with faith.

2. It's significant that the truth of regeneration is foretold in the Old Testament. When speaking of Israel's returning to their land, God said, "I will give you a new heart. . . . And I will remove the heart of stone from your flesh. . . . And I will put my Spirit within you" (Ezek. 36:26–27).

3. For a beautiful treatment of this theme, see James S. Stewart, *A Man in Christ* (New York: Harper and Brothers, 1935).

4. Adoption may also be used in Scripture to describe the special relationship of the Israelites to God (Rom. 9:4). The reference here is to the descendants of Abraham through Isaac who are "children of the promise" (vv. 7–8). Christians, too, may be identified as children of the promise (Gal. 4:28, 31; cf. 1 Pet. 3:6). The term may also have a future reference when finally the redeemed are glorified (Rom. 8:23).

5. By contrast, unbelievers are not children of God in any redemptive sense. Rather they are called "children of wrath" (Eph. 2:3; cf. v. 2; 5:6).

Regarding unbelieving Jews who were hostile toward Christ, Jesus said their father was the devil (John 8:42–44).

6. A clear exposition of the concept of God as Father is by Allen Coppedge, *Portraits of God: A Biblical Theology of Holiness* (Downers Grove, IL: InterVarsity, 2001), especially pp. 244–99.

7. In the case of infants who cannot consciously have faith, baptism is seen as an extension of the promises given to the parents (Acts 2:38). It may be noted that Jesus wished to receive little children into his presence (Luke 18:16). As a matter of record, too, whole households were baptized in the early church (Acts 10:33; 18:8; 1 Cor. 1:16). Baptism will be discussed further in the chapter on the church.

8. Quoted by Ludwitt Ott, *Fundamentals of Catholic Dogma*, trans. Patrick Lynch (Rockford, IL: Tan Books and Publishers, Inc., 1960), 257.

9. A. A. Hodge, *Outlines of Theology for Students and Laymen* (c. 1860; repr., Grand Rapids: Zondervan, 1972), 460.

10. It is well to note that not all Calvinists accept this view of imputation. Many late-seventeenth-century Puritans, like Richard Baxter, Christopher Cartwright, John Goodwin, and Benjamin Woodbridge, held to the imputation of faith as the formal cause of justification. If one wants to go deeper into this subject through able defenders of the traditional Reformed position, among others, consult the writings of R. C. Sproul, D. A. Carson, Wayne Grudem, or John Piper. Taking exception to this point of view, with variations, would be Robert H. Gundy, Mark A. Seifrid, N. T. Wright, and Scott Hafemann. Needless to say, the debate over this issue still goes on. A good summary of the differences is an article by Michael F. Bird, "Incorporated Righteousness: A Response to Recent Evangelical Discussion concerning the Imputation of Christ's Righteousness in Justification," *Journal of the Evangelical Society* 47, no. 2 (June 2004): 243–75.

11. There is considerable difference of opinion regarding Luther's position on justification and the resulting life of obedience. Some scholars, like Karl Hall, contend that Luther believed justification involved actual moral transformation of sinner into saint. Approaching the justification of man analytically, he held that God's judgment is viewed eschatologically on the basis of what man shall become. Theologians like Barth take strong exception to this interpretation, believing that it is

little different from the Roman Catholic teaching. The problem centers in subjectivizing the act of God's grace. However, this does not have to be the case, it seems to me, if the norm of God's truth in Jesus Christ is kept clearly in focus. Perhaps it would be best not to strain the basic forensic sense of justification, but to note the inseparable relation of justifying faith to regeneration and sanctification. See the discussion of this issue in G. C. Berkouwer, *Faith and Justification* (Grand Rapids: Eerdmans, 1954), 9–22.

12. Malcolm Muggeridge, quoted in *Christianity Today*, December 17, 1990, 47.

13. Narrated by Paul Rees in an editorial in *World Vision*, December 1971, 31.

14. Martin Luther, quoted in *The Joy of the Saints: Spiritual Readings throughout the Year*, arranged by Robert Flewelyn (Springfield, IL: Templegate, 1989), 315.

15. Adapted from Raymond C. Ortlund Jr., *When God Comes to Church: A Biblical Model for Revival Today* (Grand Rapids: Baker, 2000), 136.

## Chapter 13  Sanctification

1. I heard this story years ago in a sermon by Paul Rees, though my memory fails me in recalling the time and occasion.

2. Altogether believers are called "saints" about fifty-five times in the New Testament, even when still carnal (e.g., 1 Cor. 6:2; 14:33; 16:1). The degree of godliness in the Christian life does not determine sainthood, but rather the state to which the believer has been introduced by grace. Though sainthood more commonly is associated with Christians, the term also can be applied to persons "set apart" for God in the Old Testament (e.g., Ps. 16:3; 97:10; Dan. 7:18).

3. A helpful treatment of major Protestant approaches to this subject is Stanley N. Gundry, ed., *Five Views on Sanctification* (Grand Rapids: Zondervan, 1987). In this volume the Wesleyan position is treated by Melvin E. Dieter, the Reformed view by Anthony A. Hoekema, the Pentecostal understanding by Stanley M. Horton, the Keswick position by J. Robertson McQuilkin, and the Augustinian-Dispensational approach by John F. Walvoord. While the distinctives of each position are defended, it is interesting how these major schools of thought coalesce around the necessity of Christians living a holy life.

4. Let it be admitted that with God nothing is impossible. There are some within the Roman Catholic tradition who believe that by faith in Christ and meritorious works, cultivated through godly disciplines and the means of grace in the church, one can attain complete sanctification (justification) in this life. Very, very few, however, obtain this state, called the beatific vision. Believers who die not having reached this heavenly spirituality must be purged of their remaining sin after death, hence, the teaching on purgatory. When purgation is complete, the soul goes into the presence of God. Protestants find no support for the teaching of purgatory in the sixty-six inspired books of the Bible.

5. For an excellent treatment of the Keswick movement and its message, see Steven Barabas, *So Great Salvation* (Grand Rapids: Eerdmans, 1952). Critical of the movement is B. B. Warfield, *Studies in Perfectionism* (New York: Oxford, 1931). Though the movement has its origin in moderate Calvinistic leadership, Warfield contends that Keswick has taken an Arminian turn in theology. I suspect that he is right. In assessing the movement, J. Robertson McQuilkin says, "If ambiguous terms are defined in a particular way, classical Wesleyan teaching and the Keswick approach are quite compatible. If sin is any falling short of God's glorious character, no one is perfect. Yet, every Spirit-empowered believer may consistently refrain from deliberately violating God's known will." *Five Views on Sanctification*, 55.

6. This confrontation with truth is a part of the ongoing sanctifying process. However, because this point in Christian obedience requires the deepest commitment of the will, the decision it forces for some stands out as a monumental crisis. For others the decision may come so gradually, interwoven with so many other things, that knowledge of its reality may be only the quiet assurance that it is settled. To speak of it as a deeper work of grace is not meant to depreciate the grace already received. Rather, it indicates that when a saint comes to recognize the conflict caused by selfishness, and brings that problem to God, the Spirit who is already working in his or her life can also meet this deeper need.

7. Underscoring the definiteness of this action is the use of the aorist tense in the Greek text, which speaks of something that is completed; it is done. For example, cleansing instantly follows faith in Acts 15:9. It is not a long, drawn-out

sentence of getting better over time. Similarly, in 1 John 1:9, on confession of sin, there is immediate forgiveness and cleansing. When the conditions for heart purity are met, no one has to go to bed at night under condemnation. For an excellent summary of tense readings regarding sanctification in the Greek New Testament, see Daniel Steele, *Mile-Stone Papers* (Minneapolis: Bethany Fellowship, n.d.), 41–72.

8. For the best description of this teaching, see John Wesley, *A Plain Account of Christian Perfection as Believed and Taught by the Reverend Mr. John Wesley, The Works of John Wesley*, vol. 11 (Peabody, MA: Hendrickson, 1984), 366–446. An excellent summary is his "Brief Thoughts on Christian Perfection," ibid., 446.

9. Hannah Whitall Smith, *The Christian's Secret of a Happy Life* (New York: Grosset and Dunlap, n.d.), 23–24.

10. It may be well to note that the wicked really do not love themselves in any true sense, for they have rejected God's grace by which they would come to know their true and eternal happiness.

11. In this connection, Blaise Pascal perceptively observes that "self-will will never be satisfied, though it should have command of all it would; but we are satisfied from the moment we renounce it. Without it we cannot be discontented; with it we cannot be content," *Pensées*, 131.

12. For a modern treatment of these conditions, see Anthony Campolo, *Seven Deadly Sins* (Wheaton: Victor, 1987).

13. Probably the greatest Reformed theologian in America, Jonathan Edwards deals incisively with this issue in his *Treatise on Religious Affections*, vol. 4 (New York: Robert Canter and Brothers, 1879), 332–416. Commenting on his view, John H. Gerstner says, "Edwards observes that a Christian is never satisfied with anything less than being perfectly holy. For him, any remaining sin is a great burden and he will not be fully happy until it is removed. He does not 'allow' any sin, but on the contrary, fights against all remaining sin relentlessly. He will not neglect any known duty, for he is opposed to sins of omission as of commission. He will make an effort, not to know as little as possible of his duty, but as much as possible, and will come as close to perfection as it is possible in his present state." *Jonathan Edwards: A Mini-Theology* (Wheaton: Tyndale, 1987), 87.

14. To further explore this concept, see the chapter on "Impartation" in my book *Master Plan of Evangelism*, 53–61.

15. Alan Redpath, "Independent Evangelicalism—An Evaluation," *The Sunday School Times* (November 10, 1962), 826.

16. Frank Colquhoun, "Great Britain: The Spiritual Situation Today," *Christianity Today*, July 31, 1961, 916.

17. Billy Graham, "Stains on the Altar," in *One Race, One Gospel, One Task*, eds. Carl F. Henry and W. Stanley Mooneyham (Minneapolis: World Wide Publications, 1967), 158.

18. Ibid., 159.

## Chapter 14 Perseverance of the Saints

1. Quoted by Dr. D. James Kennedy, *Truths That Transform* (Old Tappan, NJ: Revell, 1974), 99.

2. This story was published in England and has been widely circulated. I have no reason to question its authenticity. The account cited here is taken from a tract, "Can We Be Sure?" (Tract Club of America, 411 South Wells, Chicago, IL).

3. Probably no issue provokes more controversy among sincere believers than the question of perseverance. Basically one can go in the direction either of the Reformed or the Arminian tradition. An interactive summary of the main viewpoints, showing where they agree and disagree, is in *Four Views on Eternal Security*, ed. J. Matthew Pinson (Grand Rapids: Zondervan, 2002). Classical Calvinism is presented by Michael S. Horton. He goes back to the covenant of redemption made in eternity past between the persons of the Trinity (no human partner involved) to elect, redeem, and restore a people for God's glory, and restates the traditional TULIP thesis (total depravity, unconditional election, limited atonement, irresistible grace, and perseverance of the saints). A moderate view of Calvinism is given by Norman L. Geisler, who affirms each point of TULIP, while reinterpreting them to come out with a position sometimes called "one point Calvinism." A Reformed Arminian perspective is discussed by Stephen M. Ashby, taking exception to most of the TULIP points and their implications for perseverance. J. Steven Harper concludes the dialogue with Wesleyan Arminianism. While the distinctions between the last two reviews are not overwhelming, the sources from which the

scholars draw I found most helpful, for Dr. Ashby cites primarily Jacob Arminius and Dr. Harper refers mostly to John Wesley. Other useful works that bring out the distinctive differences of these two major theological positions are Jerry L. Walls and Joseph R. Dongell, *Why I Am Not a Calvinist* (Downers Grove, IL: InterVarsity, 2004); and Robert A. Peterson and Michael D. Williams, *Why I Am Not an Arminian* (Downers Grove, IL: InterVarsity, 2004).

4. Influenced by Augustine, particularly his last two works, *On the Predestination of the Saints* and *On the Gift of Perseverance* (AD 429), John Calvin hardened the doctrine of predestination into a double decree by which God ordained both the salvation of the elect and the damnation of the nonelect. To use his words: "By predestination we mean the eternal decree of God, by which he determined with himself whatever he wished to happen with regard to every man. All are created on equal terms, but some are preordained to eternal life, others to eternal damnation." *Institutes of the Christian Religion*, vol. 2, book 3, chapter 21, Article 5, 206. The perseverance of the elect can be logically inferred from this teaching. Not all Calvinists, however, hold to the idea of double predestination in support of eternal security. With them the focus is on an initial conversation or continuing faith. For a concise statement on the Reformed position, see Grudem, *Systematic Theology*, 788–809.

5. Some claim, for example, as does Charles Stanley, quoting Zane Hodges, that "Satan can completely shipwreck a believer's faith but this in no way affects the believer's security." He adds, "The Bible clearly teaches that God's love for his people is of such magnitude that even those who walk away from the faith have not the slightest chance of slipping from his hand"; cited by Norman L. Geisler, "A Moderate Calvinist View," in Pinson, ed., *Four Views of Eternal Security*, 110; cf. Charles Stanley, *Eternal Security: Can You Be Sure?* (Nashville: Thomas Nelson, 1990), 121–29.

6. For a good presentation of the Arminian understanding of perseverance, contrasted to Calvinism, see Robert Shank, *Life in the Son* (1960; repr., Minneapolis: Bethany, 1989).

7. To see how this passage can be used to support both Arminian and Reformed scholars, see Grant R. Osborne, *Grace Unlimited*, ed. Clark H. Pinnock (Minneapolis: Bethany, 1975), 170–71; and Grudem, *Systematic Theology*, 789.

8. Here again, from a Reformed perspective, showing how texts are interpreted differently, the persons described here are either not believers (Grudem, *Systematic Theology*, 796–802) or immature Christians who in judgment will lose rewards (Geisler, in Pinson, ed., *Four Views of Eternal Security*, 98–100). An excellent treatment of the issue focusing on Hebrews 6:4–6 is the article by David B. Armistead, "The 'Believer' Who Falls Away: Hebrews 6:4–6 and the Perseverance of the Saints," *Journal of the Evangelical Theological Society* (November 1996): 139–46. And from a different angle, Casey W. Davis, "Hebrews 6:4–6 from an Oral Critical Perspective," *Journal of the Evangelical Theological Society* (December 2008): 753–67.

9. An apt term used to describe this position by W. T. Purkiser, *Security: The False and the True* (Kansas City, MO: Beacon Hill Press, 1956), 24.

10. After going through the warning passages of Hebrews, citing especially Hebrews 6:1, 11, and 10:22, Dale Moody concludes three things: (1) It is possible to press on to maturity and full assurance; (2) it is possible for believers who do not press on to commit apostasy; and (3) there is no remedy for the sin of apostasy. *The Word of Truth: A Summary of Christian Doctrine Based on Biblical Revelation* (Grand Rapids: Eerdmans, 1981), 352.

11. Charles H. Spurgeon, cited in a printed lecture, "Some Considerations in the Matter of the Security of the Believer," by Dr. Stephen W. Paine, President of Houghton College, Houghton, NY, n.d.

12. Ibid.

13. Called antinomianism, it is the idea that the moral law of God is no longer binding on those who believe in Christ. For support, Romans 10:4 may be cited: "Christ is the end of the law for righteousness to everyone who believes." It is claimed that in choosing the latter, one has no further commitment to the former. This teaching has caused considerable social and political disruption through church history.

14. Thomas Oden, *John Wesley's Scriptural Christianity* (Grand Rapids: Zondervan, 1994), 341.

15. Cited by G. Ray Jordan, *The Supreme Possession* (New York: Abingdon, 1945), 14–15.

16. Cited by Paul B. Kern, *Methodism Has a Message!* (Nashville: Abingdon, 1966), 15–16.

17. Reported by Thomas A. Carroth, "By All Means," in *One Divine Moment*, ed. Coleman, 85.

18. Steele, *Mile-Stone Papers*, 145–46.

19. Taken from *90 Days with the Christian Classics*, comps. Michael Bauman, Lawrence Kinbrough, Martan I. Klauber, and Keith P. Wells (Nashville: Holiness Reference, 1999), Day 32.

20. Samuel Moor Shoemaker, "An Apologia for My Life," in the biography of his life written by his wife, Helen Smith Shoemaker, *I Stand by the Door* (Waco: Word, 1967), 11–12.

21. On more than one occasion I have heard this illustration, so presumably it has some original source. However, the written story from which this account comes is Herb Hodges, *Tally Ho the Fox! The Foundation for Building World-Visionary, World-Impacting, Reproducing Disciples* (Memphis: Spiritual Life Ministries, 2001), 101.

## Chapter 15 The Church and Her Ministry

1. Samuel J. Stone, from his hymn, "The Church's One Foundation."

2. An illustration used by Manford George Gutzke, *Plain Talk about Christian Works* (Grand Rapids: Zondervan, 1965), 195.

3. Those with a dynamic view generally make a distinction between the two, as does George Eldon Ladd: "The kingdom is the rule of God; the church is a society of men" (*Jesus and the Kingdom* [New York: Harper and Row, 1964], 258). The same idea is held by John Bright in *The Kingdom of God* (New York: Abingdon, 1953), 236. Some say that Jesus had no idea of establishing a church, but that it was the kingdom of God he planned. For example, see A. Loisy, *The Gospel and the Church*, trans. Christopher Home (New York: Charles Scribner, 1909), 166. Dispensationalists, like J. F. Walvoord and J. B. Pentecost, contend that the Jews rejected the earthly Davidic kingdom of heaven, which then caused Jesus to form the church and introduce the idea of the kingdom of God to all. In this view, the church has no direct lineage with Israel. However, most scholars follow Augustine and believe that the kingdom in its spiritual aspects is identical with the church. See Geerhardus Vos, *The Teaching of Jesus concerning the Church and the Kingdom* (Grand Rapids: Eerdmans, 1951), 77–90; and James Orr, *The Christian View of God and the World* (1867; reprint, Grand Rapids: Eerdmans, 1963), 358.

4. Oscar Cullman, *Salvation in History* (London: SCM Press, 1965), 166–236.

5. Huber L. Drumwright Jr. and R. Allen Killan, "Worship" in *Wycliffe Bible Encyclopedia* 2 (Chicago: Moody, 1975), 1823.

6. For a study of the doxologies recorded around the throne of God in the book of Revelation, see Robert E. Coleman, *Singing with the Angels* (Grand Rapids: Revell, 1998); reprint of *The Songs of Heaven* (1980).

7. It is not without significance that all of the disciples called by Jesus were laymen. They were not members of the officially recognized priesthood of their day. Not until sometime after Pentecost is there any indication that members of the professional clergy joined his company (Acts 6:7). Of course, Jesus ordained some of his disciples to positions of leadership, as did the early church, but the ordination did not set them apart for the ministry that they already shared nor did it make them a counterpart to the Old Testament priest. In the apostles' fellowship every Christian was a ministering priest before God and man. The distinction between clergy and laity does not appear in the New Testament at all.

8. Quoted by Leighton Ford, *The Christian Persuader* (New York: Harper and Row, 1960), 49.

9. In coming to this definition, I have utilized insights from the Church of England's 25th Article of Religion; The Westminster Assembly's Larger Catechism Questions 162 and 163; A. A. Hodge, *Outlines of Theology*, chapter XLI (1860; repr., Grand Rapids: Zondervan, 1972); and H. Orton Wiley and Paul T. Culbertson, *Introduction to Christian Theology* (Kansas City, MO: Beacon Hill Press, 1949), 386.

10. The most notable exceptions to Protestant nonobservance of the sacraments are the Quakers and the Salvation Army. They do not see why ceremonies are necessary to express spiritual reality. In their thinking, all of life should be a sacrament of grace.

11. "Invitation to the Lord's Supper," ritual of the United Methodist Church.

12. The universal dimension of God's plan flows through the Bible. That God will not be defeated is evident in the call to Noah (Gen. 6:7–8; 8:16; 9:1, 9). He renews his promise to Abraham and his posterity (Gen. 12:1–3; 22:15–18; 26:2–5; 28:10, 15). The mission of Israel finds fulfillment in the promised Messiah (Gen. 49:10; Ps. 2:8; 46:10; 86:9; Isa. 55:4–5; Jer. 10:7; Dan. 7:13–14;

Zech. 9:10). The Great Commission consummates the unfolding plan of God from the beginning.

13. A study of the way Christ made disciples is in my book *Master Plan of Evangelism*. The trade edition has a study guide by Roy Fish. Reiterating this theme is *The Great Commission Lifestyle: Conforming Your Life to Kingdom Priorities* (Grand Rapids: Revell, 1992). A number of other authors have addressed this subject, many of whom are noted in the footnotes of the above books. A recent survey of various approaches is by Bill Hull, *The Complete Book of Discipleship* (Colorado Springs: NavPress, 2006).

14. The word is *kleros*. This noun form has the meaning of "a share, a land received by lot or inheritance." The verb *kleronomeo* refers to the activity of dividing by lot or obtaining an inheritance. A related term indicates "the one receiving the allotment" or "heir." In the Old Testament, the word may be used to determine God's will by casting lots, a reference also seen in the New Testament when the soldiers cast lots for the garments of Jesus (Matt. 27:35; Mark 15:24; Luke 23:34), and the lots used by the disciples to select a replacement for the traitor (Acts 1:16–17, 25–26). When the reference is to recipients of God's promise to the church, the terms relate to all believers who have received the inheritance of Christ (Acts 20:32; 26:18; Rom. 4:13–14; 8:16; Gal. 3:18, 29; 4:1, 7; Eph. 1:11; Col. 1:12; 3:24; Titus 3:7; Heb. 6:17; 9:15; 11:7–8; James 2:5; 1 Pet. 1:4; 5:4). In the New Testament usage of those terms, then, everyone in the church is a clergyperson or an heir of God (*The New International Dictionary of New Testament Theology*, vol. 2 [Grand Rapids: Zondervan, 1976], 295–303).

15. A review of various ways to interpret this passage can be found in Coleman, *Master Plan of Evangelism*, 90–91, 119.

16. Told by Peter Emmons, *Pattern of Things to Come*, ed. D. McConnell (New York: Friendship Press, 1954), 4.

17. What can and cannot be done in effective personal evangelism is painfully evident in the little book by Joseph Bayly, *The Gospel Blimp* (Grand Rapids: Zondervan, 1966). It is a walloping satire on artificial evangelism that focuses on a real problem among Christians. As to the best way we can practice soul winning without being repulsively professional, each person will have to let the Holy Spirit teach the most natural way in any given situation. For a listing of selected books on basic evangelism, see the bibliography in the 2008 printing of Coleman, *Master Plan of Evangelism*, 187–91.

18. There is no end to helpful books, DVDs, films, and other materials on church growth and evangelism. Check with your church or Christian bookstore for recommendations.

19. For a review of mission history, especially since the Edinburgh Missionary Conference in 1910, see Arthur P. Johnston, *World Evangelism and the Word of God* (Minneapolis: Bethany Fellowship, 1974). A concise appraisal of the problem is given by Rick Richardson, "Evangelism and Social Concern: How Do We Maintain a Healthy Balance of Witness?" *Journal of the Academy for Evangelism in Theological Education* 24 (2010): 19–34.

20. See Carl F. H. Henry, *The Uneasy Conscience of Modern Fundamentalism* (Grand Rapids: Eerdmans, 1947).

21. For example, evangelical leadership gave impetus to the movement for the abolishment of slavery, the organization of trade unions, abolition of child labor, women's suffrage, the start of hundreds of benevolent and missionary societies, the YMCA, to say nothing of the colleges and hospitals scattered across the world. See Timothy L. Smith, *Revivalism and Social Reform* (New York: Abingdon, 1957); J. Edwin Orr, *The Second Evangelical Awakening in Britain* (London: Marshall, Morgan & Scott, 1949).

22. This is the basic idea in "apostolic succession." The word *apostle* means "sent one," and it is as we go into the world with the Gospel that we truly reflect the continuity of our lives with the apostles' faith and witness. There is, of course, the necessary relationship between doctrine and ministry, but merely to regard the succession as an adherence to the apostles' doctrine is not enough. Nor can the typical continuity with the apostles through the laying on of hands fulfill the intent of the matter. The succession is in the way the teachings of the apostles are carried into the world through our lives, and only this kind of practical reproduction of the apostolic witness through the grace of God assures the ongoing movement of the church.

23. Elton Trueblood, *The Company of the Committed* (New York: Harper and Row, 1961), 72.

24. Much has been said in recent years about spiritual gifts, not without controversy. Never-

theless, it is a matter that cannot be ignored in considering the ministry of the church. Some are of the opinion, following the lead of most of the Reformation leaders, that the gifts, or at least some of them, passed away with the apostolic age. To contend that these endowments of grace would cease with the death of the original apostles or even after the first centuries seems arbitrary to me, and, I think, lacks objective support. Not only did gifts continue to be manifest through the church, especially in times of spiritual awakening, but they are in evidence today. That there have been some misrepresentations of the teaching should not distract us from seeking the truth.

25. Lewis Sperry Chafer, *True Evangelism* (London: Marshall, Morgan & Scott, 1919), 93.

26. The Old Testament word for revival comes from a term meaning "to live," which originally conveyed the idea of breathing. Hence, it could be said of the dry bones, "I will cause breath to enter you, and you shall live" (Ezek. 37:5; cf. 1 Kings 17:22; Job 33:4; Ezek. 37:6, 14). The comparable New Testament word means "to come alive" (Rom. 7:9; 14:9; Rev. 20:5). As Jesus used the term, it denotes the change in the life of a persistent prodigal who returns to the father's house (Luke 15:24, 32). Other words liken revival to the rekindling of a slowly dying fire (2 Tim. 1:6) or to a relationship that has flourished again (Phil. 4:10). For a basic description of revival, how it comes, and its patterns in the Bible, see Robert Coleman, *The Coming World Revival* (1985; repr., Wheaton: Crossway, 1995). Other works that speak to this subject are noted in the extensive footnotes in the book.

27. Stephen F. Olford, *Heart Cry for Revival* (Westwood, NJ: Revell, 1962), 7.

28. The story of American revivals has been treated by many historians. A few of the more general works are F. G. Beardsley, *A History of American Revivals* (New York: American Tract Society, 1904); W. L. Muncy, *A History of Evangelism in the United States* (Kansas City, KS: Central Seminary Press, 1945); Fred Hoffman, *Revival Times in America* (Boston: W. A. Wilde, 1956); Bernard A. Weisberger, *They Gathered at the River* (Boston: Little, Brown, 1958); and for a more biographical approach, see Keith J. Hardman, *The Spiritual Awakeners* (Chicago: Moody, 1983). For an excellent bibliography on revival from the Great Awakening to the present, especially focused on the American scene, see Earle E.

Cairns, *An Endless Line of Splendor* (Wheaton: Tyndale, 1986). Further bibliographic information on revival may be found in Richard O. Roberts, *Revival* (Wheaton: Tyndale, 1982).

29. For a reasoned challenge to believe God for revival in our day, read Collin Hansen and John Woodbridge, *A God-Sized Vision: Revival Stories That Stretch and Stir* (Grand Rapids: Zondervan, 2010). It will be a tonic for your faith.

## Chapter 16 The Return of the King

1. Though a different account, these same words were said at the Evanston Assembly of the World Council of Churches in 1945, cited in Thomas C. Oden, *Life in the Spirit: Systematic Theology*, vol. 3 (San Francisco: Harper and Row, 1992), 409.

2. The victorious day of Christ's second coming has been likened to V-Day in World War II when the German army surrendered, though the decisive event in winning the war was D-Day when the allied troops came ashore at Normandy. In this analogy, Christ's triumph over sin and the powers of darkness was complete at Calvary, though the devil continues to fight on as a defeated foe until finally vanquished at Christ's return. See Bloesch, *Jesus Is Victor!* 180, and footnote on p. 205.

3. That Christ's robe will be bathed in blood can be variously interpreted. Some see in it the fury executed on his enemies. Others give the description a more general reference to the atoning work of Christ, which highlights a theme running through the written Word of God.

4. This deceiver has the mark of an "antichrist" (1 John 4:3; 2 John 7) and world dictator (Rev. 13:7). In keeping with the deception, "scoffers . . . in the last days" will commonly deny the teaching of the Lord's return (2 Pet. 3:1–4).

5. Many see the possibility of a mighty cosmic revival before the end of the age, when the church in all parts of the world will know the overflow of God's presence. Drawing on the prophecy of Joel that the Spirit would be poured out on "all flesh" (Joel 2:28–29), a promise cited by Peter at Pentecost (Acts 2:16–17), though only partially fulfilled at the time, it is believed that complete fulfillment awaits a day to come. According to this reasoning, the church age begins and will end in a powerful spiritual baptism. What happened at the first Pentecost may be seen as the "early" display of the refreshing rain from heaven, while

the closing epic is the "late rain" (Joel 2:23; Hosea 6:3; Zech. 10:1; James 5:7). Water or rain, it will be remembered, is often symbolic of the Holy Spirit (John 7:37–39). This, and other aspects of this last great revival, is discussed in Coleman, *Coming World Revival*, 149–64.

6. The Jews' general repentance and acceptance of Christ may be seen differently and especially in reference to the millennium. Both the Old and New Testaments speak of the restoration of Israel (Isa. 1:24–27; 60:15–22; Jer. 3:12–18; Ezek. 20:40–42; 2 Cor. 3:15–16). Some see this alluded to after "the times of the Gentiles are fulfilled" (Luke 21:24; cf. Rom. 11:11–12, 24, 26). The budding of the fig tree, likened to the Jewish nation, also has been associated with this expectation (Mark 11:13; Luke 21:29), as well as the dry bones coming alive in Ezekiel 37:1–14 (cf. Isa. 11:11–12:1; Jer. 30:11; Amos 9:14–15). These passages do point to a return of the Jews to their homeland, which has been fulfilled, but a mass acceptance of their Messiah is less clear. The restoration of a national Israel also is linked to some views on the millennium.

7. For a well-documented history of Bible prophecy pertaining to eschatology, see David L. Larson, *The Company of Hope: A History of Bible Prophecy in the Church* (Bloomington, IN: AuthorHouse, 2004).

8. The word *parousia*, taken from the Greek, means "presence," and in the New Testament generally refers to the glorious coming of the Lord at the end of the age (Matt. 24:3, 27, 37, 39; 1 Cor. 15:23; 1 Thess. 2:19; 3:13; 4:15; 5:23; 2 Thess. 2:1, 8; James 5:7–8; 2 Pet. 1:16; 3:4, 12; 1 John 2:28). In Greek literature, the term often was used for a visit of a king, hence an appropriate word for the advent of Christ. See G. Abbott-Smith, *A Mutual Greek Lexicon of the New Testament* (Edinburgh: T&T Clark, 1948), 347.

9. Persons with a premillennial perspective generally believe that the resurrection of the saints and their judgment will come before the resurrection and judgment of the wicked, hence two separate events. Post- and amillennialists, on the other hand, relegate all judgment to a last great final day.

10. A full treatment of the variant views of the millennium, with their scriptural support, can be found in any good systematic theology. A helpful analysis of the views is by Craig A. Blaising (premillennialism), Kenneth L. Gentry Jr. (post-

millennialism), and Robert B. Strimple (amillennialism), interacting with each other in *Three Views on the Millennium and Beyond*, ed. Darrell L. Bock (Grand Rapids: Zondervan, 1999). For a concise summary, see the article by Timothy P. Weber, "Millennialism," in *The Oxford Handbook of Eschatology*, ed. Jerry L. Walls (New York: Oxford University Press, 2000), 365–83.

11. In a dispensational premillennial interpretation, there are actually two comings of Christ, or appearances of the Lord, one for the saints at the rapture and the second when he returns with his church to set up the millennial kingdom on earth.

12. Arguments for these ways of seeing the rapture, while intriguing, do not fall within the evangelical focus of this study. However, for those wanting to go into the subject, see the presentations of each position by Gleason L. Archer Jr., Paul D. Feinberg, and Douglas J. Moo, in *Three Views on the Rapture*, ed. Richard Reiter (Grand Rapids: Zondervan, 1996).

13. Forms of premillennialism characterized most of the ante-Nicene fathers but faded away by the Middle Ages. In the sixteenth and seventeenth centuries, it was revived among the Anabaptists and Plymouth Brethren and came to be associated with dispensationalism. With many variations it remains popular today. Among prominent advocates are George Eldon Ladd, Charles Ryrie, Dwight Pentecost, David Larson, and Walter Kaiser.

14. Different forms of amillennialism can be seen among early church leaders and became the dominant view in the Roman Catholic Church as well as in much of Reformation teaching. Contemporary exponents include such well-known scholars as G. C. Berkouwer, George Murray, Anthony Hoekema, Leon Morris, and Thomas Torrance.

15. This position can be found in the early church, though overshadowed by premillennialism. It experienced an upsurge during the Middle Ages and really began to flower in the seventeenth and eighteenth centuries among the Pietists, Puritans, and Wesleyans. In more recent times it can be seen in men like B. B. Warfield, Charles Finney, James Orr, T. A. Kantonen, and Iain Murray.

16. Altogether there are eighty-two occurrences of the description in thirty-six parallel accounts. Outside the parables and Beatitudes, it seems well distributed through the Gospels. Some scholars view the Son of Man as a symbol

representing a people devoted to their heavenly king. However, an association with the saints need not rule out his individual personage. For further treatment of this self-preferred title of Jesus, see Coleman, *Mind of the Master*, 104–7.

17. Pascal, *Pensées*, Article 756, 226.

18. I have come across this story in at least two different versions and have taken the liberty to fashion yet another. I cannot vouch for its historic accuracy, but the lesson learned from it is no less valid.

19. Charles Wesley, from his hymn "Rejoice, All Ye Believers."

## Chapter 17 The Providence of God

1. Phyllis Matthewman, *Robert Morrison* (Grand Rapids: Zondervan, 1957), 30.

2. Thomas C. Oden, drawing from the writings of Cyril of Jerusalem, in *The Living God: Systematic Theology*, vol. 1 (San Francisco: Harper and Row, 1987), 273.

3. An interesting observation has come from St. John of Damascus. He makes a distinction between God's "antecedent" will and pleasure, which springs from himself, and his "consequent" will and permission, which has its origin in us. Of the actions that are in our hands, the good ones depend on God's antecedent will, while the wicked ones depend on our choices and are a concession to our free will (Philip Schaff and Henry Wallace, eds., *Nicene and Post-Nicene Fathers*, second series, vol. 9 [New York: Cosimo Classics, 2007]).

4. Oden, reflecting on the thought of Thomas Aquinas, in *The Living God*, 294.

5. Ibid., 296.

6. I am indebted to Thomas C. Oden for this analysis in ibid., 300–302.

7. Unfortunately, the word has sometimes been associated with both the salvation and the damnation of people (so-called "double predestination"). The idea that some persons were alternatively predetermined by God to be saved while others to be lost is an unjustified inference. It blurs the difference between election and reprobation, while also casting a shadow on the goodness of God.

8. St. Justin Martyr, "To Gratian, on the Christian Faith," in *A Selected Library of Nicene and Post-Nicene Fathers of the Christian Church*, vol. 10 (Grand Rapids: Eerdmans, 1979), 159.

9. St. John Chrysostom points out two ways of seeing God's will. His first will is that all be saved; the second that the wicked perish. In his commentary on Ephesians 1:5, he writes: "The word 'good pleasure' everywhere means the precedent will, for there is also another will. As for example, the first will is that sinners should not perish; the second will is that if men become wicked, they shall perish" (*Letters to the Ephesians*, trans. W. V. Jurgens, The Faith of the Early Fathers, vol. 2 [Collegeville, MN: Liturgical Press, 1979], 120).

10. St. Augustine championed this view in the fourth century. "It is not in the choice of man's will to believe or not to believe," he says, "but because in the elect the will is prepared by the Lord." He goes on to add, "This gift is given to some (i.e., those who believe), while to some it is not given" ("On the Predestination of the Saints," in *Selected Library of Nicene and Post-Nicene Fathers*, vol. 5, 503, 506).

11. Jonathan Edwards, "A Careful and Strict Enquiry into the Prevailing Notions of That Freedom of Will, Which Is Supposed to Be Essential to Moral Agency, Virtue and Vice, Reward and Punishment, Praise and Blame," in *Puritan Sage*, 480–515.

12. An excellent, concise description of the Arminian position with its variations is by Robert E. Picirilli, "Foreknowledge, Freedom and the Future," *Journal of the Evangelical Theological Society* 93, no. 2 (June 2000): 259–71.

13. An interesting insight comes from St. Jerome. He raises the question of why Jesus chose Judas, knowing that he would betray him. His answer: "God judges the present, not the future. He does not make use of his foreknowledge to condemn a man though he knows that he will hereafter displease him; but such is his goodness and unspeakable mercy that he chooses a man, who he perceives, will meanwhile be good, and who, he knows will turn out badly, thus giving him the opportunity of being converted and repenting. . . . For Adam did not sin because God knew that he would do so; but, God, in as much as he is God, foreknew what Adam would do of his own free choice" ("Dialogue against the Pelagians," in *Selected Library of Nicene and Post-Nicene Fathers*, vol. 6, 474–75).

14. John Oxenham, "God's Handwriting," *Bees in Amber* (New York: American Tract Society).

15. The complete story of the mission of these men is told in Elisabeth Elliot, *Through Gates of Splendor* (Wheaton: Tyndale, 1956). The life

and death of one of these men is told in Elisabeth Elliot, *Shadow of the Almighty: The Life and Death of Jim Elliot* (New York: Harper and Brothers, 1958).

16. The complete account of the accidental death of Dawson Trotman, including his heroic effort to keep the girl from drowning, is in the biography *Daws* by Betty Lee Skinner (Grand Rapids: Zondervan, 1974), 377–81.

## Chapter 18  The Coming Glory

1. The song was written by T. Ramsey, with music by C. E. Durham, copyright 1956, by Broadman Press. The lines alluded to above go like this: "When I cross the river at the ending of day, / When the last winds of summer have blown, / There'll be somebody waiting to show me the way, / I won't have to cross Jordan alone."

2. Though considerably shortened and changed in wording, the idea of the story comes from Peter Marshall's sermon, "Go Down Death," included in Catherine Marshall, *A Man Called Peter* (New York: McGraw-Hall, 1951), 260–61.

3. John Bunyan, *The Pilgrim's Progress* (New York: Peter Pauper Press), 148–49.

4. The word *new* often gives expression to this idea—for example, "the New Testament" of Christ's blood (Matt. 26:28; Mark 14:24; Luke 22:20; 1 Cor. 11:26), the "new creation" Christ makes in redemption (2 Cor. 5:17; Gal. 6:15), among others. See Colin Brown, ed., *The New International Dictionary of New Testament Theology*, vol. 2 (Grand Rapids: Zondervan,

1977), 669–70; cf. Kittel, *Theological Dictionary of the New Testament*, vol. 3, 447.

5. Erich Sauer, *The Triumph of the Crucified* (Grand Rapids: Eerdmans, 1951), 179.

6. Anne R. Cousin, from her hymn "The Bride Eyes Not Her Garment."

7. Randy Alcorn, *Safely Home* (Wheaton: Tyndale, 2001). Though written as a novel, the accounts of suffering in the house church movement in China are realistic.

8. Some details of this event have been omitted for the sake of brevity. The complete account is in J. E. Church, *Forgive Them: The Story of an African Martyr* (London: Hodder & Stoughton, 1966), 12–16. The story is also found in James and Manti Hefley, *By Their Blood: Christian Martyrs of the 20th Century*, 2nd ed. (Grand Rapids: Baker, 1996).

9. Reported by Charles S. Nutter and Wilber Fisk Tillett, *The Hymns and Hymn Writers of the Church* (New York: Eaton and Mains, 1911), 440.

10. Account written by Betsy Ritchie, "Wesley's Last Hours," in *The Heart of John Wesley's Journal*, ed. Percy Livingston Parker (New Canaan, CT: Keats, 1979), 29.

11. If you would like to study the worship hymns of praise around the throne of heaven, you may appreciate my attempt to describe them in *Singing with the Angels* (Grand Rapids: Revell, 1998).

12. Francis of Assisi, from his hymn "All Creatures of Our God and King," translated by William H. Draper.

# Index

**Robert E. Coleman** is distinguished professor of evangelism and discipleship at Gordon-Conwell Theological Seminary. For many years he served as dean of the Billy Graham International Schools of Evangelism as well as director of the Billy Graham Center Institute of Evangelism at Wheaton College. He was also professor of evangelism at Trinity Evangelical Divinity School, where he directed the School of World Mission and Evangelism.

Dr. Coleman is a graduate of Southwestern University, Asbury Theological Seminary, and Princeton Theological Seminary, and has a PhD from the University of Iowa. He has received honorary doctorates from Trinity International University and Asbury Theological Seminary.

He is a founding member of the Lausanne Committee of World Evangelization and a past president of the Academy for Evangelism in Theological Education. He presently serves on the Facilitation Committee of Mission America and several international mission boards.

Twenty-four books and hundreds of articles have come from Dr. Coleman's pen. His books have been published in many languages around the world. A seasoned teacher, pastor, and evangelist, he hopes to be remembered simply as a disciple of Christ.

ALSO BY

# ROBERT E. COLEMAN

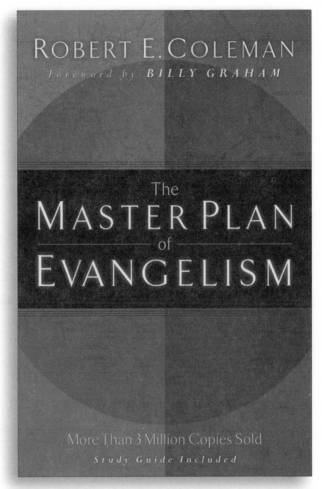

9780800731229

"Few books have had as great an impact on the cause of world evangelization in our generation as Robert Coleman's *The Master Plan of Evangelism*."

—**BILLY GRAHAM**

BakerBooks
*a division of Baker Publishing Group*
www.BakerBooks.com